VISUAL QUICKSTART GUIDE

Microsoft
WINDOWS VISTA

Chris Fehily

 Peachpit Press

Visual QuickStart Guide
Microsoft Windows Vista
Chris Fehily

Peachpit Press
1249 Eighth Street
Berkeley, CA 94710
510/524-2178
800/283-9444
510/524-2221 (fax)
Find us on the Web at: www.peachpit.com
To report errors, please send a note to errata@peachpit.com
Peachpit Press is a division of Pearson Education

Managing editor: Clifford Colby
Editor: Kathy Simpson
Production editor: Andrei Pasternak
Compositor: Owen Wolfson
Indexer: Rebecca Plunkett
Cover design: The Visual Group

ISBN 0-321-43452-8

9 8 7 6 5 4 3 2

Printed and bound in the United States of America

*For Brian, Ken, Steve,
Stu, Cliff, and Darren*

Special Thanks to...

Kathy Simpson for staying ahead of me

Cliff Colby for working backstage

Andrei Pasternak for coordinating

Owen Wolfson for squashing

Rebecca Plunkett for rotating terms

CONTENTS AT A GLANCE

TABLE OF CONTENTS

TABLE OF CONTENTS

INTRODUCTION

Windows Vista, the successor to Windows XP, is the latest Microsoft operating system for PC users at home, work, and school. Feature for feature, Vista is better than XP, but to make people *want* to upgrade to Vista, Microsoft put special effort into:

The user interface. The new UI, called Aero, is slick and lets you find and launch your stuff instantly no matter how your files and folders are organized (or disorganized). The Start menu, the taskbar, Windows Explorer, and other redesigned controls retain enough of their old personalities to let you jump in.

Security. Vista protects you against malicious websites, viruses, spyware, and other online threats. You also can control what your children or guests view and play. Vista's reduced-privilege mode (turned on by default) defends even administrators against attacks.

Connectivity. It's easy to connect quickly (and wirelessly) to people, data, and devices that you need to interact with.

Performance. Vista scales to your machine's hardware and, provided that you feed it enough memory, is faster than XP. Vista's broad driver support means that your existing hardware and software will work right (in most cases).

What Windows Does

Windows—like every operating system, Microsoft or otherwise—is software that controls:

The user interface. Windows manages the appearance, behavior, and interaction of the windows, buttons, icons, folders, mouse pointers, cursors, menus, ribbons, and other visual elements on your computer screen, either directly or indirectly through another program.

Storage. Windows' file system allocates space for and gives access to files—programs and documents—stored on disk or in memory.

Other software. Windows is a launching platform for programs. When you run Microsoft Word, Adobe Photoshop, The Sims, or any other Windows program, it relies on the services and building blocks that Windows provides for basic operations such as drawing a user interface, saving files, and sharing hardware.

Peripheral devices. Windows controls or syncs with peripheral hardware such as your mouse, keyboard, monitor, printer, scanner, USB flash drives, digital camera, PDA, and iPod.

Networks and security. Windows controls the interaction of a group of computers and peripheral devices connected by a communications link such as Ethernet or wireless. Windows also protects your system and data from harm or loss.

System resources. Windows handles the allocation and use of your computer's low-level hardware resources such as memory (RAM) and central processing unit (CPU) time.

Task scheduling. Windows acts like a traffic cop, setting priorities and allocating time slices to the processes running on your PC.

Freeware and Shareware

Many of the third-party (meaning non-Microsoft) programs that I recommend in this book are freeware or shareware. *Freeware* is software that you can use for an unlimited time at no cost, whereas *shareware* is software that you can use for a tryout period—usually 30 days—before you're expected to pay for it. I say "expected to" because much shareware keeps working beyond the trial period, so you can escape payment. Paying the fee, however, often gets you a keycode that unlocks features or turns off nag messages. If you pass along copies of shareware to others, they're expected to pay too.

Freeware and shareware are copyrighted and have licenses that may impose restrictions ("free for personal, noncommercial use," for example). Unlike commercial software, freeware and shareware isn't shrink-wrapped or sold in stores but is downloaded from the internet (or provided on magazine cover disks). I give the publisher's website for each recommended program, but you also can browse download sites like www.download.com, www.tucows.com, and www.fileforum.com or an index like http://dmoz.org/Computers/Software. http://sourceforge.net has lots of free high-quality software. Also, to keep up with the latest releases, try www.betanews.com, http://freshmeat.net, and www.microsoft-watch.com.

If a popular free program isn't labeled "public domain," "public license," or "open source" (www.opensource.org), you should check it for spyware. See "Defending Against Viruses and Spyware" in Chapter13.

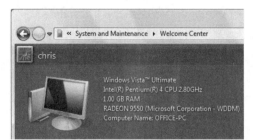

Figure i.1 The edition of Windows Vista that you're using is displayed with your computer details near the top of the window.

The Editions of Windows Vista

The editions of Windows Vista are:

◆ Windows Vista Home Basic

◆ Windows Vista Home Premium

◆ Windows Vista Business

◆ Windows Vista Enterprise

◆ Windows Vista Ultimate

The home editions have entertainment features that aren't in the business editions, which themselves have management features that aren't in the Home editions. Ultimate edition combines the Home and Business features, for a complete package, and lets you get additional programs and services by using the Windows Ultimate Extras utility in Windows Update.

The core features in the different Vista editions look and work alike, so most discussions apply to all editions equally. This book points out the differences among the editions where necessary. To find out which edition you're running, choose Start > Control Panel > System and Maintenance > Welcome Center (**Figure i.1**).

✔ Tips

■ Windows Anytime Upgrade, new in Vista, lets you upgrade your copy of Vista to another edition. You can upgrade from Home Basic to either Home Premium or Ultimate, for example. Choose Start > Control Panel > System and Maintenance > Windows Anytime Upgrade.

■ There's also an inexpensive—and severely hamstrung—Starter edition, sold only in developing countries and not covered in this book.

THE EDITIONS OF WINDOWS VISTA

What's New in Windows Vista

If you're familiar with earlier versions of Windows, here are Vista's significant new and updated features and programs.

New programs and features

◆ Welcome Center. See "Using Welcome Center" in Chapter 1.

◆ Taskbar thumbnail previews. See "Customizing the Taskbar" in Chapter 2.

◆ Sidebar and gadgets. See "Using the Sidebar" in Chapter 2.

◆ Aero color scheme. See "Setting the Window Color and Color Scheme" in Chapter 4.

◆ Live icons. See "Using Windows Explorer" in Chapter 5.

◆ File tagging. See "Tagging Files" in Chapter 5.

◆ Filtering and stacking files. See "Filtering, Sorting, Stacking, and Grouping Files" in Chapter 5.

◆ Instant search. See "Searching for Files and Folders" in Chapter 5.

◆ Saved searches. See "Saving Searches" in Chapter 5.

◆ Flip 3D. See "Switching Programs" in Chapter 6.

◆ Windows Ultimate Extras. See "Using the Free Utility Programs" in Chapter 6.

◆ XPS document support. See "Installing a Printer" in Chapter 7.

◆ Windows DVD Maker. See "Publishing a Movie" in Chapter 11.

◆ Windows Defender. See "Defending Against Viruses and Spyware" in Chapter 13.

◆ Parental Controls. See "Using Parental Controls" in Chapter 13.

◆ Windows Contacts (replaces Address Book). See "Managing Your Contacts" in Chapter 15.

◆ Windows Calendar. See "Creating a Personal Calendar" in Chapter 15.

◆ User Account Control. See "Using User Account Control" in Chapter 17.

◆ Sync Center and Windows Mobility Center. See "Using Laptop Utilities" in Chapter 19.

◆ ReadyBoost. See "Boosting Memory" in Chapter 20.

Major updates

◆ Speech recognition. See "Using Speech Recognition" in Chapter 4.

◆ Power Options utility. See "Conserving Power" in Chapter 4.

◆ Windows Explorer. See Chapter 5.

◆ Windows Photo Gallery (replaces Windows Picture and Fax Viewer). See Chapter 9.

◆ Internet Explorer. See Chapter 14.

◆ Network setup. See Chapter 18.

◆ Task Scheduler. See "Scheduling Tasks" in Chapter 20.

◆ Backup and Restore Center (formerly Windows Backup). See "Backing up Your Files" in Chapter 20.

◆ Problem Reports and Solutions (replaces Error Reporting and Dr. Watson). See "Reporting and Solving Problems" in Chapter 20.

Moderate updates

◆ Start menu. See "Exploring the Start Menu" in Chapter 2.

◆ Windows Help and Support. See Chapter 3.

◆ Control Panel. See "Using Control Panel" in Chapter 4.

◆ Taskbar clock. See "Setting the Date and Time" in Chapter 4.

◆ Ease of Access (formerly Accessibility). See "Accommodating Disabled Users" in Chapter 4.

◆ Personal folder (reorganizes My Documents, My Music, and so on). See "Storing Stuff in Your Personal Folder" in Chapter 5.

◆ Disc burning. See "Burning CDs and DVDs" in Chapter 5.

◆ Programs and Features (formerly Add or Remove Programs). See "Removing Programs" in Chapter 6.

◆ Meeting Space (formerly NetMeeting). See "Using the Free Utility Programs" in Chapter 6.

◆ Windows Fax and Scan (formerly Windows Fax). See "Scanning and Faxing" in Chapter 6.

◆ Windows Media Player. See Chapter 10.

◆ Windows Movie Maker. See Chapter 11.

◆ Internet connections. See "Connecting to the Internet" in Chapter 12.

◆ Windows Mail (formerly Outlook Express). See Chapter 15.

◆ Windows Live Messenger (formerly Windows Messenger). See Chapter 16.

◆ System Restore. See "Restoring Your System" in Chapter 20.

◆ Windows Easy Transfer (formerly Files and Settings Transfer Wizard). See "Transferring Existing Files and Settings" in the appendix.

WHAT'S NEW IN WINDOWS VISTA

Upgrading to Windows Vista

If you're moving to Vista from an earlier version of Windows, Microsoft gives you upgrade options that depend on the version that you're currently running. A Windows Vista version upgrade is much cheaper than a full copy. You can upgrade from only Windows XP or Windows 2000; if you have an earlier version, you must install a full copy of Vista. You have two ways to upgrade:

◆ An *upgrade* lets you install Vista and keep your programs, files, and settings as they were in your previous edition of Windows.

◆ A *clean install* overwrites your current copy of Windows with Vista, erasing everything. You can use Windows Easy Transfer (see the appendix) to reload your files and settings on your upgraded PC.

Table i.1 tells you which Windows versions qualify for an upgrade to Vista Home, Business, or Ultimate editions.

Not Eligible to Upgrade?

If you're not eligible to upgrade because you're a first-time Windows customer or your current Windows version doesn't qualify, then it's cheaper to buy the Vista *upgrade* version *and* get Windows 2000 —from a friend, coworker, computer swap meet, www.craigslist.org... there are plenty of copies around. (You can get a copy of Windows XP instead, but you might have trouble with its activation key if it's already been used.)

Install Windows 2000 on your PC and then apply the Vista upgrade, first making sure that your hardware meets Vista system requirements (see the appendix). Don't throw out Windows 2000; you may need it to reinstall Vista someday.

Table i.1

Upgrading from Earlier Windows Versions

Current Version	Home Basic	Home Premium	Business	Ultimate
Windows XP Professional	○	○	●	●
Windows XP Home	●	●	●	●
Windows XP Media Center	○	●	○	●
Windows XP Tablet PC	○	○	●	●
Windows XP Professional x64	○	○	○	○
Windows 2000	○	○	○	○

○ Clean install only.
● In-place upgrade or clean install.

About This Book

This book is for you if you're new to Windows, moving or upgrading to Vista from a previous Windows version, or need a quick reference at hand. My audience is beginning and intermediate Windows Vista users, including people who are buying Vista along with their first computers. Windows veterans can look up specific tasks quickly or scan the tips and sidebars for tricks, shortcuts, and subtleties. Wherever possible, I give step-by-step instructions for using features and programs.

Conventions used in this book

Commands. I use shorthand instructions rather than list steps separately. Here's a command that opens a nested folder:

◆ Choose Start > Computer > Local Disk (C:) > Users > Public.

This sequence means: Click the Start button (on the taskbar, in the bottom-left corner of the desktop) to reveal the Start menu; then click Computer. Inside the Computer window, double-click the drive icon labeled Local Disk (C:) to open it. Inside that window, double-click the icon Users to open it. Inside *that* window, double-click the icon Public to open it.

Each shorthand element (between the > symbols) refers to an icon, window, dialog box, menu, button, check box, link, tab, or some other user-interface component; just look for the component whose label matches the element name. Whenever a particular step is unclear or ambiguous, I spell it out rather than use shorthand.

Here's a command that launches the Notepad program:

◆ Choose Start > All Programs > Accessories > Notepad.

This one shows file extensions:

◆ Choose Start > Control Panel > Appearance and Personalization > Folder Options > View tab > uncheck Hide Extensions for Known File Types > OK.

Keyboard shortcuts. Use keyboard shortcuts so that you don't waste time moving your hand from keyboard to mouse repeatedly. These shortcuts involve the modifier keys that sit at the bottom corners of the keyboard's main section. Press these keys—Shift, Ctrl (Control), and Alt (Alternate)—together with other keys to change the action. The C key pressed by itself types a lowercase c; pressed along with the Shift key, it types an uppercase C; and pressed along with the Ctrl key, it issues the Copy command.

Modifier keys are joined to other keys with a plus sign. Ctrl+C, for example, means "Press the Ctrl key, hold it down while you press the C key, and then release both keys." A three-key combination such as Ctrl+Alt+Delete means "Hold down the first two keys while you press the third one; then release all three." The modifiers always are listed first. An Alt-key shortcut joined by commas rather than plus signs (Alt, F, O, for example) means press and release each key in succession rather than pressing them all at once.

The *Windows logo key*, next to the Alt key on most PC keyboards, pulls up the Start menu when pressed by itself, but it also can be used as a modifier. Windows logo key+D, for example, minimizes all windows. When I give a Windows-logo-key shortcut, mentally add "if my keyboard has one," because not all keyboards do.

✔ Tip

■ Use Windows Help and Support to view or print a list of keyboard shortcuts: Choose Start > Help and Support, and search for *keyboard shortcuts*.

Default settings

Throughout this book, I refer to Vista's *defaults*, or predefined settings, that Microsoft set when it shipped Windows from the factory. In some cases a middleman—such as your PC's manufacturer, a network administrator, or whoever unpacked your computer—will have changed some default options, so your initial Windows setup might look or behave a little differently than I describe.

Companion website

For corrections and updates, go to www.fehily.com. Click the Contact link to send me questions, suggestions, corrections, and gripes related to this book.

ABOUT THIS BOOK

GETTING STARTED

"Windows needs your permission to continue"

Windows Vista has a new security feature, named User Account Control (UAC), that interrupts program installations and attempts to make significant changes to your computer's setup. UAC alerts you to system changes and gets your approval via the User Account Control prompt:

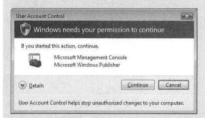

If you're logged on as an administrator, UAC asks you to click Continue or Allow. If you're a standard user, the UAC prompt provides a space for you to type an administrator password. When the UAC prompt appears, the rest of the screen darkens until you consent to (or deny) the action. Windows marks administrator actions with a shield icon:

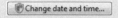

UAC, administrators, and standard users are covered in Chapter 17.

Windows Vista is complex software, but its user interface—the aspects of it that you see and hear and use to control Vista—is designed to let you wield a lot of power with a modest amount of learning. The secret is understanding the underlying consistency of the ways that Windows works. As you use Windows, techniques like switching programs, searching for files, resizing windows, drag-and-drop, and copy-and-paste will become familiar.

This chapter and the next one get you up and running and introduce you to Windows fundamentals. Chapter 3 tells you how to get help with learning and configuring Windows, on or off the internet. After that you're on your way to becoming a power user.

Logging On and Logging Off

Logging on is the process of starting a session in Windows Vista—the first thing you do after turning on your computer. After your computer powers up—or *boots*—you'll see the Welcome screen, in which you enter your user name and (optional) password. Windows *user accounts* identify who has permission to use a particular computer (or network). User accounts are covered in Chapter 17, but for now you need to know only your user name and password, which depend on your installation:

- If your PC came with Windows Vista installed, either the Welcome screen will appear with a factory-installed account name or the computer will start in Windows Setup (see the appendix) the first time you turn it on. Follow the manufacturer's instructions.

- If you upgraded to Windows Vista from Windows XP by doing an in-place installation, your existing accounts migrated to the new installation and appear on the Welcome screen.

- If you did a clean install of Windows Vista, you set up an account during installation. Use that user name and password.

- If you're on a large network at work or school, ask your network administrator how to log on.

- If your computer has only one user account with no password, Windows bypasses the Welcome screen and boots to that account's desktop directly. (Vista comes with hidden Guest and Administrator accounts, but they don't apply here.)

Logging on Automatically

You can set up your computer to log on automatically at startup even if it has more than one account or if your account is password-protected. You may like automatic logon if you're the main user but sometimes others log on, or if you keep your own separate accounts for different tasks.

To log on automatically at startup:

1. Choose Start, type `control userpasswords2` in the Search box, and then press Enter.

   or

   If you're connected to a network domain, choose Start > Control Panel > User Accounts > Advanced Options.

   If a security prompt appears, type an administrator password or confirm the action.

2. In the User Accounts dialog box, on the Users tab, uncheck Users Must Enter a User Name and Password to Use This Computer.

   This check box won't appear if your computer doesn't support automatic logon or if your network administrator has disabled it.

3. Click OK.

4. In the Automatically Log On dialog box, type the user name and password (twice) of the account that you want to log on to automatically; then click OK.

Now the system invisibly enters your user name and password at power-up. Anyone who turns on your computer can access the same files and resources that you do.

You can use the other accounts on the computer by using Fast User Switching or by logging off and then logging on to another account.

LOGGING ON AND LOGGING OFF

Logging on

Logging on to a computer identifies you uniquely so that Windows can load your personal settings and grant you certain permissions. You use the Welcome screen to log on to Windows; it lists all the accounts on your computer.

To log on to Windows:

1. On the Welcome screen, click your user name or picture.

2. If your account is password-protected, type your password in the Password box and then press Enter or click the arrow.

   Your personalized Windows desktop appears.

✔ Tips

- If you've set a password hint (see "Setting up User Accounts" in Chapter 17), it appears below the password box if you mistype your password.

- The bottom portion of the Welcome screen shows the edition of Vista that you're running and offers the options listed in **Table 1.1**.

- To cancel logon after you've started typing your password, press Esc.

- Windows XP lets you turn off the Welcome screen and use the classic logon prompt; Vista doesn't.

Table 1.1

Welcome Screen Options	
BUTTON	**CLICK TO**
	Adjust your computer for vision, hearing, and mobility, and use speech recognition. See "Accommodating Disabled Users" in Chapter 4.
	Choose a turn-off option: Restart, Sleep, Hibernate, or Shut Down. See "Turning off your computer" later in this section.
Cancel	Return to the CTRL + ALT+ DELETE screen if secure logon is enabled.

Domain Logons

If you're a home or small-business user, you're probably using a stand-alone computer or one that's part of a small workgroup network (Chapter 18), so you log on by using the Welcome screen. If you're on a large network at work or school, your machine is part of a centrally administered domain. You can log on to any computer in the domain without needing an account on that machine. Your network administrator or IT department will give you logon instructions, but here are a few basics:

◆ Windows Vista Business, Enterprise, and Ultimate editions can join domains (Home editions can't).

◆ Secure logon usually is enabled on domains; press Ctrl+Alt+Delete to display the logon screen.

◆ The domain logon screen, unlike the standard Welcome screen, doesn't list everyone's account (doing so would be insecure and impractical). Instead, you have a single place to enter your user name and password.

◆ By default, the logon screen shows the last account to log on and gives you the option to log on as a different user. Include the domain name with your user name: Log on as *user_name@domain_name* or *domain_name\user_name*. To log on to the local machine, type *.\user_name*, where *user_name* is a local (not domain) account.

◆ After logon, you can connect to the domain's shared network resources (printers, servers, and so on). Your computer might run an automated logon script to handle permissions, security, maintenance, updates, system scans, or whatever else your network administrator wants.

◆ To find the domain that you're on, choose Start > Control Panel > System and Maintenance > System (or press Windows logo key+Break). If your computer is connected to a domain, under Computer Name, Domain, and Workgroup Settings, you'll see the domain name; otherwise, you'll see a workgroup name.

◆ To connect to a domain, choose Start > Control Panel > System and Maintenance > System (or press Windows logo key+Break). Under Computer Name, Domain, and Workgroup Settings, click Change Settings. (If a security prompt appears, type an administrator password or confirm the action.) On the Computer Name tab, click Network ID to start the Join a Domain or Workgroup wizard and then follow the onscreen instructions. (Alternatively, click Change instead of Network ID to set the domain quickly without using the wizard.)

◆ If your computer was a member of a workgroup before you joined a domain, it is removed from the workgroup.

Switching users

Fast User Switching lets more than one person log on at the same time. If you step away from your computer for a short time, you can leave your programs running *and* let someone else log on to, say, check email. When you log back on, Windows resumes your session where you left off.

Only one person at a time—the *active user*—actually can *use* the computer (type at the keyboard). People who are logged on but not active—*disconnected users*—can keep their programs running and files open in the background, invisible to the active user.

To switch users without logging off:

1. Choose Start, click the arrow next to the Lock button, and then click Switch User (**Figure 1.1**).

   or

   Press Windows logo key+L.

   or

   Press Ctrl+Alt+Delete; then click Switch User.

2. If secure logon is enabled, press Ctrl+Alt+Delete.

3. In the Welcome screen, click another account name or picture; then log on normally.

Figure 1.1 Choose Switch User to keep all your work running in background memory while someone else uses the computer.

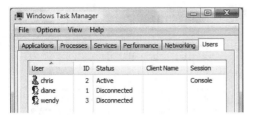

Figure 1.2 The Users tab tells you who else is logged on via Fast User Switching.

✔ Tips

■ Save all your work before switching. If the other user shuts down the computer or logs you off, Windows won't save your open files automatically.

■ In Vista (unlike Windows XP), Fast User Switching works if you're on a network domain.

■ To turn off Fast User Switching, choose Start, type `gpedit.msc` in the Search box, and then press Enter. (If a security prompt appears, type an administrator password or confirm the action.) In the Group Policy Object Editor, choose Local Computer Policy > Computer Configuration > Administrative Templates > System > Logon > enable Hide Entry Points for Fast User Switching > OK.

To find out who else is logged on to your computer:

1. Right-click an empty area of the taskbar and choose Task Manager.

   or

   Press Ctrl+Shift+Esc.

2. Click the Users tab to view users and their status (**Figure 1.2**).

LOGGING ON AND LOGGING OFF

7

If your computer is running slowly, use Task Manager to see the programs that other logged-on users are running and how much memory they're chewing up. Task Manager lists filenames (*winword.exe*, for example) in the Image Name column and program names (*Microsoft Word*) in the Description column.

To find out which programs other users are running:

1. Right-click an empty area of the taskbar and choose Task Manager.

   or

   Press Ctrl+Shift+Esc.

2. Click the Processes tab.

3. Click Show Processes from All Users (**Figure 1.3**).

   If a security prompt appears, type an administrator password or confirm the action.

✔ Tips

■ If Task Manager is missing its menus and tabs, double-click the window border to bring them back.

■ To identify the active user quickly, click Start and read the user name in the top-right section of the Start menu.

■ To log off another user, see "Logging off" later in this section.

■ Fast way to switch users: Right-click a user name in Task Manager's Users tab and choose Connect or Disconnect from the shortcut menu (see Figure 1.6 later in this chapter).

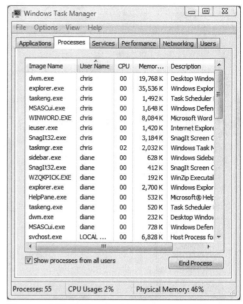

Figure 1.3 This list is sorted by user name. Click any column heading to sort by that column, or drag the headings to rearrange columns.

Figure 1.4 Your programs continue to run while your computer is locked.

Locking your computer

Without logging off, you can *lock* your computer—that is, set it so that the keyboard and mouse won't change anything—to protect your programs and personal information while you're away from your PC. Locking lets others know that you're using the computer and prevents everyone except you (or an administrator) from viewing your files or programs, though other users still can log on via Fast User Switching.

To lock your computer:

◆ Choose Start > Lock button (**Figure 1.4**).

or

Press Windows logo key+L.

or

Press Ctrl+Alt+Delete; then click Lock This Computer.

Windows displays a Locked screen with your user name until you return.

To unlock your computer:

◆ On the Locked screen, type your password in the Password box; then press Enter or click the arrow. (If secure logon is enabled, press Ctrl+Alt+Delete to display the Locked screen.)

✔ Tips

■ You can set your screen saver to lock your computer automatically after a set period of idle time; see "Setting the Screen Saver" in Chapter 4.

■ A locked computer still is subject to power-management settings; see "Conserving Power" in Chapter 4.

■ A locked computer doesn't interfere with shared printers or other network resources.

LOGGING ON AND LOGGING OFF

Logging off

Logging off ends your session in Windows Vista. When you log off your user account:

◆ Windows closes all your open programs and files. (Each program prompts you to save any unsaved work.)

◆ Windows disconnects your dial-up and other external connections.

◆ You prevent curious or malicious passersby from using your user account to access your files or network.

◆ Your computer remains turned on.

To log off:

1. Choose Start, click the arrow next to the Lock button, and then click Log Off (**Figure 1.5**).

   or

   Press Ctrl+Alt+Delete; then click Log Off.

2. If there's a problem logging off (usually because you haven't saved your work in some program), Windows displays a dialog box listing the currently running programs and explaining the problem. Do one of the following:

   ▲ Click Cancel to cancel the logoff. Resolve the issue with the problem program (by saving your work and exiting the program, for example).

   or

   ▲ Click Log Off Now to continue logging off. Windows forces the problem program to close. You might lose your work as a result.

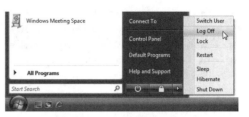

Figure 1.5 After you log off, Windows displays the Welcome screen (or the Secure Logon screen, if enabled) to let the next person log on.

Figure 1.6 Logging other users off without warning is impolite because it kills their programs without saving their unsaved work.

If other users are logged on to your machine (via Fast User Switching), you can use Task Manager to log them off.

To log off someone else:

1. Right-click an empty area of the taskbar and choose Task Manager.

   or

   Press Ctrl+Shift+Esc.

2. Click the Users tab to view logged-on users.

3. Select a user; then click Logoff.

   or

   Right-click a user and choose Log Off (**Figure 1.6**).

4. Confirm the logoff in the message box that appears.

Turning off your computer

Windows prepares itself for shutdown by saving session and system information and by disconnecting network, dial-up, and other external connections. Windows still can recover if you lose power suddenly or yank your PC's plug from the wall, but you may get an "improper shutdown" message when you return (and your unsaved work will be lost). For peace of mind, always use one of the official Windows turn-off options.

By default, turning off your computer puts it in a power-saving state called Sleep. Sleep, new in Vista, differs from the Shut Down (power-off) state used by default in earlier Windows versions.

To turn off your computer:

◆ To put your computer to sleep, choose Start; then click the Power button ( ). On laptop PCs, closing the lid puts the computer to sleep by default.

   or

   To use a different turn-off option, choose Start, click the arrow next to the Lock button (**Figure 1.7**), and then choose one of the options listed in **Table 1.2**.

Figure 1.7 Choose Restart, Sleep, Hibernate, or Shut Down.

Table 1.2

Turn-Off Options	
OPTION	WHAT IT DOES
Sleep	Turns off the display, stops the hard disks and fan, and enters low-power-consumption mode. Windows saves your work automatically, so you don't have to save your files and exit programs before putting your computer to sleep. A light on your computer case may blink slowly or turn yellow while the computer sleeps. A sleeping computer springs to life quickly—with your desktop exactly as you left it—when you start working again. Use Sleep to stop using your computer for a short time and save power (especially useful for laptops).
Shut Down	Ends your session and shuts down Windows so that you can turn off the power safely. Most computers turn off the power automatically; if yours doesn't, push the power button on the computer after the "It's safe" message appears. This option quits your programs, prompting you to save any unsaved work. After shutdown, it may take several minutes to turn on your computer, log on, and then start the programs that you were using. Use Shut Down when you're done for the day or when you need to muck around inside your computer.
Restart	Ends your session, shuts down Windows, and starts Windows again automatically. This option quits your programs, prompting you to save any unsaved work. Use Restart if you've installed hardware or software that requires a restart, or if Windows is acting erratically or sluggishly.
Hibernate	Hibernate saves your session to a file on your hard disk before turning off the power. When you restart the computer, your desktop is restored quickly and exactly as you left it. Older computers may not support this option.

To wake a computer from sleep state:

◆ Press the power button on the computer's case, press a key on the keyboard, click the mouse, or (for a laptop PC) open the lid. The computer usually will wake within seconds.

✔ Tips

■ A sleeping computer uses a tiny amount of power to maintain your work in memory. Sleeping laptops lose about 1 or 2 percent of battery power per hour. If a laptop has been sleeping for a few hours or its battery is low, Windows saves your work to hard disk and turns off your computer, drawing no power. To learn about power options for laptops, see "Conserving Power" in Chapter 4.

■ If the Power button looks like this, your computer will shut down instead of sleep because either your hardware doesn't support the sleep option (possibly because you have an old video card or outdated video driver) or an administrator has set the Power button to always shut down (see "Conserving Power" in Chapter 4).

■ A shield on the Power button means that automatic updates are ready to be installed on your computer (see "Updating Windows" in Chapter 13). Clicking this button ends your session, installs the updates, and then shuts down your computer.

■ The turn-off options also are available on the Welcome screen; see "Logging on" earlier in this section.

- If the desktop is active, you can press Alt+F4 to chose a turn-off option (**Figure 1.8**).

- For reasons of convenience, parts wearout, power consumption, power interruption, and heat stress, it's unclear whether you should leave your PC on or shut it down overnight. (I know people who rarely turn off their PCs.) Either way, you should always turn off your monitor when you're done.

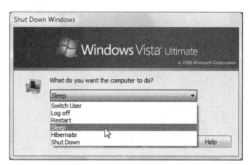

Figure 1.8 The old-style Shut Down Windows dialog box still is available.

When Installing Hardware

You should follow the manufacturer's instructions when installing hardware on your PC, but here are a few general rules (see Chapter 8 for details):

- Before you install hardware inside your computer (memory, disk drive, sound card, video card, and so on), shut down your computer *and* unplug it.

- Before you attach a peripheral device (printer, monitor, external drive) that does *not* connect to a USB or IEEE 1394 (FireWire) port, shut down your computer (no need to unplug it).

- When adding a USB or IEEE 1394 device (most newer devices), you don't have to shut down.

Using Welcome Center

At startup, Windows displays Welcome Center (**Figure 1.9**) to help you set up your computer for the first time. Common tasks include connecting to the internet (Chapter 12), adding user accounts for other people (Chapter 17), transferring files and settings from another computer (appendix), and personalizing Windows (Chapter 4).

Welcome Center appears automatically when you log on for the first time. If you don't want to see it on future starts, uncheck Run at Startup in the bottom-left corner. You can always bring it back.

Figure 1.9 Welcome Center puts tasks that help you get started using Windows Vista in one easy-to-find place. Click a task, and a description and link appear in the top pane. Click the link to get started.

USING WELCOME CENTER

To open Welcome Center:

◆ Choose Start > Control Panel > System and Maintenance > Welcome Center.

✔ Tips

■ By default, only some tasks are shown. To see them all, click the Show All Items link in the Get Started with Windows section.

■ Below Get Started with Windows is at least one Offers section with more tasks and (free or pay) offers from Microsoft or your computer's manufacturer.

■ Some Welcome Center tasks depend on your Windows setup. Add New Users won't appears if you're on a network domain, for example, and Windows Ultimate Extras appears only in Vista Ultimate edition.

Exploring the Windows Interface

Figure 1.10 shows the basic elements that you'll find on the Windows Vista desktop.

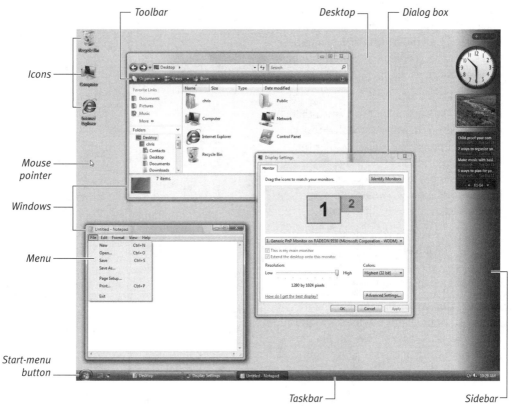

Figure 1.10 Basic elements of the Windows Vista desktop. The desktop lets you move items and manage your tasks vaguely the same way that you would on a physical desktop.

Microsoft modeled Windows on a real-world office environment: You have a desktop, on which you work and use tools, and folders, in which you organize files.

Desktop. After you log on to Windows, the *desktop*—a work area that uses menus, icons, and windows to simulate the top of a desk—appears automatically.

Start menu. The *Start menu* is the central menu that lets you access the most useful folders, programs, and commands on your computer. Chapter 2 covers the Start menu.

Taskbar. The *taskbar* lets you switch among open programs and documents. It also lets you launch programs and alerts you to certain events, such as appointment reminders or incoming email. Chapter 2 covers the taskbar.

Sidebar. The *sidebar,* new in Vista, is a long vertical bar on the edge of the desktop. It holds mini-programs, called *gadgets,* that show live information (time, weather, headlines, and so on) and provide access to frequently used tools (calendar, contacts, notes). Chapter 2 covers the sidebar.

Mouse pointer. Use your mouse, stylus, trackball, touchpad, or similar input device to move the *mouse pointer* to select items, drag icons, or choose commands onscreen.

Menus. A *menu* is a list of related commands. Most programs use menus to provide an easy-to-learn, easy-to-use alternative to memorizing instructions.

Toolbars. A *toolbar* is a row, column, or block of buttons or icons. When you click one of these buttons or icons, the program carries out a command or task.

Icons. An *icon* is a small image that represents an item to be opened, such as a file, folder, disk, program, or the Recycle Bin. An icon's picture is a visual cue designed to help you recall what the icon represents.

Windows. A *window* is a rectangular portion of your screen where a program runs. You can open many windows at the same time. Each window can be independently resized, moved, or closed; maximized to occupy the entire screen; or minimized to a button on the taskbar.

Dialog boxes. A special type of window called a *dialog box* contains text boxes, buttons, tabs, scrolling lists, or drop-down lists that let you set preferences or run commands. Some dialog boxes—such as Open, Save As, and Print—are similar in every Windows program. Others, such as the Properties dialog box shown in Figure 1.10, depend on the program or context.

The User Interface

You work with Windows through its *graphical user interface* (GUI, pronounced *gooey*), which offers pictures along with words to help you perform tasks. To make learning easier, Windows displays visual clues about how things work. Often, these clues are analogous to those you see in the real world. If a door has a flat plate rather than a handle to grasp, it's a clue to push that door, not pull it. The three-dimensional (3D) look of buttons on your screen implies that you're supposed to push them (click them). You'll recognize similar hints throughout the user interface. This chapter and the next introduce Windows' standard GUI elements.

EXPLORING THE WINDOWS INTERFACE

The Mouse

The mouse is one of two primary input devices in Windows (the other is the keyboard). Moving the mouse on your physical desk controls the motion of the mouse pointer on your screen. By moving the mouse pointer over an icon or control and then clicking, you can select an item, open or move a file, run a program, or throw something away, for example.

A mouse has a left and a right button. You'll use the left button for most actions, but skillful use of the right button, which displays a shortcut menu, is a key to working quickly. Advanced mice have extra buttons for other functions.

✔ Tips

- Most mice have a *scroll wheel* (a small wheel between the two main buttons) that helps you scroll through documents and webpages. On some mice, you can press the scroll wheel as a third button.

- Instead of a mouse, you may have a touchpad (used on laptops), trackball, or stylus (used on Tablet PCs).

- Lefties can swap the functions of the left and right mouse buttons. See "Configuring the Mouse" in Chapter 4.

- The pointer's shape changes depending on what it's pointing to. **Table 1.3** shows the default pointers. To change the shapes, see "Configuring the Mouse" in Chapter 4.

- In text documents, don't confuse the cursor, which blinks steadily, with the mouse pointer, which never blinks. The *cursor* (also called the *insertion point*) indicates where text will be inserted when you type (**Figure 1.11**).

Figure 1.11 The cursor—the vertical bar at the end of the text—marks the insertion point for newly typed text. To move the insertion point, click the mouse pointer—the I-beam on the right—at a new insertion point or use the arrow keys.

Table 1.3

Mouse Pointers

Shape	When It Appears
◦	The normal pointer. Click the area or item that you want to work with.
◦	Appears when you click the question mark (?) in the top-right corner of a dialog box. Click any dialog-box item to get "What's This?" help.
◦	Windows is doing something in the background—opening or saving a temporary file, for example. You can keep doing your own work, but response time may be longer than usual.
○	Windows is busy with a task and will ignore you until it finishes. Typically, this pointer will appear in only one program window at a time; if it appears everywhere, your computer is indeed busy.
↕ ↔ ↘	Appears when you point to a window's border (side or corner). Drag the border to resize the window. See "Windows" later in this chapter.
☝	Appears when you point to a word or image linked to a help page, command, or website. Click the link to jump to a related destination or display pop-up information.
⊘	The action that you're trying to perform is forbidden, or the item that you're pointing to is unavailable.
I	The I-beam or I-bar appears where you can select or edit text. Click to set the insertion point, or click and drag to select (highlight) text.
+	Helps you move an item precisely. This pointer often appears in drawing programs.
✛	Appears when you choose Move or Size from a window's control menu. When it does, use the arrow keys to move or resize the window and then press Enter, or press Esc to cancel. Also see "Windows" later in this chapter.

Figure 1.12 One tiny pixel is the pointer's hot spot, which you use to point precisely. For an arrow pointer, it's the tip of the arrow. In Microsoft's wilder alternative pointer schemes, finding the hot spot takes a little practice.

Figure 1.13 Click to select an icon...

Figure 1.14 ...or activate a dialog-box item.

Figure 1.15 Right-click an item to display its shortcut menu.

Figure 1.16 Drag to move items such as icons and folders. What this action actually accomplishes depends on where you drag to.

To point:

◆ Move the tip of the pointer over the item to which you want to point (**Figure 1.12**).

To click:

◆ Point to an item; then press and release the left mouse button without moving the mouse (**Figure 1.13** and **Figure 1.14**).

To double-click:

◆ Point to an item and click the left mouse button twice in rapid succession without moving the mouse.

✔ Tip

■ Double-click too slowly, and Windows interprets it as two single clicks, which isn't the same thing. To change the speed of what Windows recognizes as a double-click, see "Configuring the Mouse" in Chapter 4.

To right-click:

◆ Point to an item; then click the *right* mouse button without moving the mouse (**Figure 1.15**).

To drag:

◆ Point to an item; press *and hold* the left mouse button while you move the pointer to a new location; then release the button (**Figure 1.16**).

✔ Tips

■ Drag an object with the right mouse button to display a shortcut menu when you reach the new location.

■ Press Esc during a drag to cancel it.

■ Drag in a folder window or on the desktop to draw a rectangular *marquee* around icons. Releasing the mouse button selects the enclosed icons.

THE MOUSE

The Keyboard

The keyboard isn't just for typing text. Experienced Windows users use keystrokes instead of the mouse to issue commands. Windows provides hundreds of *keyboard shortcuts* that replicate almost every common mouse maneuver. You can use keyboard shortcuts to open, close, and navigate the Start menu, desktop, menus, windows, dialog boxes, programs, documents, and webpages. Using a keyboard shortcut usually is faster than using the mouse to do the same thing

In addition to keys for letters, numbers, and symbols, your keyboard has other types of keys:

◆ **Modifier keys** alter the meaning of the other key(s) being pressed (**Table 1.4**).

◆ **Function keys** are the keys along the keyboard's top or left side labeled F1, F2, and so on. Their functions depend on the program that you're using.

◆ **Navigation keys** scroll windows and move things around (**Table 1.5**).

Table 1.4

Modifier Keys	
KEY	**PRESS TO**
Shift	Type symbols or uppercase letters, or extend the selection when used with the mouse.
Ctrl	Modify the function of other keys. (Ctrl stands for Control.)
Alt	Access menus or modify the function of other keys. (Alt stands for Alternate.)

Table 1.5

Navigation Keys	
KEY	**PRESS TO**
Home	Scroll to the beginning or move to the start of a line or row
End	Scroll to the end or move to the end of a line or row
Page Up	Scroll up one page or windowful
Page Down	Scroll down one page or windowful
Arrow keys	Scroll in that direction, move the insertion point or selected item(s), or select the adjacent item.

The Esc Key

The Esc (for *Escape*) key, at the keyboard's top-left corner, usually means "Never mind" or "Stop what you're doing." Press it to cancel commands, interrupt long processes, cancel dialog boxes, close menus, and dismiss message boxes. Sometimes Esc does nothing. Its exact function depends on the context and the active program.

THE KEYBOARD

To use a keyboard shortcut:

1. Hold down the modifier key(s) Shift, Ctrl, or Alt.

2. Press the specified letter, number, symbol, or function key.

3. Release all the keys.

✔ Tips

■ For a list of keyboard shortcuts, choose Start > Help and Support; then search for *keyboard shortcuts*.

■ Alt behaves a little differently from Shift and Ctrl. Shift or Ctrl does nothing when pressed by itself, but Alt pressed by itself activates the menu bar or ribbon. (If you press Alt accidentally, press Alt again to get back to normal.)

■ Most PC keyboards have extra Windows-specific keys on either side of the spacebar. Press the *Windows logo key* alone to open the Start menu or press it in combination with letter keys for other actions, which I discuss where they're appropriate.

The *Application key* displays the shortcut menu for the selected item (the same as right-clicking).

■ Some keyboard shortcuts are consistent across all programs (F1 for help and Ctrl+C to copy, for example), but programs also define custom shortcuts.

■ Some keyboard shortcuts won't work if Sticky Keys is turned on in Ease of Access Center. See "Accommodating Disabled Users" in Chapter 4.

THE KEYBOARD

Modifier keys also work with mouse clicks.

To Shift-click:

◆ Hold down Shift; then click before releasing the key.

To Shift-drag:

◆ Hold down Shift; then drag and drop before releasing the key.

✔ Tip

■ Windows also has Ctrl+click, Alt+click, Ctrl+drag, and Alt+drag commands for file operations.

Keyboard Tricks

If you were raised on IBM 84-key, nonstandard laptop, or ergonomic keyboards, you may be near madness from the placement of the Caps Lock, Ctrl, and Windows logo keys on standard 102-key keyboards.

PC Magazine's TradeKeys utility ($8 U.S.; www.pcmag.com) lets you change, swap, or disable keyboard keys (including modifier keys) in almost any way. Different users can switch among different mappings quickly.

A few keyboard utilities automate repetitive typing and reduce errors:

◆ ShortKeys ($20 U.S.; www.shortkeys.com) lets you set up replacement text for keystrokes that you define. ShortKeys autoreplaces the keystrokes with the text as you type (like Word's AutoCorrect feature).

◆ Keyboard Express ($25 U.S.; www.keyboardexpress.com) lets you define keyboard *macros*, which are keystroke sequences that run automatically.

◆ Microsoft's IntelliType Pro (free; www.microsoft.com/hardware/mouseandkeyboard/ Download.mspx) works with some non-Microsoft keyboards too. Use it to reassign or disable keys, issue common commands, open programs and webpages, and more.

◆ If you, like me, are a fan of the old IBM Model M keyboards, with their heavy-duty casings and springy clacky keys, you can buy them at www.clickykeyboards.com or www.pckeyboard.com.

Menus

Windows uses menus to list commands in groups (**Figure 1.17**). Menus are especially convenient when you're new to a program because they show you what commands are available and make experimenting easy.

Experienced users prefer to use keyboard shortcuts instead of the mouse to choose menu commands. Programs often provide a keyboard shortcut for a frequently used command, which appears to the right of the command on its menu line. To choose Copy, for example, press Ctrl+C. If no shortcut key is listed for the command, you can use Alt+ the command's underlined menu letter instead.

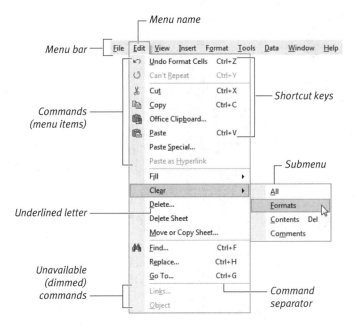

Figure 1.17 Menus are located in the menu bar at the top of a program's window.

✔ Tips

- Commands with a triangular arrowhead next to them have additional choices listed in a *submenu*. To open a submenu, click or point to the command.

- Checked commands (**Figure 1.18**) represent on/off options or mutually exclusive choices.

- Dimmed commands are unavailable in the current context. Cut and Copy are unavailable if nothing is selected, for example.

- Within individual menus, commands are grouped logically by horizontal lines called *command separators*.

- Some menus are consistent across programs. The File menu almost always has the commands New, Open, Save, Save As, Print, and Exit; the Edit menu has the commands Undo, Cut, Copy, and Paste.

To choose a menu command:

1. Click the menu name.

   The menu appears, displaying its commands.

2. Point to the desired menu command.

3. Click to choose the command.

   The menu disappears.

Figure 1.18 A checked command indicates an option that's turned on or selected.

•••

Most menu commands take effect as soon as you choose them. If a command needs more information to complete, it's followed by an ellipsis (...), which lets you know that a dialog box will appear to let you enter more information. The Find command in Figure 1.17, for example, has an ellipsis because the command isn't complete until you specify what you want to find.

Some commands, such as Properties and Help > About, show a dialog box but have no ellipsis because no more information is needed to run the command.

To choose a menu command by using the keyboard:

1. Hold down Alt, press the underlined letter in the menu name, and then release both keys.

   In some programs, the underlines or menu bar won't appear until you press Alt.

2. On the keyboard, press the underlined letter of a menu command.

3. If a submenu appears, press the underlined letter of a submenu command.

✔ Tips

■ To display underlines in dialog boxes and other windows, choose Start > Control Panel > Ease of Access > Ease of Access Center > Make the Keyboard Easier to Use > check Underline Keyboard Shortcuts and Access Keys > Save.

■ If two or more menu commands have the same underlined letter, press the letter repeatedly until you select the right command; then press Enter.

■ Another way to use the keyboard: Press F10 or Alt (by itself) to activate the menu bar, use the arrow keys to navigate to a command, and then press Enter.

■ In some Vista programs—Windows Explorer, Internet Explorer, and Windows Media Player, for example—you have to press and release Alt to make the menu bar appear.

■ To close a menu without choosing a command, press Esc twice (or click outside the menu).

MENUS

Shortcut menus

A *shortcut menu* (also called a *right-click menu* or *context menu*) is a context-sensitive menu that appears when you right-click an item (**Figure 1.19**). Windows provides shortcut menus for nearly all interface elements: icons, files, folders, disks, desktop, taskbar, Start button, Start-menu items, Recycle Bin, and so on. Shortcut menus are among the most useful features in Windows. Try right-clicking any item to see whether a shortcut menu pops up.

✔ Tips

- Shortcut-menu commands apply only to the item (or group of items) to which you point.

- Programs provide their own custom shortcut menus. Right-click a link in Internet Explorer, selected text in Notepad or Microsoft Word, or an image in Adobe Photoshop, for example.

- Right-clicking a taskbar button or a title bar displays the control menu (sizing menu) for that program's window. See "Windows" later in this chapter.

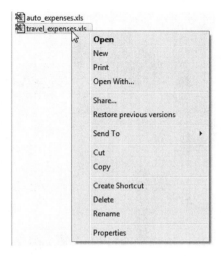

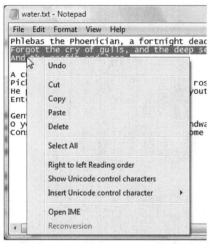

Figure 1.19 The right mouse button's shortcut menus offer common commands quickly. Here are shortcut menus for a Microsoft Excel file in Explorer, the Recycle Bin, and selected text in Notepad. Figure 1.15 shows the Computer shortcut menu.

To choose a shortcut-menu command:

1. Right-click an item.
   The shortcut menu appears, displaying its commands.

2. Point to the desired menu command.

3. Click to choose the command.
   The menu disappears.

To choose a shortcut-menu command by using the keyboard:

1. Select (highlight) an item.

2. [icon] Press the Application key (or press Shift+ F10).

3. Press the underlined letter of a menu command.
   or
   Use the arrow keys to navigate to a command; then press Enter.

✔ Tips

- Some shortcut menus have a default command in boldface; you can press Enter to choose this command.

- To close a shortcut menu without choosing a command, press Esc or left-click outside the menu. (Right-clicking outside the menu only makes the menu jump to the pointer.)

- If multiple icons are selected, right-click any one of them to open the shortcut menu for the group.

Uninvited Shortcut-Menu Entries

Utilities, shareware, and other programs often add their own entries to shortcut menus with or without your permission. If a shortcut menu gets too crowded, you usually can remove items via the programs' Options or Preferences dialog boxes; look for options labeled *context menu*. WinZip, for example, adds commands (such as Add to Zip) to Explorer's shortcut menus. WinZip's Option > Configuration > Explorer Enhancements tab lets you show or hide these commands.

If no context-menu option is available, you can edit the registry (see "Editing the Registry" in Chapter 20). Many context-menu commands are in *HKEY_CLASSES_ROOT\Directory\shell* and *HKEY_CLASSES_ROOT\Folder\shell*. Double-click *shell* to reveal the keys corresponding to each menu command. (You won't see and can't remove Windows' built-in commands.) Delete the keys that you don't want.

In some cases, the keys are hidden elsewhere in *HKEY_CLASSES_ROOT*, and you'll have to hunt for the program's key (sometimes tricky—*Adobe.Acrobat. ContextMenu*, for example) or choose Edit > Find to find the menu-item text (Scan for Viruses or whatever). For instructions, see the software publisher's website or search the web by using the terms *context menu, registry,* and the name of the program. Sometimes no keys are available, and you must live with the custom menu item. Back up your registry before you edit it.

MENUS

Menu buttons

In Vista you'll also find *menu buttons,* which look like ordinary buttons except that they have a menu drop-down arrow within them. In some cases, clicking the button reveals a menu (**Figure 1.20, top**). In others, hovering the mouse pointer "splits" the button into two parts: a larger part that runs the main command and a smaller one (with the drop-down arrow) that shows a small menu of related commands and options (**Figure 1.20, middle**). Some task-pane buttons and links have menus that are displayed within the pane (**Figure 1.20, bottom**).

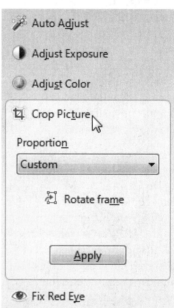

Figure 1.20 A menu button in Windows Photo Gallery (top), a split menu button in Windows Media Player (middle), and a task-pane menu in Windows Photo Gallery (bottom).

Ribbons

In Microsoft Office 2007, released about the same time as Windows Vista, Microsoft introduced the *ribbon* to replace the traditional menus and toolbars. A ribbon (**Figure 1.21**) is organized as a set of tabs that exposes many more commands than the system of menus, toolbars, task panes, and dialog boxes that people worked with in earlier Office versions. The ribbon appears in Word 2007, Microsoft PowerPoint 2007, Excel 2007, and Microsoft Access 2007. If it catches on, expect to see the ribbon in other Windows applications.

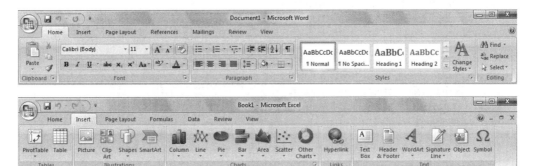

Figure 1.21 The ribbons in Word 2007 (top) and Excel 2007 (bottom) make it easier to find commands that previously were buried deep in the interface.

MENUS

Toolbars

A *toolbar* is a row, column, or block of buttons with icons that you click to perform some action, choose a tool, or change a setting (**Figure 1.22**). Toolbar buttons often duplicate menu functions, but they're more convenient because they're always visible—generally at one edge of the work area. Programs typically have several toolbars, each responsible for a group of tasks. In a word processor, for example, there's one toolbar for formatting text and paragraphs, and there's another for performing file operations.

✔ Tips

- Many programs display *tooltips* or *screentips*—short descriptions of toolbar buttons and icons that appear temporarily when the mouse pointer pauses on them (**Figure 1.23**).

- A toolbar button with a small triangular arrow pointing right or down will reveal its own small, self-contained menu when clicked (**Figure 1.24**). See also "Menu buttons" earlier in this chapter.

- Often, you can customize toolbars, create new ones, and move them around onscreen to suit your preferences. Experiment. Right-click a toolbar to see whether a shortcut menu appears. Click an empty area of a toolbar (usually its left side), and try dragging to dock it at an edge of the window or just let it float in the middle.

- Some toolbars have *toggle buttons* that push in (turn on) with one click and pop out (turn off) with the next. They can set global options or conditions that apply to only the current selection (**Figure 1.25**).

- Toolbars can appear and disappear automatically, depending on what you're doing in the program.

Figure 1.22 Toolbars from Windows Explorer (top) and Photoshop (middle). The bottom toolbar shows Microsoft's standard Office icons, which many programs adopt for consistency. Left to right: New, Open, Save, Print, Print Preview, Spell Check, Cut, Copy, Paste, Format Painter, Undo, and Redo.

Figure 1.23 A word-processing tooltip. Some tooltips also give the keyboard shortcut for the command.

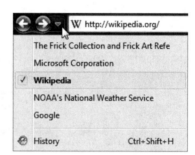

Figure 1.24 In Internet Explorer, the Recent Pages button's menu lets you revisit websites that you've seen recently.

Figure 1.25 Toggle buttons stay pressed until they're clicked a second time. These pushed-in buttons boldface and left-align the selected text in a word processor.

Figure 1.26 An icon's image depends on what it represents. System objects such as Computer, Control Panel, and the Recycle Bin have default images. All documents of the same type—text (.txt) files, for example— have the same icon. Programs (.exe) files such as Internet Explorer have icons that the software publisher built into the program.

Figure 1.27 Click an icon to select it.

Icons

An *icon* is a small picture that represents an item you can manipulate. Windows uses icons on the desktop and in folders to represent folders, files, disks, documents, programs, the Recycle Bin, and hardware devices (**Figure 1.26**).

You select (highlight) an icon or group of icons to perform an action. Left-click to select; right-click to open the shortcut menu.

What happens when you open an icon depends on the icon's type. A *folder, drive, removable-storage* or *portable-device* icon opens in a Windows Explorer window. A *document, picture, video,* or *music* icon opens in its associated program, launching that program if it's not already open. A *program* icon launches the program. A *saved search* icon, new in Vista, searches your computer and lists all files that match what you're looking for. The *Recycle Bin* icon displays the items to be deleted when you empty the bin.

To select an icon:

◆ Click it (**Figure 1.27**).

or

Press the arrow keys until the icon is selected.

or

Press the first letter of the icon's name. If two or more icons have the same initial letter, press the letter repeatedly until you select the right icon.

✔ Tips

■ Selecting an icon deselects any other selected icons.

■ You can configure Windows to select an icon just by pointing at it. See "Using Alternative Mouse Behavior" in Chapter 4.

ICONS

To select multiple icons:

◆ Ctrl+click each icon that you want to select (**Figure 1.28**).

or

Drag a selection rectangle around the icons (**Figure 1.29**). The area always is a rectangle; you can't surround an odd-shaped area.

or

Click the first icon that you want to select; then Shift+click the last icon. All icons in between are selected automatically—at least by Windows' definition of "in between."

✔ Tip

■ In Windows Explorer it's easiest to work with multiple icons in details or list view, in which all icons appear in columns: Choose Views > Details or Views > List (on the toolbar). See "Using Windows Explorer" in Chapter 5.

To select all icons in a window:

◆ Choose Organize > Select All (on the toolbar) or Edit > Select All (on the menu bar), or press Ctrl+A.

To deselect an icon:

◆ If the icon is the only one selected, click anywhere in the window or desktop other than the selected icon.

or

If the icon is part of a multiple selection, Ctrl+click it to remove it from the selection.

✔ Tips

■ To select *almost* all the icons in a window, press Ctrl+A; then Ctrl+click the icons you *don't* want.

■ Choose Edit > Invert Selection (or press Alt, E, I) to reverse which icons are selected and which are not.

Figure 1.28 Ctrl+click to select multiple (nonconsecutive) icons. This window shows icons in details view.

Figure 1.29 You can drag across icons in any direction to create a selection. Icons within the rectangle darken to confirm that they're selected.

ICONS

Figure 1.30 Drag and drop an icon to move it to...

Figure 1.31 ...a new position in the window (or on the desktop).

To move an icon:

◆ Drag it to a new position (**Figure 1.30** and **Figure 1.31**).

✔ Tips

■ Click the column headings (Name, Date Modified, Type, Size, and so on) to sort the icons within a window.

■ You can't drag icons to new positions within a window set to list view.

■ You can move multiple icons at the same time by dragging any icon in a multiple selection.

To open an icon:

◆ Double-click it.

or

Select it; then press Enter.

✔ Tips

■ To open multiple icons at the same time, select the icons; then press Enter.

■ To open a document or picture with something besides its associated (default) program, right-click its icon and choose Open With.

■ You can configure Windows to open an icon with a single click. See "Using Alternative Mouse Behavior" in Chapter 4.

ICONS

Windows

The Windows interface takes its trademark name from the rectangles on your screen—the windows—in which you work. **Figure 1.32** shows a typical window with its parts labeled. When you work with Windows Vista you'll have multiple (overlapping) windows open at the same time so that you can, say, alternate working with a word processor, email program, and web browser.

In a window for an application (such as Internet Explorer, Word, or Photoshop), you identify the window by its *title bar,* which lists the name of the program and the current document. In a folder window (such as Documents or Control Panel), the title bar is blank, and the *address bar* displays your current location as a series of links separated by arrows (**Figure 1.33**).

Each window has its own boundaries and can present different views of its contents. To manage multiple windows, you need to learn a few basic skills.

✔ Tips

■ The windows that you actually work with often are crowded with other items, such as menus, toolbars, status bars, and navigation and other panes.

■ Windows don't *have* to be rectangular. Some applications (Windows Media Player, for example) let you apply odd-shaped "skins."

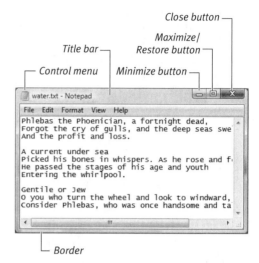

Figure 1.32 An application window.

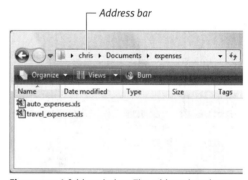

Figure 1.33 A folder window. The address bar shows the current location.

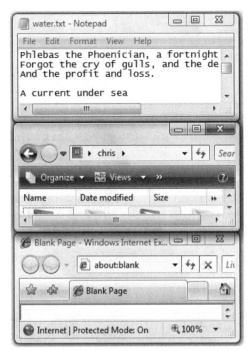

Figure 1.34 You can tell which window is active by looking for the darker color of the title bar and borders—the center one, in this case.

Activating a window

If you have multiple windows open, only one window is active at any time. The *active window* is the one that receives your keystrokes (text entry, navigational movements, or commands). You can identify the active window by its dark-colored title bar and border; the edges of inactive windows have a washed-out color. If you're using the Aero color scheme, the active window has a heavier shadow that makes it look like it's floating above the inactive ones (**Figure 1.34**). An inactive window can be hidden partially or entirely behind another window, where it remains inactive until you bring it to the foreground.

To activate a window:

◆ Click anywhere on the window (but don't click a button or menu lest you activate it accidentally).

or

Click the window's taskbar icon.

or

In the Quick Launch toolbar on the taskbar, click the Switch Between Windows button (▦), use the arrow keys to select a window, and then press Enter.

or

Hold down Alt, press Esc repeatedly until the desired window appears, and then release both keys.

or

Hold down Alt, press Tab repeatedly until the desired program icon is highlighted in the pop-up selection bar, and then release both keys. (This common technique is called *Alt-tabbing*.)

or

If you're using the Aero color scheme, hold down the Windows logo key, press Tab repeatedly until the desired program window appears, and then release both keys.

WINDOWS

✔ Tips

■ Programs whose windows are inactive can still carry out tasks—called *background tasks*—such as downloading files or printing documents. *Inactive* means that *you* are ignoring the window, but Windows still gives it the resources to do its job.

■ Generally, the active window is in front of all other windows. But some windows, such as Task Manager and Help, can be set to stay on top—in the foreground— even when inactive.

■ See also "Switching Programs" in Chapter 6.

Resizing, moving, and closing windows

You can *maximize* a window to the size of your whole screen (**Figure 1.35**), *minimize* it to a button on the taskbar (**Figure 1.36**), or *restore* it to a free-floating rectangle on your screen (**Figure 1.37**). To change the size of a restored window, drag its corners or edges.

To resize a window:

◆ Drag any window border (side or corner). The pointer changes to a double-headed arrow when it's moved over a border. See "The Mouse" earlier in this chapter.

or

Activate the window, press Alt+spacebar, press S, use the arrow keys to resize the window, and then press Enter. (Hold down Ctrl to make the arrow keys resize in fine increments.)

Figure 1.35 A maximized window reduces the need for scrolling but hides other windows. When a window is maximized, its Maximize button changes to the Restore button.

Figure 1.36 A minimized window reduces screen clutter and reveals other windows hidden behind it.

Figure 1.37 You can resize or move a restored window to work with multiple windows conveniently. When a window is restored, its Restore button changes to the Maximize button.

WINDOWS

Figure 1.38 Right-clicking a taskbar button displays its window's control menu.

To maximize a window:

◆ If the window is minimized, right-click its taskbar button and choose Maximize (**Figure 1.38**).

   or

   If the window is restored, click its Maximize button ( ) or double-click its title bar.

   or

   If the window is restored, activate it; press Alt+spacebar; and then press X.

To minimize a window:

◆ Click its Minimize button ( ).

   or

   Activate the window, press Alt+spacebar, and then press N.

To restore a window:

◆ Right-click its taskbar button and choose Restore.

   or

   If the window is maximized, click its Restore button ( ) or double-click its title bar.

   or

   If the window is maximized, press Alt+spacebar and then press R.

✔ Tips

■ If you use Alt+spacebar+(underlined letter) to maximize or restore a window, that window remains active; if you minimize it, it doesn't.

■ You can resize only restored windows, not maximized or minimized ones.

■ To arrange multiple (restored) windows neatly on your desktop, see "Managing Windows by Using the Taskbar" in Chapter 2.

■ Some utility programs, such as Calculator and Character Map, can't be maximized or resized.

WINDOWS

To move a window:

◆ Drag its title bar (**Figure 1.39**).

or

Activate the window, press Alt+spacebar, press M, use the arrow keys to move the window, and then press Enter. (Hold down Ctrl to make the arrow keys move in fine increments.)

✔ Tips

■ You can move only restored windows, not maximized or minimized windows.

■ You can move a window so that a portion of it lies off the screen's edge.

To close a window:

◆ Click its Close button ( ).

or

Right-click its taskbar button and choose Close (refer to Figure 1.38).

or

Right-click its title bar and choose Close from the control menu.

or

Double-click the icon or an empty area at the far-left end of the title bar.

or

Activate the window and press Alt+F4.

or

Activate the window, press Alt+spacebar, and then press C.

or

Choose File > Close (or press Alt, F, C) to close the file or File > Exit (Alt, F, X) to quit the application, whichever is appropriate. (This distinction between Close and Exit isn't consistent across programs.) You'll be prompted to save any unsaved work.

Figure 1.39 The title bar provides convenient ways to move and resize a window: Drag it to move the window, double-click it to alternate between restored and maximized states, or right-click it (or left-click near the left corner) to show the control menu.

Figure 1.40
If a document window is maximized, its window controls appear directly below the program's window controls.

✔ Tips

- The desktop itself is a window open under all other windows; you "close" it by logging off or shutting down. Pressing Alt+F4 when the desktop is active displays the Shut Down Windows dialog box.

- Many programs, such as Word and Photoshop, let you have more than one document or picture open at the same time. Each document window has its own title bar and dedicated controls, letting you work in it without affecting other windows (**Figure 1.40**).

Scrolling

If a window is too small to display all its contents, scroll bars appear. A *scroll bar* is a vertical or horizontal bar at the side or bottom of a window that you can move with the mouse to slide that window's contents around.

A scroll bar has three components: *scroll arrows* at its ends for moving incrementally, a sliding *scroll box* for moving to an arbitrary location, and the scroll-bar *shaft* (gray background) for jumping by one windowful at a time (**Figure 1.41**).

To scroll a window's contents:

◆ To scroll up or down line by line, click the up or down scroll arrow.

or

To scroll up or down incrementally, press an arrow key.

or

To scroll up or down by a windowful, click the shaft above or below the vertical scroll box, or press Page Up or Page Down.

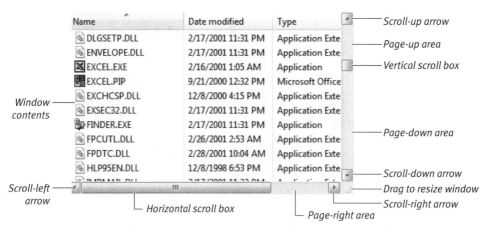

Figure 1.41 The size of a scroll box is proportional to the fraction of the window contents displayed, so the scroll box indicates visually how much you *can't* see, as well as showing you where you are.

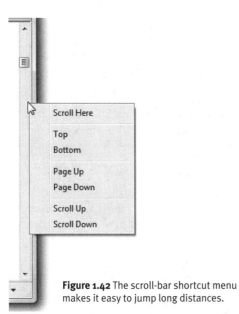

Figure 1.42 The scroll-bar shortcut menu makes it easy to jump long distances.

Automatic Scrolling

Many programs scroll automatically in the following situations:

◆ When you drag highlighted text or graphics near the window's edge, the area scrolls in the direction of the drag.

◆ When you extend a highlighted selection by dragging past an edge, the area scrolls in the direction of the drag (sometimes at high velocity).

◆ When you drag an object past the edge of a scrollable window, the area autoscrolls at a speed proportional to how far past the edge you drag.

◆ When you tab to a text box or type or paste text into a partially hidden text box, the form autoscrolls to reveal the whole box.

◆ Using Find, Replace, or a similar command autoscrolls to show the matching selection or new cursor location.

or

To scroll left or right incrementally, click the left or right scroll arrow.

or

To scroll left or right by a windowful, click the shaft to the left or right of the horizontal scroll box.

or

To move to an arbitrary location, drag a scroll box to the place you want. (Some programs show the scrolling content or a location indicator while you drag so you know when to stop; other programs make you guess.)

✔ Tips

■ If your mouse has a wheel, you can scroll up or down by turning it.

■ In many programs you can press Ctrl+Home and Ctrl+End to go to a document's beginning or end. If yours won't, the fastest way to scroll is to drag the scroll box to the top or bottom of the scroll bar.

■ In Windows Explorer, Internet Explorer, Notepad, and some other programs, you can right-click anywhere on a scroll bar to show a navigation shortcut menu (**Figure 1.42**).

■ Holding down the mouse button on a scroll arrow or shaft autorepeats the scrolling behavior. (If you lean on the shaft for more than a few seconds, Windows can lose track of video memory, and the window contents will appear distorted or sliced up before Windows recovers.)

■ You can use the mysterious Scroll Lock key for keyboard scrolling. When Scroll Lock is toggled on (its keyboard indicator is lit) and you press a navigation key, some programs scroll the view without affecting the cursor or selection.

WINDOWS

Dialog Boxes

Dialog boxes let you enter new information or view or change existing settings. A dialog box is a small temporary window that a program displays to respond to a command or event (**Figure 1.43**).

✔ Tips

■ Dialog boxes appear when you must enter more information to complete a command. See the sidebar in "Menus" earlier in this chapter.

■ The specialized dialog boxes for saving and opening files are covered in "Saving Documents" and "Opening Documents" in Chapter 6.

OK, Cancel, Apply

Most dialog boxes have an OK button and a Cancel button, and many have an Apply button too. The differences are:

OK. Saves your changes and closes the dialog box (often equivalent to pressing Enter).

Cancel. Discards your changes and closes the dialog box (equivalent to pressing Esc).

Apply. Saves your changes and leaves the dialog box open for more changes. Apply is handy if you want to try out a change with the chance to change it right back.

The Apply button's behavior has a slight wrinkle: If you click Apply and then click Cancel, changes made *before* you click Apply are saved, but changes made *after* you click Apply are lost—usually, that is. Some programs behave differently.

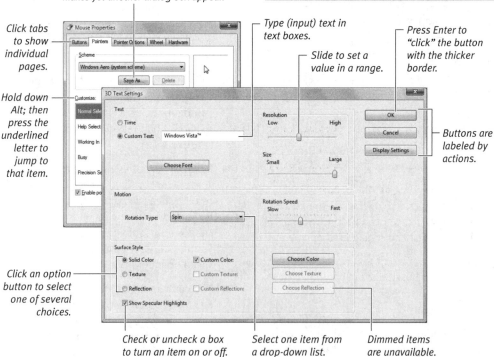

Clicking a button with an ellipsis (...) makes yet another dialog box appear.

Click tabs to show individual pages.

Type (input) text in text boxes.

Slide to set a value in a range.

Press Enter to "click" the button with the thicker border.

Hold down Alt; then press the underlined letter to jump to that item.

Buttons are labeled by actions.

Click an option button to select one of several choices.

Check or uncheck a box to turn an item on or off.

Select one item from a drop-down list.

Dimmed items are unavailable.

Figure 1.43 Dialog boxes let you change settings by using buttons, check boxes, text boxes, lists, and other controls.

Table 1.6

Dialog-Box Keyboard Shortcuts	
PRESS	To
Ctrl+Tab	Select the next tab
Ctrl+Shift+Tab	Select the previous tab
Tab	Select the next option
Shift+Tab	Select the previous option
Alt+underlined letter	Select the corresponding option or click the corresponding button
Spacebar	Click a button, toggle a check box, or choose an option button (if that option is active)
Arrow keys	Select an item in an option-button group or list, or move a slider
F1	Display Help
F4	Display list items
Enter	Click the selected button (with the dotted outline) or the default button (with the shadow)
Esc	Click the Cancel button

Figure 1.44 The purpose of each wizard page is stated clearly at the top. Many pages have links that you can click for help. The Back button is in the top-left corner.

Figure 1.45 Message boxes bring your program to a halt. You must respond before the program can do anything further.

The differences between dialog boxes and normal windows are:

◆ File Open and File Save As dialog boxes usually are resizable, to let you vary the number of files that they display. Most other dialog boxes aren't resizable.

◆ Some open dialog boxes won't let you keep working in their program until you close them. You still can use other programs, though.

◆ When you edit text in a dialog box, you can't use the Edit menu to cut, copy, and paste, but you can use keyboard shortcuts (Ctrl+X, Ctrl+C, and Ctrl+V) or right-click to use a shortcut menu.

◆ Use keyboard shortcuts to navigate dialog boxes quickly (**Table 1.6**).

◆ A *wizard* is a series of interactive dialog boxes that steps you through a complex task (**Figure 1.44**).

◆ Windows uses a *message box* to notify you of events or ask for a decision (**Figure 1.45**).

Properties

Almost every object in Windows has a Properties dialog box full of information about its contents and settings. Items with properties include files, folders, drives, documents, programs, hardware devices, fonts, the taskbar, the Start menu, the sidebar, the desktop, the notification area, Computer, and Network.

To display an item's properties:

◆ Right-click the item and choose Properties (**Figure 1.46**).

   or

   Select (highlight) the item and press Alt+Enter.

   or

   Hold down Alt and double-click the item.

Figure 1.46 You can choose an item's properties from its shortcut (right-click) menu. The Properties command usually is at the bottom of the menu.

PROPERTIES

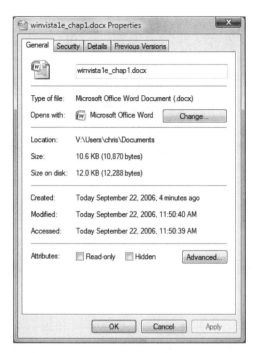

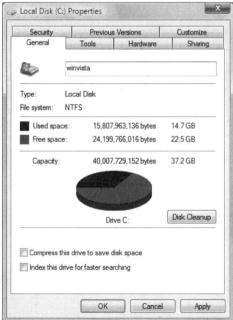

Figure 1.47 The properties information shown is appropriate for the item you select. Here are properties for a Word document (top) and a hard disk (bottom).

Figure 1.47 shows Properties dialog boxes for a Word file and a hard disk. Windows lets you change some properties; you can rename the file or compress the hard disk, for example. Many properties are *read-only*, however, meaning that Windows sets them and you can't change them. You can inspect—but not change—a hard disk's capacity or a file's creation date, for example.

✔ Tips

■ A read-only property usually is shown as black text on a gray background; a modifiable (read–write) property is set in a text box, check box, drop-down list, or similar control. If it's not obvious whether you can change a property, try to click it or tab to it. You can copy the text of some read-only properties by dragging across the text to select it and pressing Ctrl+C. Paste it somewhere with Ctrl+V.

■ Some dialog boxes have a button labeled Restore, Restore Defaults, Defaults, or Reset. Clicking this button changes your current settings back to Windows' factory-installed settings. Be careful, because you (or the programs that you've installed) have probably made more changes than you remember—or even know about.

■ Some programs let you add file properties such as comments and custom name-value attributes. In the Properties dialog box of a Word document, for example, click the Details tab (or choose File > Properties inside Word itself). Also see "Tagging Files" in Chapter 5.

■ To see how much disk space a group of files or folders occupies, select the files' or folders' icons; then display the properties for the selected group.

Transferring Data

One thing you'll do regularly in Windows is move data around: copy webpage text to an email message, put graphics-editor images in a word-processing document, move paragraphs around in a text file, export spreadsheet rows to a database, embed a chart in a presentation slide, and so on. Windows gives you a few ways to do so.

Cut, copy, and paste

Cut, copy, and paste, which are second nature to experienced Windows users, are used to organize documents, folders, and disks.

Cut-and-paste removes (cuts) information and places it on the clipboard so that it can be moved (pasted) elsewhere. Cutting deletes the data from its original location.

Copy-and-paste copies information to the clipboard so that it can be duplicated (pasted) elsewhere. Copying leaves the original data intact (nothing visible happens).

You'll find Cut, Copy, and Paste commands in a program's Edit menu (**Figure 1.48**), but each program may handle these operations differently. In Windows Explorer, for example, you can copy or move files and folders from one disk or folder to another. In Word, you can copy or move text or graphics to another part of a document or to a different document. In Internet Explorer, you can only copy material from webpages, not cut it.

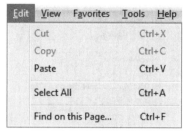

Figure 1.48 If nothing is selected, the Cut and Copy commands are dimmed.

To cut:

1. Select (highlight) the material to remove.

2. Choose Edit > Cut.

or

Press Ctrl+X.

or

Right-click the selection and choose Cut.

To copy:

1. Select (highlight) the material to copy.

2. Choose Edit > Copy.

or

Press Ctrl+C.

or

Right-click the selection and choose Copy.

To paste:

1. Click the mouse (or move the cursor to) where you want to the material to appear.

2. Choose Edit > Paste.

or

Press Ctrl+V.

or

Right-click and choose Paste.

TRANSFERRING DATA

If you mean to copy (Ctrl+C) something and accidentally cut (Ctrl+X) it instead, or if you paste something in the wrong place, you can recover by undoing your action.

To undo a cut or paste:

◆ Immediately after you cut or paste, choose Edit > Undo (or press Ctrl+Z).

✔ Tips

■ Keyboard shortcuts save time, but they're especially useful when the Edit menu is unavailable (**Figure 1.49**).

■ Many programs have an Edit > Paste Special command that pastes, links, or embeds the clipboard contents in a document in the format you specify. The Paste Special command in Word, for example, lets you strip all formatting from pasted text, for example.

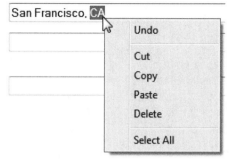

Figure 1.49 In windows that have no Edit menu, such as this dialog box, you can cut, copy, and paste by using keyboard shortcuts or the shortcut (right-click) menu.

The Clipboard

The *clipboard* is the invisible area of memory where Windows stores cut or copied data, where it remains until it's overwritten when you cut or copy something else. This scheme lets you paste the same thing multiple times in different places. You can transfer information from one program to another provided that the second program can read data generated by the first. A little experimenting shows that you often can combine dissimilar data; you can paste text from Notepad or Word into Photoshop, for example. Note that you can't paste something that you've *deleted* or *cleared* (as opposed to cut), because Windows doesn't place that something on the clipboard.

If you're a writer, editor, researcher, or graphic artist, try something more powerful than the standard clipboard: ClipCache Pro ($25 U.S.; www.clipcache.com), ClipMate ($35 U.S.; www.thornsoft.com), Clipboard Recorder (free; www.lw-works.com), or Ditto (free; http://ditto-cp.sourceforge.net). These alternatives let you save, organize, combine, preview, and control many persistent clips.

Dolore quis aliquip dolore te velit ad, sed ut illum nibh autem vel. Minim nulla ex lobortis nulla odio qui tation eros dol, duis qui adipiscing. Erat aliquip, consectetuer tation suscipit dignissim dolor praesent nulla ut vero ut dignissim, consequat ut commodo, dolore in ea vel iriure facilisi. WHAT COLOR IS AN ORANGE?

Dolore quis aliquip dolore te velit ad, sed ut illum nibh autem vel. WHAT COLOR IS AN ORANGE? Minim nulla ex lobortis nulla odio qui tation eros dolore, duis qui adipiscing. Erat aliquip, consectetuer tation suscipit dignissim dolor praesent nulla ut vero ut dignissim, consequat ut commodo, dolore in ea vel iriure facilisi.

Figure 1.50 Click in the middle of some highlighted text (top), and drag it elsewhere within the same document (bottom) or to a different window or program.

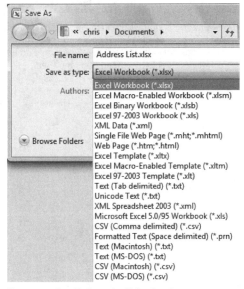

Figure 1.51 Excel's Save As dialog box lets you save a spreadsheet in formats other than the native Excel format.

Drag-and-drop

WordPad, Windows Mail, Microsoft Outlook, Word, PowerPoint, and many other email and word-processing programs let you drag-and-drop as a faster alternative to cut-and-paste. **Figure 1.50** shows you how. Move any amount of text, from single character to epic poem. This technique doesn't involve the clipboard and won't change its contents.

✔ Tips

- Press Ctrl as you drag to *copy*, rather than move, the highlighted material.

- When you drag highlighted material near the window's edge, the document auto-scrolls until you move (usually jerk) away from the edge. See the "Automatic Scrolling" sidebar earlier in this chapter.

Intermediate formats

Another way to exchange data between programs is to save it in a format that both the source and target programs can read and write. To read a list of addresses into a mailing-list program from a spreadsheet or database, for example, save the addresses in a CSV-format file (a text file of comma-separated values); then open it in the mailing-list program. The source program's Save As dialog box lists the format types that you can save (**Figure 1.51**). The target program usually autoconverts the CSV file when you open it with File > Open, but you may have to step through a wizard to organize the incoming data. Image-editing programs such as Photoshop and Microsoft Paint can exchange files in JPEG, GIF, TIFF, PNG, and other popular graphic formats.

Import/export

Use import and export tools to transfer large amounts of data or data in incompatible formats. Most address-book, browser, email, spreadsheet, database, and statistical programs have Import and Export commands, typically in the File menu. The commands vary by program (they're not part of Windows), so read the documentation for both the source and target programs. Import/export operations can be routine—most database and accounting programs can skip the CSV step and export to the native Excel format directly, for example—but they're superlative when no standard exchange-format exists. If you want to try new email and browser programs, import/export is the only practical way to transfer all your addresses, messages, bookmarks, cookies, and other information (**Figure 1.52**).

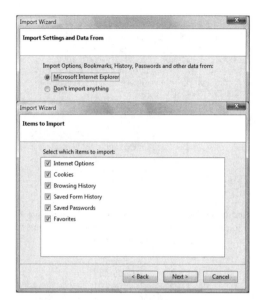

Figure 1.52 The Import wizard in the Mozilla Firefox browser (free; www.mozilla.com) imports settings, cookies, bookmarks (favorites), passwords, and other items from Internet Explorer and other browsers.

Figure 1.53 Click the Create New tab to insert a new object; click the Create from File tab to insert an existing file. Check Link to File if you want the data to self-update when the source file is edited. The Result box explains the inserted object's behavior.

OLE

OLE (pronounced *oh-lay*), for Object Linking and Embedding, lets you insert self-updating material from a source document in one program into a target document running in another. If you insert an Excel spreadsheet as a linked object into a Word document, for example, any changes that you make to the spreadsheet separately in Excel appear in the Word document automatically.

To insert an OLE object:

1. Open or create a document in a program that supports OLE (WordPad, Word, Excel, or PowerPoint, for example).

2. Click or move the cursor to where you want the inserted object to appear.

3. Choose Insert > Object.
   This command may appear elsewhere in non-Microsoft programs.

4. In the Object dialog box, choose the object type and link type that you want to create (**Figure 1.53**).

5. Click OK.

✔ Tips

- You can cut, copy, and paste OLE objects. To delete one, click it; then press Delete.

- To edit an OLE object, double-click it. If it's linked to a file, the document opens in its own window. If it's not linked, the source program's menus appear in place of the current program's menus; click off the object or press Esc when you're done editing, and the original menus reappear.

- After editing a linked object, you may have to "encourage" it to update itself. Select it; then use the program's Update function (the F9 key in Microsoft Office programs).

THE DESKTOP

After you log on, Windows displays the desktop (**Figure 2.1**). The *desktop* is the backdrop of your working environment and lets you organize the resources on your computer. The *Start menu* is the central location that lists the most useful folders, programs, and commands. The *taskbar* tells you what programs are running on your computer and lets you activate or close them. The *sidebar* contains handy mini-programs called *gadgets*.

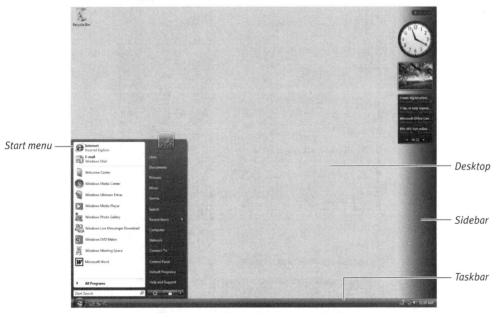

Start menu

Desktop

Sidebar

Taskbar

Figure 2.1 Basic desktop elements. Your desktop may have a different background or icons, depending on your setup and regular use.

Exploring the Start Menu

The Start menu (**Figure 2.2**) lets you:

◆ Start programs

◆ Open commonly used folders

◆ Search for files, folders, and programs

◆ Get help

◆ Adjust computer settings

◆ Switch users, lock your computer, log off, or turn off your computer

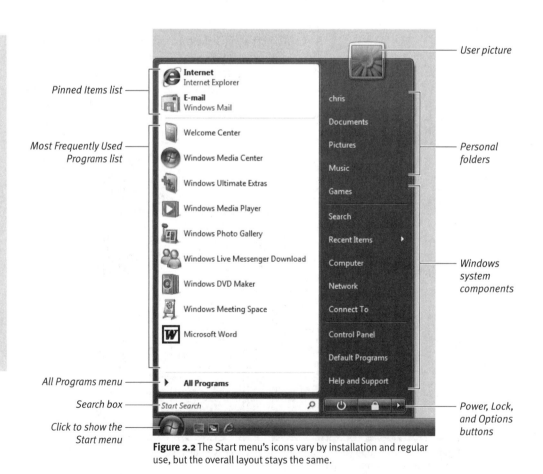

Figure 2.2 The Start menu's icons vary by installation and regular use, but the overall layout stays the same.

Start Menu: What's New?

Here are the main changes that Vista makes to the Start menu:

- The redesigned Start button now holds the Windows logo. The button actually extends past the logo, so you can click at either side of the "orb" or at the edge of the screen.

- The search box lets you search your entire computer for files, folders, or programs.

- The All Programs menu now expands as a single in-place list rather than as cascading submenus.

- The "My" has been dropped from folder names: *My Documents* is now just *Documents, My Computer* is *Computer,* and so on.

- The logoff and turn-off buttons in Windows XP have been replaced by the Power, Lock, and Options buttons.

- The picture at the top of the menu, which used to display only the user-account picture, now changes to the icon of what you're pointing to. You still can click it to access your user account.

- The Run command is no longer in the Start menu, but you can get it back: Right-click the Start button and choose Properties > Customize > check Run Command > OK. (Alternatively, press Windows logo key+R to open the Run dialog box at any time.)

EXPLORING THE START MENU

To open the Start menu:

♦ Click the Start button (at the left end of the taskbar), or press Ctrl+Esc.

or

Press and release the Windows logo key.

The left side of the Start menu lists programs and has a search box (**Table 2.1**). The right side has links to personal folders and Windows system components (**Table 2.2**). The Power, Lock, and Options buttons are described in "Logging On and Logging Off" in Chapter 1.

To close the Start menu without choosing a command:

♦ Press and release the Windows logo key, or press Esc.

or

Click anywhere off the menu (on the desktop or in a program, for example).

✔ Tips

■ Hover your mouse pointer over an item in the Start menu, and you'll get a pop-up tip describing that item. If these tips distract you, you can turn them off: Choose Start > Control Panel > Appearance and Personalization > Folder Options > View tab > uncheck Show Pop-up Description for Folder and Desktop Items > OK.

■ In Windows XP, personal folders are stored in \Documents and Settings*username*. In Vista, they're in \Users*username*.

Table 2.1

Start Menu Left Column

SECTION	DESCRIPTION
Pinned Items list	Items in the top section of this column remain there, always available to open. You can select programs to appear here, as well as their order. By default, your web browser and email program are in the list. See "Adding items to the Start menu" in the next section.
Most Frequently Used Programs list	Windows maintains this list by appending programs as you use them. Each added program replaces one that you haven't used recently. You can delete items from this list and set the number of items displayed, but you can't reorder or add them manually.
All Programs menu	This menu lists all the programs that you've installed and that come with Windows. Click or hover over All Programs to expand the menu. Click the word *Back* to collapse it. Use the menu's scroll bar or your mouse's scroll wheel to move up and down the list.
Search box	This feature find files, folders, and programs on your computer. Type search text in the Search box. As you type, items that match your text appear instantly in the menu's left column. Search looks at your personal folder, offline files, email, contacts, calendar events, and internet favorites and history, basing its search on the filename, the program title (*excel*, for example), text in the file, tags, and other file properties. Click an item in the results list to open it, or press Esc to cancel the search. For details, see "Searching for Files and Folders" in Chapter 5.

Table 2.2

Start Menu Right Column

SECTION	DESCRIPTION
User picture	Shows your account picture. This picture initially shows your user-account picture and changes to the icon of whatever you're pointing to on the right side of the menu. If you click the picture, the User Accounts tool opens to let you make changes to your account.
Personal folder	Opens your personal folder. This link (chris, in **Figure 2.2**) shows the user name of the currently logged-on user—you, usually. See "Storing Stuff in Your Personal Folder" in Chapter 5.
Documents, Pictures, and Music	Opens subfolders in your personal folder that contain specific types of files.
Games	Lets you play games (this entry doesn't appear in Vista Business editions).
Search	Opens a window where you can search your computer by using advanced options. See "Searching for Files and Folders" in Chapter 5.
Recent Items	Shows a menu of your recently opened files; click any entry to reopen that file.
Computer	Opens a window that lets you access disk drives, cameras, and other hardware connected to your computer. See "Exploring Your Computer" in Chapter 5.
Network	Opens a window that lets you access the computers and devices on your network, and provides quick access to Network and Sharing Center. See Chapter 18.
Connect To	Shows the Connect to a Network dialog box for connecting to wireless and other networks. See Chapter 18.
Control Panel	Opens Control Panel, which lets you configure and manage your system. See "Using Control Panel" in Chapter 4.
Default Programs	Shows the Default Programs window, which lets you choose the programs that Vista uses by default for web browsing, email, documents, pictures, and more. You also can associate file types with programs, change AutoPlay settings, and set program access.
Help and Support	Gets Windows help. See Chapter 3.

EXPLORING THE START MENU

Using the Start Menu

Start-menu commands are a click away. If you don't like the Start menu's default layout, you can change it. Changes you make apply only to you, the logged-on user.

To choose a Start-menu item:

◆ Click the item.

or

Use the arrow keys to navigate to the item and then press Enter.

or

Press any arrow key once to move out of the Search box, press the key of the item's first letter, and then press Enter.

If two or more items have the same first letter, press that letter repeatedly until the desired item is highlighted and then press Enter.

✔ Tips

■ A menu item with a right-pointing arrow (such as Recent Items in Figure 2.2) opens a submenu when you click or point to it.

■ If you open the All Programs menu, you can click the word *Back* to close it again.

■ If you prefer the old one-column Start menu, right-click the Start button and choose Properties > Classic Start Menu > OK. See also "Restoring the Old Windows Look" in Chapter 4.

Figure 2.3 You can right-click a program in the Start menu, in Windows Explorer, in Computer, or on the desktop. For documents, pictures, folders, and disks, use drag-and-drop.

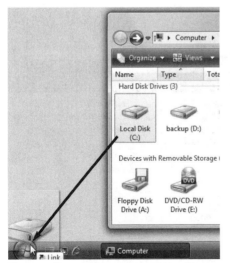

Figure 2.4 You can pin a program, folder, file, or even a disk to the Start menu by dropping it on the Start button.

Adding items to the Start menu

Icons in the Start menu are *shortcuts*—links to computer or network items such as programs, files, folders, disks, webpages, printers, connected hardware, and other computers. You can add items to the Start menu by dragging and dropping or by pinning. You also can remove or reorder items.

✔ Tip

- Changing or deleting a shortcut has no effect on the item that it's linked to. Removing a shortcut won't uninstall a program, delete a file or folder, or erase a disk, for example.

To pin an item to the Start menu:

1. Locate the item (icon) that you want to display at the top of the menu.

2. Right-click the icon and choose Pin to Start Menu (**Figure 2.3**).

   or

   Drag the item to the Start button (**Figure 2.4** and **Figure 2.5**).

Figure 2.5 The Start menu pops open if you pause on the Start button while dragging, letting you drop the item in the desired position.

✔ Tips

- If you don't know the item's location, choose Start > Search, use the Search box to find it, and then drag it from the results list to the Start button. If you're looking for a program (rather than a document, folder, or disk), type the program name in the Start menu's Search box, right-click it in the results list, and choose Pin to Start Menu.

- If you can't drag icons onto the Start menu, or if right-clicking the menu has no effect, turn on Start-menu dragging and dropping: Right-click the Start button and choose Properties > Customize > check Enable Context Menus and Dragging and Dropping > OK.

- Hold down Shift when you right-click a file in a folder window, and Pin to Start Menu will appear in the shortcut menu.

- You can't pin items to the classic (one-column) Start menu.

To move a pinned item:

- Drag the item to a new position (**Figure 2.6**).

To remove a pinned item:

- Right-click the item and choose Remove from This List (**Figure 2.7**).

Figure 2.6 The horizontal black line shows where the item will land when it's dropped.

Figure 2.7 This technique works in both the Pinned Items and Most Frequently Used Programs lists. In the Pinned Items list, you also can choose Unpin from Start Menu.

Figure 2.8 The All Programs menu superimposes itself over the left side of the Start menu.

Modifying the All Programs menu

The All Programs menu, which appears when you click or point to All Programs in the Start menu (**Figure 2.8**), displays all the programs that you, Windows Setup, your PC manufacturer, and/or your administrator have installed on your computer. Program installers add their own icons to the All Programs menu, but you can add, delete, or reorder them manually. The menu accepts not only program icons, but also document, folder, and disk icons.

By default, Windows keeps the All Programs menu sorted automatically: files alphabetically at top, followed by folders alphabetically. If you want to add an item to a specific place without having it jump to its sorted position, or if you want to move an item within the menu, turn off autosorting.

To turn off All Programs autosorting:

◆ Right-click the Start button and choose Properties > Customize > uncheck Sort All Programs Menu by Name > OK.

To add an item to the All Programs menu:

1. Locate the item (icon) that you want to add.

2. Drag the icon over the Start button and pause until the Start menu opens.

3. Continue to drag and pause over All Programs until the menu opens.

continues on next page

4. Drag the icon to the place in the All Programs menu where you want it to appear.

You can drag near the menu's top or bottom edge to autoscroll up or down, or pause over a folder to open it.

A black horizontal line shows where the icon will appear when you drop it (**Figure 2.9**).

5. Hold down Alt.

Holding down the Alt key guarantees that Windows will create a link (shortcut) in the All Programs menu rather than moving or copying the item to the All Programs folder.

6. Drop the icon on the All Programs menu and release Alt.

✔ Tips

■ Instead of dragging in step 2, you can right-drag instead. When you drop the icon, a shortcut menu appears to let you create the link (you don't have to hold down Alt).

■ Adding a folder to the All Programs menu creates a subfolder that lists its contents.

■ The default name for an item's shortcut ends with - *Shortcut* (Downloads - Shortcut, for example). To change the name, right-click the item and choose Rename.

■ If you can't drag icons onto the All Programs menu, or if right-clicking the menu has no effect, turn on Start-menu dragging and dropping: Right-click the Start button and choose Properties > Customize > check Enable Context Menus and Dragging and Dropping > OK.

■ If you're using the classic (one-column) Start menu, you can manage icons with the Customize Classic Start Menu dialog box: Right-click Start and choose Properties > Customize.

Figure 2.9 If All Programs autosorting is turned off, the item stays where you drop it; otherwise, it jumps to its proper position in the sort order.

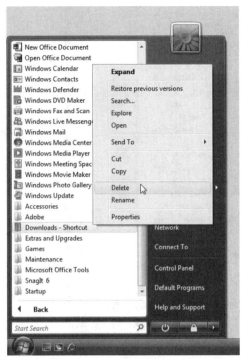

Figure 2.10 If your desktop is clear, you also can drag an item off the menu and drop it into the Recycle Bin to delete it.

To delete an item from the All Programs menu:

1. Right-click the item and choose Delete (**Figure 2.10**).

2. Confirm the deletion if a message box appears.

✔ Tip

■ To undelete an item from the Recycle Bin, see "Deleting Files and Folders" in Chapter 5.

To move an item in the All Programs menu:

1. Make sure that All Programs autosorting is turned off (described earlier in this section).

2. Drag the item to a new position.

   This technique works as shown in Figure 2.6.

To sort the All Programs menu alphabetically:

◆ Right-click any menu item and choose Sort by Name. (This command isn't available if autosorting is turned on.)

   Windows sorts files in alphabetical order at the top, followed by folders in alphabetical order.

✔ Tip

■ You can use this command to sort any subfolder individually within the All Programs menu.

Managing All Programs items with folders

To keep your All Programs menu from growing too long, you can consolidate menu items into submenus (**Figure 2.11**). You add submenus by creating folders.

Every item that appears in the Start menu is contained in one of two folders: a folder that applies only to you, the logged-on user (which only you can access); and a folder that applies to all users (which everyone who has a user account can access).

To add or delete All Programs items:

1. Right-click the Start button (**Figure 2.12**).

2. To add or delete items for only you, choose Open or Explore.

   or

   To add or delete items for everyone with a user account, choose Open All Users or Explore All Users.

Figure 2.11 A menu item with a folder icon spawns a submenu when you click it.

Figure 2.12 You can add or delete items that are visible only to you or to all users.

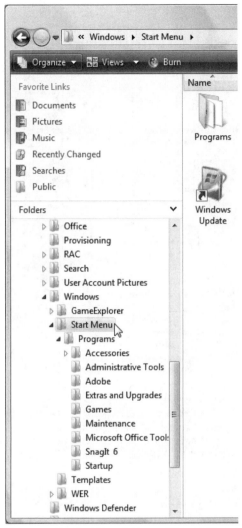

Figure 2.13 The Start Menu folder and its subfolders determine what appears in the All Programs menu. Click the right-pointing triangle next to a folder (or double-click the folder icon itself) to reveal its nested folders.

3. To add (or delete) menu items, drag icons into (or delete icons from) the Start Menu folder, the Programs folder, or any folder nested in the Start Menu or Programs folders (**Figure 2.13**).

Icons placed inside the Start Menu folder or the Programs folder appears in the All Programs menu. Subfolders inside the Programs folder appear as submenus.

To add an All Programs submenu:

1. Right-click the Start button (refer to Figure 2.12).

2. To add a submenu for only you, choose Open or Explore.

   or

   To add a submenu for everyone with a user account, choose Open All Users or Explore All Users.

3. Click Organize (on the toolbar) > New Folder, or press Alt, F, W, F.

   or

   Right-click an empty area in the right pane and choose New > Folder.

   or

   Right-click the Start Menu folder or one of its subfolders in the Folders list (on the left) and choose New > Folder. (If the list is hidden, click the Folders bar at the bottom left.)

   If a security prompt appears, type an administrator password or confirm the action.

4. Type the name of the folder and press Enter.

   You create an empty folder, which is an empty submenu (**Figure 2.14**).

5. To make a particular item appear in the new submenu, drop a shortcut to it on the new folder and then close the Explorer window.

6. Choose Start > All Programs to see the new submenu (**Figure 2.15**).

✔ Tip

- To create a nested submenu, create a new folder inside the first folder that you added.

Figure 2.14 A subfolder within the Start Menu folder or the Programs folder appears as a submenu in the All Programs menu.

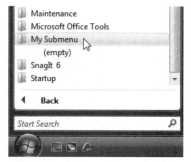

Figure 2.15 The new folder appears as an empty submenu in the All Programs menu. If All Programs autosorting is turned off, you can drag the folder up or down the menu to reposition it.

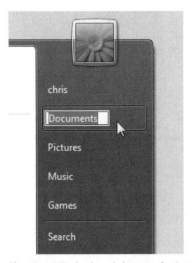

Figure 2.16 The keyboard shortcuts for Cut, Copy, and Paste (Ctrl+X, Ctrl+C, and Ctrl+V) work when you're editing the name.

Figure 2.17 Besides letting you configure the Start menu, this dialog box lets you choose the old-style, one-column Classic Start menu.

Customizing the Start Menu

The Start menu's Windows components and default behavior are easy to change. You can, for example, change the name of your Documents folder, decide which icons the menu displays, and highlight recently installed programs.

To rename a Start-menu item:

1. Right-click a menu item and choose Rename.

   If the Rename command doesn't appear in the shortcut menu, you can't rename that item.

2. Type a new name or edit the existing one, and press Enter (**Figure 2.16**).

✔ Tips

- Don't rename the Startup folder. If you do, Windows won't launch programs automatically when the computer starts.

- To cancel renaming an item, press Esc while editing.

To customize the Start menu:

1. Right-click the Start button and choose Properties (**Figure 2.17**).

   or

   Choose Start > Control Panel > Appearance and Personalization > Taskbar and Start Menu > Start Menu tab.

   continues on next page

2. In the Privacy section, clear one or both check boxes if you don't want someone else to know what you've been running or working on.

The Files check box applies to the Recent Items submenu (in the right column of the Start menu). The Programs check box applies to the Most Frequently Used Programs list (in the left column) and the Run command history (if it's displayed). Checking these boxes again makes Windows repopulate the lists over time.

3. Make sure that Start Menu (not Classic Start Menu) is selected, and click Customize to open the Customize Start Menu dialog box (**Figure 2.18**).

4. Choose the desired options, described in **Table 2.3**.

5. For Start Menu Size, type or select the number of frequently used programs to display in the menu's left column.

Displaying more programs gives you quicker access but takes up more vertical space.

6. If you want to revert to the Start menu's original factory settings, click Use Default Settings.

7. In the Show on Start Menu section, check the boxes if you want your web browser and email program pinned at the top of the menu's left column. Use the drop-down lists to choose among the installed browsers and email programs.

8. Click OK in each open dialog box.

Figure 2.18 The Customize Start Menu dialog box affects what you see in the menu's left column, where programs are listed, and the right column, where your personal folders and the Windows system components are listed.

✔ Tips

■ You still can open a folder even if you've chosen Display As a Menu: Right-click it in the Start menu and choose Open.

■ To clear the Recent Items list, right-click Recent Items in the Start menu and choose Clear Recent Items List. To clear an individual item in the list, right-click it in the Recent Items submenu and choose Delete. Clearing recent items from the list doesn't delete the originals from your computer.

■ In the classic Start menu, Recent Items is named Documents.

Table 2.3

Start-Menu Options

Computer, Control Panel, Documents, Games, Music, Personal Folder, Pictures

OPTION/SETTING	DESCRIPTION
Display As a Link	Displays a shortcut that opens that folder.
Display As a Menu	Opens a submenu (**Figure 2.19**).
Don't Display This Item	Removes that folder from the Start menu.

Connect To, Default Programs, Help, Run Command, Search

OPTION/SETTING	DESCRIPTION
Checked	Item appears in the Start menu's right column.
Unchecked	Item doesn't appear in the Start menu. (If you use these commands rarely or invoke them with keystrokes, clear their check boxes to save menu space.)

Enable Context Menus and Dragging and Dropping

OPTION/SETTING	DESCRIPTION
Checked	Lets you drag icons on, off, and within the Start menu, and also display their shortcut (right-click) menus.
Unchecked	Locks Start-menu items in place.

Favorites Menu

OPTION/SETTING	DESCRIPTION
Checked	Adds a link to your Favorites folder, which contains shortcuts to webpages, documents, and folders that you've bookmarked.
Unchecked	The Favorites menu doesn't appear.

Highlight Newly Installed Programs

OPTION/SETTING	DESCRIPTION
Checked	Highlights new programs in orange for a few days.
Unchecked	Doesn't distinguish new programs.

Table continues on next page

Figure 2.19 Display As a Menu makes a Start-menu folder expand as a submenu that displays its contents (rather than open as a window).

CUSTOMIZING THE START MENU

Table 2.3 *continued*

Start-Menu Options

Network

OPTION/SETTING	DESCRIPTION
Checked	Shows a link to shared resources on your network.
Unchecked	Shows this computer and its peripherals only.

Open Submenus When I Pause on Them with the Mouse Pointer

OPTION/SETTING	DESCRIPTION
Checked	Displays a submenu when you point to it or click it.
Unchecked	Displays a submenu when you click it.

Printers

OPTION/SETTING	DESCRIPTION
Checked	Adds a link to the Printers folder.
Unchecked	Displays printers only in Control Panel.

Search Files (affects searches from the Start-menu Search box)

OPTION/SETTING	DESCRIPTION
Don't Search for Files	Excludes your documents from searches.
Search Entire Index	Searches everything that Windows has indexed.
Search This User's Files	Includes your documents in searches.

Search Communications/Favorites and History/Files/Programs

OPTION/SETTING	DESCRIPTION
Checked	Searches for these items when you type in the Start-menu Search box.
Unchecked	Omits these items from the results when you use the Start-menu Search box.

Sort All Programs Menu by Name

OPTION/SETTING	DESCRIPTION
Checked	Windows keeps the All Programs menu sorted automatically: files alphabetically at top, followed by folders alphabetically.
Unchecked	Windows doesn't sort the All Programs menu, letting you add or move a menu item to a specific place without having it jump to its sorted position.

System Administrative Tools

OPTION/SETTING	DESCRIPTION
Display on the All Programs Menu	Tools appear in the All Programs menu and Control Panel.
Display on the All Programs Menu and the Start Menu	Tools appear in the All Programs menu, Start menu, and Control Panel.
Don't Display This Item	Tools appear only in Control Panel.

Use Large Icons

OPTION/SETTING	DESCRIPTION
Checked	Uses large icons in the Start menu's left column. The menu is easier to read, and its icons are easier to click. (This setting doesn't affect the All Programs menu, which always uses small icons.)
Unchecked	Uses small icons in the Start menu's left column. The menu displays its items compactly (like the All Programs menu) but is harder to read.

Exploring the Taskbar

The taskbar provides quick access to programs and the status of background processes. It appears at the bottom of your screen by default and is divided into segments with distinct functions (**Figure 2.20**):

Start button. Click this button to open the Start menu.

Quick Launch toolbar. This customizable toolbar lets you display the desktop or launch a program with a single click. The taskbar has a few other toolbars that you can show or hide.

Taskbar buttons. Buttons on the taskbar represent all open windows. You can use these buttons to resize, switch among, or close programs.

Notification area. This area displays the clock and shows the status of programs and activities.

Empty area. The taskbar has its own short-cut menu, which you reach by right-clicking an empty area. If your taskbar is crowded, right-click just to the left or right of the Start-button "orb," where there's always an unoccupied sliver.

✔ Tip

■ Point (without clicking) to any icon on the taskbar to show a helpful tooltip or thumbnail view of the window contents (if you're using the Aero color scheme).

Start-menu button   Quick Launch toolbar   Taskbar buttons   Empty area   Notification area (system tray)

Figure 2.20 The parts of the taskbar.

Managing Windows by Using the Taskbar

The windows of multiple open programs tend to overlap or hide one another, making them hard to tell apart or find. When you launch a program, its button appears on the taskbar; you can use the taskbar to manage open programs and switch among windows easily.

To view several windows at the same time, you can drag and resize them or use taskbar controls to tile them on your desktop. To clear your desktop, you can minimize all windows to taskbar buttons.

To activate a window:

◆ Click the taskbar button representing that window (**Figure 2.21**). If the button shows a menu when you click it (**Figure 2.22**), click the name of the desired window in the menu.

✔ Tips

■ The active window's taskbar button appears pressed in; other buttons appear normal (popped out) whether their windows are minimized, restored, or maximized.

■ If a window is active, clicking its taskbar button minimizes (hides) it.

■ If a program is busy, clicking its taskbar button may not activate the window.

■ Right-click a taskbar button to open the window's control menu (**Figure 2.23**).

■ To switch windows without using the taskbar, press Alt+Tab, or see "Switching Programs" in Chapter 6.

■ Some programs—usually, programs that run all the time—have notification-area icons (covered later in this chapter) instead of taskbar buttons.

Figure 2.21 Clicking a window's toolbar button brings the window to the top of the pile, if it happens to be hidden by other windows.

Figure 2.22 A group button on the taskbar will display a pop-up menu of window choices rather than activate a particular window.

Figure 2.23 Among other things, the control menu lets you close a window, sometimes without restoring it first.

■ To press taskbar buttons by using the keyboard: Press Ctrl+Esc to open the Start menu, press Esc to close it, and then tab to the first taskbar button. Next, use the arrow keys to highlight the desired button; then press the spacebar to activate the window or Shift+F10 to open its control menu.

Figure 2.24 Showing the desktop even minimizes dialog boxes (which don't appear as taskbar buttons).

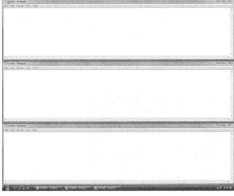

Figure 2.25 Arrange windows in a cascade (top), vertical stack (center), or side by side pattern (bottom). Minimized windows aren't arranged, so your taskbar may have more buttons than are tiled on the desktop.

To minimize all windows:

◆ Right-click an empty area of the taskbar and choose Show the Desktop.

or

If the Quick Launch toolbar is displayed, click the Show Desktop icon (**Figure 2.24**).

or

Press Windows logo key+D or Windows logo key+M.

To restore minimized windows:

◆ Right-click an empty area of the taskbar and choose Undo Minimize All or Show Open Windows.

or

Click the Show Desktop icon on the Quick Launch toolbar.

or

Press Windows logo key+D or Windows logo key+Shift+M.

To arrange windows on your desktop:

1. Minimize the windows that you *don't* want arranged on the desktop.

2. Right-click an empty area of the taskbar and choose Cascade Windows, Show Windows Stacked, or Show Windows Side by Side (**Figure 2.25**).

or

Right-click a group button on the taskbar (refer to Figure 2.22) and choose Cascade, Show Windows Stacked, or Show Windows Side by Side.

✔ Tips

■ To reverse the arrangement, right-click an empty area of the taskbar and choose the Undo command.

■ To display the Quick Launch toolbar, right-click an empty area of the taskbar and choose Toolbars > Quick Launch.

Customizing the Taskbar

You can change many aspects of the taskbar. A space-saving feature groups similar windows in one menulike taskbar button rather than crowding the taskbar with one truncated button for each open window.

To customize the taskbar:

1. Right-click an empty area of the taskbar and choose Properties (**Figure 2.26**).

   or

   Choose Start > Control Panel > Appearance and Personalization > Taskbar and Start Menu > Taskbar tab.

2. Check Lock the Taskbar to keep the taskbar at its current size and position; uncheck it if you want to resize or move the taskbar or any of its toolbars.

3. Check Auto-Hide the Taskbar to hide the taskbar when you're not using it.

   The taskbar disappears until you point to the edge of the screen where it's located.

4. Check Keep the Taskbar on Top of Other Windows to prevent other windows—even maximized windows—from covering the taskbar.

5. Check Group Similar Taskbar Buttons to reduce taskbar clutter.

   Windows rearranges taskbar buttons for each program so that they're all adjacent. If the taskbar becomes so crowded that button text is truncated, buttons for the same program are consolidated into one button displaying the number of program instances or documents (**Figure 2.27**).

Figure 2.26 The Taskbar and Start Menu Properties dialog box lets you change the taskbar's appearance and behavior.

Figure 2.27 A group button displays a small arrow and the number of open documents for the program. Click the button to show the document that you want. Button grouping won't work in a taskbar docked to the screen's left or right edge. You can right-click each window name in a group menu to display a control menu.

Figure 2.28 Thumbnail previews, new in Vista, appear if you're using the Aero color scheme. Thumbnails show static images for documents and pictures or playing images for videos, movies, animations, and progress bars. Pointing to a grouped taskbar button shows a stack of previews, but only the topmost one is visible. Click a group button and hover your mouse pointer over each window name to see its individual preview.

6. Check Show Quick Launch to display the Quick Launch toolbar on the taskbar.

Quick Launch lets you show the desktop or open a program with a single click. See "Adding Toolbars to the Taskbar" later in this chapter.

7. Check Show Window Previews (Thumbnails) to show a small pop-up image of a window's contents when you hover the mouse pointer over its taskbar button (**Figure 2.28**).

A thumbnail is useful when you can't identify a window by its title alone. This setting works only if you're using the Aero color scheme.

8. Click OK (or Apply).

Taskbar Recommendations

As the uniform command center for all your running programs, the taskbar is one of the most powerful features of Windows and among the ones that you'll use most often. The right taskbar settings can make using your computer more pleasant. Here are my recommendations for taskbar Properties settings.

Lock the Taskbar: On.

Auto-Hide the Taskbar: Off, unless you're working with a small screen or want to devote every pixel to a particular window.

Keep the Taskbar on Top of Other Windows: On.

Group Similar Taskbar Buttons: On, unless you work regularly with few open windows.

Show Quick Launch: On.

Show Window Previews (Thumbnails): On, unless they annoy you or you're low on memory or battery power.

✔ Tips

■ To show an autohidden taskbar by using the keyboard, press Ctrl+Esc or the Windows logo key.

■ To toggle the taskbar lock on or off quickly, right-click an empty area of the taskbar and choose Lock the Taskbar.

■ Right-click a group button to manage multiple windows as a group (**Figure 2.29**).

■ If the taskbar becomes *too* crowded, Windows hides some taskbar buttons and displays scroll buttons instead (**Figure 2.30**).

■ The taskbar won't group a program's windows into one button if there's enough room for a separate button for each window.

To move the taskbar:

1. If the taskbar is locked, unlock it (right-click an empty area of the taskbar and then uncheck Lock the Taskbar).

2. Point to an empty area of the taskbar and drag to any edge of your screen (**Figure 2.31**).

✔ Tip

■ Try docking the taskbar to the screen's left edge. It may feel awkward at first, but it reduces the amount of mousing needed for routine tasks, shows the day and date (not just the time), and displays more icons in the Quick Launch toolbar and notification area.

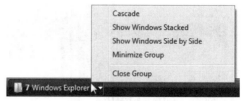

Figure 2.29 A group button's shortcut menu lets you arrange all the group's windows, minimize them, or close them (without affecting other windows).

Figure 2.30 These scroll buttons let you access hidden buttons on a jam-packed taskbar.

Figure 2.31 The taskbar widens automatically when you drag it to the left or right edge. Open windows self-adjust to accommodate the taskbar's new location.

Figure 2.32 Taskbars at the screen's top or bottom resize in button-height increments. Taskbars to the left or right resize without constraints.

To resize the taskbar:

1. If the taskbar is locked, unlock it (right-click an empty area of the taskbar and then uncheck Lock the Taskbar).

2. Point to the inside edge of the taskbar (the pointer becomes a double-headed arrow), and drag toward the desktop for a larger taskbar or toward the screen edge for a smaller one (**Figure 2.32**).

✔ Tip

■ If you make your taskbar more than one line deep, truncated buttons and toolbars will expand.

Using the Notification Area

The *notification area* lives at the right end of the taskbar, holding the clock and small icons that monitor activities on your computer or network (**Figure 2.33**).

Windows and other programs use icons here to let you know things—that you've received new email, for example. Some icons flash to get your attention, whereas others appear for the duration of an event (such as printing a document). Hover the mouse pointer over an icon to find out what it represents (**Figure 2.34**).

These icons have no standard controls. Some, you click; others, you double- or right-click; and some ignore clicks.

✔ Tips

- Programs can display what they please in the notification area (and some abuse the privilege). You can dismiss some icons with a right-click, whereas others cling like barnacles. A program's options or preferences (usually listed in the Edit or Tools menu) may let you control notification-area settings.

- Before Windows XP, the notification area was called the *system tray* (or just *tray*). Some programs still call it that in their documentation and dialog boxes.

Figure 2.33 Notification-area icons give the status of background programs, tasks, and services. The number of icons grows as you install more programs.

Figure 2.34 The tooltip for the Network icon shows your computer's connection status.

Figure 2.35 A < button indicates that Windows has hidden some notification-area icons (refer to Figure 2.33). Click the button to expand the notification area and display all icons, as shown here. (Note that the < button changes to >.)

Figure 2.36 The Notification Area tab lets you change the notification area's appearance and behavior.

Figure 2.37 You can specify the notification behavior for items displayed currently as well as in the past.

Windows manages the notification area by watching you work. If you don't use an icon regularly, Windows calls it inactive and hides it, but you can control icon display rather than accept the default behavior (**Figure 2.35**). You also can control the display of the Windows system icons.

To customize the notification area:

1. Right-click an empty area of the notification area (clicking to the right of the clock is easiest) and choose Properties (**Figure 2.36**).

    or

    Choose Start > Control Panel > Appearance and Personalization > Taskbar and Start Menu > Notification Area tab.

2. In the System Icons section, check or uncheck the icons that you want always to show or hide.

3. In the Icons section, to always show all icons, uncheck Hide Inactive Icons, click OK, and then skip the remaining steps.

4. To customize the behavior of icons, click Customize.

    The Icon column shows the programs (**Figure 2.37**).

5. In the Behavior column, click each program that you want to customize and choose Hide When Inactive, Hide, or Show from the drop-down list.

    or

    Click Default Settings to restore the icons' standard behavior.

6. Click OK in each open dialog box.

✔ Tips

■ If Hide Inactive Icons is turned on, you can customize notifications directly. Right-click an empty area of the notification area and choose Customize Notification Icons.

■ A taskbar on the left or right screen edge (or a tall one at the top or bottom) displays the day and date automatically (**Figure 2.38**).

■ Occasionally, an icon in the notification area will display a small pop-up window (called a *notification*) to tell you about something (**Figure 2.39**).

■ Point to the clock to show the day and date, or click it to show a calendar and an analog clock.

Figure 2.38 A tall or vertical taskbar displays the day, the date, and more icons.

Figure 2.39 You may see this message after adding a new hardware device to your computer. Click the Close button (X) in the top-right corner of the notification to dismiss it, or do nothing, and the notification will fade away on its own after a few seconds.

Adding Toolbars to the Taskbar

Specialized toolbars are available on the taskbar (**Figure 2.40**):

Quick Launch. Provides one-click access—much quicker than the Start menu—to commonly used items. It also lets you minimize all windows to show the desktop and switch among windows. By default, only this toolbar is displayed.

Address. A text box that accepts any address on the web, on your network, or on your computer. Enter a web address (URL) to launch or activate Internet Explorer (or your default browser), a program name to launch the program, a document name and path to open the document in its associated program (launching the program if necessary), or a folder name to open it in Windows Explorer.

Desktop. Links to all desktop shortcuts, so that you don't have to minimize all windows to reach them.

Links. Links to Internet Explorer's Favorites folder. You can drag file or webpage shortcuts onto this toolbar or right-click to delete links.

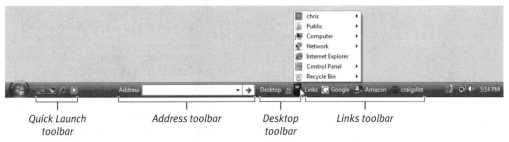

Quick Launch toolbar   *Address toolbar*   *Desktop toolbar*   *Links toolbar*

Figure 2.40 Toolbars occupy a lot of taskbar space. Click the chevron button (⟫) that appears at a toolbar's right end to display a menu of items or commands that won't fit on the taskbar

✔ Tips

■ The Address toolbar autocompletes—
that is, proposes matching entries that
you've typed before. You can keep typing,
or you can use arrow keys to select a
match and then press Enter. If you type
something that Windows doesn't understand, Windows searches and either
finds what you want or displays an error
message.

■ Many tasks in this section require an
unlocked taskbar. Right-click an empty
area of the taskbar. If Lock the Taskbar is
checked, uncheck it.

Other Toolbars

These toolbars also are available:

◆ The Windows Media Player toolbar
appears on the taskbar only when
Media Player (Chapter 10) is open and
minimized. Use it to control the
player's main functions.

◆ If you're using a Tablet PC, the
Tablet PC Input Panel toolbar
provides a quick way to enter text
without a keyboard.

Figure 2.41 You can show or hide each toolbar independently of the others.

To show or hide taskbar toolbars:

◆ Right-click an empty area on the taskbar, point to Toolbars, and then check or uncheck a name in the submenu to toggle that toolbar (**Figure 2.41**).

✔ Tips

■ Resize a toolbar by dragging the vertical rib at its left end.

■ To create a custom toolbar, right-click an empty area of the taskbar, choose Toolbars > New Toolbar, navigate to a folder whose contents you want to make into a toolbar, and then click Select Folder. Sadly, this toolbar vanishes when you close it or log off; you repeat the New Toolbar process to get it back.

■  To create a custom shortcut toolbar on the desktop, right-click an empty area of the desktop, choose New > Folder, type a folder name, press Enter, and then drag the folder to the very edge of the screen. The folder will look like a new toolbar. Drag shortcuts to it or right-click it to display a shortcut menu.

To customize a taskbar toolbar:

◆ Right-click an empty area of the toolbar and choose one of these commands at the top of the shortcut menu (**Figure 2.42**):

View. Shows large (double-size) or small (default) toolbar icons.

Open Folder. Opens the folder that the toolbar represents. Adding, changing, and deleting shortcuts in the folder is easier than manipulating the toolbar's small icons.

Show Text. Displays a text label next to each toolbar icon, which takes a lot of space. This feature is on by default for Links but not for Quick Launch.

Show Title. Shows the toolbar name—generally a waste of space except as an extra empty area for right-clicking.

Close Toolbar. Closes the toolbar.

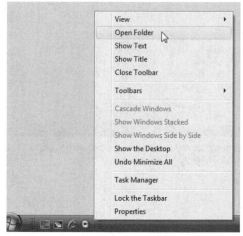

Figure 2.42 The Open Folder command works with only the Links and Quick Launch toolbars (and with custom toolbars created with Toolbars > New Toolbar).

Figure 2.43 (Left to right) The Show Desktop button hides all windows; click it again to restore them to their original positions (keyboard shortcut: Windows logo key+D). The Switch Between Windows button changes the active window (keyboard shortcut: Windows logo key+Tab or Alt+Tab). The next two buttons launch Internet Explorer (Chapter 14) and Windows Media Player (Chapter 10)

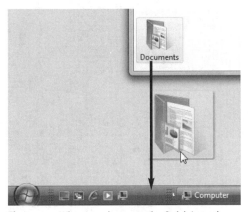

Figure 2.44 When you drag over the Quick Launch toolbar, an I-beam will appear to show where the item will land when you drop it.

Figure 2.45 If you don't see the Add to Quick Launch command in the shortcut menu, you can drag a Start-menu icon directly to the Quick Launch toolbar.

Using the Quick Launch Toolbar

Quick Launch begins with four Microsoft-supplied buttons (**Figure 2.43**). You can add buttons for instant one-click access to favorite files and folders or delete buttons that you don't need.

To add a button to Quick Launch:

◆ Locate the item (icon) that you want to add, drag it over the toolbar, and then drop it where you want it to appear (**Figure 2.44**).

or

Locate the icon in the Start menu, right-click it, and then click Add to Quick Launch (**Figure 2.45**).

✔ Tips

■ You can add almost anything to the Quick Launch toolbar: a program, file, folder, disk, web address (URL), hardware device, Control Panel program, and so on.

■ Drag buttons within the toolbar to reorder them.

■ Hold down Shift when you right-click a file in a folder window, and Add to Quick Launch will appear in the shortcut menu.

■ If, instead of buttons that you've added, you see the chevron button (**»**), it means that the hidden buttons won't fit on the toolbar. You can click the chevron to reveal the hidden buttons or—better—preserve one-click access by resizing the toolbar. To do that, right-click an empty area of the taskbar and make sure the taskbar is unlocked; then drag Quick Launch's ribbed sizing handle (refer to Figure 2.43) to the right until you see all your buttons.

USING THE QUICK LAUNCH TOOLBAR

To delete a button from Quick Launch:

1. Right-click the button and choose Delete.

2. Confirm the deletion if a message box appears.

✔ Tips

- Deleting a shortcut doesn't remove the file or uninstall the program that it represents.

- You can drag an unwanted button from the toolbar to the Recycle Bin.

- Don't delete the Show Desktop button; it's a command, not a shortcut. If you delete it accidentally, go to http://support.microsoft.com/?kbid=190355, "How to Re-Create the Show Desktop Icon on the Quick Launch Toolbar."

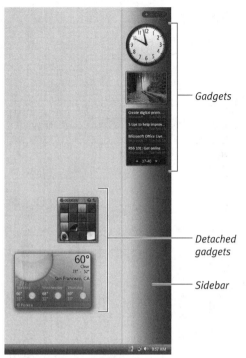

Gadgets

Detached gadgets

Sidebar

Figure 2.46 When you start Windows, the sidebar appears on the desktop's right edge with the Clock, Slide Show, and Feed Headlines gadgets. You can open and close the sidebar, and decide which gadgets to put on it and which to remove.

Using the Sidebar

Windows Sidebar (**Figure 2.46**), new in Vista, is a long, vertical strip along the edge of your desktop that holds mini-programs called *gadgets,* such as slide-show viewers, scrolling headlines, weather forecasts, search boxes, games, and sticky notes. Windows comes with a small collection of gadgets, and you can get more online.

You can customize the sidebar (and individual gadgets) to organize the information that you want to access quickly without cluttering your screen with open windows. You also can detach gadgets from the sidebar and place them on your desktop so that they're still visible when the sidebar is closed.

✔ Tips

- You need an internet connection for continuously updating or "live" gadgets like news feeds and stock tickers. An always-on connection like DSL or cable works best, but a regular dial-up modem works too, in a creaky sort of way.

- Windows Sidebar replaces the Active Desktop feature (live web content embedded in the desktop) of earlier Windows versions.

USING THE SIDEBAR

To open the sidebar:

◆ Choose Start > All Programs > Accessories > Windows Sidebar.

or

 Click the Windows Sidebar button in the notification area of the taskbar.

or

Press Windows logo key+spacebar (brings all gadgets to the front and selects the sidebar).

or

Press Windows logo key+G (opens the sidebar and cycles through the gadgets).

or

Choose Start, type sidebar in the Search box, and then select Windows Sidebar in the results list.

Figure 2.47 The sidebar's shortcut menu is available even if the sidebar is closed.

✔ Tip

■ You can right-click the Windows Sidebar button to display the sidebar's shortcut menu (**Figure 2.47**).

To close the sidebar:

◆ Right-click the sidebar and choose Close Sidebar (**Figure 2.48**).

Closing the sidebar won't close detached gadgets on your desktop.

To exit the sidebar:

◆ 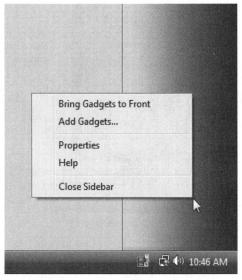 Right-click the Windows Sidebar button in the notification area of the taskbar and choose Exit.

Exiting removes the sidebar from the desktop and the sidebar button from the notification area. It also shuts down the gadgets so that they're not using memory, as they do invisibly when the sidebar is closed.

Figure 2.48 Right-click the sidebar (but not a gadget) to show the sidebar's shortcut menu.

USING THE SIDEBAR

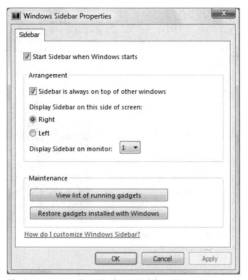

Figure 2.49 Use the Windows Sidebar Properties dialog box to control the position and behavior of the sidebar. If you're using multiple monitors, you can choose which one the sidebar appears on.

Figure 2.50 The Gadget Gallery initially displays the gadgets that come with Windows.

To customize the sidebar:

1. Right-click the sidebar and choose Properties.

   or

   Right-click the Windows Sidebar button in the notification area of the taskbar and choose Properties.

   or

   Choose Start > Control Panel > Appearance and Personalization > Windows Sidebar Properties.

   or

   Choose Start, type `sidebar` in the Search box, and then select Windows Sidebar Properties in the results list.

2. Set the desired options and click OK (**Figure 2.49**).

✔ Tip

■ If you check Sidebar Is Always on Top of Other Windows, maximized windows lock against the sidebar automatically.

To add a gadget:

1. Right-click the sidebar and choose Add Gadgets.

   or

   Right-click the Windows Sidebar button in the notification area of the taskbar and choose Add Gadgets.

   or

   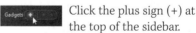 Click the plus sign (+) at the top of the sidebar.

2. Double-click a gadget to add it (**Figure 2.50**).

   or

   Right-click a gadget and choose Add.

   or

   Drag a gadget to the sidebar or desktop.

USING THE SIDEBAR

✔ Tips

■ To download and install more gadgets, in the Gadget Gallery, click the link Get More Gadgets Online to open the Microsoft Gadgets website.

■ If you have a lot of gadgets installed, click the arrows in the top-left corner of the Gadget Gallery to page through them, or type a gadget name in the Search box in the top-right corner. (You can narrow the search further by clicking the arrow to the right of the Search box. Choosing Recently Installed Gadgets, for example, narrows the search to gadgets installed in the past 30 days.)

■ You can add multiple instances of a particular gadget and customize each one. You can add clocks set to different time zones, for example.

■ To uninstall a gadget, right-click it the Gadget Gallery and choose Uninstall. If you uninstall gadgets that came with Windows, you can restore them by clicking Restore Gadgets Installed with Windows in the sidebar's Properties dialog box (refer to Figure 2.49).

To remove a gadget:

◆ Right-click the gadget and choose Close Gadget (**Figure 2.51**).

   or

 Click the Remove button that appears when you hover your mouse pointer over the gadget.

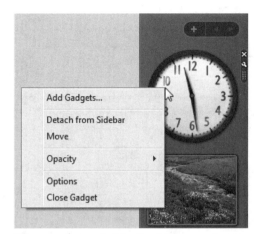

Figure 2.51 Each gadget (on the sidebar or on the desktop) has its own shortcut menu.

Figure 2.52 Each gadget has its own individual options. These are the options for the Clock gadget.

To place a gadget on the desktop:

◆ Right-click the gadget on the sidebar and choose Detach from Sidebar.

or

Drag the gadget to the desktop from the sidebar or from the Gadget Gallery.

✔ Tips

■ You can reposition detached gadgets by dragging them around on the desktop.

■ To make a detached gadget always float on top of other windows, right-click it and choose Always on Top.

■ To move a detached gadget back to the sidebar, drag it to the sidebar, or right-click it and choose Attach to Sidebar.

To customize an individual gadget:

◆ Right-click the gadget and choose Options (**Figure 2.52**).

or

 Click the Options (wrench) button that appears when you hover your mouse pointer over the gadget.

✔ Tip

■ If a gadget is distracting, you can dim it by displaying its shortcut menu and lowering its opacity (refer to Figure 2.51). The gadget returns to full brightness temporarily when you hover your mouse pointer over it.

Managing Shortcuts

I've covered creating, editing, and deleting shortcuts in the Start menu and Quick Launch toolbar. Shortcuts also can appear on the desktop and in folders. A shortcut can link to a program, file, folder, disk, printer or other device, web address (URL), or system folder (such as Computer). When you double-click a shortcut, its linked file opens. You can create and modify a shortcut to any item and store it anywhere; it's a tiny file.

Windows offers two types of shortcut files: Windows shortcuts (.lnk files) to items on your computer or network, and internet shortcuts (.url files) to webpages. A shortcut shares the icon of the original but adds a small boxed arrow in one corner (**Figure 2.53**).

Figure 2.53 You can distinguish a shortcut from the original file to which it's linked by the small curved arrow. This makes it easy to identify the shortcut so that you don't mistakenly delete the original when you meant to delete the shortcut.

✔ Tips

■ You can make several shortcuts to the same object and store them in different places.

■ You can make shortcuts to network-accessible items, not just items on your local computer.

■ Don't confuse a shortcut *icon,* which is a placeholder for an object, with a shortcut (right-click) *menu* or a *keyboard* short-cut, which is a command keystroke.

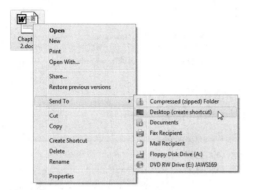

Figure 2.54 The shortcut menu lets you create a desktop shortcut quickly.

To create a shortcut:

1. Locate the item (icon) that you want to create a shortcut to.

2. Right-drag the icon to a destination (typically, the desktop or a folder) and choose Create Shortcut(s) Here.

   or

   Right-click the icon and choose Send To > Desktop (Create Shortcut) (**Figure 2.54**).

   or

   Right-click the icon and choose Copy; then right-click where you want the shortcut to appear and choose Paste Shortcut.

   or

   Right-click the icon and choose Create Shortcut.

   This method creates a shortcut in the same location as the original. You can move the shortcut anywhere.

   or

   Right-click an empty area of the desktop or a folder window and choose New > Shortcut.

   The Create Shortcut wizard starts. Follow the onscreen instructions.

   or

   Alt+drag the icon to a destination.

   or

   Ctrl+Shift+drag the icon to a destination.

MANAGING SHORTCUTS

To create a shortcut to a webpage:

1. In your web browser, go to the page that you want to create a shortcut to.

2. Drag the small icon on the left end of the address bar to the desktop or a folder window.

Before you drag, move or resize your browser window so you can see the shortcut's destination.

✔ Tips

- If you create a shortcut and its icon doesn't have a small curved arrow, it's not a shortcut; you've moved or copied the original. Press Ctrl+Z to undo your action and try again.

- If you create a shortcut to a shortcut, the new shortcut points to the original target.

- If you double-click a shortcut and the Problem with Shortcut dialog box appears (**Figure 2.55**), the original file has been moved or deleted.

Figure 2.55 You can delete the shortcut or restore the original file (if it's in the Recycle Bin).

Creating Shortcuts to Programs

If you want to create a shortcut to a program, the easiest way is to right-click it on the left side of the Start menu (or in the All Programs submenu) and choose Send To > Desktop (Create Shortcut).

If you can't find a program in the Start menu, look for it—specifically, for its .exe file (Word's executable file is winword.exe, for example)—in a folder nested in the \Program Files folder or, for the small utility programs that come with Windows, in the \Windows or \Windows\System32 folder.

Figure 2.56 You can bring back the common icons that were on the desktop by default in earlier versions of Windows.

To display system-folder shortcuts on the desktop:

1. Right-click an empty area of the desktop and choose Personalize.

   or

   Chose Start > Control Panel > Appearance and Personalization > Personalization.

2. Click the Change Desktop Icons link (in the left pane).

3. In the Desktop Icons section, check the boxes for the shortcuts that you want on the desktop (**Figure 2.56**) and then click OK (or Apply).

✔ Tip

- The Desktop Icon Settings dialog box also lets you change the system icons. Select the icon and click Change Icon to choose a new icon. (To restore the original icon, select the icon and click Restore Default.)

To rename a shortcut:

1. Right-click the shortcut and choose Rename.

   or

   Select (highlight) the shortcut and press F2.

   or

   Click the shortcut's title (not its icon) twice slowly; don't double-click.

2. Retype or edit the name and press Enter (**Figure 2.57**).

   You can use the Cut, Copy, and Paste keyboard shortcuts (Ctrl+X, Ctrl+C, and Ctrl+V) while editing.

✔ **Tips**

■ To cancel renaming a shortcut, press Esc while editing.

■ Shortcut names can include letters, numbers, spaces, and some punctuation marks but not these characters: \ / : * ? " > < |.

■ You can rename a shortcut in the General tab of the shortcut's Properties dialog box.

To delete a shortcut:

◆ Right-click the shortcut and choose Delete.

   or

   Select (highlight) a shortcut or multiple shortcuts and press Delete.

✔ **Tip**

■ To recover (undelete) a shortcut from the Recycle Bin, see "Deleting Files and Folders" in Chapter 5.

Figure 2.57 Getting rid of *- Shortcut* usually is the first objective in renaming.

MANAGING SHORTCUTS

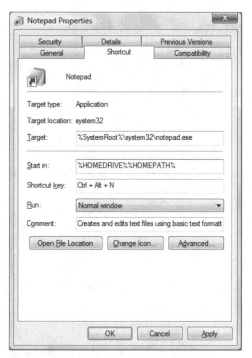

Figure 2.58 The Properties dialog box for Windows shortcuts (to documents and programs) has a Shortcut tab, whereas...

Figure 2.59 ...Properties dialog boxes for internet shortcuts (URLs) have a Web Document tab. For details, see the "Shortcut Properties" sidebar.

To view or change a shortcut's properties:

◆ Right-click the shortcut and choose Properties.

or

Select (highlight) the shortcut and press Alt+Enter (**Figure 2.58** and **Figure 2.59**).

✔ Tips

■ Privacy tip: An internet shortcut's Web Document tab (refer to Figure 2.59) shows the number of times that you've visited the page.

■ Run Maximized is useful for programs that "forget" to run in full-screen mode when you start them from the shortcut.

■ If you use Run Minimized for Startup-folder icons, programs will start automatically as taskbar buttons, and your logon desktop won't be cluttered with windows.

■ You can update the target (path) of the object that a shortcut points to, but usually it's easier to create a new shortcut.

MANAGING SHORTCUTS

Shortcut Properties

Information in a shortcut's Properties dialog box depends on what the shortcut represents. Here are some common properties:

Target. The name of the item that the shortcut points to. A shortcut to a file needs the full path to its location (unless the file is in a Windows system folder).

Start In. The folder in which the program looks for files to open or save, by default.

Shortcut Key. The keyboard shortcut with which to open (or switch to) the program. Press any key to make Ctrl+Alt+*key* appear here. You can assign Ctrl+Alt+E to Windows Explorer, for example, to open it without hunting for its shortcut. A shortcut key requires at least two of Ctrl, Shift, and Alt but can't use Esc, Enter, Tab, spacebar, Delete, Backspace, or Print Screen.

Shortcut keys work for desktop and Start-menu shortcuts. Pick shortcuts that don't conflict with program-defined or other shortcut keys.

Run. Tells the program to open in a normal (restored), minimized, or maximized window.

Comment. Provides the descriptive text (tooltip) that appears when your mouse pointer hovers over the shortcut.

Open File Location. Opens the folder containing the target file that the shortcut points to. The file will be selected in the folder window that appears.

Change Icon. Allows you to change the default icon of a shortcut, which is the same as that of the target. Changing this icon doesn't change the target's icon.

URL. Displays the target web address (URL) of an internet shortcut.

Details tab. Displays more properties and their associated values.

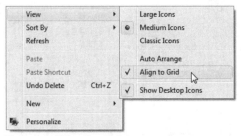

Figure 2.60 This submenu lets you resize your desktop shortcuts, align them, or hide them temporarily.

Tidying Your Desktop

Over time, shortcuts tend to accumulate on your desktop. Microsoft's productivity elves have provided cleanup tools.

To arrange desktop shortcuts:

1. Right-click an empty area of the desktop, point to View, and then choose a command from the submenu (**Figure 2.60**):

   Large Icons, Medium Icons, or **Classic Icons.** Changes the size of all the icons on the desktop. The default is Medium. Classic icons are the smaller icons that appeared in earlier Windows versions.

   Auto Arrange. Places icons in neat columns, starting on the screen's left side. Uncheck this option to drag icons anywhere on your desktop. This option won't work if your desktop is full.

   Align to Grid. Turns on an invisible grid that makes icons snap into equally spaced alignment when you move them. Uncheck this option to turn off the grid (useful only if Auto Arrange is turned off).

   Show Desktop Icons. Uncheck this option to hide all desktop icons; check it to show them.

   continues on next page

TIDYING YOUR DESKTOP

2. Right-click an empty area of the desktop, point to Sort By, and then choose a command from the submenu (**Figure 2.61**):

Name. Sorts alphabetically by name.

Size. Sorts by file size, with the smallest first. If the shortcut points to a program, the size refers to the size of the shortcut file.

Type. Sorts by file type, which keeps files with the same file extension together (.doc for Microsoft Word files or .exe for programs, for example).

Date Modified. Sorts by the date when the shortcut (not the original) was last modified, with the most recent first.

✔ Tips

- If your icons look grainy or badly drawn, right-click an empty area of the desktop and choose Refresh to redisplay icons.

- Windows XP's Desktop Cleanup wizard has been removed from Vista.

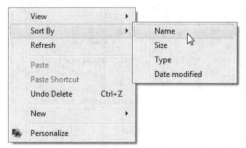

Figure 2.61 This submenu lets you choose the way Windows sorts your desktop shortcuts.

GETTING HELP

Windows' help system has changed over the years into something that's actually useful to beginning and intermediate users. Vista's Help and Support is a hybrid web-based and on-disk help system that lets you use web-style links and searches to access:

- Standard documentation

- Animated tutorials

- Troubleshooting guides

- Windows Help websites

- Help from other Windows users

Also, the Remote Assistance program lets a remote user view your screen—or even control your PC—to help you solve problems.

Starting Help and Support

The first stop in Windows Help and Support (Help for short) is the home page (**Figure 3.1**), which includes links to basic information and external help resources. Your home page may differ slightly from the one pictured because Microsoft sometimes updates Help through Windows Update.

To start Help and Support:

◆ Choose Start > Help and Support.

or

Press Windows logo key+F1.

or

If the desktop is active, press F1.

or

Choose Start, type `help` in the Search box, and then select Help and Support in the results list.

✔ Tip

■ Help and Support won't help you with a program that's not part of Windows; for that, you'll need to consult the program's own help system (which almost every program has). To open a program's help system, use its Help menu or press F1. If you have an older program that uses Windows Help format (.hlp files), see `http://support.microsoft.com/ ?kbid=917607`, "Windows Help program (WinHlp32.exe) is no longer included with Windows."

Figure 3.1 The home page for Windows Help and Support.

Table 3.1

Help Keyboard Shortcuts	
PRESS	**To**
Alt+A	Show the customer support page
Alt+C	Show the table of contents
Alt+N	Show the Connection Settings menu
Alt+O or F10	Show the Options menu
Alt+left arrow	Move back to the previously viewed topic
Alt+right arrow	Move forward to the next previously viewed topic
Alt+Home	Show the home page
Home	Go to the beginning of the current topic
End	Go to the end of the current topic
Ctrl+A	Select all the text of the current topic
Ctrl+C	Copy the selected text of the current topic
Ctrl+F	Search the current topic
Ctrl+P	Print the current topic
F3	Move to the Search box

Browsing Help and Support

You navigate Help and Support by using weblike buttons, icons, and links. The Help toolbar always is visible at the top of the window. You can also navigate via the keyboard (**Table 3.1**).

To use the toolbar:

◆ In Help and Support, click the following buttons on the toolbar:

Move back and forward through recently viewed topics.

Show the home page (refer to Figure 3.1).

Print the current help topic.

Show the table of contents.

Show links to customer support and other types of help.

Print, show the table of contents, change the text size, search the current topic, or change the default help settings.

Getting Help in Dialog Boxes and Windows

If you see a question mark inside a circle or square, or a colored and underlined text link, click it to open the Help topic. You'll see the following Help links in some dialog boxes and windows:

To browse Help by subject:

1. 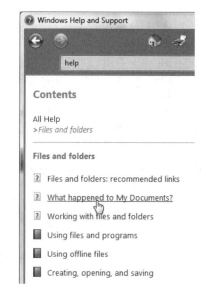 Click the Browse Help button on the toolbar (or press Alt+C).

2. Click an item in the list of subject headings that appears (**Figure 3.2**).

✔ Tips

■ If you see a blue compass at the top of a Help topic (**Figure 3.3, top**), it means that *guided help* is available to let you actually see the steps required to do something instead of reading them. **Figure 3.3, bottom,** shows a step in guided help.

■ Help commands also are available in the shortcut menu; right-click anywhere in the topics area.

Figure 3.2 Subject headings contain Help topics (?) or other subject headings (■). Click a Help topic to open it, or click another heading to dig deeper into the subject list.

Figure 3.3 Guided help, new in Vista, can perform the steps for you by opening menus, starting programs, and clicking buttons—just watch and learn. Or it can show you each step but let you do the actual opening, starting, or clicking.

Figure 3.4 The most relevant results are at the top of the list. At the bottom of a long list, you can click a link to see more results.

Searching Help and Support

Help's search function is easy; faster than browsing by subject; and usually finds a wide range of related topics, which can acquaint you with features that you were unaware of.

To search for help topics:

1. In Help and Support, type or paste a search phrase (one or more keywords) in the Search box and then press Enter or click the magnifying glass.

   Help displays a list of results (**Figure 3.4**).

2. Click one of the results to read the topic.

✔ Tips

- If your search phrase contains multiple words, Help searches for topics that contain all the words. A search for *keyboard shortcuts,* for example, yields pages that contain *keyboard* and *shortcuts,* though not necessarily adjacent in the text. To find an exact phrase, enclose it in quotes (*"keyboard shortcuts"*).

- Searches include common synonyms. The search phrases *erase file* and *delete file* and *remove file,* for example, all return similar results (the official term is *delete*). Help handles some misspelled keywords too.

- Search for *troubleshoot* to see a long list of topics that help you identify and resolve hardware, software, and networking problems.

- Search terms aren't case sensitive.

- Help ignores a long list of articles, prepositions, and other noise words: *a, the, of, like, from,* and so on.

Getting Up-to-Date Help

If you're connected to the internet, you can include the latest content from Microsoft's Windows Online Help and Support website (http://windowshelp.microsoft.com) when you search so that you have a better chance of getting your question answered:

1. Choose Start > Help and Support > Options (on the toolbar) > Settings.

2. Check Include Windows Online Help and Support When You Search for Help, and click OK.

   The words *Online Help* appear in the bottom-right corner of the Help and Support window when you're connected.

Getting Help on the Web

You can get Windows help from several websites:

◆ **Windows Online Help and Support.** An online version of Help and Support, plus instructional videos, columns, and other odds and ends. Go to `http://windowshelp.microsoft.com`.

◆ **Microsoft Help and Support.** A collection of solutions to common problems, how-to topics, troubleshooting steps, and the latest downloads. Go to `http://support.microsoft.com`.

◆ **Microsoft Knowledge Base.** A huge searchable database of articles with detailed solutions to specific problems and computer errors. Go to `http://support.microsoft.com` and click Search Knowledge Base.

◆ **Microsoft TechNet.** A resource for technical professionals. Go to `http://technet.microsoft.com` and click the link for Windows Vista.

◆ **Google.** A search engine that often indexes Windows pages, articles, and help topics better than Microsoft does. Go to `www.google.com` and type a search phrase.

If all else fails, you can get help—free or paid—from a technical support professional by phone, email, or online chat. If you bought a new computer with Windows already installed, your PC manufacturer provides support; if you purchased Windows separately, Microsoft does.

Click the Ask button on the Help and Support toolbar to see which support options apply to your computer.

Newsgroups

A *newsgroup* is a free internet discussion group where people from all over the world talk about a specific topic. To get help from other Vista users, go to `www.microsoft.com/communities/newsgroups/default.mspx` and click the link for Windows Vista. Search the newsgroup to get a feeling for how it works; then see whether someone else has already asked your question and had it answered. If not, post a message and check back later for an answer (likely, but not certain). You can use a web-based newsreader or Windows Mail (Chapter 15) to read and post messages.

GETTING HELP ON THE WEB

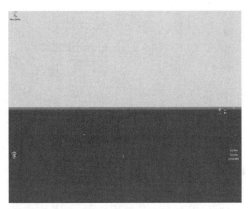

Figure 3.5 This image shows a problem—a greatly oversized taskbar taking up half the desktop—that an experienced Windows user could diagnose in a moment by looking at a screen shot. A beginner would have difficulty explaining the problem by using only words.

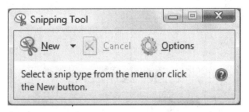

Figure 3.6 Snipping Tool, new in Vista, lets you capture, annotate, save, and share screen images. Choose Start > All Programs > Accessories > Snipping Tool.

Capturing Screen Images

If you want to ask a friend or colleague for help over email, he may be able to solve your problem better if you send him a *screen shot*—an image of what's on all or part of your screen.

The simplest way to take a screen shot is to use your keyboard: Press the Print Screen (PrntScrn) key to capture the entire screen (**Figure 3.5**) or Alt+Print Screen to grab only the active window. The screen image is now stored on the invisible clipboard, ready for pasting into an email message (or a graphics program, if you want to edit, save, or print it).

Serious screen-shooters use more sophisticated tools: Try Snipping Tool (**Figure 3.6**), SnagIt ($40 U.S.; www.snagit.com), or Gadwin PrintScreen (free; www.gadwin.com).

Allowing Others to Connect to Your Computer Remotely

You'll appreciate Remote Assistance if you've ever endured the friendship-dissolving stress of giving or receiving tech support over the phone. *Remote Assistance* lets you invite a friend or technical helper—anyone you trust who's running Windows Vista, Windows XP, or Windows Server 2003—to help you by connecting to your PC over the internet or a network. That person can swap messages with you, view your screen, or (with your permission) use his mouse and keyboard to control your computer. All sessions are encrypted and password protected.

Remote Assistance relieves novices of having to explain problems in jargon they haven't learned, and lets helpers cut the chatter and work on the novice's machine directly. Helpers can even install software, update hardware drivers, and edit the registry.

✔ Tip

- Remote Assistance isn't the same as Remote Desktop (see Chapter 19). Among other differences, in Remote Assistance, both parties must be present at their PCs and agree to the connection.

Security Concerns

Like all remote-control technologies, Remote Assistance has security implications beyond the ordinary issues of strong passwords and firewalls. When you invite someone to take control of your PC, you must balance your trust with others' inclinations toward malice. That person is free not only to fix your problem, but also to, say, erase your hard drive or steal your files. You can view everything he's doing onscreen, and if you don't like what you see, press Esc or click Cancel to break the connection immediately.

Still, damage done in a moment can take ages to undo. Even if that person can't control your PC, you could follow his bad advice and delete critical files or turn off security features yourself. Furthermore, you may not be able to confirm the identity of the other person.

Figure 3.7 If you're paranoid, uncheck this box to turn off Remote Assistance.

Figure 3.8 If you're worried about security at the helper's end, you can shorten the maximum expiration period to a few minutes or hours.

Before starting a Remote Assistance session, set invitation and time limits.

To configure Remote Assistance:

1. Choose Start > Control Panel > System and Maintenance > System > Remote Settings (on the left) > Remote tab.

   or

   Press Windows logo key+Break and then click Remote Settings (on the left) > Remote tab.

   If a security prompt appears, type an administrator password or confirm the action.

2. If it's unchecked, check Allow Remote Assistance Connections to This Computer (**Figure 3.7**).

3. Click Advanced to open Remote Assistance Settings (**Figure 3.8**).

4. If you're the novice, and you don't want the helper to control your computer (only to see your desktop), uncheck Allow This Computer to Be Controlled Remotely.

   Even with this box checked, you must approve each request for control of your computer explicitly.

5. Use the two Invitations drop-down lists to set the maximum duration of Remote Assistance invitations that you send.

   The default expiration is 6 hours.

   continues on next page

ALLOWING OTHERS TO CONNECT REMOTELY

6. If you want to connect only to people running Windows Vista or later (not Windows XP or Server 2003), check the Create Invitations check box.

7. Click OK in each open dialog box.

✔ Tip

■ If your firewall is blocking Remote Assistance, you'll need to create an exception to unblock it. If Windows Firewall (Vista's built-in firewall) is blocking Remote Assistance, the Windows Remote Assistance wizard will give you unblocking instructions. See also "Using a Firewall" in Chapter 13.

In a Remote Assistance session, the two connected parties—the novice and the helper—must:

◆ Be using Windows Vista, Windows XP, or Windows Server 2003 (subject to the restrictions given in the "Remote Assistance and Windows XP and Server 2003" sidebar)

◆ Be on the same local area network (LAN) or have active internet connections

◆ Not be blocked by a firewall (Chapter 13)

The order of events in a Remote Assistance session is:

1. The novice sends the helper an invitation via email.

2. The helper accepts the invitation.

3. Remote Assistance opens a window that shows the novice's desktop to the helper.

4. The helper views the novice's desktop and exchanges messages with the novice or, with permission, takes control of the novice's computer.

5. Either party disconnects to end the session.

Remote Assistance and Windows XP and Server 2003

If you're connecting from a Vista computer to one running Windows XP or Windows Server 2003, be aware of these restrictions:

◆ XP and Server 2003 can't pause a Remote Assistance session, so if you pause the session, the XP/Server user won't know it.

◆ XP and Server 2003 support voice capability, but Vista doesn't; nothing happens if the XP/Server user clicks the Start Talk button.

◆ You can't offer Remote Assistance from Vista to XP or Server 2003.

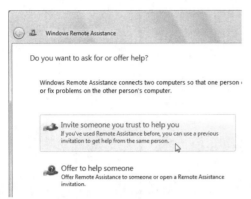

Figure 3.9 The Remote Assistance wizard steps you through the process of inviting a helper via email. (Note that you can detour here if you want to give help rather than get it.)

Figure 3.10 If you've configured your email program, Windows will start it for you to send the invitation when you're finished with the wizard; otherwise, it will prompt you to set up Windows Mail.

To get help by using Remote Assistance:

1. Choose Start > All Programs > Maintenance > Windows Remote Assistance.

   or

   Choose Start > Help and Support > click Use Windows Remote Assistance to Get Help from a Friend or Offer Help (under Ask Someone).

   or

   Choose Start, type `remote assistance` in the Search box, and then press Enter.

   The Windows Remote Assistance wizard starts.

2. Click Invite Someone You Trust to Help You (**Figure 3.9**).

3. If you've already set up an email program (such as Windows Mail; see Chapter 15), click Use E-Mail to Send an Invitation (**Figure 3.10**).

   or

   If you want to send the invitation as an attachment via web-based email (such as Yahoo or Gmail), click Save This Invitation As a File.

4. Type and retype a password (and set a disk location if you're saving the invitation as a file), and then click Next.

continues on next page

ALLOWING OTHERS TO CONNECT REMOTELY

5. Give the password to the helper in person or on the phone; email and instant messaging are insecure ways to send passwords (**Figure 3.11**).

   If your email program is set up, Remote Assistance launches it and creates a message with boilerplate text telling the helper how to respond to your invitation; you can add some personal text if you like.

6. Type the helper's email address in the To box and send the message (**Figure 3.12**).

   or

   If you're using web-based email, attach the invitation file that you created in step 3 to a message and send it to the helper. (Instead of emailing it, you can transfer this file over a network, on a floppy disk or USB flash drive, or via instant messaging.)

   After you send the invitation, the Windows Remote Assistance window will appear (**Figure 3.13**). It will notify you when the helper accepts your invitation.

7. Approve the invitation to start the session.

   If you let the helper use his mouse and keyboard to control your desktop, you'll see ghostly pointer movements, self-typing text, and self-opening windows as he fixes your problem.

8. To end the session (which either you or the helper can do at any time), click Cancel, click Stop Sharing, or press Esc.

Figure 3.11 All Remote Assistance sessions are password protected. This password is used by the person you're inviting to help you and is valid for the duration of the session.

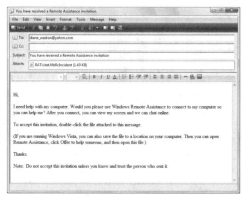

Figure 3.12 The helper must open (double-click) the attachment (a .MsRcIncident file) to accept your invitation, sending a response message back to you.

Figure 3.13 Remote Assistance will notify you when the helper accepts your invitation, which you must approve to start the session.

✔ Tips

- The helper can use (and reuse) your invitation until it expires. If he doesn't respond to your invitation within the specified time period, it expires. To see how to set the expiration time, refer to Figure 3.8.

- If you check Allow *<helper>* to Respond to User Account Control Prompts when the helper asks to control your desktop, he can run administrator-level programs without your participation. You can allow him to run these programs only if you can run them yourself, so you'll be asked for consent or credentials before giving him these abilities. He can't see your desktop while you provide them.

- If *you* are the helper and want the Remote Assistance window out of your way briefly while you're helping the novice, don't close it; you'll break the connection. Minimize it instead.

- When you invite a helper via email, you're actually transmitting your IP address, which identifies you uniquely on the internet. If you have a dynamic (rather than static) IP address, which changes every time you connect to the internet, the helper won't be able to connect to your PC if you've broken your connection since sending the invitation or if you share an internet connection through a router.

ALLOWING OTHERS TO CONNECT REMOTELY

PERSONALIZING YOUR WORK ENVIRONMENT

Each new version of Windows makes its designers assume more about the preferences and abilities of the "average" user. Because this user doesn't exist, Microsoft lets you change Windows Vista's factory settings.

You can configure Windows in hundreds of ways ranging from superficial to meaningful. Changes to graphics, colors, and animation usually are cosmetic, whereas some other settings—the language used or adaptations for disabled users—change the way you work with Windows.

Using Control Panel

Control Panel is the central container of tools for changing preferences, configurations, and settings. These miniature programs commonly are called *applets* or *extensions*. Experienced Windows users are familiar with the interface in **Figure 4.1**, now called *classic view*. Windows Vista's Control Panel defaults to *category view,* much improved since Windows XP (**Figure 4.2**). In either view, you can hover your mouse pointer over a category heading or icon to see a pop-up description of it.

To open Control Panel:

◆ Choose Start > Control Panel.

or

Choose Start, type control panel in the Search box, and then press Enter.

or

Press Windows logo key+R; type control and press Enter.

or

If you're using the classic (one-column) Start menu, choose Start > Settings > Control Panel.

Figure 4.1 Classic view consolidates all Control Panel tools in one window.

Figure 4.2 Category view groups Control Panel tools into functional categories.

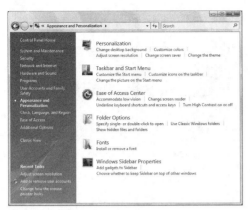

Figure 4.3 Clicking the Appearance and Personalization category heading displays this page.

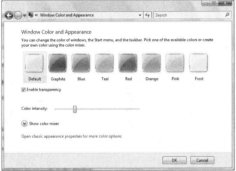

Figure 4.4 Clicking Customize Colors (under the Appearance and Personalization category heading) bring you right to this page.

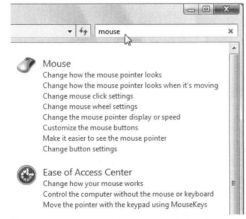

Figure 4.5 This search lists mouse-related tasks. The Search box, new in Vista, works best in category view.

To open an item in category view:

◆ Click a category heading or icon to display a list of related tasks and Control Panel tools (**Figure 4.3**).

or

Click a task link under a category heading to go right to that task (**Figure 4.4**).

To open an item in classic view:

◆ Double-click the item.

or

Use the arrow keys to navigate to the desired item; then press Enter.

or

Press the key of the item's first letter; then press Enter.

If multiple items have the same first letter, press that letter repeatedly until the desired item is highlighted; then press Enter.

To search for a Control Panel item:

◆ In the top-right corner of Control Panel, type search text (one or more keywords) in the Search box.

Control Panel shows the matching tasks as you type. Click any link in the results list (**Figure 4.5**).

See also "Searching for Files and Folders" in Chapter 5.

USING CONTROL PANEL

To switch Control Panel views:

1. Open Control Panel.

2. In the left pane, click Classic View (for classic view) or Control Panel Home (for category view) (**Figure 4.6**).

✔ Tips

■ When you're browsing a category, the left pane includes a link to take you to the Control Panel Home page, links for each category, and links for recently performed tasks (refer to Figure 4.3).

■ Unlike the Search box in the Start > Search window or the Start menu (which searches your whole computer), the Control Panel Search box finds only tasks related to Control Panel. Some example searches to try: *screen resolution, add a printer,* and *connect internet.*

■ If you're using a laptop computer, you have an additional Control Panel category— Mobile PC—that desktop users don't.

■ Some icons are appear in more than one category. You can find Power Options, for example, in both the Hardware and Sound category and the Mobile PC category, and Windows Firewall appears in both Security and in Network and Internet.

■ If you can't find the item you want in category view, click the Additional Options category (or switch to classic view).

■ In either view, you can drag an item to the desktop to create a shortcut.

■ A guided-help animation is available for Control Panel: Choose Start > Help and Support, type `tour the control panel` in the Search box, and then press Enter. In the results list, click Tour the Control Panel.

Figure 4.6 It's easy to switch the current view. Windows veterans may no longer prefer classic view now that Control Panel has a Search box.

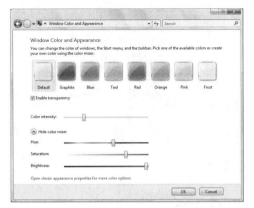

Figure 4.7 The color and transparency of window borders and title bars change dynamically as you adjust these controls.

Setting the Window Color and Color Scheme

You can fine-tune the color and style of the frames of your windows, and choose one of the built-in color schemes.

To set window colors and the color scheme:

1. Choose Start > Control Panel > Appearance and Personalization > Personalization > Window Color and Appearance (**Figure 4.7**).

   or

   Right-click an empty area of the desktop and choose Personalize > Window Color and Appearance.

2. Click a color in the list or click Show Color Mixer to create your own color.

   Drag the Color Intensity slider to dilute or deepen the chosen color.

3. Check Enable Transparency if you want to see through the edges of windows; uncheck it for opaque edges (which uses less computer horsepower).

   continues on next page

SETTING THE WINDOW COLOR AND COLOR SCHEME

4. Click Open Classic Appearance Properties for More Color Options.

The Appearance Settings dialog box (**Figure 4.8**) lets you choose the color scheme. Windows picks one for you automatically based on your computer's memory, display hardware, and video card, but you can change it manually in the Color Scheme list. **Table 4.1** describes the options.

The Effects button changes font smoothing, menu shadows, and window-dragging animation. The Advanced button changes individual interface elements if you're using the Classic scheme.

5. Click OK in each open dialog box.

✔ Tips

■ To get the hardware requirements for Aero, choose Start > Help and Support, type aero in the Search box, and then press Enter. In the results list, click How Do I Get Windows Aero? Other relevant topics to search for: *Video Cards: Frequently Asked Questions* and *Ways to Improve Display Quality*.

■ If you open a program that won't run in the current scheme, Vista downgrades the scheme temporarily and displays a message in the notification area (**Figure 4.9**).

Figure 4.8 Without Aero you lose only flash, not function, so you may want to change to a less-fancy scheme if it makes your computer's response snappier.

Figure 4.9 Windows changes the scheme back to normal when you quit the incompatible program. You also might see this message if you're running low on memory (quit some programs to reclaim the memory).

Table 4.1

Color Schemes

SCHEME	DESCRIPTION
Aero	The top-tier display, with advanced visual effects like transparent-glass windows and Start menu; real-time thumbnails on taskbar buttons and in the Alt+Tab window switcher, Flip 3D (Windows logo key+Tab); subtle animations; dynamic reflections; drop shadows; and color gradients. This scheme is available in all Vista editions except Home Basic and only with suitable display hardware.
Standard	Like Aero but without transparency, live thumbnails, Flip 3D, and other gee-whizzery. It has the same hardware requirements as Aero. If you're using a laptop, use Standard or Basic to save battery power.
Basic	A basic desktop with no hardware requirements beyond those of Windows Vista itself.
Classic	Mimics the look of Windows 98/2000. It changes only appearance, not functionality; you still get Search boxes, column controls, and so on. See also "Restoring the Old Windows Look" later in this chapter.
High Contrast	For people with vision problems. See also "Accommodating Disabled Users" later in this chapter.

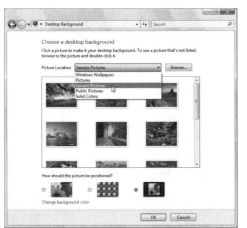

Figure 4.10 By default, Windows looks for background pictures in your personal Pictures folder (\Users*username*\Pictures), the shared Pictures folder (\Users\Public\Pictures), and \Windows\Web\Wallpaper.

Setting the Desktop Background

You can change the image, or *wallpaper,* that appears under the icons on your desktop. If you don't like the desktop backgrounds that Windows or your PC manufacturer provides, you can use one of your own pictures.

To set the desktop background:

1. Choose Start > Control Panel > Appearance and Personalization > Personalization > Desktop Background (**Figure 4.10**).

   or

   Right-click an empty area of the desktop and choose Personalize > Desktop Background.

2. Choose a location from the Picture Location drop-down list, and click the picture or color that you want for your background.

   or

   To use your own picture, click Browse, find the picture file on your computer or network, and then double-click it to make it your background. It will appear in the list of desktop backgrounds.

3. In the How Should the Picture Be Positioned? section, choose an option:

    Resize the image to fit your screen (with some distortion). This option works best with large images and photos.

   Tile the image repeatedly over the entire screen. This option works best with small images.

    Center the image on the desktop background.

   continues on next page

4. If you chose to center the image in the preceding step, click Change Background Color to select a desktop color to fill the space unoccupied by the picture.

5. Click OK.

✔ Tips

■ You can use bitmap (.bmp/.dib) or JPEG (.jpeg/.jpg) files as background pictures.

■ If you choose Solid Colors from the Picture Location drop-down list, the More button lets you pick a custom color.

■ To make any picture on your computer your desktop background, right-click the picture and choose Set As Desktop Background.

■ To use a web image as wallpaper, right-click the image in Internet Explorer and choose Set As Background. The downloaded image appears in the Picture Location list. Each new internet image you define as a background replaces the old one.

■ To save a web image permanently and use it as wallpaper, right-click the image in Internet Explorer, choose Save Picture As, save the image in Pictures or a folder of your own, and then proceed as described.

■ Go to "Managing Visual Effects and Performance" later in this chapter and experiment with Use Drop Shadows for Icon Labels on the Desktop to see which setting makes your desktop icons' text labels easier to read against your background.

Resizing Desktop Images

If the photos from your digital camera are larger than your screen, here's how to trim them to use as wallpaper:

1. Right-click an empty area of your desktop and choose Personalize > Display Settings.

2. Under Resolution (bottom left), note the number of pixels (for example, 1024×768).

3. Find the icon or thumbnail of the image that you want to use for wallpaper, and hover the pointer over it until its file-information tooltip appears. (Alternatively, right-click the icon and choose Properties > Details tab > Dimensions property.)

Dimensions gives the image's width and height size in pixels (for example, 1600×1200).

If the image's dimensions exceed your computer's screen resolution, Windows fills your screen with the center portion of the image, and the edges go wherever leftover pixels go. This result will be fine with you if the image edges are uninteresting. But if you want the uncropped image to be your wallpaper, make a copy and use the Resize function of a graphics program (Windows Paint, GIMP, or Adobe Photoshop, for example) to shrink it to the same size as your screen (or close).

Figure 4.11 Set your screen saver's wait time carefully so your boss won't realize how long it's been since you did anything.

Setting the Screen Saver

A *screen saver* is a utility that causes a monitor to blank out or display images after a specified time passes without keyboard or mouse activity. (Pressing a key or moving the mouse deactivates the screen saver.) Screen savers were developed to prevent hardware damage to your monitor, but today's monitors don't need that protection, so modern screen savers provide decoration or entertainment instead. A screen saver also can password protect your computer and hide your screen when it takes effect.

To set a screen saver:

1. Choose Start > Control Panel > Appearance and Personalization > Personalization > Screen Saver (**Figure 4.11**).

   or

   Right-click an empty area of the desktop and choose Personalize > Screen Saver.

2. Choose a screen saver from the drop-down list.

   (To turn off the screen saver, choose None from the list, click OK, and then skip the remaining steps.)

3. Specify how long your computer must be idle before the screen saver activates.

   Try 15 to 20 minutes.

4. Click Settings to see any options for the selected screen saver—to change color or animation style, for example.

5. *(Optional)* Check On Resume, Display Logon Screen to display a logon window when you begin using your computer after screen-saver activation.

   continues on next page

SETTING THE SCREEN SAVER

6. Click Preview to see a full-screen preview of the screen saver.

Press a key or move your mouse to end the test.

7. Click OK (or Apply).

✔ Tips

■ Your screen-saver password is the same as your logon password. If you have no logon password, you can't set a screen-saver password.

■ Appearances aside, screen savers—particularly complex ones such as 3D Text—waste energy and processor time. To save resources, turn off your monitor manually or automatically after a certain period of inactivity. See "Conserving Power" later in this chapter.

To use personal pictures as a screen saver:

1. Make sure you have two or more pictures in a folder on your computer (usually, your Pictures folder).

2. In the Screen Saver Settings dialog box (refer to Figure 4.11), choose Photos from the drop-down list.

3. Click Settings to pick the folder containing your pictures and set other options (**Figure 4.12**).

4. Click OK or Save in each open dialog box.

Figure 4.12 The Photos screen saver scrolls through all the pictures and videos in the selected folder or Photo Gallery (Start > All Programs > Windows Photo Gallery).

Idly Folding Proteins

Forget screen savers. Instead, put your idle PC to work solving great math and science problems. By participating in *distributed*—or *grid*—*computing* projects, you (and thousands of others) donate bits of your computer's spare processing power to large-scale, not-for-profit research projects. It's fascinating, free, and doesn't interfere with your normal computer use. Visit www.grid.org, http://gridcafe.web.cern.ch, or www.distributedcomputing.info to learn about grid projects worldwide. You'll find projects for researching cancer, AIDS, anthrax, and smallpox; predicting climate change; searching for ETs; folding proteins; finding prime numbers; and more.

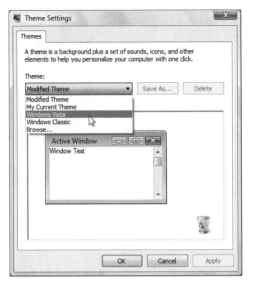

Figure 4.13 Each person with a user account can pick or create a distinct theme.

Setting the Desktop Theme

If Windows' default appearance and sounds aren't to your taste, you can change them with a different desktop *theme*—a stored set of colors, icons, fonts, sounds, and other elements that redecorate your desktop. You can pick a predefined theme or create your own.

To set a theme:

1. Choose Start > Control Panel > Appearance and Personalization > Personalization > Theme (**Figure 4.13**).

   or

   Right-click an empty area of the desktop and choose Personalize > Theme.

2. From the Theme drop-down list, choose a theme.

3. Click OK (or Apply).

✔ Tips

- To populate the Theme list, Windows looks in your Documents folder and in \Windows\Resources\Themes. Choose Browse from the Theme drop-down list to open a theme located elsewhere.

- Windows comes with only two themes, but many others are freely available. Try www.dowtheme.com and the Themes section of www.download.com or www.tucows.com. Movie and game sites have them too. Choose Browse from the Theme drop-down list to load a downloaded theme (.theme file). For an extreme makeover, try WindowBlinds ($20 U.S.; www.windowblinds.net).

- Select the Windows Classic theme to restore the look of Windows 98/2000.

To create a custom theme:

1. Choose Start > Control Panel > Appearance and Personalization > Personalization > Theme.

   or

   Right-click an empty area of the desktop and choose Personalize > Theme.

2. From the Theme drop-down list, choose an existing theme as a starting point for creating a new one.

3. Choose the desired settings in Control Panel to change the theme (see the "Theme Settings" sidebar).

4. When you're finished making changes, click Apply in the Theme Settings dialog box (refer to Figure 4.13).

5. Click Save As, type a theme name, and then click Save.

   By default, Windows saves the theme in your Documents folder (Start > Documents).

6. Click OK (or Apply).

To delete a custom theme:

1. Choose Start > Control Panel > Appearance and Personalization > Personalization > Theme (refer to Figure 4.13).

   or

   Right-click an empty area of the desktop and choose Personalize > Theme.

2. From the Theme drop-down list, choose the theme that you want to delete; then click Delete.

   You can delete only the themes that you created or installed, not the ones that Windows provides.

SETTING THE DESKTOP THEME

Theme Settings

The following Control Panel settings become part of your theme:

♦ Window color and appearance (see "Setting the Window Color and Color Scheme" earlier in this chapter)

♦ Desktop background (see "Setting the Desktop Background" earlier in this chapter)

♦ Screen saver (see "Setting the Screen Saver" earlier in this chapter)

♦ Mouse pointers (see "Configuring the Mouse" later in this chapter)

♦ Sounds (see "Configuring Sound and Audio Devices" later in this chapter)

♦ Desktop icons (Choose Start > Control Panel > Appearance and Personalization > Personalization > Change Desktop Icons [on the left])

LCD Monitors and Laptop Screens

If you're using a flat-panel LCD (liquid crystal display) monitor or laptop screen rather than a traditional bulky CRT (cathode ray tube) monitor, you can ignore some of the discussions here:

- LCD displays produce sharp images only at *native resolution* (and possibly some fractions of native resolution, depending on your model). Running at other resolutions makes the screen image blurry or blocky. The monitor manufacturer will tell you the native resolution, but it's usually the maximum resolution available.

- The refresh rate doesn't apply to LCDs, because they work with a continuous stream of light and pixels don't dim unless instructed to. CRT pixels begin to dim as soon as the electron gun's beam passes them.

- ClearType, Microsoft's font-smoothing technology, makes text appear sharper on LCD and plasma screens. (Results vary on CRTs.) ClearType is turned on by default. To use the ClearType control, choose Start > Control Panel > Appearance and Personalization > Personalization > Window Color and Appearance > Open Classic Appearance Properties for More Color Options > Effects button > Use the Following Method to Smooth Edges of Screen Fonts.

  More information about ClearType is at www.microsoft.com/typography/cleartype. You can download ClearType Tuner to fine-tune your display. See also "Managing Fonts" later in this chapter.

Configuring the Monitor

Windows lets you adjust your display hardware with these settings:

Screen resolution is the amount (fineness) of detail in your screen's image, expressed in pixels wide by pixels high. (A *pixel* is the smallest building block of the display.) Conventional screens have resolutions of 640 × 480 (largely useless except in emergencies), 800 × 600, 1024 × 768, and 1152 × 864. High-end monitors support much higher resolutions.

Color quality ranges from 16 ugly colors for archaic Standard VGA to 4 billion colors (32 bits per pixel) for the best monitors and video cards. The number of colors available correlates to your resolution setting—most video cards display fewer colors at higher resolutions—so you may have to reduce resolution to get higher color quality. The available resolution and color choices adjust automatically. If your digital photos look blotchy, increase the color quality.

Refresh rate is the frequency at which the screen is redrawn to maintain a steady image. Higher refresh rates yield less flicker. A refresh rate below 72 hertz, or 72 times per second, can tire your eyes if you look at the screen too long.

Color matching ensures that colors are represented accurately and consistently across color printers, scanners, cameras, monitors, and programs. Without color management, onscreen and printed colors may vary: Orange can appear brown, green can appear blue, and so on. Graphic designers love color matching because it does away with trial and error in resolving color differences. Color matching requires a separate color profile (.icm file) for each device connected to your computer. This profile conveys the device's color characteristics to the color management system every time colors are scanned, displayed, or printed.

✔ Tips

- Changing these settings affects all users who log on to your computer.

- On CRT monitors, don't always choose the maximum resolution available. If you spend most of your time typing memos or reading email, you may find that medium resolution reduces eyestrain. For general use, try 800 × 600 on a 15-inch monitor, 1024 × 768 on a 17-inch monitor, or 1152 × 864 on a 19-inch monitor.

- Video-card memory largely determines the maximum resolution and color quality that you can use. To see how much video memory you have, choose Start > Control Panel > Appearance and Personalization > Personalization > Display Settings > Advanced Settings > Adapter tab > Adapter Information table (**Figure 4.14**).

- To access a monitor's device driver, choose Start > Control Panel > Hardware and Sound > Device Manager. If a security prompt appears, type an administrator password or confirm the action. In Device Manager, double-click Monitors; then double-click the name of the monitor. See "Managing Device Drivers" in Chapter 8.

- To adjust the monitor for vision impairments, see "Accommodating Disabled Users" later in this chapter.

- For general information about installing and configuring hardware, see Chapter 8.

Figure 4.14 Better video cards have 128 MB or more of dedicated memory—overkill for word processing and email but just enough for gaming and digital video. High-end video cards add extra tabs to this dialog box or install their own Control Panel program or Start-menu item.

Figure 4.15 Increasing the number of pixels displays more information on your screen, but icons and text get smaller.

To set screen resolution and color quality:

1. Choose Start > Control Panel > Appearance and Personalization > Personalization > Display Settings (**Figure 4.15**).

   or

   Right-click an empty area of the desktop and choose Personalize > Display Settings.

2. Drag the Resolution slider to set the display size.

3. From the Colors drop-down list, choose the number of colors.

   Choose 16-bit or higher color; otherwise, photographic images will appear grainy *(dithered)*.

continues on next page

Scaling for Easier Reading

Dots per inch (dpi) is the standard way to measure screen and printer resolution—the more dots per inch, the better the resolution. By increasing dpi, you can make text, icons, and other screen items larger and easier to see. Decreasing dpi makes them smaller, fitting more on your screen. To adjust dpi scaling:

1. Start > Control Panel > Appearance and Personalization > Personalization > Adjust Font Size (DPI) (on the left).

2. If a security prompt appears, type an administrator password or confirm the action.

3. In the DPI Scaling dialog box, choose Default Scale (96 DPI) or Larger Scale (120 DPI), or click Custom DPI to set a custom scale.

4. Click OK.

5. To see the changes, close all your programs; then restart Windows.

Recycle Bin
96 dpi

Recycle Bin
120 dpi

CONFIGURING THE MONITOR

4. Click Apply.

Your screen turns black briefly and refreshes with the new settings.

5. After your settings change, you have 15 seconds to accept the changes (**Figure 4.16**).

✔ Tips

■ If you have more than one monitor (driven by multiple video cards or by a single card that supports multiple monitors), the Monitor tab displays a monitor icon for each monitor. Click a monitor icon to activate it before choosing its resolution and color settings.

■ If you need a 256-color display to run an old DOS game or program, don't set your entire system to 256 colors even if that option is available. Instead, use the Compatibility feature; see "Running Older Programs" in Chapter 6.

■ The Advanced Settings button lets you view the hardware properties of your monitor and video card. You can adjust some settings, but you usually don't need to unless you're installing a new driver, setting color matching, or changing the refresh rate. The Troubleshoot tab lets you control graphics-hardware acceleration manually.

Figure 4.16 If your new screen settings look good, click Yes; otherwise, click No or just wait to revert to your previous settings.

Figure 4.17 To reduce eyestrain, choose the highest refresh rate that your monitor and video card support, but check the documentation or the manufacturer's website to find out what the hardware will accept.

To set the refresh rate:

1. Choose Start > Control Panel > Appearance and Personalization > Personalization > Display Settings > Advanced Settings > Monitor tab (**Figure 4.17**).

   or

   Right-click an empty area of the desktop and choose Personalize > Display Settings > Advanced Settings > Monitor tab.

2. If you have multiple monitors, in the Monitor Type section, select the monitor that you're working with currently.

3. In the Monitor Settings section, choose a refresh rate from the drop-down list.

4. Click Apply.

   Your screen turns black briefly.

5. After your refresh rate changes, you have 15 seconds to accept the change (refer to Figure 4.16).

✔ Tip

- Don't uncheck Hide Modes That This Monitor Cannot Display to choose a higher refresh rate. A refresh rate that exceeds the capabilities of your monitor or video card can distort images and damage hardware.

CONFIGURING THE MONITOR

To manage color profiles:

1. Choose Start > Control Panel > Appearance and Personalization > Personalization > Display Settings > Advanced Settings > Color Management tab > Color Management button > Devices tab (**Figure 4.18**).

   or

   Right-click an empty area of the desktop and choose Personalize > Display Settings > Advanced Settings > Color Management tab > Color Management button > Devices tab.

2. To add a color profile, click Add; then use the Associate Color Profile dialog box to select a color profile to associate with the current monitor (**Figure 4.19**).

   or

   To remove a profile, select it and click Remove.

   or

   To set a profile as the default for the current monitor, select it and click Set As Default Profile.

3. Click OK in each open dialog box.

✔ Tips

- I've only touched on color management here. To learn more, click Understanding Color Management Settings in Figure 4.18 or choose Start > Help and Support and search for *color management*.

- Right-click a color profile (.icc or .icm file) in a folder window to install it or associate it with a device.

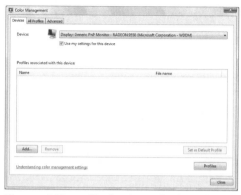

Figure 4.18 The profiles list shows all color profiles associated with the current monitor and video card (none, in this case, which is fine for most people and everyday use).

Figure 4.19 Color profiles installed with a monitor and video card are stored in the folder \Windows\System32\ spool\drivers\color.

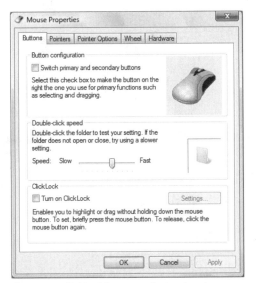

Figure 4.20 ClickLock is a mercy for touchpad users.

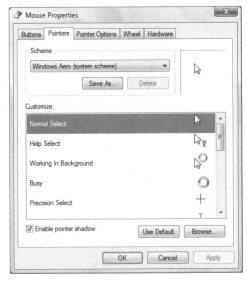

Figure 4.21 This tab lets you select predefined pointer schemes (which range from cute to practical), create your own pointer schemes, or browse to select an individual pointer (rather than an entire scheme).

Configuring the Mouse

Use the Mouse utility in Control Panel to control settings such as button configuration, double-click speed, mouse pointers, responsiveness, and wheel behavior.

To configure the mouse:

1. Choose Start > Control Panel > Hardware and Sound > Mouse.

   or

   Choose Start, type mouse in the Search box, and then press Enter.

2. To swap the left and right mouse-button functions, choose Buttons tab > check Switch Primary and Secondary Buttons.

3. If Windows often interprets your double-clicks as two single clicks, choose Buttons tab > drag the Double-Click Speed slider toward Slow.

4. To make dragging easier, choose Buttons tab > check Turn on ClickLock (**Figure 4.20**); then you can select text or drag icons without holding down the mouse button continuously.

5. To customize mouse pointers, choose Pointers tab > Scheme to set or create a new pointer scheme (**Figure 4.21**).

   Use the Customize list to change individual pointers (see "The Mouse" in Chapter 1).

   continues on next page

6. On the Pointer Options tab, adjust how the pointer responds to the mouse's physical actions (**Figure 4.22**).

7. If your mouse has a wheel, on the Wheel tab, adjust its scroll behavior (**Figure 4.23**).

8. Click OK (or Apply).

✔ Tips

■ Fancy mice from Microsoft, Logitech, Kensington, and other manufacturers come with their own driver software. Installing these drivers adds new options and can change some default mouse settings. A cordless mouse may add a tab that indicates remaining battery life, for example. Some drivers add their own Control Panel programs or Start-menu items.

■ A computer with a special default pointing device—such as a touchpad on a laptop—may replace the Wheel tab with a tab of controls for that device.

■ When you install an alternative pointing device such as a stylus or tablet, look for a Control Panel program or Start-menu item devoted for that device.

■ To drag an icon with ClickLock turned on, point to the icon, press the left mouse button for the ClickLock interval, release the button, drag the icon to a destination, and then press the button again for the ClickLock interval.

■ To adjust the mouse and insertion point for mobility impairments, see "Accommodating Disabled Users" later in this chapter.

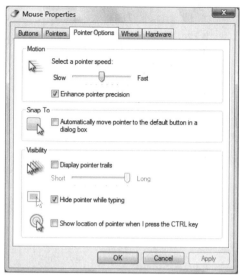

Figure 4.22 If the pointer distracts you while you type, check Hide Pointer While Typing. If you need to keep track of the pointer as it moves, check Display Pointer Trails (useful for laptop screens). Adjust the pointer's speed to have it respond more quickly or slowly to mouse movements.

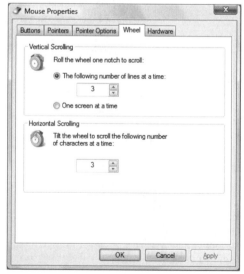

Figure 4.23 A mouse wheel can stand in for scroll bars; roll the wheel to scroll up or down a list, document, or webpage. The wheel on some mice can tilt left or right for horizontal scrolling. If your mouse has no wheel, these settings are ignored.

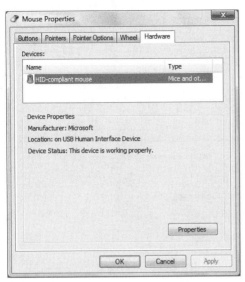

Figure 4.24 Click Properties and then click Change Settings to access the same dialog box as the one in Device Manager.

Figure 4.25 Like all other peripherals, mice have device drivers that you may want to inspect or update from time to time. See "Managing Device Drivers" in Chapter 8.

- The Hardware tab lists the pointing devices attached to your computer (**Figure 4.24**).

- To access a mouse's device driver, choose Start > Control Panel > Hardware and Sound > Device Manager. If a security prompt appears, type an administrator password or confirm the action. In Device Manager, double-click Mice and Other Pointing Devices; then double-click the name of the mouse (**Figure 4.25**).

- For general information about installing and configuring hardware, see Chapter 8.

CONFIGURING THE MOUSE

Configuring the Keyboard

A standard keyboard should work after you plug it in, with no adjustments in software. You can use Control Panel's Keyboard utility to change some settings after installation.

To configure the keyboard:

1. Choose Start > Control Panel > Hardware and Sound > Keyboard (**Figure 4.26**).

   or

   Choose Start, type keyboard in the Search box, and then select Keyboard in the results list.

2. On the Speed tab, update the following settings:

   Repeat Delay controls the amount of time that elapses before a character begins to repeat when you hold down a key.

   Repeat Rate adjusts how quickly a character repeats when you hold down a key.

   Cursor Blink Rate controls the blink rate of the text cursor (insertion point). To stop the cursor from blinking, set the blink rate to None.

3. Click OK (or Apply).

Figure 4.26 If you type rapidly, drag the Character Repeat sliders to the right to make your keyboard more responsive.

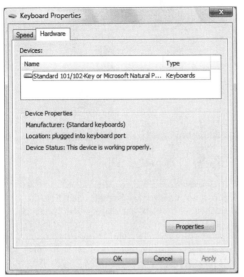

Figure 4.27 Click Properties and then click Change Settings to access the same dialog box as the one in Device Manager.

Figure 4.28 Like all other peripherals, keyboards have device drivers that you may want to inspect or update from time to time. See "Managing Device Drivers" in Chapter 8.

✔ Tips

■ Fancy keyboards from Microsoft, Logitech, Kensington, and other manufacturers come with their own driver software. Installing these drivers adds new options and can change some default keyboard settings. A cordless keyboard may add a tab that indicates remaining battery life, for example. Some drivers add their own Control Panel programs or Start-menu items.

■ To choose an international keyboard layout, see "Localizing Your System" later in this chapter.

■ To adjust the keyboard for mobility impairments, see "Accommodating Disabled Users" later in this chapter.

■ The Hardware tab lists the keyboards attached to your computer (**Figure 4.27**).

■ To access a keyboard's device driver, choose Start > Control Panel > Hardware and Sound > Device Manager. If a security prompt appears, type an administrator password or confirm the action. In Device Manager, double-click Keyboards; then double-click the name of the keyboard (**Figure 4.28**).

■ For general information about installing and configuring hardware, see Chapter 8.

Configuring Sound and Audio Devices

Most computers have audio recording and playback devices such as sound cards, microphones, headphones, and speakers (built-in or external). Use Control Panel's Sound program to configure these devices.

You also can customize system sound effects, which are audio clips (beeps, chords, or music snippets) associated with system events such as emptying the trash or error messages.

To control sound volume:

1. Choose Start > Control Panel > Hardware and Sound > Adjust System Volume (under Sound) (**Figure 4.29**).

   or

   Click the Volume icon in the taskbar's notification area (**Figure 4.30**).

2. Drag the slider to lower or raise the volume.

   or

   ◀) Click the Mute button to turn off sound.

✔ Tips

- If the Volume icon doesn't appear in the notification area, right-click an empty area of the notification area and choose Properties > Notification Area tab > check Volume > OK.

- Hover your mouse pointer over the Volume icon to see the current volume level and playback device (**Figure 4.31**).

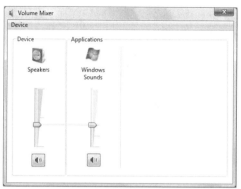

Figure 4.29 The Volume Mixer lets you adjust the master volume (at left) and, independently, the volume of individual programs that appear in the Applications section (at right).To open the mixer quickly, right-click the Volume icon in the notification area and choose Open Volume Mixer.

Figure 4.30 This slider controls the volume for your speakers or headphones.

Figure 4.31 The current volume level is given on a scale from 0 (muted) to 100 (loudest).

Figure 4.32 The Volume icon's shortcut menu provides quick access to sound functions.

Figure 4.33 A playback device's shortcut menu lets you set up the device—usually speakers or headphones. Click Properties for more options.

To configure playback devices:

1. Choose Start > Control Panel > Hardware and Sound > Sound > Playback tab.

   or

   Right-click the Volume icon in the taskbar's notification area and choose Playback Devices (**Figure 4.32**).

   or

   Choose Start, type sound in the Search box, and then select Sound in the results list.

2. Right-click a device in the list and choose a command to configure or test the device, or to inspect or change its properties (**Figure 4.33**).

3. When you're done, click OK in each open dialog box.

To configure recording devices:

1. Choose Start > Control Panel > Hardware and Sound > Sound > Recording tab.

   or

   Right-click the Volume icon in the taskbar's notification area and choose Recording Devices (refer to Figure 4.32).

2. Right-click a device in the list and choose a command to configure or test the device, or to inspect or change its properties (**Figure 4.34**).

3. When you're done, click OK in each open dialog box.

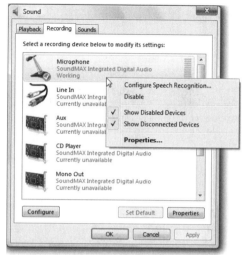

Figure 4.34 A recording device's shortcut menu lets you set up the device—usually a microphone or a line-in. Click Properties for more options.

Audio Hardware

Depending on your computer's audio hardware, you may see all or some of these devices (or others not listed here) in the Playback and Recording tabs:

◆ **CD Player** controls the volume of audio CDs (if your CD drive is connected to the sound card directly with a cable).

◆ **Line In/Aux** controls the volume of the sound card's Line-In or Aux input (usually used to record from a stereo or other external playback device).

◆ **Microphone** controls the sound card's microphone input volume (usually used with a microphone or dictation headset).

◆ **Speakers/Headphones** controls the volume of your PC's headphones or external or built-in speakers (connected to a USB port, motherboard audio port, or a sound card).

◆ **SW Synth** controls the volume of music produced by the sound card's MIDI synthesizer or wavetable.

◆ **Wave Out Mix** sounds are generated by Windows, games, MP3s, Windows Media Player, and many other programs.

Figure 4.35 You can choose (or mute) each sound individually or use a sound scheme to apply a group of sounds.

To configure system sounds:

1. Choose Start > Control Panel > Hardware and Sound > Sound > Sounds tab.

   or

   Right-click the Volume icon in the taskbar's notification area and choose Sounds (refer to Figure 4.32).

2. To choose a predefined group of sound effects, choose a scheme from the Sound Scheme drop-down list (**Figure 4.35**).

3. To change a sound for a particular event, click the event in the Program list; then choose the sound from the Sounds drop-down list.

   or

   Select the event and click Browse to select another sound file (in .wav audio format) on your system.

   or

   Choose (None) from the Sounds drop-down list to remove a sound.

4. To preview a sound for a particular event, select the event in the Program list and click Test.

5. To save a changed sound scheme, click Save As, type a name, and then click OK.

6. To delete a custom sound scheme, select the scheme and click Delete.

   You can delete only the schemes that you created or installed, not the ones Windows provides.

7. Click OK (or Apply).

CONFIGURING SOUND AND AUDIO DEVICES

✔ Tips

■ Place .wav files in the folder \Windows\Media to have them appear in the system sounds list.

■ To adjust sounds for hearing impairments, see "Accommodating Disabled Users" later in this chapter.

■ To access an audio device's device driver, choose Start > Control Panel > Hardware and Sound > Device Manager. If a security prompt appears, type an administrator password or confirm the action. In Device Manager, double-click Sound, Video, and Game Controllers; then double-click the name of the audio device (**Figure 4.36**).

■ For general information about installing and configuring hardware, see Chapter 8.

Figure 4.36 Like all other peripherals, audio devices have device drivers that you may want to inspect or update from time to time. See "Managing Device Drivers" in Chapter 8.

Figure 4.37 You have to be an administrator to change the date or time, but not the time zone.

Figure 4.38 To set the time in the Time box, type new numbers, press the up- and down-arrow keys, or click the small up and down arrows. Click the small arrow at the top of the calendar to change months.

Setting the Date and Time

Keep your system time accurate, because Windows uses it to time-stamp files and email, schedule tasks, and record events.

✔ Tip

- If the clock doesn't appear in the notification area, right-click an empty area of the notification area and choose Properties > Notification Area tab > check Clock > OK.

To set the date and time:

1. Choose Start > Control Panel > Clock, Language, and Region > Date and Time.

   or

   Click the clock in the taskbar's notification area; then click Change Data and Time Settings.

   or

   Right-click the taskbar clock and choose Adjust Date/Time.

   or

   Choose Start, type date and time in the Search box, and then press Enter.

2. On the Date and Time tab (**Figure 4.37**), click Change Date and Time (if a security prompt appears, type an administrator password or confirm the action), adjust the date and time as needed (**Figure 4.38**), and then click OK.

continues on next page

SETTING THE DATE AND TIME

3. On the Date and Time tab, click Change Time Zone, choose your time zone from the drop-down list (**Figure 4.39**), and then click OK.

4. On the Additional Clocks tab, you can add more clocks that show the time in other time zones (**Figure 4.40** and **Figure 4.41**).

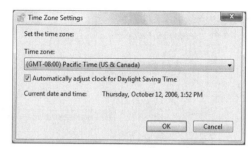

Figure 4.39 Windows assumes that you want to Automatically Adjust Clock for Daylight Saving Time. Uncheck this box if you don't want to use daylight saving time.

Figure 4.40 Add clocks that show the time in other parts of the world and view them by...

Figure 4.41 ...clicking the taskbar clock.

Figure 4.42 When your computer is shut down, the motherboard battery maintains the time.

Figure 4.43 Additional-clock times appear too, if you've set them.

5. On the Internet Time tab, click Change Settings (if a security prompt appears, type an administrator password or confirm the action), check Synchronize With an Internet Time Server to synchronize your computer clock with a highly accurate clock (**Figure 4.42**), and type or choose any time-server address in the Server box.

Once a week is the only interval you get unless you click Update Now.

6. Click OK (or Apply) in all open dialog boxes.

✔ Tips

■ Internet-time synchronization occurs regularly only if you have a full-time internet connection such as DSL or cable. If you use dial-up, click Update Now while you're connected to the internet to synchronize your clock immediately.

■ A time server won't synchronize your system time if your date is incorrect.

■ Hover your mouse pointer over the taskbar clock to see the current day and date (**Figure 4.43**).

■ The sidebar has a Clock gadget. See "Using the Sidebar" in Chapter 2.

■ For hyperaccurate system time, use Tardis 2000 ($20 U.S.; www.kaska.demon.co.uk) or Dimension 4 (free; www.thinkman.com) to synchronize the clock at fine intervals.

SETTING THE DATE AND TIME

Localizing Your System

Windows supports many international standards, formats, and languages. Use Control Panel's Regional and Language Options utility to adjust country-specific settings such as unit of measurement; currency, number, and date formats; and keyboard and display language.

To set formats for numbers, currencies, times, and dates:

1. Choose Start > Control Panel > Clock, Language, and Region > Regional and Language Options > Formats tab (**Figure 4.44**).

   or

   Choose Start, type `regional and language` in the Search box, and then press Enter.

2. Choose a language from the Current Format drop-down list.

3. To change individual settings, click Customize this Format (**Figure 4.45**).

4. Click OK in each open dialog box.

✔ Tip

■ You can't save customized regional settings as though they were themes. If you customize and then choose another language in the list, you lose your customized settings.

Figure 4.44 The language that you choose affects how programs format numbers, currencies, times, and dates.

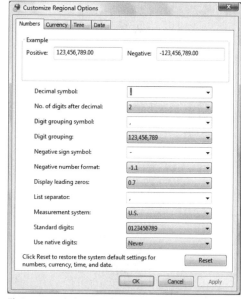

Figure 4.45 The Example section shows how selected settings affect the appearance of quantities.

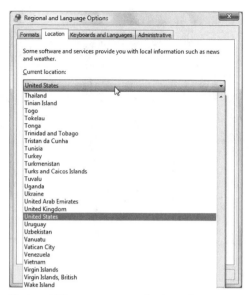

Figure 4.46 Some programs and web services use this location to deliver you local information such as news and weather.

To set your location:

1. Choose Start > Control Panel > Clock, Language, and Region > Regional and Language Options > Location tab (**Figure 4.46**).

2. Choose your location from the Current Location drop-down list.

3. Click OK (or Apply).

To set the keyboard language:

1. Choose Start > Control Panel > Clock, Language, and Region > Regional and Language Options > Keyboards and Languages tab (**Figure 4.47**).

2. Click Change Keyboards.

continues on next page

Figure 4.47 The input language controls the language used when you type on your keyboard.

LOCALIZING YOUR SYSTEM

149

3. On the General tab, click Add, specify the language(s) and keyboard layout(s) to install, and then click OK (**Figure 4.48**).

You can click the preview button to look at the keyboard layout of each language before you add it.

4. On the Language Bar tab, set the location and appearance of the language bar (**Figure 4.49**).

Figure 4.48 Keyboard layouts rearrange the keys' character assignments. Pressing the [key on a U.S. keyboard with a German layout, for example, types the ü character.

Figure 4.49 The default location—on the taskbar—is the most sensible place for the language bar.

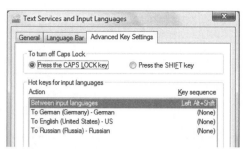

Figure 4.50 Defining hotkeys makes it easy to switch among languages on the fly.

Figure 4.51 Click the language bar and choose the language or keyboard layout that you want to switch to; switch by pressing the left Shift and left Alt keys at the same time; or press the language's hotkey (if you defined one).

Figure 4.52 This wizard shows you how to get additional languages.

5. On the Advanced Key Settings tab, define a hotkey for each language (**Figure 4.50**).

6. Click OK (or Apply).

7. On the taskbar, click the language bar to choose a keyboard layout (**Figure 4.51**).

✔ Tip

- Use the Character Map program to view the characters available on your keyboard; see "Using the Free Utility Programs" in Chapter 6.

To set the display language:

1. Choose Start > Control Panel > Clock, Language, and Region > Regional and Language Options > Keyboards and Languages tab (refer to Figure 4.47).

2. In the Display Language section, choose a language from the list and click OK.

or

If you don't see the list of display languages, you need to install additional language files first. Click Install/Uninstall Languages (if a security prompt appears, type an administrator password or confirm the action) and follow the onscreen instructions (**Figure 4.52**).

LOCALIZING YOUR SYSTEM

To set the preferred language for older programs:

1. Choose Start > Control Panel > Clock, Language, and Region > Regional and Language Options > Administrative tab (**Figure 4.53**).

2. In the Language for Non-Unicode Programs section, click Change System Locale (if a security prompt appears, type an administrator password or confirm the action), choose your preferred language in the list, and then click OK.

3. To apply your Regional and Language settings to all new user accounts or to system accounts, click Copy to Reserved Accounts (if a security prompt appears, type an administrator password or confirm the action), check the desired account boxes, and then click OK.

4. Click OK (or Apply).

Figure 4.53 If an older program is unable to recognize your preferred language, Windows can swap the character set.

Accommodating Disabled Users

Windows can be set up to assist disabled users. *Ease of Access* is Microsoft's umbrella term for tools that make a computer easier to use for people with poor eyesight, hearing, or mobility. Ease of Access Center is the main switchboard that teaches you about ease-of-access options and lets you turn them on or off. **Table 4.2** describes the main features.

The easiest way to learn about Ease of Access options is to answer a questionnaire that recommends settings based on your answers. If you prefer to skip the questionnaire, you can explore and set each option individually.

Table 4.2

Ease of Access Features	
FEATURE	DESCRIPTION
Magnifier	Enlarges part of the screen in a small separate window while you work, leaving the rest of your desktop in a standard display.
Narrator	Reads onscreen text aloud and describes some computer events (such as error messages) when they happen.
On-Screen Keyboard	Displays a picture of a keyboard with all the standard keys so you can type with mouse clicks or a joystick.
High Contrast	Makes things easier to read by increasing the contrast of colors. Keyboard shortcut: Press left Alt+left Shift+Print Screen (or PrntScrn).
Speech Recognition	Lets you give commands and dictate text by using your voice. See "Using Speech Recognition" later in this chapter.
Mouse Keys	Lets you use the arrow keys on your keyboard or the numeric keypad to move the mouse pointer around the screen. Keyboard shortcut: Press left Alt+left Shift+Num Lock.
Sticky Keys	Lets you press key combinations, such as Ctrl+Alt+Delete, one key at a time. Keyboard shortcut: Press Shift five times.
Toggle Keys	Plays an alert each time you press the Caps Lock, Num Lock, or Scroll Lock key. Keyboard shortcut: Press Num Lock for 5 seconds.
Filter Keys	Removes unintentional repeated keystrokes when you hold down a key too long. Keyboard shortcut: Press right Shift for 8 seconds.

ACCOMMODATING DISABLED USERS

To open Ease of Access Center:

◆ Choose Start > All Programs > Accessories > Ease of Access > Ease of Access Center (**Figure 4.54**).

or

Choose Start > Control Panel > Ease of Access > Ease of Access Center.

or

Choose Start, type ease of access in the Search box, and then press Enter.

or

Press Windows logo key+U.

Figure 4.54 Ease of Access Center starts by reading its own text aloud. You can mute it by unchecking Always Read This Section Aloud.

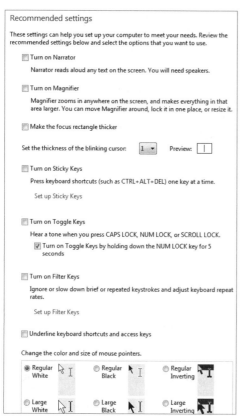

Figure 4.55 When you finish the questionnaire, Windows presents you with a list of Ease of Access options that you can turn on or off.

To use the Ease of Access questionnaire:

1. In Ease of Access Center, click Get Recommendations to Make Your Computer Easier to Use.

2. Follow the onscreen instructions (**Figure 4.55**).

To set Ease of Access options individually:

◆ In Ease of Access Center, click the links under Explore All Settings (the bottom portion of Figure 4.54). Each link will take you to a page of controls that lets you turn on or off related Ease of Access options (**Figure 4.56**).

✔ Tips

■ Some Ease of Access tools are for everyone. Graphic designers and developers can use Magnifier for pixel-level design work, and On-Screen Keyboard is handy if you find yourself with a broken keyboard.

■ Ease of Access options also are available on the Welcome screen. See "Logging On and Logging Off" in Chapter 1.

■ Ease of Access was called Accessibility Options in Windows XP. Ease of Access Center replaces XP's Utility Manager, and the questionnaire replaces the Accessibility wizard.

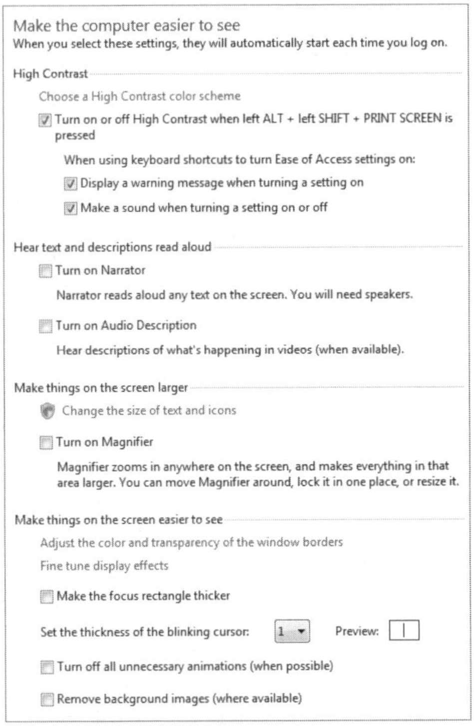

Figure 4.56 These options appear if you click Make the Computer Easier to See. (One assumes that Microsoft actually is referring to the screen image rather than the computer itself.)

Using Speech Recognition

Control Panel's Speech utility controls Windows' speech-recognition and text-to-speech (speech synthesizer) features.

Speech recognition lets you speak into a microphone to control your computer; you can give commands that the computer will carry out or dictate text that will self-type on your screen. You can create a voice profile that trains your computer to understand you better. You can use speech recognition to dictate documents and email messages, use your voice to control programs and browse the web, and avoid repetitive-strain injuries by reducing the use of your mouse and keyboard.

Currently, speech recognition works for:

◆ Nearly all applications that come with Windows Vista

◆ Microsoft Word and Outlook (but not Excel and PowerPoint)

Windows' Text-to-Speech (TTS) utility reads aloud onscreen text, buttons, menus, filenames, keystrokes, and other items by using a speech synthesizer. The only built-in program that reads to you is Narrator, which has its own voice controls (see "Accommodating Disabled Users" earlier in this chapter). You can find other TTS programs at www.microsoft.com/enable.

✔ Tips

■ In addition to a microphone, you'll need a sound card if your computer's motherboard doesn't have a built-in microphone jack.

■ Use a high-quality microphone such as a USB headset microphone or an array mic. Get a mic with noise-cancellation technology if you work in a noisy place like a call center or trading floor.

■ A better speech-recognition product is Dragon NaturallySpeaking (www.scansoft.com).

To set up speech recognition for first use:

1. Choose Start > All Programs > Accessories > Ease of Access > Windows Speech Recognition.

   or

   Choose Start, type speech recognition in the Search box, and then press Enter.

   The Set Up Speech Recognition wizard opens. **Figure 4.57** shows the wizard's first two pages.

2. Follow the onscreen instructions.

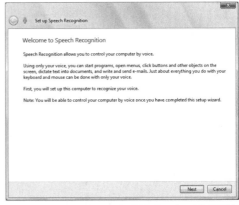

Figure 4.57 This wizard helps you set up your microphone, learn how to talk to your computer, and train your computer to understand your speech.

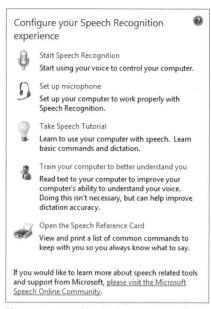

Configure your Speech Recognition experience

🎙 **Start Speech Recognition**
Start using your voice to control your computer.

🎧 **Set up microphone**
Set up your computer to work properly with Speech Recognition.

💡 **Take Speech Tutorial**
Learn to use your computer with speech. Learn basic commands and dictation.

👤 **Train your computer to better understand you**
Read text to your computer to improve your computer's ability to understand your voice. Doing this isn't necessary, but can help improve dictation accuracy.

🖨 **Open the Speech Reference Card**
View and print a list of common commands to keep with you so you always know what to say.

If you would like to learn more about speech related tools and support from Microsoft, please visit the Microsoft Speech Online Community.

Figure 4.58 Use this window to start, configure, and get help for speech recognition.

Figure 4.59 You must train a speech recognizer to adapt to the sound of your voice, word pronunciation, accent, and speaking manner.

✔ Tips

- To set up the parts of speech recognition individually, choose Start > Control Panel > Ease of Access > Speech Recognition Options (**Figure 4.58**). Click Set Up Microphone, Take Speech Tutorial, and Train Your Computer to Better Understand You. Follow the onscreen instructions that appear after you click each link.

- The speech tutorial takes about 30 minutes to complete. Make sure that you have enough uninterrupted free time to finish it.

To set speech options:

1. Choose Start > Control Panel > Ease of Access > Speech Recognition Options > Advanced Speech Options (on the left) > Speech Recognition tab (**Figure 4.59**).

2. In the Language section, choose a speech-recognition engine from the drop-down list or click Settings (if available) to show additional engine properties.

3. In the Recognition Profiles section, click New to create a new recognition profile for your voice; then follow the onscreen instructions when the wizard opens.

4. In the Microphone section, set and configure your audio input device.

5. Click OK (or Apply).

USING SPEECH RECOGNITION

To use speech recognition:

1. Choose Start > Control Panel > Ease of Access > Speech Recognition Options (refer to Figure 4.58).

2. Click Open the Speech Reference Card to use a quick reference while you give commands and dictate text.

3. Switch back to Speech Recognition Options and click Start Speech Recognition.

   If you haven't yet set up speech recognition, the Set Up Speech Recognition wizard opens; see "To set up speech recognition for first use" earlier in this section.

   See the sidebar for an example session.

✔ Tips

■ To correct mistakes while dictating text, say "Correct" and the word that the computer typed by mistake; then select the correct word in the list offered by Speech Recognition or repeat the correct word again. If the computer misrecognized "speech" as "peach," say "Correct peach," and then select the right word in the list or say "speech" again.

■ When you say a command that can be interpreted in a few ways, the system displays a disambiguation interface to clarify what you intended.

■ Speak directly into your microphone, and make sure that it's properly attached and not muted. If your computer still can't hear you, check the input level on the Levels tab of the mic's Properties dialog box (see "To configure recording devices" in "Configuring Sound and Audio Devices" earlier in this chapter).

An Example Session

The most common way to use speech recognition is to dictate a document. Here's a quick example that starts WordPad, dictates the body of a document, names and saves the document, and exits WordPad:

◆ "Start listening." (This makes the computer listen to you.)

◆ "Open WordPad."

◆ "This is a test of speech recognition period." (Remember to pronounce punctuation.)

◆ Say "File," then "Save As," then "My test document," and then "Save."

◆ "Close WordPad."

◆ "Stop listening." (This makes the computer stop listening to you.)

Figure 4.60 For U.S. English, the robotic voice of Windows is named Microsoft Anna.

To set TTS options:

1. Choose Start > Control Panel > Ease of Access > Speech Recognition Options > Advanced Speech Options (on the left) > Text to Speech tab (**Figure 4.60**).

2. In the Voice Selection section, choose one of the available TTS voices from the drop-down list or click Settings (if available) to display additional voice properties.

   The selected voice speaks the text in the "preview voice" box.

3. In the Voice Speed section, drag the slider to adjust the voice's rate of speech.

4. Click Audio Output to set the preferred device for voice playback.

5. Click OK (or Apply).

USING SPEECH RECOGNITION

Using Alternative Mouse Behavior

The mouse behavior described in "The Mouse" and "Icons" in Chapter 1 is the default. Windows' alternative setting is a weblike interface, letting you open icons by single-clicking—instead of double-clicking, which can be awkward for beginners. (Right-clicking and dragging remain unchanged.)

To open items with a single click:

1. Choose Start > Control Panel > Appearance and Personalization > Folder Options > General tab (**Figure 4.61**).

   or

   Choose Start, type folder options in the Search box, and then press Enter.

2. In the Click Items As Follows section, select Single-Click to Open an Item (Point to Select).

3. Choose icon title underlining: permanent (like links on a webpage) or temporary (only when you point to icons).

4. Click OK (or Apply).

The instructions in this book assume that you use the default behavior, but if you choose the alternative:

◆ There's no more double-clicking. To open an icon, click it. To select an icon, move the pointer over it; don't click.

◆ To select multiple icons, hold down the Ctrl or Shift key while moving the pointer over each desired icon; again, don't click. Ctrl selects individual icons; Shift selects a range of icons.

◆ To rename an icon, point to it, press F2, type the name, and then press Enter.

   or

   Right-click it, choose Rename, type the name, and then press Enter.

Figure 4.61 You can open items in folders and on the desktop by single-clicking them, just as you click a link on a webpage. To select an item without opening it, move the pointer over it.

Conserving Power

Environmental and money concerns make power management an issue for desktop as well as laptop users. Control Panel's Power Options utility lets you configure hardware features that reduce power consumption, affect how the power switch works, and extend the life of computer parts by turning them off or switching them to a low-power state.

To optimize your computer's power use, Windows uses a *power plan*—a collection of settings that reduces the power consumption of certain system devices or of your entire system. (Power plans were called *power schemes* in earlier Windows versions.) You can use the default power plans provided with Windows or create your own by using one of the default plans as a starting point. You can change settings for any of your custom plans or the default plans to, for example:

◆ Make your computer go to sleep or turn off the display after a specified idle period

◆ Adjust the brightness of your display

◆ Require a password to unlock the computer when it wakes from sleep

◆ Choose what your computer does when you press the hardware power and sleep buttons or (for a laptop) close the lid

Uninterruptible Power Supply

An Uninterruptible Power Supply (UPS) is a sealed backup battery—connected between the computer and the electrical outlet—that kicks in to keep your computer running if power fails. The UPS's capacity is expressed in minutes available to save your work and shut down normally during a power outage—about 5 minutes for a cheaper UPS and up to about 30 minutes for better ones. UPSes also protect against power surges, spikes, and brownouts (low voltage), which damage hardware more than blackouts.

Don't forget to plug your monitor into the UPS. You also can plug in a power strip for extra sockets and keep your modem, printer, and electric stapler safe too.

A UPS doesn't really *have* to interact with Windows, but Windows includes built-in support for monitoring that sounds power-failure alerts, displays remaining UPS-battery time, and—if power becomes very low—shuts down the computer automatically. A UPS that plugs into a USB port will install its driver and may come with its own power-management software.

✔ Tips

■ Some computers may not be able to use all the Power Options features. Windows identifies your hardware configuration automatically and makes available only the settings that you can change.

■ See also "Turning off your computer" in "Logging On and Logging Off" in Chapter 1.

To set a power plan:

◆ Choose Start > Control Panel > Hardware and Sound > Power Options and select a power plan (**Figure 4.62**).

or

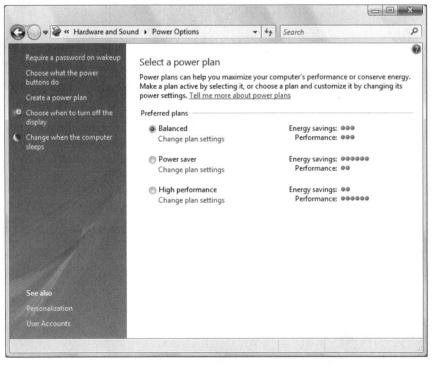

Figure 4.62 The Power Options page is the main switchboard for choosing, creating, and editing power plans.

Figure 4.63 Click the battery icon to pick a power plan.

Choose Start, type `power options` in the Search box, press Enter, and select a power plan.

or

If the battery icon appears in the notification area on the taskbar, click it and select a power plan (**Figure 4.63**).

Table 4.3 describes the plans that come with Windows. Your PC manufacturer or system administrator may have added others (or customized the battery icon).

Table 4.3

Power Plans	
PLAN	**DESCRIPTION**
Balanced	Offers full performance when you need it and saves power during periods of inactivity. This plan is fine for most people's needs.
Power Saver	Maximizes battery life by reducing system performance. If you're a laptop user, use this plan if you travel often and rely on battery power for long periods.
High Performance	Maximizes system performance and responsiveness. If you're a desktop user, use this plan for processor-intensive tasks like editing video, playing 3D games, and doing engineering or scientific calculations.

CONSERVING POWER

✔ Tips

- If you're on a network domain, your administrator can block you from changing the power plan.

- The battery icon appears on all laptop computers. On desktop computers, it appears only if you're using a short-term battery, such as a UPS supply that plugs into a USB port.

- The battery icon also responds to hovering and right-clicks (**Figure 4.64**). If your laptop has more than one battery, click the battery icon to see the charge remaining on each battery. Hover over the icon to see the combined charge.

- To show or hide the battery icon, right-click an empty area of the notification area, choose Properties, and then check or uncheck Power in the Notification Area tab. (The Power check box is unavailable if no battery is installed.) You also can open this dialog box from the battery icon's shortcut menu (refer to Figure 4.64).

- The battery icon is a graphical "fuel gauge" that tells you the battery's remaining power and charging state (**Table 4.4**). If you've customized your power plan to let you know when your battery is low, that notification appears above the battery icon. System-intensive tasks (like watching DVDs) drain a battery a lot faster than mundane ones (like reading and writing email). Over time you'll learn how accurate the battery meter is for your laptop, battery, and computing tasks.

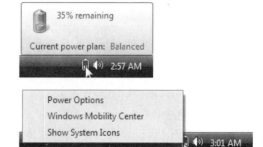

Figure 4.64 Hover your mouse pointer over the battery icon for a status report (top) or right-click it for a shortcut menu (bottom). Choosing Power Options from the shortcut menu is a quick way to open the Power Options page (refer to Figure 4.62).

Table 4.4

Battery Icons

Icon	What It Means
	Your laptop is plugged in, and the battery is charging.
	Your laptop is plugged in, and the battery is fully charged.
	Your laptop isn't plugged in, and the battery is draining.
	The battery is low (yellow caution sign). See "To set low and critical battery behavior."
	The battery is critically low (red circled x). See "To set low and critical battery behavior."
	Your laptop is plugged in, but the battery isn't charging. (If the battery icon doesn't fill for a long time, you may have an old battery or a hardware problem.)
	Windows can't determine the battery charge (empty battery).
	Windows can't find a battery in the battery bay (red x). Check the documentation that came with your battery or laptop to know when it's safe to remove or insert the battery.

CONSERVING POWER

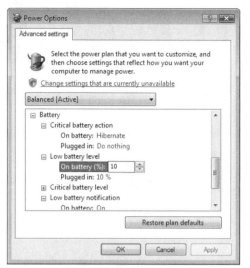

Figure 4.65 Windows monitors your battery's charge and warns you when it reaches low and critical levels. Don't set these levels so low that you won't have a chance to install a charged battery, find a power outlet, or save your work and turn off your laptop. Try 25% (low) and 10% (critical) initially.

To set low and critical battery behavior:

1. Choose Start > Control Panel > Hardware and Sound > Power Options (refer to Figure 4.62).

2. Under the selected plan, click Change Plan Settings.

3. Click Change Advanced Power Settings.

4. On the Advanced settings tab, expand Battery (**Figure 4.65**).

5. To set the charge levels at which battery notifications occur, expand Low Battery Level and Critical Battery Level; then choose the percentage that you want for each level.

   or

   To set what to do when a battery notification occurs, expand Low Battery Action and Critical Battery Action; then choose the action that you want for each level.

   or

   To turn battery-level notifications on or off, expand Low Battery Notification, click On Battery, and then choose On or Off.

6. Click OK.

7. Click Save Changes.

✔ Tips

- To extend a battery's charge, use the Power Saver power plan, reduce your display brightness, and unplug the USB and PC Card devices that you're not using.

- The Hibernate state is described in "Turning off your computer" in "Logging On and Logging Off" in Chapter 1.

CONSERVING POWER

To create your own power plan:

1. Choose Start > Control Panel > Hardware and Sound > Power Options (refer to Figure 4.62).

2. Click Create a Power Plan (on the left).

3. On the Create a Power Plan page, select the plan that's closest to the type of plan that you want to create (**Figure 4.66**).

4. In the Plan Name box, type a name for your plan; then click Next.

5. On the Change Settings for the Plan page, choose the display and sleep settings that you want to use when your computer is running on battery and when it's plugged in; then click Create (**Figure 4.67**).

✔ Tips

■ The plan that you just created automatically becomes the active plan.

■ If you're using a laptop, your plan appears under Plans Shown on the Battery Meter. If you're using a desktop computer, your plan appears under Preferred Plans. The plan that you based your new plan on is moved under Additional Plans (**Figure 4.68**).

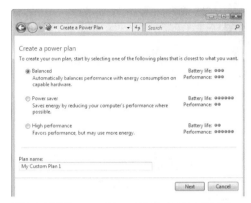

Figure 4.66 If you want to create a plan to conserve energy, for example, start with Power Saver.

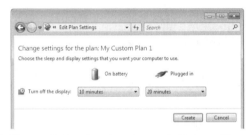

Figure 4.67 If you're using a laptop, On Battery will appear.

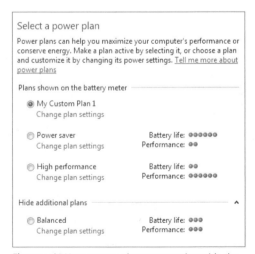

Figure 4.68 Your custom plans appear alongside the default plans.

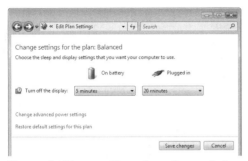

Figure 4.69 This page will vary depending on whether you're using a laptop or a desktop computer.

Figure 4.70 Expand the category that you want to customize, expand each setting that you want to change, and then choose the values that you want to use when your computer is running on battery and when it's plugged in.

To change an existing power plan:

1. Choose Start > Control Panel > Hardware and Sound > Power Options (refer to Figure 4.62).

2. Under the plan that you want to change, click Change Plan Settings.

3. On the Change Settings for the Plan page, choose the new settings (**Figure 4.69**).

4. If you don't want to change any more settings, click Save Changes.

   or

   To change additional power settings, click Change Advanced Power Settings; then complete steps 5 and 6.

5. Change the settings on the Advanced Settings tab (**Figure 4.70**).

6. Click OK.

7. Click Save Changes.

To delete a power plan:

1. Choose Start > Control Panel > Hardware and Sound > Power Options (refer to Figure 4.62).

2. If the active plan is the one that you want to delete, make a different plan the active plan.

3. Under the plan that you want to delete, click Change Plan Settings.

4. On the Change Settings for the Plan page, click Delete This Plan.

5. When prompted, click OK.

✔ Tips

- You can't restore a plan after deleting it.

- You can't delete any of the three default plans (Balanced, Power Saver, or High Performance).

CONSERVING POWER

To configure system settings for power options:

1. Choose Start > Control Panel > Hardware and Sound > Power Options (refer to Figure 4.62).

2. Click Require a Password on Wakeup (on the left).

3. Choose the settings for the power and sleep buttons, laptop lid, and password protection (**Figure 4.71**).

   If any settings are unavailable, click Change Settings That Are Currently Unavailable, and type an administrator password or confirm the action when prompted.

4. Click Save Changes.

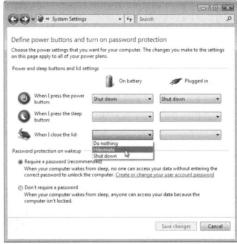

Figure 4.71 These settings apply to all power plans. To apply them to only a specific plan, use the Advanced Settings dialog box for that plan (refer to Figure 4.70).

Managing Fonts

A *font* is a collection of letters, numbers, symbols, and other characters that describes a certain typeface, along with size, spacing, and other qualities. Windows includes dozens of fonts used to display text onscreen and in print. Most of these are *TrueType* or *OpenType* fonts, which look smooth and clear in all sizes and on all output devices. Windows also supports *PostScript* fonts, with no need for Adobe Type Manager. You'll also find a few hideous bitmapped fonts, called *raster* fonts, included for compatibility with older programs. You manage fonts in the Fonts folder.

If you want a font that prints well and is easy to read on the screen, use a TrueType or OpenType font. If you need a large character set for language coverage and fine typography, use an OpenType font. For printing glossy magazines and professional-quality publications, use an OpenType or PostScript font.

For more font information, visit `www.microsoft.com/typography`. Look for a list of font foundries where you can buy high-quality fonts online. You also can download lots of free fonts, but they're rarely of good quality. (Make sure that you trust the source when you download a font.)

✔ Tips

■ To make your onscreen fonts clearer, you can increase dpi scaling and use ClearType; see the sidebars in "Configuring the Monitor" earlier in this chapter. The Windows fonts designed to work well with ClearType include Constantia and Cambria (serif); Corbel, Candara, and Calibri (sans serif); Consolas (monospace); and Segoe UI (used throughout the Windows interface).

■ Windows uses the font Segoe UI—new in Vista—in menus, icons, and other screen elements. To change the Windows font, choose Start > Control Panel > Appearance and Personalization > Personalization > Window Color and Appearance > Open Classic Appearance Properties for More Color Options > Advanced button. In the Item list, choose the part of Windows where you want to change the font; then pick a font, size, and color.

To open the Fonts folder:

◆ Choose Start > Control Panel > Appearance and Personalization > Fonts (**Figure 4.72**).

or

Choose Start, type fonts in the Search box, and then press Enter.

or

In Windows Explorer, open the folder \Windows\Fonts.

✔ Tip

■ To match the font names with their filenames and paths, choose Views > Details (on the toolbar), right-click a column heading in the file list, and then check Font File Names (**Figure 4.73**). If a font icon has a shortcut arrow, the font is installed but located elsewhere; the Font File Names column tells you where.

Figure 4.72 Choose Views > Tiles (on the toolbar) to see each font's name, type, and file size.

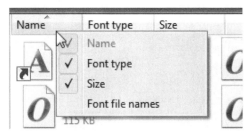

Figure 4.73 Right-click the column header to pick which columns to show in details view. Click any column header to sort by that criterion (in any view, not just details). Click again to reverse the sort.

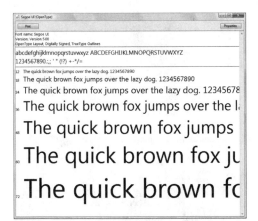

Figure 4.74 Font Viewer shows a font's summary information along with a preview.

To view or print a font:

◆ In the Fonts folder, double-click the font's icon (**Figure 4.74**).

or

In the Fonts folder, select one or more font icons; then press Enter.

Windows displays font statistics, the full alphabet, and a type sample at various sizes. Click Properties to get more information or Print to print a font sample.

✔ Tips

■ Font Viewer displays only a predefined set of characters. To display every character in a font, use Character Map. See "Using the Free Utility Programs" in Chapter 6.

■ To view fonts with a program other than Windows Font Viewer, right-click a font icon, choose Properties, and then click Change.

To install a new font:

◆ In the Fonts folder, choose File > Install New Font (press Alt if the File menu isn't visible); then navigate to and select the font files to install (**Figure 4.75**).

or

Drag a font file into the Fonts folder.

✔ Tips

■ You also can open Add Fonts by right-clicking an empty area in the file list of the Fonts folder and choosing Install New Font.

■ After a font is installed, it appears in your programs' Font dialog boxes and lists. You may have to close and reopen a program for the font to show up.

■ If a new font appears unexpectedly in your Fonts folder, a recently installed program probably put it there.

■ If you install a TrueType font and a PostScript font with exactly the same name, Windows won't know which one to access when you use it. Avoid installing different fonts with the same name; install only one.

To remove a font:

◆ In the Fonts folder, right-click the font's icon and choose Delete.

or

In the Fonts folder, select one or more font icons; then press the Delete key.

or

Drag one or more font icons out of the Fonts folder to the Recycle Bin or another folder.

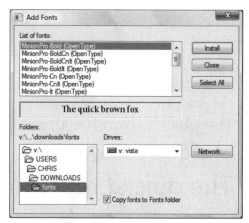

Figure 4.75 To install fonts from a network drive without using disk space on your computer, uncheck Copy Fonts to Fonts Folder.

Font Utilities

If you work with fonts regularly or your font lists are getting crowded, try a font-management utility such as Suitcase ($80 U.S.; www.extensis.com).

To convert PostScript Type 1 and TrueType fonts between Windows and Mac, try CrossFont ($45 U.S.; www.asy.com).

To create your own fonts, try FontCreator ($80 U.S.; www.high-logic.com).

For enthusiasts, Metafont, TeX, and LaTeX—the best typography and typesetting programs on the planet—are free and available at www.tug.org.

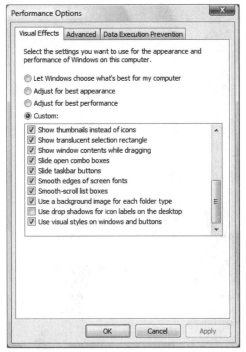

Figure 4.76 The Performance Options dialog box lets you turn visual effects on and off.

Managing Visual Effects and Performance

The Windows interface offers many visual effects, such as animation, fading, and shadows. These effects can be entertaining or useful, but they chew up processor time and can degrade performance noticeably (particularly if you're short on RAM, video processor speed, or battery power). Windows lets you turn off individual visual effects, perhaps making your system more responsive. It's worth experimenting.

To turn off visual effects:

1. Choose Start > Control Panel > System and Maintenance > System > Advanced System Settings (on the left).

   If a security prompt appears, type an administrator password or confirm the action.

2. On the Advanced tab, in the Performance section, click Settings > Visual Effects tab (**Figure 4.76**).

3. Select Custom, uncheck the boxes for the effects that you want to turn off, and then click OK in each open dialog box.

Restoring the Old Windows Look

If you prefer the appearance of Windows 98/2000 to Windows Vista's redesigned look, you can revert to the classic look (**Figure 4.77**). I've collected the settings here for quick reference. They apply only to the logged-on user.

To switch to the classic Start menu:

◆ Right-click the Start button > Properties > Classic Start Menu > click OK (**Figure 4.78**).

To switch to classic Control Panel view:

◆ Choose Start > Control Panel > Classic View (on the left) (**Figure 4.79**).

Figure 4.77 A Windows Vista desktop with the classic Start menu, Control Panel, and visual style.

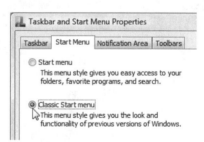

Figure 4.78 This setting activates the classic single-column Start menu.

Figure 4.79 Classic view removes the extra layer of fluff in category view, but Control Panel's Search box won't work as well.

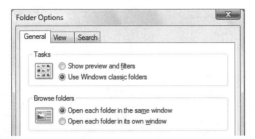

Figure 4.80 This Classic Folders option shows the classic menu bar and hides space-consuming panes in folder windows. The Same Window option keeps your desktop from becoming cluttered with folder windows.

Figure 4.81 This setting restores the squared-off, muted look of windows and buttons. Click the Advanced button to change the appearance of individual elements.

To show the menu bar and hide the Details and Preview panes in all folder windows:

◆ Choose Start > Control Panel > Appearance and Personalization > Folder Options > General tab > Use Windows Classic Folders (**Figure 4.80**).

To browse folders by using a single window:

◆ Choose Start > Control Panel > Appearance and Personalization > Folder Options > General tab > Open Each Folder in the Same Window (refer to Figure 4.80).

To switch to the classic visual scheme:

◆ Choose Start > Control Panel > Appearance and Personalization > Personalization > Window Color and Appearance > Open Classic Appearance Properties for More Color Options > Windows Classic color scheme (**Figure 4.81**).

RESTORING THE OLD WINDOWS LOOK

To show system icons on the desktop:

◆ Choose Start > Control Panel >
   Appearance and Personalization >
   Personalization > Change Desktop Icons
   (on the left) > Desktop Icons section
   (**Figure 4.82**).

To use earlier versions of desktop icons:

1. Choose Start > Control Panel >
   Appearance and Personalization >
   Personalization > Change Desktop Icons
   (on the left).

2. Select an icon and click Change Icon.

3. Browse to \Windows\System32\shell32.dll,
   which contains most of the old icons
   (**Figure 4.83**).

4. Select an icon and click OK.

To use classic mouse pointers:

◆ Choose Start > Control Panel >
   Appearance and Personalization >
   Personalization > Mouse Pointers, and
   choose (None) from the Scheme drop-
   down list.

✔ Tip

■ When you upgrade to Vista, Windows
   Setup hijacks some file-type associations
   without telling you. Your default program
   for .htm and .html (web) files, for example,
   changes to Internet Explorer. To change
   your settings back, see "Associating
   Documents with Programs" in Chapter 6.

Figure 4.82 Check the icons that you want to appear on your desktop.

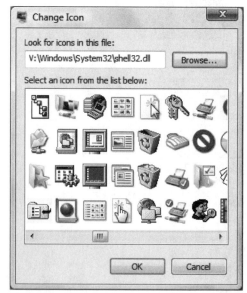

Figure 4.83 Windows Vista still contains a treasure trove of classic-style icons, if you want to go retro.

Figure 4.84 This page gives basic information about your Windows edition, processor, RAM, network, and product registration.

Figure 4.85 A computer's base score is determined by the lowest subscore (here, the Gaming Graphics subscore); it's not an average.

Getting General System Information

Control Panel's System page is a helpful information-only window that displays:

◆ Your Windows edition (including Service Packs)

◆ Information about your processor and physical memory (RAM)

◆ Your computer's name and network (workgroup or domain)

◆ Windows registration information

You'll need some of this information when you request tech support over the phone, particularly if you're talking to Microsoft.

To display general system information:

◆ Choose Start > Control Panel > System and Maintenance > System (or press Windows logo key+Break) (**Figure 4.84**).

✔ Tips

■ Click Windows Experience Index in Figure 4.84 to get your computer's *base score:* Microsoft's numeric rating of your computer's capabilities (**Figure 4.85**). Click the Help button (❷) in the top-right corner for an explanation.

■ Another way to get basic system information: Choose Start > All Programs > Accessories > Command Prompt, type systeminfo at the prompt, and then press Enter. To redirect the output to a text file in the current directory, type systeminfo > info.txt. This command may not work in Home editions of Vista.

■ To get detailed system information, see "Getting System Information" in Chapter 20.

ORGANIZING FILES AND FOLDERS

Like all modern operating systems, Windows uses files and folders to organize your information so that you aren't overwhelmed by long file lists and can distinguish one set of information from another. A *file* is the basic unit of computer storage; it can be a program, a program's configuration data, a log that the computer itself maintains, or a document that you create or receive. You organize files in containers called *folders* (or *directories*), which can hold additional folders (called *subfolders*) to form a treelike hierarchy. Folders in turn are stored on *disks,* or *volumes*—such as hard drives, floppy disks, CDs, DVDs, USB flash drives, and network servers.

Windows creates a few system folders to store its own files and settings but otherwise doesn't care how you structure your tree of folders and files. In this chapter, I explain how to use Windows Explorer to navigate and manage your stored information.

Exploring Your Computer

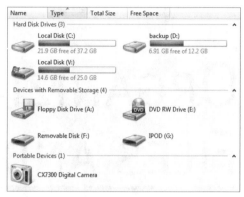

Computer (**Figure 5.1**), a top-level folder, is the window to your computer's data structure. From it you can open files, folders, and disks on your computer (or network), which are categorized as follows:

Hard Disk Drives lists the hard drives installed on this computer.

Devices with Removable Storage lists floppy disks, CDs, DVDs, flash memory, tapes, and other removable media.

Portable Devices shows icons for connected digital cameras, personal digital assistants (PDAs), and other portable devices. It's not always clear whether a gadget is a portable device or removable storage; note that Windows classifies the iPod music player shown in Figure 5.1 as storage.

Depending on how your PC is configured, more categories (such as Other and Network Drives) may appear.

Figure 5.1 The Computer window shows the top-level folders and disks on your PC, including network drives and other storage devices. This window's appearance varies by computer and changes over time as you add or remove drives and devices.

USB Flash Drives

USB flash drives are small devices (about the size and weight of a car key) that are similar in use to a hard drive. Just plug one into a USB port, and its icon appears in Computer—Removable Disk (F:) in Figure 5.1, for example.

USB flash drives have largely supplanted floppy disks and CD-Rs for portable storage. They currently can hold up to 4 GB of data—about six times the content of a standard CD or about 1,300 3-minute MP3 files (66 hours). Like digital-camera memory cards, these drives have no moving parts and can outlast spinning hard disks by years.

Flash drives also are called pen drives, thumb drives, keychain drives, key drives, or memory keys. They cost between $20 and $200 (U.S.), depending on capacity. See also "Connecting Devices to Your Computer" in Chapter 8.

Figure 5.2 Double-clicking a camera icon displays this dialog box, asking whether you want to copy photos to your hard drive or browse them on the camera.

Windows System Folders

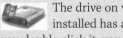 The drive on which Vista is installed has a Windows logo. If you double-click it, you can browse the top-level system folders that Windows Setup created during installation:

Program Files contains all the programs —Microsoft Word, Internet Explorer, or Adobe Photoshop, for example—that you, Windows Setup, or your PC's manufacturer installed, along with all the support files needed to run those programs. In general, you shouldn't need (or want) to touch files in this folder.

Users (named Documents and Settings in earlier Windows versions) contains a subfolder for each user account or for each user who has logged on to a network domain. These subfolders contain the users' personal settings and files. If you're not an administrator, you can't open or see other users' subfolders (see Chapter 17). The Public folder (in Users) stores files available to every user, administrator or not.

Windows contains critical operating-system files. Look but don't touch (with the exception of the Fonts subfolder; see "Managing Fonts" in Chapter 4).

To see what's on your computer:

1. Choose Start > Computer.

   or

   Press Windows logo key+E.

2. To see what's on a hard drive, in the Hard Disk Drives section, double-click the drive that you want to see.

   or

   To find a file or folder on a floppy disk, CD, DVD, USB flash drive, or other removable media, in the Devices with Removable Storage section, double-click the item you want to see. (You'll get an error message if there's no disk in the drive.)

   or

   To see what's on a portable device, in the Portable Devices section, double-click the device that you want to see.

   Windows may open a dialog box asking you what you want to do (**Figure 5.2**).

3. Keep double-clicking folders to burrow to the file or folder you want.

   To return to the previous folder, press Backspace or click the Back button (⊙) in the window's top-left corner.

✔ Tips

- When you double-click a folder, Windows replaces the original window with a new one or opens a separate window atop the current one. Opening new windows makes it easy to move or copy files but clutters the screen quickly. To choose the behavior you prefer, in Computer, choose Organize (on the toolbar) > Folder and Search Options > General tab and then select an option under Browse Folders.

- Hard Disk Drives (3) ⌃

  The horizontal separator for each category lists the number of disks or devices in that category. Click a separator to select all the icons in that category, or double-click it or click its arrow button (ⓐ) to show or hide them.

- To make Computer appear as a submenu in the Start menu, right-click the Start button, choose Properties > Customize > Computer > Display As a Menu > OK (**Figure 5.3**).

- To show the Computer icon on the desktop, open the Start menu, right-click Computer, and then choose Show on Desktop.

- To rename a drive icon, right-click it and choose Rename.

- Tiles view (shown in Figure 5.1 and available from the Views button on the toolbar) shows you how much free space remains on each hard disk drive. In other views, right-click a drive icon and choose Properties.

- *Computer* was called *My Computer* in earlier Windows versions.

Figure 5.3 Even when Computer is set to expand as a menu, you can right-click its icon in the Start menu to open it in a window.

Drive Letters

Like all Windows versions, Vista inherits its drive-naming conventions from DOS. Drives are named by a letter followed by a colon.

A: is the first floppy-disk drive.

B: is the second floppy-disk drive (if present).

C: is the first hard-disk drive or the first partition of the first physical hard-disk drive. This drive usually contains Windows itself if you have only one operating system on your machine.

D: through Z: are assigned to other hard-disk drives, partitions, CD/DVD drives, USB flash drives, mapped network drives, removable storage, and portable devices.

Windows assigns drive letters consecutively, but you can use Computer Management to change them; see "Managing Disks" in Chapter 20.

Figure 5.4 Your personal folder comes with several specialized subfolders meant for storing certain types of files.

Storing Stuff in Your Personal Folder

Your *personal folder* (**Figure 5.4**) is a convenient location for storing your files and folders in one place. The folder isn't actually called "personal"; it's labeled with your logon name. This folder is associated with the user account (Chapter 17) of whoever is logged on, so its contents are unique for every user. Other users (besides administrators) can't see what's in your personal folder; neither can you see what's in theirs.

The personal folder includes a handful of specialized subfolders, each of which is intended for the type of file that its name suggests. Here's a list of the most commonly used subfolders and what Microsoft suggests you store in them:

- Documents—Word-processing files, spreadsheets, presentations, and text files

- Downloads—Files and programs downloaded from the internet

- Music—MP3s and digital music, downloaded or ripped from a CD

- Pictures—Digital pictures from a camera, scanner, or email message

- Videos—Videos and clips from your digital camera or camcorder, or video files downloaded or ripped from a DVD

These folders are just helpful anchors to help you organize your files without having to start from scratch, but this storage scheme doesn't really work when things get complicated. It's better to ignore file types and nest folders deeply. If you create a shallow or "flat" folder structure, you're forced to use long, descriptive filenames rather than succinct ones. A flat structure also makes you fill folders with so many subfolders that it's hard to discern the structure quickly.

Suppose that your new advertising campaign for olive oil includes files for photos, graphics, text copy, layouts, video ads, radio spots, and spreadsheets. It's more sensible to organize them in one place than to scatter them about the factory-installed subfolders. You could create your own hierarchy of folders in your personal folder—something like Projects > Clients > Genco Olive Oil Company > June 2007 Campaign > More Subfolders—and put everything in there.

✔ Tips

- Vista has some new features—file tagging and instant search, covered later in this chapter—that *do* let you scatter related files around your hard drive and then quickly list them all in a single window. But any pro on a deadline will tell you that nothing provides utility and peace of mind like a well-designed folder hierarchy.

- Even if your needs are more modest than those of someone running an ad campaign, you still can create subfolders anywhere in your personal folder to organize your files better. In your Pictures folder, for example, you might create subfolders to organize photos by date, by event, by location, by the names of people in the photos, or by any other scheme that works for you.

- Reduce clutter. Don't store documents on the desktop. Reserve your desktop for shortcuts to your pending projects. In general, don't put anything—even shortcuts—in the root C:\ folder.

Why to Use Your Personal Folder

You don't *have* to store your stuff in your personal folder (Windows doesn't care where you put it), but doing that is a good idea, because the folder:

- ◆ Is easy to open from the Start menu, Windows Explorer Navigation pane, and other parts of Windows.

- ◆ Has specialized subfolders (Music, Videos, Pictures) that are optimized for faster searching and organizing, and are preset to display their contents best.

- ◆ Is indexed by Windows automatically so you can find files instantly by using the Search box.

- ◆ Is where programs expect you to save and open files.

- ◆ Segregates your work and programs (which are stored in \Program Files), preventing accidental document deletion when you remove or upgrade programs.

- ◆ Makes it easier to back up your work by archiving only your personal folder (and its subfolders) rather than folders scattered about your hard disk.

- ◆ Keeps your personal files private. (To share files, move them to the Public folder.)

Opens your personal folder

Open personal subfolders

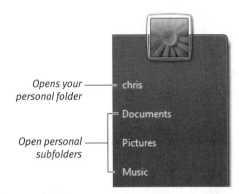

Figure 5.5 The Start menu is the easiest way to open your personal folder and its subfolders.

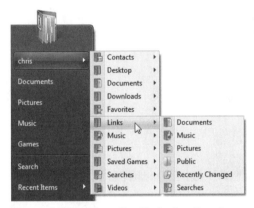

Figure 5.6 Choose the option Display As a Menu to show a cascading menu for your personal folder (or its subfolders). Even when a folder is set to expand as a menu, you can right-click its icon in the Start menu to open it in a window.

To open your personal folder:

1. Choose Start.

2. To open your personal folder, click your user name (below the icon in the top-right section of the menu).

   or

   To open a personal subfolder, click one of the links below your user name (**Figure 5.5**).

✔ Tips

- The path to your personal folder is \Users*username*.

- To see your files in one place instead of opening different folders to see different kinds of files, see "Searching for Files and Folders" later in this chapter.

- If you back up your personal folder regularly, it might be convenient to create a top-level folder—say, C:\nobackup—to store miscellaneous files that you don't want archived.

- To show or hide your personal folder and subfolders in the Start menu, right-click the Start button; choose Properties > Customize; choose an option under Documents, Music, Personal Folder, or Pictures; and then click OK (**Figure 5.6**).

- Vista drops the *My* from the folder names of earlier Windows versions: *My Documents* is now just *Documents, My Music* is *Music,* and so on.

Using Windows Explorer

Windows Explorer, or simply *Explorer,* is the key tool for working with files and folders on your local machine or network. **Figure 5.7** shows the parts of an Explorer window, and **Table 5.1** describes them.

When Windows Help and Support or this book refers to a *folder window,* it actually means a Windows Explorer window. It's common to have several instances of Explorer open at the same time, each one looking a little different depending on the settings and filters in effect for that folder. Microsoft presets folders to show their contents a certain way; you'll see panes show or hide themselves and icons grow or shrink or regroup, depending on which folder you click. But you can change the view by setting the options described here and in the next few sections.

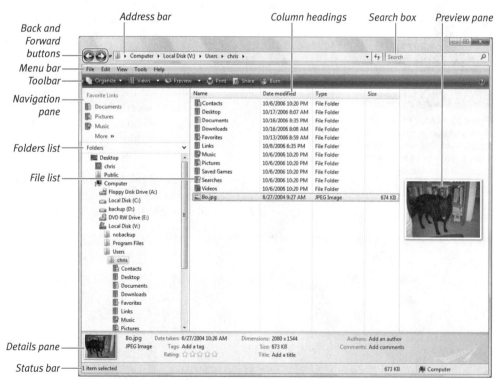

Figure 5.7 Windows Explorer gets a new look for Vista but retains its core functions.

Table 5.1

Parts of Windows Explorer	
PART	DESCRIPTION
Back and Forward buttons	Moves among previously visited locations. See "Navigating in Windows Explorer" later in this chapter.
Address bar	Shows or changes the current location. See "Navigating in Windows Explorer" later in this chapter.
Search box	Finds files in the current folder and its subfolders. See "Searching for Files and Folders" later in this chapter
Menu bar	Shows the classic folder menus. The menu bar is hidden by default. To show it, press Alt. To always show it, choose Organize > Layout > Menu Bar (or choose Organize > Folder and Search Options > View tab > check Always Show Menus).
Toolbar	Shows the most frequently used commands. The Organize and Views buttons always appear. The other buttons change to show only what's useful for what you've selected. If you click a picture file, for example, the toolbar shows different buttons than it would if you clicked a music file. (The toolbar replaces Windows XP's task pane.)
Column headings	Determines what information appears in details view and changes the way that the files in the file list are filtered and arranged. See "Filtering, Sorting, Stacking, and Grouping Files" later in this chapter.
Navigation pane	Lets you navigate directly to the folder that contains the files you want. To show or hide this pane, choose Organize > Layout > Navigation Pane. See "Navigating in Windows Explorer" later in this chapter.
Folders list	Part of the Navigation pane; shows your folders organized in a treelike structure. To show or hide the tree, click Folders in the Navigation pane.
File list	Shows the contents of the selected folder or files filtered by using column headings or the Search box.
Preview pane	Shows the contents of the selected file. To show or hide this pane, choose Organize > Layout > Preview Pane.
Details pane	Shows details about the selection and lets you add or edit them. This pane is a shortened version of the Properties dialog box. To show or hide this pane, choose Organize > Layout > Details Pane. See "Tagging Files" later in this chapter.
Status bar	Shows settings and statistics about the selection. It's divided into sections that show different information. To show or hide the status bar, choose View > Status Bar (press Alt if the View menu isn't visible). The status bar displays a short explanation of any menu command that you point to. Double-clicking the Computer icon on the status bar displays the Internet Security Properties dialog box.

To open Windows Explorer:

◆ Choose Start > All Programs > Accessories > Windows Explorer.

or

Right-click the Start button and choose Explore or Open.

or

Choose Start, type windows explorer in the Search box, and then press Enter.

or

Press Windows logo key+R; type explorer and then press Enter.

✔ Tips

■ 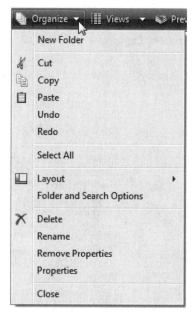 Click the Organize button on the toolbar to display a menu of commands for managing your files and folders (**Figure 5.8**).

Figure 5.8 This menu shows the basic tasks: moving, copying, renaming, deleting, and so on. If you can't find what you want on the toolbar, try the menu bar or try right-clicking a file, folder, or an empty area of the window.

■ Each time you click the Views button on the toolbar, it changes the size or arrangement of the file and folder icons in the folder window, cycling through List, Details, Tiles, and Large Icons views. Click the down arrow next to the word *Views* for more choices (**Figure 5.9**).You also can change views by right-clicking an empty area of the file list and making a choice from the View submenu.

■ Shortcut: Hold down the Ctrl key and spin your mouse wheel in either direction to cycle through all the views.

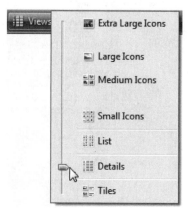

Figure 5.9 The slider moves smoothly between Extra Large Icons and Small Icons. List, the most compact display, lists only the names of files and folders, preceded by small icons. Details displays a columnar list of files, folders, and their properties (this view shown in Figure 5.7). Tiles displays medium icons with three lines of descriptive text that vary by file type.

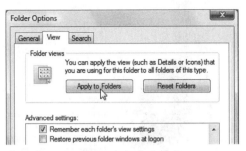

Figure 5.10 You still can apply distinct views to individual folders after clicking Apply to Folders. To return all folders of the same type to their default views, click Reset Folders.

■ To make all folders of the same type use the same view, set up one folder the way you want it and then choose Organize > Folder and Search Options > View tab > Apply to Folders button (**Figure 5.10**). Each folder remembers its own view when revisited. To make folders forget their views between visits, in the View tab, uncheck Remember Each Folder's View Settings (under Advanced Settings).

■ Click Organize and use the Layout submenu to show or hide the various panes of the folder window. To resize panes, drag the vertical and horizontal separators. (When you're over a separator, your mouse pointer changes to a double-headed arrow.) The amount of information shown in the Details pane increases or decreases with the size of the pane.

■ As you type in the Search box, the folder's contents are filtered to show only those files that match what you typed. The Search box doesn't automatically search your entire computer, however—only the current folder and its subfolders (if any). If the folder view is already filtered (if it's showing files only by a certain author, for example), the Search box will search only within that limited view. See "Searching for Files and Folders" later in this chapter.

Using Windows Explorer

- Live icons let you see a preview of a file's or folder's actual contents without having to open it (provided that previewing is supported for the file type or creating application). This feature, new in Vista, improves on generic system and program icons. What's displayed depends on the type of file selected: the opening text of a text file or Microsoft Word document, the first slide of a Microsoft PowerPoint presentation, the first worksheet of a Microsoft Excel spreadsheet, the first frame of a video, the album art of a song, or a scaled-down image of a photo. Folder icons show previews of the individual files that they contain (**Figure 5.11**). The Details and Preview panes show the same images.

- To view Explorer full-screen with minimal clutter, press F11. The Address bar appears when you move your pointer near the top edge of the screen. Press F11 again to restore normal view.

- ⚙ Click the Help button at the right end of the toolbar to get online help.

Sample Pictures

Figure 5.11 This folder icon shows high-resolution thumbnails of the actual photos that the folder contains. Larger icons provide clearer previews.

Printing Directory Listings

Windows Explorer lacks the simple capability to print the contents of a folder; the Print button on the toolbar or the Print command in the File menu, if it appears, prints the selected file, not the file list. You can create a file listing if you're Command Prompt-savvy, however (see "Using the Free Utility Programs" in Chapter 6). At a prompt, use the cd command to change to the desired directory and then type:

```
dir /a /o:neg /-p > list.txt
```

This command creates the file list.txt in the current directory. Open list.txt in Notepad (or any text editor) for a printable list of the files and folders in the directory. To change the command to suit your preferences, search for *command-line reference* in Help and Support, and look for the *dir* command and *command redirection*.

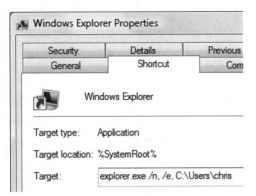

Figure 5.12 This setting opens Explorer at my personal folder. If you see the text %SystemRoot%\ in front of explorer.exe, you can leave it alone or remove it, as desired.

Explorer usually opens with your Documents folder selected, but you can modify an Explorer's shortcut icon to highlight a folder of your choice initially.

To open Windows Explorer with a specific folder selected:

1. Right-click a Windows Explorer shortcut (in the Start menu, on the desktop, or in a folder) and choose Properties.

2. In the Target box, type:

   explorer.exe /n, /e, C:\myfolder

   Replace C:\myfolder with the pathname of the folder to select initially (**Figure 5.12**). The folder can be on a local, removable, or network drive. If C:\myfolder contains spaces, surround it with double quotes.

3. Click OK.

   When you double-click the shortcut, Explorer opens with the specified folder selected.

✔ Tip

- Another way to open Explorer in a specific folder: Choose Start or press Windows logo key+R, type or paste the folder's pathname in the box, and then press Enter.

USING WINDOWS EXPLORER

Navigating in Windows Explorer

You can use Windows Explorer's address bar or Navigation pane to move among the folders on your computer or network.

Address bar

The address bar appears at the top of every folder window and displays your current location as a path or "breadcrumb trail" of links separated by arrows. The address bar shows your current location on the computer or on a network (**Figure 5.13**).

To click a new location:

◆ To go directly to a location that's already visible in the address bar, click the link in the address bar (**Figure 5.14**).

or

To go to the subfolder of a link that's visible in the address bar, click the arrow to the right of the link and then click the new location in the list (**Figure 5.15**).

To type a new location:

1. Click an empty area in the address bar to the right of the text that displays the current location (**Figure 5.16**).

or

Press Alt+D.

The address bar changes to display the pathname of the current location (see the "Pathnames" sidebar).

2. Type or paste the pathname of the new location and press Enter.

or

To go to a common location, type its name and press Enter. The valid names are *Computer, Contacts, Control Panel, Documents, Favorites, Games, Music, Pictures, Recycle Bin,* and *Videos*.

Figure 5.13 The location of a personal folder might appear like this in the address bar.

Figure 5.14 Click any of the links between the arrows to go directly to that location.

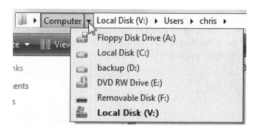

Figure 5.15 Clicking the arrow to the right of a location displays a list of that location's subfolders. The boldface item is the current link.

Figure 5.16 You also can click the small icon at the left end of the location to display the pathname.

Figure 5.17 Click any location in the list to return to a recently visited page. The item with the check mark is the current location.

Figure 5.18 This menu shows the links that the address bar doesn't have room to show. Click any link to go to that location.

✔ Tips

- Like a web browser, Explorer records your recently visited locations, which you can revisit by clicking Back or Forward. Click the Recent Pages button (right of the Forward button) to jump directly to any of these locations (**Figure 5.17**).

- ◾ Click the Previous Location button at the right end of the address bar (or press F4) for a drop-down list of your location history, including web addresses. Click any list item to go to that location. To clear this list, choose Start > Control Panel > Network and Internet > Internet Options > General tab > Delete (under Browsing History) > Delete History > Yes.

- ◾ Click the Refresh button (or press F5) if some icons are badly drawn or if you think that the folder window is out of date (which happens sometimes for network locations).

- « If the address bar is too narrow to display the entire location, click the chevron button that appears to the left of it (**Figure 5.18**).

- If you type a web address (URL) in the address bar, Internet Explorer opens and displays the webpage.

Pathnames

Windows locates and identifies each file or folder by its unique address, called its *pathname*. A pathname is a listing of the folders that lead from the top-level or *root* directory of a disk drive to a particular file or folder. C:\ represents the C drive's root directory, for example. A backslash (\) separates the pathname components. The pathname C:\Users\Public\Pictures\Sample Pictures\ Creek.jpg traces the route from the file Creek.jpg to the C drive's root directory. For files on a network, the pathname can begin with a double backslash and a computer or server name instead of a disk drive (\\someserver instead of C:, for example).

To see a pathname, right-click an icon and choose Properties (the pathname is in the Location box). To copy a pathname, hold down Shift while you right-click an icon and then choose Copy As Path.

Navigation pane

By using the Navigation pane, you can navigate directly to the folder that contains the files you want. To show or hide the Navigation pane, choose Organize > Layout > Navigation Pane.

Favorite Links (**Figure 5.19**), at the top of the Navigation pane, offers one-click access to commonly used folders. The top three links are shortcuts to your Documents, Pictures, and Music folders. The next link, Recently Changed, is a saved search; click it to display items from your personal folder that you've created or modified in the past 30 days (see "Saving Searches" later in this chapter). The next link, Searches, opens your Searches folder, which contains your saved searches. The Public link opens a folder containing files shared by all users.

Figure 5.19 To open a saved search, click Searches and then double-click the saved search that you want to open.

To customize the Favorite Links list:

◆ To reorder the list, drag links higher or lower.

or

To add a link, drag a folder or a saved search from its original folder to the list. You also can drag folders from the Folders list.

or

To rename a link, right-click it, choose Rename, type the new name, and then press Enter. (Only the link is renamed, not the original folder or saved search.)

or

To remove a link, right-click it and choose Remove Link. (Only the link is deleted, not the original folder or saved search.)

or

To restore the default list, right-click an empty area of the list and choose Restore Default Favorite Links.

Figure 5.20 This tree is expanded to show the user's personal folder.

The Folders list (**Figure 5.20**), at the bottom of the Navigation pane, represents your files, folders, and disks as a hierarchical structure called a *tree*. A fully expanded tree is unwieldy, so by default, the Folders list shows only the tree's top few levels. You can use the mouse or keyboard to collapse and expand individual branches selectively. To show or hide the tree, click Folders in the Navigation pane.

To navigate by using the Folders list:

◆ To show a folder's contents, click its icon in the tree.

or

To expand or collapse a branch, click an arrow (▷ or ◢) to the left of an icon in the tree.

✔ Tips

■ **Table 5.2** lists the keyboard shortcuts for using the Folders list. For others, see "Using Keyboard Shortcuts" later in this chapter.

■ A security prompt may appear when you try to navigate to some folders. If it does, type an administrator password or confirm the action.

■ If no arrow appears next to an icon, that branch can't be expanded further because it has no subfolders.

■ If the Folders bar is too narrow to show its contents, drag the right edge of the pane to widen it. If you point to a partially hidden folder, a pop-up tip displays its full name.

■ Press F5 to refresh the display if you notice that a folder is missing or that an arrow appears next to a folder that has no subfolders (which happens sometimes for network folders).

Table 5.2

Folders List Keyboard Shortcuts	
To	**Press**
Expand or collapse the selected branch	Right arrow or left arrow
Jump to parent branch without collapsing	Backspace
Jump from top to bottom of expanded branch	Alt+Right arrow
Jump from bottom to top of expanded branch	Alt+Left arrow
Move up visible branches	Up arrow
Move down visible branches	Down arrow
Expand all branches below the selection	* (on numeric keypad)
Go to a visible branch	The branch's initial letter
Cycle through visible branches with same initial letter	The initial letter repeatedly
Cycle through the parts of a folder window	Tab or F6

Tagging Files

You saw in "Properties" in Chapter 1 that every file has properties—bits of information about the file, some of which you can edit. Windows also lets you define tags. *Tags* are properties that you can attach to your files to help you find and filter them. Unlike predefined properties, a tag can be anything you choose and, when created and attached to a file, becomes one of the file's properties. Like predefined properties, tags aren't part of the actual contents of a file; they're called *metadata* (data about data).

The easiest way to add tags is to use the Details pane in Windows Explorer (if the pane isn't visible, choose Organize > Layout > Details Pane). You also can add or change properties to a file when you create and save it. If you share files, you can remove the properties that you don't want others to see.

✔ Tips

- You can apply multiple tags to a single file or apply a single tag across multiple files.

- You can't add tags to text (.txt), RTF (.rtf), and some other types of files.

- See "Searching for Files and Folders" later in this chapter to see how to use tags and other properties to find files.

- You also can add tags by using Windows Photo Gallery (see "Finding Photos" in Chapter 9) or Windows Media Player (see "Organizing Your Library" in Chapter 10).

TAGGING FILES

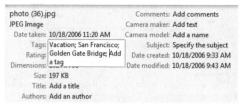

Figure 5.21 Editing the tag of a photograph in the Details pane. You can click the other properties in this pane to change them. Some intrinsic properties—such as Size, Dimensions, and Date Created—are read-only.

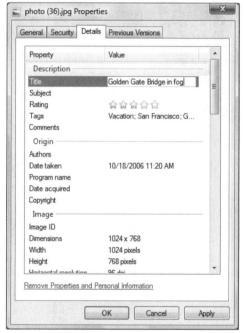

Figure 5.22 Scroll down the list to see and change a large number of properties.

To add or change properties by using the Details pane:

1. Click a file or select a group of files to apply properties to.

2. In the Details pane at the bottom of the folder window, click the property that you want to change, type the new property, and then click Save (**Figure 5.21**).

   To add more than one property, separate the entries with a semicolon (;). To rate a file by using the Ratings property, click a star.

✔ Tip

- To resize the Details pane, drag the horizontal separator at the top edge of the pane. You also can right-click an empty area of the pane and make a choice from the Size submenu.

To add or change properties that don't appear in the Details pane:

1. Right-click a file or a group of files and choose Properties.

2. In the Properties dialog box, click the Details tab, click the properties box that you want to change, and then type a word or phrase (**Figure 5.22**).

   To add more than one property, separate the entries with a semicolon (;). To rate a file by using the Ratings property, click a star.

3. Click OK (or Apply).

✔ Tips

- If you don't see any text for the property that you want to add, point to the place where you would expect to see it, and a box will appear.

- For more ways to open the Properties dialog box, see "Properties" in Chapter 1.

To add or change properties when saving a file:

1. In the program that you're using, choose File > Save As (press Alt if the File menu isn't visible).

2. In the Save As dialog box, type tags and other properties in the appropriate boxes (**Figure 5.23**).

3. Type a name for the file and click Save.

To remove properties:

1. Right-click a file or a group of files and choose Properties.

2. In the Properties dialog box, click the Details tab.

3. Click Remove Properties and Personal Information (at the bottom of Figure 5.22).
   The Remove Properties dialog box opens (**Figure 5.24**).

4. Select Create a Copy with All Possible Properties Removed and click OK.
   This lets you keep the original file with all its properties and make a copy with all the properties removed that you can share.
   or
   Select Remove the Following Properties from This File, check each property to remove (or click Select All), and then click OK.

Figure 5.23 Not every Save As dialog box lets you define properties.

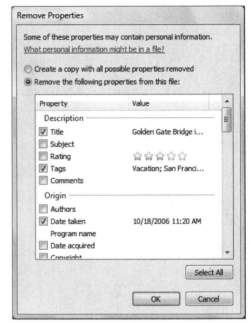

Figure 5.24 Stripping individual properties from a file.

Figure 5.25 Column headings appear in all views in Windows Explorer.

Figure 5.26 Right-click any column heading to choose which columns to display.

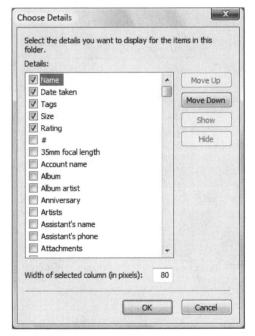

Figure 5.27 The Choose Details dialog box offers dozens of properties to display, many of which apply only to specific file types. You also can reorder headings and set their widths here, but it's more cumbersome than dragging the headings directly.

Filtering, Sorting, Stacking, and Grouping Files

Column headings (**Figure 5.25**) are more useful than their appearance suggests. In details view, which shows the most information about files, you can:

◆ Reorder columns by dragging column headings left or right.

◆ Resize a column by dragging the right edge of its heading left or right.

◆ Make a column width match its widest entry by double-clicking the right edge of its column heading (or right-clicking a column heading and choosing Size Column to Fit or Size All Columns to Fit).

By default, the columns displayed depend on the type of files in the folder—picture folders show Date Taken, for example, and document folders show Date Modified—but you can choose which columns appear.

To choose which column headings to show:

1. In Windows Explorer, right-click any column heading.

2. Check or uncheck a heading name to show or hide it (**Figure 5.26**).

   or

   Click More, check or uncheck the headings to show or hide, and then click OK (**Figure 5.27**).

✔ Tip

■ You can't hide the Name column.

You also can use column headings to filter and arrange files—in any view, not just details. Viewing files this way helps you find files that have something in common. Click the arrow to the right of a column heading to see the options (**Figure 5.28**).

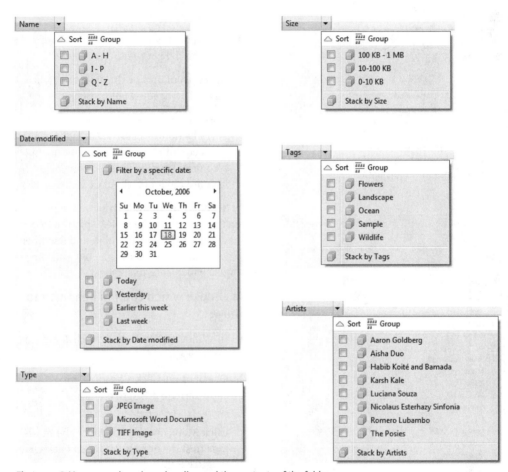

Figure 5.28 Menus vary by column heading and the contents of the folder.

Figure 5.29 A file list before and after filtering by the Wildlife tag. Note that a check mark appears in the column heading when filtering is applied.

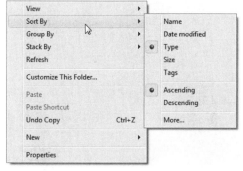

Figure 5.30 The file list's shortcut menu has menus for sorting, grouping, and stacking.

When you filter a folder's contents by file properties (such as filename, date, author, or tag), only files with those properties are displayed. To see only files written by a particular author, for example, filter by that person's name.

To filter files:

1. Open the folder that contains the files you want to filter.

2. Click the arrow to the right of the heading that you want to filter by (refer to Figure 5.28).

3. Click the name of the property that you want to filter by.

   To filter by two or more properties, check the box for each property (**Figure 5.29**).

By default, Windows Explorer sorts files alphabetically by name (listing all folders first, followed by all files), but you can sort them by any column heading.

To sort files:

1. Open the folder that contains the files you want to sort.

2. Click the arrow to the right of the heading that you want to sort by and then click Sort (refer to Figure 5.28).

   To reverse the sort order, repeat this action.

   or

   Click the heading of the column to sort by. To reverse the sort order, click it again.

   or

   Right-click an empty area of the file list and make a choice from the Sort By submenu (**Figure 5.30**).

✔ Tips

- Name ☐ Subtle shading indicates the sort column. A small arrowhead above the column name points up for ascending sort or down for descending sort.

- You can sort filtered, stacked, or grouped files.

- In the Computer window, you can sort by the disks' free space or total size.

Stacking files arranges into them into piles, called *stacks*, that correspond to a column heading. If you stack by Author, for example, you'll see one stack for each author. If you want to see only the files written by a particular author, open that author's stack.

To stack files:

1. Open the folder that contains the files you want to stack.

2. Click the arrow to the right of the heading that you want to stack by and then click Stack (refer to Figure 5.28).

   or

   Right-click an empty area of the file list and make a choice from the Stack By submenu (refer to Figure 5.30).

✔ Tip

- ☐ Save Search The stacks appear in a Search Results folder (**Figure 5.31**). Click Save Search (on the toolbar) to save the stacks, or click Back (ⓖ) or press Backspace to return to the original folder. See "Saving Searches" later in this chapter.

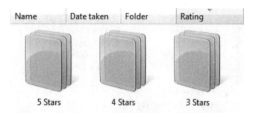

Figure 5.31 The results of stacking on the Rating column. Double-click a stack to see its files.

FILTERING, SORTING, STACKING, AND GROUPING FILES

Figure 5.32 The results of grouping on the Tag column.

Whereas a stack hides the files it contains behind an icon, a group displays a list of all the grouped files. When you group files by Author, for example, several groups appear, each one displaying all the files written by a particular author. Grouping isn't available in list view.

To group files:

1. Open the folder that contains the files you want to group.

2. Click the arrow to the right of the heading that you want to group by and then click Group (refer to Figure 5.28).

   or

   Right-click an empty area of the file list and make a choice from the Group By submenu (refer to Figure 5.30).

✔ Tip

- Unlike stacked files, grouped files appear in the original folder (**Figure 5.32**). You can click the horizontal separator at the top of each grouping category to select all the files in that category or double-click the separator to hide them.

Customizing a Folder

You can apply folder templates and custom images to folders.

To customize a folder:

1. In Windows Explorer, open the folder that you want to customize.

2. Right-click an empty area of the file list and choose Customize This Folder.

   or

   Choose View > Customize This Folder (press Alt if the View menu isn't visible).

3. Choose a folder template from the drop-down list (**Figure 5.33**), and specify whether you want the template applied to all subfolders as well.

   The All Items template is for generic folders. Other templates are designed for document, photo, video, and music folders.

4. To place a picture of your choice on the folder icon, click Choose File; then navigate to and select an image file.

   If you change your mind, click Restore Default to use default pictures.

5. To replace the standard folder icon, click Change Icon; then navigate to and select an icon.

6. Click OK (or Apply).

✔ Tip

■ Customize This Folder isn't available for the Windows and Programs Files system folders.

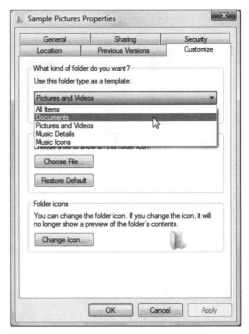

Figure 5.33 The template choice determines the view setting (Details, Large Icons, and so on) and column headings for the folder.

Figure 5.34 Some options have default values that can make Windows harder to use or drain your laptop battery faster.

Figure 5.35 A folder tip with size information.

Setting Folder Options

Windows offers a trainload of options that control how folders appear and behave.

To set folder options:

1. In Windows Explorer, choose Organize > Folder and Search Options > View tab (**Figure 5.34**).

   or

   Choose Start > Control Panel > Appearance and Personalization > Folder Options > View tab.

   or

   Choose Start, type folder options in the Search box, press Enter, and then click the View tab.

2. Select the desired options (**Table 5.3**). Changes affect all Explorer windows.

3. To restore the options to their factory settings, click Restore Defaults.

4. Click OK (or Apply).

Table 5.3

Folder Options

Option	Description
Always Show Icons, Never Thumbnails	Always shows static icons of files instead of their thumbnail previews. Turing off this option may speed your computer a little and (for laptops) drain the battery slower.
Always Show Menus	Turn on this option if you prefer always to see the classic menus above the toolbar. The menu bar is hidden by default. If this option is turned off, press Alt to show the menus.
Display File Icon on Thumbnails	Turn on this option to show file icons on thumbnail previews (applies if the option Always Show Icons, Never Thumbnails is turned off).
Display File Size Information in Folder Tips	Turn on this option to show size information in the folder tip that pops up temporarily when your mouse pointer hovers over a folder icon (**Figure 5.35**). If you turn it off, you still get pop-up contents information; to turn off folder tips, choose the folder option Show Pop-Up Description for Folder and Desktop Items.

Table continues on next page

Table 5.3 *continued*

Folder Options	
OPTION	DESCRIPTION
Display Simple Folder View in Navigation Pane	Turn off this option to restore the navigation method of earlier Windows versions, which shows vertical dotted lines in the folder tree to indicate how deeply a folder is nested.
Display the Full Path in the Title Bar (Classic Folders Only)	When this option is turned on and you're using the Classic color scheme (unlikely), Explorer's title bar shows the selected folder's full pathname: *C:\Users\diane\Documents* instead of only *Documents*, for example. To set the color scheme, see "Setting the Window Color and Color Scheme" in Chapter 4.
Hidden Files and Folders *and* Hide Protected Operating System Files (Recommended)	By default, Windows hides critical files that it doesn't want you to move, delete, or rename. If you show these files, they appear as dimmed icons so that you remember to leave them alone. (Technically, a hidden file has its Hidden attribute set; you can see this attribute in its Properties dialog box.)
Hide Extensions for Known File Types	By default, Windows hides file extensions (*.doc* for Word files and *.exe* for programs, for example). Beginners may be tempted to leave this option on to make Windows appear less intimidating, but everyone should turn it off for the reasons given in "Associating Documents with Programs" in Chapter 6.
Launch Folder Windows in a Separate Process	By default, only one copy of `explorer.exe` is ever in memory, handling all Explorer windows, the Start menu, the desktop, and much more. Turn this option on to open a new program instance for each Explorer window so that if one instance crashes, the rest don't. For technical reasons, if the "wrong" one crashes, you may be left without a Start menu and desktop. Favor leaving this option turned off.
Managing Pairs of Web Pages and Folders	When you save a complete webpage in Internet Explorer, the page's text is stored in one HTML file, and its images and scripts are stored in a folder named to match (**Figure 5.36**). To make Windows Explorer treat this file-and-folder pair as a single entity, select Show and Manage the Pair As a Single File or Show Both Parts but Manage As a Single File. If you move or delete one item, for example, Windows Explorer takes the same action on the other, maintaining the connection between them. To break the file-and-folder link, select Show Both Parts and Manage Them Individually.
Remember Each Folder's View Settings	Turn on this option to make Explorer remember each folder's view settings independently. If you turn off this option, each folder inherits its view setting from its parent folder.
Restore Previous Folder Windows at Logon	Turn on this option to make Windows reopen all your previously opened folder windows when you log on, preserving your desktop setup from session to session. Turn off this option for a clean desktop every logon.

Table continues on next page

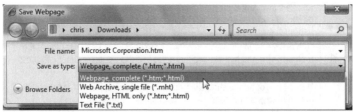

Figure 5.36 When I save Microsoft's complete home page in Internet Explorer (that is, visit www.microsoft.com and choose File > Save As), IE creates an HTML file named Microsoft Corporation.htm and a folder named Microsoft Corporation_files that contains the accompanying image (GIF and JPEG) and script files.

Table 5.3 *continued*

Folder Options	
OPTION	DESCRIPTION
Show Drive Letters	Turn off this option if you want to hide the drive letter of each drive or device in the Computer folder. Drive letters are useful in many situations (particularly if you need technical support); you should turn on this option unless you want to see only the friendly name of each drive.
Show Encrypted or Compressed NTFS Files in Color	Turn on this option to show NTFS-encrypted and NTFS-compressed files and folders in identifying colors. Turn off this option to turn all files the same color. See "Compressing Files and Folders" later in this chapter and "Encrypting Data" in Chapter 13.
Show Pop-Up Description for Folder and Desktop Items	Turn on this option to see pop-up information about almost any icon you point to. Turn it off if the little pop-up boxes bug you.
Show Preview Handlers in Preview Pane	Turn off this option to never show the contents of files in the Preview pane. Turning off this option may speed your computer a little and (for laptops) drain the battery slower.
Use Check Boxes to Select Items	Turn on this item to add check boxes to file views to make it easier to select multiple files. This option is useful if it's difficult for you to hold the Ctrl key while clicking to select multiple files (**Figure 5.37**).
Use Sharing Wizard	Turn on this option to use the friendly File Sharing wizard when you share your files. Experienced network administrators may prefer to turn off this option. See "Sharing Files" in Chapter 18.
When Typing in List View	When the file list is active in a folder window, this option determines whether your keystrokes are used to select files in the list or are redirected to the Search box to filter the files in the list.

Figure 5.37 Check boxes appear when you hover the mouse pointer over a file of folder. To select all the files, check the box in the column heading.

Creating Folders

If you're creating a hierarchy of folders, see "Storing Stuff in Your Personal Folder" earlier in this chapter for some advice on organizing your files and folders.

To create a folder:

1. In Windows Explorer, open the folder where you want to create a subfolder.

2. Right-click an empty area of the file list and choose New > Folder (**Figure 5.38**).

   or

   Choose File > New > Folder (press Alt if the File menu isn't visible).

3. Type a name for the new folder and press Enter.

   While editing, you can use the keyboard shortcuts for Cut, Copy, Paste, Undo, and Select All (Ctrl+X, Ctrl+C, Ctrl+V, Ctrl+Z, and Ctrl+A, respectively).

✔ Tips

■ To create a new folder on the desktop, right-click an empty area of the desktop and choose New > Folder.

■ The New submenu lets you create new empty documents too, depending on which programs are installed.

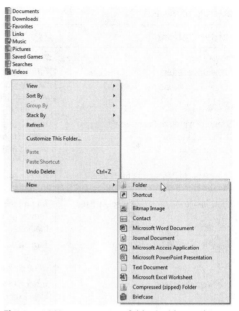

Figure 5.38 You can create a folder inside another folder, on the desktop, at the root of a hard disk, or on a USB flash drive or floppy.

Figure 5.39 To replace the current name, just start typing. To change a few characters in the existing name, use the arrow keys to move to a specific position and then insert, delete, cut, or paste characters.

Naming Rules and Tricks

A file or folder name can contain up to 260 characters, including the extension (the part after the last dot). Spaces and punctuation are permitted but names can't contain these characters: \ / : * ? " < > |. (Note that this paragraph contains 260 characters.)

The 260-character limit actually applies to the complete pathname (for example, *C:\downloads\myfile.txt*). Avoid using very long filenames.

A folder can't contain two items with the same name. Windows is case insensitive (it considers `MyFile.txt` and `myfile.txt` to be identical), but it preserves the case of each letter you type.

If you select multiple items and rename one of them, say, `MyFile.txt`, Windows renames the others `MyFile (1).txt`, `MyFile (2).txt`, and so on. If you bulk-rename a bunch of files accidentally, press Ctrl+Z repeatedly to revert to the original names.

Use Better File Rename ($30 U.S.; `http://publicspace.net`) or Lupas Rename (free; `www.azheavymetal.com/~lupasrename`) for major surgery on filenames. You can find and replace a common phrase in a set of filenames, for example, or add dates and sequence numbers to them. You can preview your changes before you commit them.

Naming Files and Folders

You can rename a file or folder to make its name longer, shorter, or more explicit.

To rename a file or folder:

1. In Windows Explorer, select the file or folder that you want to rename.

2. Right-click the file or folder and choose Rename (or press F2).

   or

   Choose File > Rename (press Alt if the File menu isn't visible).

   or

   Click the file or folder's name (not its icon) twice, slowly (don't double-click).

3. Type a new name and press Enter or click outside the name area (**Figure 5.39**).

   While editing, you can use the keyboard shortcuts for Cut, Copy, Paste, Undo, and Select All (Ctrl+X, Ctrl+C, Ctrl+V, Ctrl+Z, and Ctrl+A, respectively).

✔ Tips

- You can rename a file or folder in the General tab of its Properties dialog box.

- Press Esc while editing to revert to the original name.

- You can't rename the system folders Program Files, Users, or Windows.

- In applications, you can rename files and folders in the Open and Save As dialog boxes.

- If the folder option Hide Extensions for Known File Types is turned on, Windows tracks the file association automatically. See "Setting Folder Options" earlier in this chapter.

Moving and Copying Files and Folders

You can move or copy files and folders to reorganize your folder structure, make backup copies in a safe location, or move files to the Public folder to share them with other users. To copy or move items, you must select (highlight) them. For an icon-selection refresher, see "Icons" in Chapter 1.

To move or copy items by choosing a destination:

1. In Windows Explorer, select the item(s) that you want to move or copy.

2. To move the items, choose Edit > Move to Folder (press Alt if the Edit menu isn't visible).

   To copy the items, choose Edit > Copy to Folder.

3. Navigate to the destination folder; then click Move (or Copy) (**Figure 5.40**).

To move or copy items by using cut, copy, and paste:

1. In Windows Explorer or on the desktop, select the item(s) that you want to move or copy.

2. To move the items, press Ctrl+X (or right-click a selected item and choose Cut).

   To copy the items, press Ctrl+C (or right-click a selected item and choose Copy).

3. Select the destination folder, disk, or window.

4. Press Ctrl+V (or right-click an empty area and choose Paste).

Figure 5.40 Windows Explorer gives you several ways to move and copy files, but using a highlighted target is the easiest and most consistent.

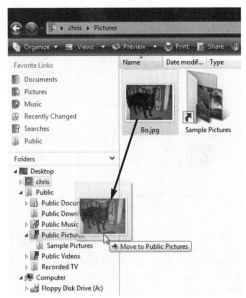

Figure 5.41 Here, I'm dragging the file Bo.jpg from my Pictures folder to Public Pictures. The destination folder in the folder tree darkens automatically as the pointer moves on or close to it. If you hover briefly over a folder that contains subfolders, it will expand.

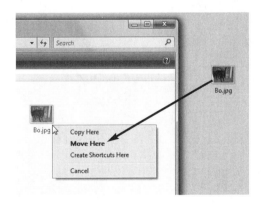

Figure 5.42 Right-dragging to copy or move items is safer than left-dragging.

Figure 5.43 The small graphic near the mouse pointer means (left to right) move, copy, and create shortcut.

To move or copy items by dragging:

1. Make sure that the destination folder, disk, or window is visible.

2. In Windows Explorer or on the desktop, select the item(s) that you want to copy or move.

3. Right-drag the items to the destination; then release the right mouse button.

4. Choose Move Here or Copy Here from the shortcut menu (**Figure 5.41** and **Figure 5.42**).

When you drag an icon, a small indicator appears when you arrive at the new location, telling you whether you're moving. copying, or creating a shortcut (**Figure 5.43**). If you use the *left* mouse button and drag normally to copy or move items (bypassing the shortcut menu in Figure 5.42), the rules that determine what happens are:

◆ If you drag an item to another place on the same disk, it's moved.

◆ If you drag an item from one disk to another, it's copied, not moved.

◆ To copy an item instead of moving it, hold down Ctrl while dragging.

◆ To move the item instead of copying it, hold down Shift while dragging.

◆ To create a shortcut to the item instead of moving or copying it, hold down Alt while dragging.

◆ If you drag a system icon such as Computer or Control Panel, it's never moved or copied; instead, a shortcut is created.

If that's too much to remember, always *right*-drag to copy or move items; it's easier and surer.

✔ Tips

■ If you move or copy an item to a folder that already has an item with the same name, Windows asks you what to do (**Figure 5.44**).

■ You can move or copy items anywhere on your computer or network, so long as you have privileges to do so. If a security prompt appears, type an administrator password or confirm the action.

■ If you copy an item to the folder in which it already exists, Windows creates a duplicate named '*itemname* - Copy'.

■ You can drag items between Explorer windows, or cut or copy from one window and paste to another.

■ Items appear dimmed when they're cut, but they don't actually move until you paste them somewhere. Press Esc to cancel a cut.

■ Press Esc during a drag to cancel it.

Figure 5.44 You can overwrite the file in the destination folder, cancel the operation, or complete the operation but rename the file being moved or copied so that its name doesn't conflict with the other file.

Figure 5.45 The Send To menu often is faster than dragging and dropping. Windows adds destinations for removable storage automatically. The bottom three menu items are a floppy disk, DVD/CD writer, and USB flash drive.

Sending Files and Folders

One of the handiest file-management tools is the Send To menu, which lets you send a copy of a file or folder quickly to:

◆ A compressed (zipped) folder (see "Compressing Files and Folders" later in this chapter)

◆ Your desktop (as a shortcut)

◆ Your Documents folder (or any folder)

◆ Another person via fax or email

◆ A USB flash drive, floppy disk, or CD/DVD for burning

◆ Other destinations, depending on the programs installed

To send an item:

1. In Windows Explorer or on the desktop, select the item(s) that you want to send.

2. Right-click one item, choose Send To, and then choose a destination from the submenu (**Figure 5.45**).

✔ Tips

■ In Explorer, Send To is available in the File menu (press Alt if the File menu isn't visible).

■ To move an item instead of copying it, hold down Shift when you right-click.

If you perform the same file-management tasks regularly, you can add your own destinations to the Send To menu by adding new shortcuts to your SendTo folder (which is hidden by default). Every user on your computer has a separate SendTo folder. The destination determines what happens to the item being sent. If the destination is a program, for example, the program is launched with the selected file open. For folder and disk destinations, items are copied.

To add a destination to the Send To menu:

1. Choose Start > Computer > Local Disk (C:) > Users > *username*.

    If Windows is installed on a drive other than C, choose that drive instead. Look for the drive with the Windows logo.

2. Make sure that hidden files and folders are visible by choosing Organize > Folder and Search Options > View tab > Show Hidden Files and Folders > OK.

3. Choose AppData > Roaming > Microsoft > Windows > SendTo.

   The full pathname of your current location is C:\Users*username*\AppData\Roaming\Microsoft\Windows\SendTo.

4. Add the desired shortcuts to the folder, or right-click an empty area and choose New > Shortcut (**Figure 5.46**).

5. Close the window when you're done adding shortcuts.

   (Don't forget to rehide hidden files and folders.)

Figure 5.46 Here, I've added a few custom destinations to the standard ones. The Notepad shortcut opens any file in Notepad, regardless of the file's type. The Backups shortcut copies files to a safe place. The printer (HP LaserJet) shortcut prints documents with no need to open their associated applications. The SendTo Folder shortcut adds destinations to the Send To menu itself.

✔ Tips

■ If you have many destinations, you can nest folders to create Send To sub-submenus.

■ You can create Send To shortcuts to shared folders on other machines on your network.

■ If you put a shortcut to the SendTo folder inside the SendTo folder itself, you can create destinations quickly by sending them to the SendTo folder.

Recycle Bin   Recycle Bin

Figure 5.47 The Recycle Bin's icon tells you whether it contains deleted items (left) or is empty (right).

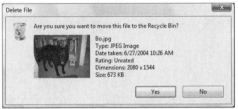

Figure 5.48 If you're deleting one item, Windows gives you a thumbnail preview of it (top). For multiple items, you're given a count but no preview (bottom).

Deleting Files and Folders

When you delete a file or folder, it's not actually erased but compressed and stored in the Recycle Bin on the desktop (**Figure 5.47**). The Recycle Bin is a safeguard from which you can restore (undelete) items if you change your mind or delete them permanently.

To delete items:

1. In Windows Explorer or on the desktop, select the item(s) that you want to delete.

2. Choose Organize > Delete (or press Delete).
   or
   Right-click one item and choose Delete.

3. If an "Are you sure?" message appears, click Yes (**Figure 5.48**).

DELETING FILES AND FOLDERS

✔ Tips

- You also can drag items to the Recycle Bin to delete them.

- To suppress the "Are you sure?" message, right-click the Recycle Bin, choose Properties, and then uncheck Display Delete Confirmation Dialog.

- To delete selected items without sending them to the Recycle Bin, press Shift+Delete (do so with care).

- You can bypass the Recycle Bin so that all deleted files are erased immediately (good for using a public computer): Right-click the Recycle Bin icon, choose Properties, and then choose Do Not Move Files to the Recycle Bin.

- Some programs let you delete items within Open and Save As dialog boxes.

- Items deleted from network drives and removable storage (such as floppies and USB flash drives) bypass the Recycle Bin, as do deletions via the command-line `del` and `erase` commands.

When You Can't Delete

A few things may stop you from deleting a file or folder:

- You lack the proper rights to delete it. If you didn't create it, you may not be able to delete it, even if it's in the Public folder. Ask the file's owner to delete it.

- A program currently is using the file. Find the program and close it. (Closing only the file but leaving the program running might not release the file lock immediately.) If you're not the only person logged on, someone else might be using the file.

- If you delete all the files in a folder but can't delete the folder itself, close all open programs and then try to delete the folder. If this doesn't work, restart the computer and try to delete it again. The folder probably wasn't deleted because it was locked by another program or system utility.

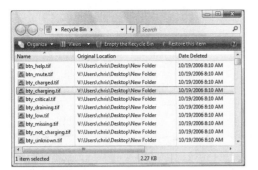

Figure 5.49 Details view tells you when items were deleted and where from.

To empty the Recycle Bin:

1. Double-click the Recycle Bin icon (**Figure 5.49**).

2. To remove all items, click Empty the Recycle Bin (on the toolbar).

   or

   To remove some items, Ctrl+click each item to remove (or click only one item); then press Delete.

3. Click Yes in the "Are you sure?" message.

✔ Tips

■ The Delete command also is available in a Recycle Bin item's shortcut menu.

■ To empty the Recycle Bin quickly without inspecting its contents, right-click its icon on the desktop and choose Empty Recycle Bin. (You can't suppress the "Are you sure?" message.)

Undead Files

Deleting files doesn't actually destroy their data; it just makes that data harder to find. When you empty the Recycle Bin, Windows doesn't erase files but *marks* them as deleted, making them invisible to you and to programs but leaving their data intact on disk. Only when Windows needs disk space later will it overwrite deleted files with newly created ones. On a large or sparsely populated drive, deleted files may survive for weeks before Windows reclaims the disk space (unless you defragment the disk, which overwrites most deleted files).

To recover deleted files, use an undelete utility soon after you've emptied the Recycle Bin. Some popular ones are SpinRite ($89 U.S.; www.grc.com/spinrite), Undelete ($30 U.S.; www.undelete.com), and PC INSPECTOR File Recovery (free; www.pcinspector.de/file_recovery/uk/welcome.htm). You can find many others by searching the web for *windows undelete files*.

On the other hand, use a *file shredder* to make your files *un*recoverable. File shredders—useful if you're selling your PC or expecting an arrest warrant—overwrite deleted files or entire disks with random data. Shredders let you overwrite a few times (to defeat ordinary undelete software) or many times (to defeat an electron microscope). To shred files, try Eraser (free; www.heidi.ie/eraser) or Sure Delete (free; www.wizard-industries.com).

Note that Windows' `format` (formerly `fdisk`) command won't shred files. If utterly destroying your data is crucial—you know who you are—smash your hard disk and throw the pieces in a river.

To restore items from the Recycle Bin:

1. Double-click the Recycle Bin icon (refer to Figure 5.49).

2. Ctrl+click the items that you want to restore (or click only one item).

3. To restore items to their original locations, click Restore the Selected Items (or Restore This Item) on the toolbar.

   or

   To restore items to a specific location, drag them out of the Recycle Bin to the desired folder (in an Explorer window or on the desktop).

✔ Tip

- The Restore command also is available in a Recycle Bin item's shortcut menu.

Figure 5.50 Every disk has its own Recycle Bin. If you have more than one drive or have a partitioned drive, you can set each disk's junk limit independently.

The Recycle Bin stores deleted items until it runs out of space, at which point the items are removed automatically, oldest first, to accommodate new items. By default, the size of the Recycle Bin folder is 10 percent of the hard drive, but you can change that percentage.

To change the Recycle Bin's capacity:

1. Right-click the Recycle Bin icon and choose Properties.

2. Click a drive in the list, choose Custom Size, and then specify how much drive storage (measured in megabytes) to allocate to the Recycle Bin (**Figure 5.50**).

3. Click OK (or Apply).

✔ Tips

■ On high-capacity drives, 10 percent is a lot of space. On a 160 GB disk, for example, 10 percent is 16 GB of junk. Unless you have a lot of music or video files, 1 GB or 2 GB should be enough.

■ The Recycle Bin's status bar shows how much space the deleted items occupy. Choose View > Status Bar (press Alt if the View menu isn't visible).

■ To hide the Recycle Bin or change its icon, choose Start > Control Panel > Appearance and Personalization > Personalization > Change Desktop Icons (in the left pane).

DELETING FILES AND FOLDERS

Compressing Files and Folders

Compressing files and folders reduces the space they occupy on your drives (fixed or removable). Windows offers two compression schemes: Microsoft's proprietary NTFS compression (the same as in Windows 2000) and industry-standard zipped folders. You can use either scheme or both; each has its relative advantages. NTFS compression is simple, transparent, and suitable for everyday use, whereas zipped folders are best for:

◆ Emailing large attachments

◆ Archiving files that you no longer need regularly

◆ Transferring files over the internet or via FTP

◆ Gaining the maximum amount of disk space

◆ Compressing encrypted files

NTFS compression

Some important points about NTFS compression are:

◆ It's available only on NTFS-formatted drives, not FAT or FAT32 drives (**Figure 5.51**). See "Getting Ready to Install Windows Vista" in the appendix.

◆ You can compress individual files and folders or an entire NTFS drive.

◆ It's easy to use but doesn't save much disk space compared with zip compression.

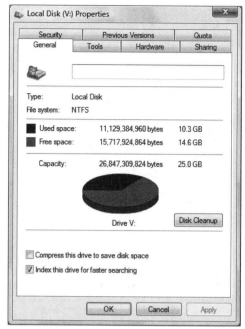

Figure 5.51 To determine whether a drive is formatted with NTFS, choose Start > Computer, right-click a drive, and then choose Properties. The file system appears on the General tab.

Figure 5.52 If the Advanced button is missing (top), the selected file or folder isn't on an NTFS drive. The Advanced Attributes dialog box (bottom) won't let you choose both compression and encryption.

◆ NTFS-compressed files and folders act normally in Explorer, programs, and dialog boxes. Windows decompresses and compresses files invisibly and on the fly when you open and close them, at the cost of a small (probably not noticeable) performance hit.

◆ Don't compress system files in the Windows folder, because Vista uses them frequently.

◆ If you send an NTFS-compressed file to a non-NTFS disk (via email or dragging, for example), Vista expands it to its normal size automatically and invisibly. A file sent to a compressed folder or disk is compressed automatically.

◆ NTFS-compressed files can't be EFS-encrypted (but you *can* encrypt zipped folders). See "Encrypting Data" in Chapter 13.

To NTFS-compress a file, folder, or drive:

1. Close all files to be compressed.

2. To compress individual files or folders, select their icons in Windows Explorer, right-click one of the selected items, choose Properties > General tab, click the Advanced button, check Compress Contents to Save Disk Space, and click OK (**Figure 5.52**).

   or

   To compress a drive, right-click its icon in Computer, choose Properties > General tab, check Compress This Drive to Save Disk Space, and click OK (refer to Figure 5.51).

continues on next page

3. In the Confirm Attribute Changes dialog box, indicate whether you want to compress subfolders too (**Figure 5.53**).

✔ Tips

■ Compressing an entire hard disk may take hours. Close all programs before you start; otherwise, Windows halts mid-process to ask you to quit a program.

■ To display compressed files and folders in a different color in Windows Explorer, choose Organize > Folder and Search Options > View tab > check Show Encrypted or Compressed NTFS Files in Color.

Zipped folders

If you've used the popular WinZip program, you're familiar with the concept of compressing files and folders in zip format. Some important points about zip files are:

◆ A zipped folder, called an *archive,* is a collection of files compressed and combined into a single file (**Figure 5.54**).

◆ You can create archives on any drive, not just an NTFS drive. Archives stay compressed when you send them elsewhere. Mac and Unix users can work with them too.

◆ Zipping squashes files much smaller than NTFS compression does. Zipping most image, video, music, and PDF files won't save much space because they're already compressed, but program, web-page, text, word-processing, spreadsheet, database, bitmap, TIFF, and WAV audio files shrink a lot.

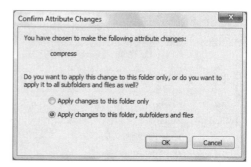

Figure 5.53 Usually, you'll want to compress all subfolders too.

Chapter 5.zip

Figure 5.54 An archive looks like a folder, except with a zipper. An archive has a .zip file extension.

COMPRESSING FILES AND FOLDERS

Figure 5.55 Details view provides compression information about each file. The Ratio column tells you how much smaller a zipped file is relative to its uncompressed size. (The closer the ratio is to 100%, the more compressed the file is.)

◆ Though they're actually files, zipped folders still behave like folders in several ways. Double-click an archive to see what's in it (**Figure 5.55**). Double-click a document in the archive to open a read-only copy of it, or extract it from the archive to work with the original (see "To extract files and folders from a zipped folder" later in this chapter).

COMPRESSING FILES AND FOLDERS

WinZip and WinRAR

If you zip files only occasionally, Windows' built-in tools work fine; otherwise, get a copy of WinZip ($30 U.S.; www.winzip.com), a superior utility that can:

◆ Zip and email in a single step

◆ Create self-extracting (.exe) archives that unpack themselves automatically when double-clicked

◆ Use wildcard file specifications—like *.doc (Word files) or *.mp3 (MP3s)—to bulk-add files to an archive instead of adding them one by one

◆ Split large archives across disks for easy reassembly later

◆ Encrypt and password-protect archives

◆ Work with many compression standards, not just zip

WinZip and zipped folders can coexist. When installed, WinZip takes over the .zip file extension and becomes the main way to handle zip archives (see "Associating Documents with Programs" in Chapter 6).

A more capable but proprietary compression format is RAR (.rar files). It's used mostly on file-sharing networks (BitTorrent, for example). To pack and unpack RAR files, use WinRAR (free; www.win-rar.com). WinRAR handles zip files too.

To create a new zipped folder:

1. In Windows Explorer, select where you want to create the new archive.

2. Choose File > New > Compressed (Zipped) Folder (press Alt if the File menu isn't visible).

   or

   Right-click an empty area of the file list and choose New > Compressed (Zipped) Folder.

3. Type a name for the new archive (keeping the .zip extension, if it appears) and press Enter.

✔ Tip

- To create a zipped folder on the desktop, right-click an empty area and choose New > Compressed (Zipped) Folder.

To create a new zipped folder from existing files or folders:

1. In Windows Explorer, select the file(s) or folder(s) that you want to archive.

2. Right-click one of the selected items and choose Send To > Compressed (Zipped) Folder.

3. Type a name for the new archive (keeping the .zip extension, if it appears) and press Enter.

Figure 5.56 Use the Extract Compressed (Zipped) Folders wizard to specify a destination folder and, optionally, open it after extraction.

To add files or folders to a zipped folder:

1. In Windows Explorer, find the zipped folder that you want to add files or folders to.

2. Right-drag the item(s) into the zipped folder and choose Copy Here or Move Here.

To extract files and folders from a zipped folder:

◆ To extract only some files or folders, double-click the zipped folder to open it and then drag the files or folders to a new location, where they return to their original sizes.

   or

   To extract all files and folders, right-click the zipped folder and choose Extract All (**Figure 5.56**).

✔ Tips

■ If a zipped folder window is already open, click Extract All Files in the task pane.

■ To compress digital photos for email, see "Emailing Photos" in Chapter 9.

COMPRESSING FILES AND FOLDERS

Searching for Files and Folders

Even if you organize your files and folders logically, sooner or later you'll need to find something: a newly installed program, a downloaded file, a file or folder whose location you forgot, or a particular photo among thousands, for example. Often, you'll also want to find all files that meet certain criteria: all or part of a filename, files containing a specific phrase, documents written by a given author, photos taken on a certain date, and so on.

Vista's Search feature greatly improves on that of earlier Windows versions. It returns results instantly and is available systemwide. You'll find Search boxes in, for example, the Start menu, Control Panel, every folder window, Help and Support (Chapter 3), Windows Photo Gallery (Chapter 9), and Windows Media Player (Chapter 10).

`Search` When you type in the Search box, Windows returns a results list or filters the view based on what you're typing. You can type things like file and folder names, program names, text contained within a file, and file tags and properties (see "Tagging Files" earlier in this chapter). **Table 5.4** lists some of the common properties that you can type in the Search box.

Search is context sensitive, basing its results on your current location and activity. Searching from the Start menu finds stuff in all your files, folders, and programs; searching from Control Panel finds only Control Panel tasks; and searching from a folder window finds items only in that folder and its subfolders. For advanced searches, use a Search folder.

Table 5.4

File Properties to Search On

PROPERTY	HOW TO USE IT IN THE SEARCH BOX
Filename	Type part or all of the filename that you're looking for. To find a file named Golden Gate Bridge.jpg, for example, you can type Gol or bridge.
Kind of file	Typically *Document*, *Picture*, or *Music*. To find all your text, word-processing, spreadsheet, and presentation files, for example, type *Document*.
Type of file	The last three letters of the filename, called the file extension, identify the file type. Common types include DOC (Word document), XLS (Excel spreadsheet), JPG (JPEG image), MP3 (music/audio file), TXT (text file), and ZIP (compressed zip file). Type the file extension. To find only MP3 files, for example, type *MP3* or (for more accurate results) *.mp3*. For details about file extensions, see "Associating Documents with Programs" in Chapter 6.
Tags	Words or phrases that you apply to your files to describe them. Type any tag to see a list of files for which that tag has been added. See "Tagging Files" earlier in this chapter.
Author	The name of the person who created the file to see a list of files by that author.

✔ Tips

- The keyboard shortcuts for Cut, Copy, Paste, Undo, and Select All work in the Search box (Ctrl+X, Ctrl+C, Ctrl+V, Ctrl+Z, and Ctrl+A, respectively).

- Search text is case insensitive: Search considers *John, john,* and *JOHN* to be the same search term.

- Type from the start of the word. Typing *cycle* finds *cycle, cycles,* and *my cycle* but not *bicycle.* Words start after any of these characters: *space* . - _ & \ / ( ) { } [ ].

- You don't have to wait until a search ends to open or use a file in the results list.

- You can use *wildcard characters* to represent one or more filename characters when you don't know what the real character is or don't want to type the entire name. ? substitutes for any single character, and * substitutes for zero or more characters. Type **.do?,* for example, to find all files that end in *.doc* (Word documents) or *.dot* (Word templates). *chapter*.doc* finds all Word documents that begin with the word *chapter,* followed by any characters (or no characters).

- In a Search Results window, you can press F5 to update the results list. If you've deleted a file or folder or changed it so that it no longer meets the search criteria, it disappears from the list (or appears in it if the change meets the criteria).

- If you're looking for a bunch of related files, finding them by using column headings might be better than using Search. See "Filtering, Sorting, Stacking, and Grouping Files" earlier in this chapter.

From the Start menu

The Search box is in the bottom-left corner of the Start menu. It searches your computer for files, folders, and programs, based on the filename, the program title (*excel*, for example), text in the file, tags, and other file properties. It looks at your personal folder, offline files, email, contacts, calendar events, and internet favorites and history. (It doesn't search the private files of other users.) To change the scope of the search, right-click the Start button, choose Properties > Customize, and then turn on or off the Search options (see "Customizing the Start Menu" in Chapter 2).

To search from the Start menu:

1. Click the Start button (or press the Windows logo key) and type text in the Search box.

   You don't need to click inside the Search box before you begin typing; just type.

   As you type, items that match your text appear in the left pane of the Start menu.

2. To open an item in the results list, click it or use the arrow keys to select it and then press Enter.

   If Search has already autoselected the item that you're looking for, just press Enter (**Figure 5.57**).

   or

   To open a Search folder with a complete list of results, click See All Results.

   or

   To open a browser window and expand your search to the internet, click Search the Internet.

   or

   Right-click an item in the results list to show its shortcut menu.

   or

   To cancel the search, press Esc, backspace over the search text, or click the close button (✖).

Figure 5.57 Search results superimpose themselves on the left pane of the Start menu. The results list narrows as you type more characters.

✔ Tip

■ Typing all or part of a program name in the Start menu's Search box often is the fastest way to launch that program.

Figure 5.58 Control Panel searches find only tasks that you can access in Control Panel; they don't search your files, applications, or other parts of Windows. This search shows tasks related to connecting to a network.

From Control Panel

The Search box is in the top-right corner of Control Panel. Use it to search for Control Panel tasks. Search works best in Category view, which is the default view (see "Using Control Panel" in Chapter 4).

To search from Control Panel:

1. Choose Start > Control Panel.

   or

   Choose Start, type control panel in the Search box, and then press Enter.

   or

   If Control Panel is already open, press Ctrl+E.

2. Type text in the Search box.

   You don't need to click inside the Search box before you begin typing; just type.

   As you type, tasks that match your text appear in the Control Panel window.

3. To open a task in the results list, click it, or tab to it and press Enter (**Figure 5.58**).

   or

   To cancel the search, press Esc, backspace over the search text, or click the close button (✖).

✔ Tip

- You can omit noise words from your search text. Type *connect internet* instead of *connect to the internet,* for example.

From a folder window

A Search box is in the top-right corner of every folder window. Use it to search in the current folder and all its subfolders, no matter how deeply nested. These searches are useful if a folder contains hundreds of files or subfolders. Search bases its search on filenames, text in the file, tags, and other file properties. See also "Using Windows Explorer" earlier in this chapter.

To search from a folder window:

1. In Windows Explorer, navigate to the folder that you want to search.

2. Click or tab to the Search box (or press Ctrl+E) and type text.

   As you type, the contents of the folder are filtered to match your text.

3. When you see the file or folder that you want, stop typing (**Figure 5.59**).

   or

   To cancel the search, press Esc, backspace over the search text, or click the close button (✖).

   The folder window goes back to its unfiltered state.

✔ Tip

■ For privacy reasons, only your own files are searched. To search for files belonging to another user, navigate to C:\Users*username* and do your search. (If necessary, change C to whatever drive Windows is installed on.) If a security prompt appears, type an administrator password or confirm the action.

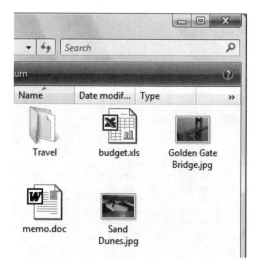

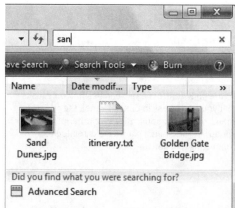

Figure 5.59 The original folder contents (top) and its contents after typing *san* in the Search box (bottom). The file Sand Dunes.jpg appears because *san* is part of its filename. itinerary.txt (from the Travel subfolder) appears because it contains the text *República de Santa Cruz*. And Golden Gate Bridge.jpg appears because it has the tag *San Francisco* applied.

From a Search folder

Use a Search folder when you want to:

◆ Get search results from more than one folder

◆ Use multiple criteria for a search

◆ Choose specific disks and other locations to search

By default, this search is based on a set of indexed locations, including everything in your personal folder (Documents, Pictures, Music, Desktop, and so on), email, offline files, and other common locations. You can add other places where you store files to indexed locations; see "Indexes" later in this section.

To search from a Search folder:

1. Chose Start > Search (or press Windows logo key+F).

   or

   In Windows Explorer or on the desktop, press F3.

2. Type text in the Search box

   You don't need to click inside the Search box before you begin typing; just type.

   As you type, files and folders from a variety of locations that match your text appear in the window.

continues on next page

SEARCHING FOR FILES AND FOLDERS

3. Click one of the filter buttons to show only certain kinds of files: E-mail, Document, Picture, Music, or Other.

or

Click the Advanced Search button (⊙) to show additional filters.

To build a more advanced search, enter search criteria in the lists and text boxes; then click the Search button (**Figure 5.60**).

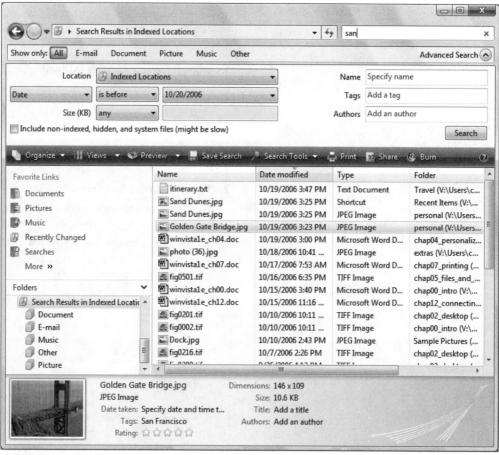

Figure 5.60 The Advanced Search pane lets you narrow your search by location, date, file size, tags, and other file properties.

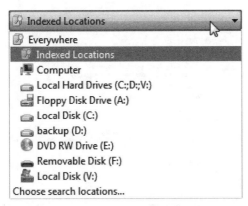

Figure 5.61 If you can't find a file that you know is on your computer, the most likely reason is that you're searching a limited set of locations. When you choose Everywhere, you get results from indexed locations quickly; then results from outside the index appear slowly as the rest of your computer is searched.

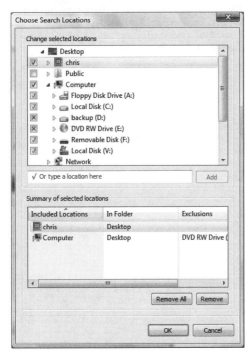

Figure 5.62 Navigate the location tree by clicking the small arrows. Use the check boxes to include a place in the search or omit a place from the search. For some network or deeply nested places, it might be quicker to type or paste the location in the box and click Add.

✔ Tips

- The default search, Indexed Locations, usually works best. Windows indexes the most common places for storing files automatically, so the search is very fast. You can use the Location list to pick a different set of search locations (**Figure 5.61**). You can search an entire drive, multiple drives, or—for a thorough search of your entire computer—Everywhere. To search in a custom set of places, click Choose Search Locations (**Figure 5.62**). You may want to add search locations for system and program files, which aren't included in the index to make routine searches faster.

- Network locations, USB flash drives, memory cards, CDs, DVDs, and other removable storage aren't indexed, so searching them is slow compared with searching on your computer. If Windows complains that it can't reach a location, check your network connection or the drive. If you're searching a location that's not indexed, you may have to press Enter to start the search.

- Windows continually updates the index with the latest information about files on your computer. If you search while the index is being updated, your results may not be up to date for files that you've created or changed recently. Wait a few seconds for the index to update.

- On the toolbar, click Search Tools > Search Options (or choose Organize > Folder and Search Options > Search tab) to change the default behavior of the Search folder (**Figure 5.63**).

Figure 5.63 Search options let you change the default settings for searches. These settings reduce or expand the scope and type of searches and can make them much faster or slower.

Table 5.5

Search Operators	
FILTER	FINDS FILES OR PROPERTIES THAT
word1 AND word2	Contain both word1 and word2, even if those words aren't next to each other. aspen AND colorado finds files that contain both those words.
word1 OR word2	Contain either word1 and word2. aspen OR tree finds files that contain either of those words.
NOT word	Don't contain word. aspen NOT tree finds files that contain aspen but not tree.
Quotes	Contain an exact phrase. "aspen tree" finds files in which aspen and tree are right next to each other, in that order.
Parentheses	Contain the specified words. (aspen tree) finds files in that contain both those words in any order. Expressions in parentheses are evaluated before expressions outside them. If parenthesized expressions are nested, the innermost expressions are evaluated first.
>	Are greater than a value or later than a date. modified:>06/22/2007 finds files changed after that date.
<	Are less than a value or earlier than a date. size:< 1.5 MB finds files smaller than 1.5 megabytes.

Advanced searches

Search results can be too broad. I typed *summer* and got photos tagged with *Summer in Aspen,* songs by Donna Summer, a file named *My Summer Vacation.doc,* a computer game named *_summer,* and a 1917 novel by Edith Wharton.

To search more selectively, you can filter your search in the Search box by specifying which file property to search: Separate the name of the property and the search term with a colon (:). Type *name:summer* to find only files that have the word *summer* in the filename, for example. *tag:summer* finds only files tagged with the word *summer.* *modified:2007* finds files changed at any time during that year (or *modified:06/22/2007* for that particular date).

You can filter on any property that appears in the column headings of a folder window. To see the complete list of properties, right-click any column heading and click More. For details, see "Filtering, Sorting, Stacking, and Grouping Files" earlier in this chapter.

Boolean and other search operators let you combine search words by using logic (**Table 5.5**). Type *AND, OR,* and *NOT* in uppercase. You can combine Boolean and property filters: *author:david AND lodge* finds files that are authored by David and any files that have Lodge in the filename or in any file property. *author:(david AND lodge)* finds only files authored by both names (not how parentheses changed the meaning). *author:"david lodge"* finds only files authored by someone with this name exactly.

Natural-language search

Natural-language search lets you type search text the way you talk. You don't have to type *AND, OR,* and *NOT* in uppercase. *kind:music artist:(beethoven OR mozart)* is equivalent to the natural-language search *music by beethoven or mozart.* You can use tags and properties in your search text. Some examples:

- *e-mail from joe sent last month*

- *documents modified today*

- *pictures of paris taken June 2007*

- *classical music rated ****

To turn on natural-language search:

- Choose Start > Control Panel > Appearance and Personalization > Folder Options > Search tab > check Use Natural Language Search (refer to Figure 5.63).

✔ Tip

- When natural-language search is turned on, you still can use the Search box in the normal way, with property names, colons, parentheses, and search operators.

Figure 5.64 The currently indexed locations are shown in the Index These Locations list.

Figure 5.65 To include a folder but not all its subfolders, expand the folder and then uncheck the box next to any folder you don't want to index. These folders appear in the Exclude column of the Summary of Selected Locations list.

Indexes

Windows invisibly and continually keeps track of the files on your computer by using an index, which stores the filename, date modified, size, file type, author, tag, properties, and other information. The index lets Windows do very fast searches; when you search, Windows consults the index instead of scanning your entire hard disk.

By default, Windows indexes the most common files on your computer, including all the files in your personal folder (such as Documents, Pictures, Music, and Videos), email, offline files, contacts, calendar events, and internet favorites and history. It doesn't index program files and system files, because you rarely need to search them.

If you frequently search in locations that aren't indexed, your searches may be slow. You can add those locations to the index to speed future searches. Bigger indexes make for slower searches, however, so you shouldn't index any more than you have to (Windows usually scans the entire index every time you search).

To add or remove index locations:

1. Choose Start > Control Panel > System and Maintenance > Indexing Options (**Figure 5.64**).

2. To add new files or locations to the index, click Modify; click Show All Locations (if a security prompt appears, type an administrator password or confirm the action); and then check the boxes in the Change Selected Locations list (**Figure 5.65**).

   or

   To remove a location from the index, uncheck its box in the Change Selected Locations list (refer to Figure 5.65).

3. Close each open dialog box.

✔ Tips

- You can't turn off or pause the index.

- You can't index network locations.

- For advanced indexed management, click the Advanced button in the Indexing Options dialog box (refer to Figure 5.64). The Index Settings tab lets you rebuild the index or change the hard disk or folder where it's stored (**Figure 5.66**). The File Types tab lets you search for a file type that's not currently being indexed (**Figure 5.67**).

Figure 5.66 Usually, your index requires no maintenance. But if Windows can't find files that you know are in an indexed location, you may need to rebuild the index. This takes a long time to complete, so avoid rebuilding until you have given the index a few hours to self-correct.

Figure 5.67 If you use an unusual file type that the index doesn't recognize, you can add it to the index yourself.

Figure 5.68 Your saved searches are available from the Favorite Links section of the Navigation pane. You can add searches here by dragging them from the file list. Windows provides a few saved searches to get you started.

Saving Searches

If you work regularly with a certain group of files and do the same search repeatedly to find them, you can save your search results. With a saved search (new in Vista), you don't have to keep rebuilding the same search manually. Just open that search. Windows repeats the search and lists the most current files that match the original search criteria.

To save a search:

1. Chose Start > Search (or press Windows logo key+F).

   or

   In Windows Explorer or on the desktop, press F3.

2. Find your files.

   For more information, see "Searching for Files and Folders" earlier in this chapter.

3. **Save Search** When the search completes, click Save Search (on the toolbar).

4. In the File Name box, type a name for the search; then click Save.

   The search is saved in your Searches folder.

To open a saved search:

1. In Windows Explorer, click Searches in the Navigation pane (**Figure 5.68**).

2. Double-click the saved search in the file list.

✔ Tips

- To make a saved search easier to find, tag it. See "Tagging Files" earlier in this chapter.

- You can move, copy, delete, rename, and treat saved searches like any other files.

SAVING SEARCHES

Burning CDs and DVDs

If your computer has a CD or DVD recorder, you can copy—or *burn*—files to a writeable disc. By default, Windows burns discs in the *Live File System* format, but you also can use the *Mastered* format (if you burned CDs in Windows XP, you used Mastered). To decide which format to use, see the "Picking a Disc Format" sidebar.

BURNING CDs AND DVDs

Picking a Disc Format

Live File System discs:

◆ Work like floppy disks or USB flash drives, meaning that you can copy files to disc immediately by dragging them

◆ Let you keep a disc in the burner and copy a few files at a time when you need to

◆ Let you delete individual files or reformat the disc to free space on CD-RW, DVD-RW, and DVD-RAM discs

◆ Don't need additional hard-disk space during burning

◆ Don't have a long recording step

◆ May need to be closed before you can use them in other computers

◆ Are compatible only with Windows XP and later

Mastered discs:

◆ Are convenient if you want to burn a large collection of files (always use this format when you're archiving backups)

◆ Don't copy files immediately, meaning that you need to select the entire collection of files that you want to copy to the disc and then burn them all at the same time

◆ Need temporary free hard-disk space at least the size of the files to be burned

◆ Have a long recording step

◆ Don't need to be closed

◆ Are compatible with older computers and devices such as CD players and DVD players

Figure 5.69 Windows displays this dialog box when you insert a blank CD or DVD. You may see other options if you've installed third-party burner software.

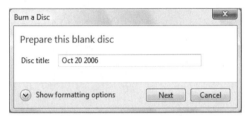

Figure 5.70 You can give the disc a name more meaningful than the current date. The default disc format is Live File System.

To burn a disc by using the Live File System format:

1. Insert a writeable CD or DVD into your computer's disc burner.

2. In the dialog box that appears, click Burn Files to Disc (**Figure 5.69**).

3. In the Burn a Disc dialog box, type a name for this disc; then click Next (**Figure 5.70**).

   It might take a few minutes for Windows to format as Live File System. When the formatting completes, an empty disc folder opens.

4. Open the folder containing the files that you want to burn, and drag the files into the empty disc folder.

   As you drag files into the disc folder, they are copied automatically to the disc.

To burn a disc by using the Mastered format:

1. Insert a writeable CD or DVD into your computer's disc burner.

2. In the dialog box that appears, click Burn Files to Disc (refer to Figure 5.69).

3. In the Burn a Disc dialog box (refer to Figure 5.70), type a name for this disc; then click Show Formatting Options.

4. Choose Mastered and then click Next (**Figure 5.71**).

   An empty disc folder opens.

5. Open the folder containing the files that you want to burn, and drag the files into the empty disc folder.

6.  On the toolbar, click Burn to Disc.

   When Windows finishes burning the files to the disc, the burner tray opens, and you can remove the disc. Then you can use it in other computers or CD/DVD players.

Figure 5.71 Clicking Show Formatting Options in Figure 5.70 reveals all the available formats.

Figure 5.72 The disc burner's Recording tab lets you pick a default burner (if you have more than one) and choose the "scratch" drive for storing temporary files during Mastered burns. You also can turn off disc autoejection.

✔ Tips

■ [Delete temporary files] If you change your mind about burning a Mastered disc after you've selected files to burn, you can delete the temporary files to recover hard disk space. To delete the files, open the disc folder, select the files, and then click Delete Temporary Files (on the toolbar).

■ To configure your disc burner, choose Start > Computer, right-click the burner drive and then choose Properties > Recording tab (**Figure 5.72**).

■ You can put a shortcut to your burner on your desktop and then drop files on the shortcut.

■ Burners are unreliable; during a Mastered burn, don't use other programs or stomp around the room. When the burn completes, test the disc immediately to see whether you can use it. (If you can't, you have a coaster.)

■ This section talks about copying *data* files to CDs and DVDs. To burn *music* CDs, use Windows Media Player. See "Burning Music CDs" in Chapter 10. To burn multimedia DVDs with video, photos, and audio, use DVD Maker (Start > All Programs > Windows DVD Maker). See also "Publishing a Movie" in Chapter 11.

■ For more recording features and verified burning, try Nero Ultra Edition ($80 U.S.; www.nero.com) or Roxio Easy Media Creator ($80 U.S.; www.roxio.com). Your computer or disc burner may have come with a stripped-down version of one of these programs.

BURNING CDS AND DVDS

Closing a Live File System disc makes it compatible with other computers and devices. (Mastered discs automatically are compatible with other computers and don't need to be closed.) You need to close only CD-R, DVD-R, and DVD+R discs (but not rewriteable discs, which end in RW). Discs that have not been closed still can be used in other disc burners but not in CD-ROM and DVD-ROM drives. Windows closes a disc automatically when you eject it.

To close a disc:

◆ Press the Eject button on your computer's burner drive.

or

Choose Start > Computer, right-click the burner drive, and then choose Eject (**Figure 5.73**).

It may take a few minutes to close the disc.

✔ Tips

■ To close a disc manually, choose Close Session from the burner drive's shortcut menu.

■ To stop closing discs automatically, click Global Settings in the burner drive's Properties dialog box (refer to Figure 5.72) and then uncheck Automatically Close the Current UDF Session When the Disc Is Ejected.

■ Some third-party burning programs offer to *finalize* your disc. Unlike a closed disc, a finalized disc can't have any more files added.

Figure 5.73 A disc burner's shortcut menu.

If you're using a CD-RW, DVD-RW, DVD+RW, or DVD-RAM disc, you can erase it and write to it many times. Live File System discs let you delete one or more files. Mastered discs are an all-or-nothing erase.

To erase all files on a disc:

1. Insert a rewriteable CD or DVD into your computer's disc burner.

2. Choose Start > Computer, right-click the burner drive, and then choose Erase This Disc (refer to Figure 5.73).

   or

   [Erase this disc] In a disc folder, click Erase This Disc (on the toolbar).

3. Follow the onscreen instructions.

To erase some files on a disc:

1. Insert a rewriteable CD or DVD into your computer's disc burner.

2. Choose Start > Computer.

3. Double-click the burner drive to display its contents.

4. Select the files or folders that you want to delete.

5. Press Delete.

BURNING CDs AND DVDs

Using Keyboard Shortcuts

Table 5.6 and **Table 5.7** list keyboard shortcuts for the desktop, Computer, Windows Explorer, and other programs. (Table 5.2 in "Navigating in Windows Explorer" earlier in this chapter contains additional Explorer-specific shortcuts.)

Table 5.6

General Keyboard Shortcuts

To	Press
Show the top of the active window or folder list	Home
Show the bottom of the active window or folder list	End
Copy	Ctrl+C
Cut	Ctrl+X
Paste	Ctrl+V
Undo	Ctrl+Z
Delete or move the selected item(s) to the Recycle Bin	Delete
Delete the selected item(s) permanently, bypassing the Recycle Bin (use only if you're sure)	Shift+Delete
Copy the selected item	Ctrl while dragging item
Create a shortcut to the selected item	Ctrl+Shift while dragging item
Rename the selected item	F2
Move the insertion point to the beginning of the next word	Ctrl+Right arrow
Move the insertion point to the beginning of the previous word	Ctrl+Left arrow
Move the insertion point to the beginning of the next paragraph	Ctrl+Down arrow
Move the insertion point to the beginning of the previous paragraph	Ctrl+Up arrow
Highlight a block of text	Ctrl+Shift+arrow key
Select more than one item in a window or on the desktop, or select text within a document	Shift+arrow key
Select all contents	Ctrl+A
Search for a file or folder	F3
Show the properties of the selected object	Alt+Enter
Close the active item or quit the active program	Alt+F4
Open the shortcut menu for the active window	Alt+spacebar
Close the active document in programs that allow you to have multiple documents open at the same time	Ctrl+F4
Switch among open windows	Alt+Tab
Use the arrow keys to switch among open windows	Ctrl+Alt+Tab
Cycle through windows in the order in which they were opened	Alt+Esc
Cycle through window panes or desktop elements	F6
Show the address-bar list in Computer or Windows Explorer	F4

Table continues on next page

Table 5.6 *continued*

General Keyboard Shortcuts	
To	Press
Toggle full-screen mode on and off	F11
Show the shortcut menu for the selected item	Shift+F10
Show the Start menu	Ctrl+Esc
Show a menu	Alt+underlined letter in the menu name
Carry out a menu command	Underlined letter in the command name in an open menu
Activate the menu bar in the active program	F10
Open the next menu to the right or open a submenu	Right arrow
Open the next menu to the left or close a submenu	Left arrow
Refresh the active window	F5
View the folder one level up in Computer or Windows Explorer	Backspace
Cancel the current task	Esc
Prevent the CD from playing automatically	Shift when you insert a CD into the CD drive

Table 5.7

Windows Logo Key Shortcuts	
To	Press
Show or hide the Start menu	Windows logo key
Show the System Properties dialog box	Windows logo key+Break
Show the desktop	Windows logo key+D
Minimize all windows	Windows logo key+M
Restore minimized windows	Windows logo key+Shift+M
Open Computer	Windows logo key+E
Search for a file or folder	Windows logo key+F
Search for computers on a network	Windows logo key+Ctrl+F
Show Windows Help	Windows logo key+F1
Lock your computer if you're on a network domain or switch users if you're not	Windows logo key+L
Open the Run dialog box	Windows logo key+R
Cycle through programs on the taskbar	Windows logo key+T
Open Ease of Access Center	Windows logo key+U
Cycle through running programs by using Flip 3D (Aero color scheme only)	Windows logo key+Tab
Use the arrow keys to cycle through running programs by using Flip 3D (Aero color scheme only)	Ctrl+Windows logo key+Tab
Bring all gadgets to the front and select the sidebar	Windows logo key+spacebar
Cycle through sidebar gadgets	Windows logo key+G
Open Windows Mobility Center (on laptops)	Windows logo key+X

INSTALLING AND RUNNING PROGRAMS

Windows, like all operating systems, is a launching pad for programs, or *applications*. More programs from more software firms are available for Windows than for any other OS. Fortunately, Microsoft and sound design enforce substantial consistency, so you can apply knowledge of a few common operations to many programs. Most programs share user-interface elements—scroll bars, copy-and-paste functions, menus, buttons, and so on—as well as setup and management options.

In this chapter, you'll learn how to install, remove, launch, and manage Windows programs. You'll also learn about *documents,* which are self-contained pieces of work (files) that you create with programs.

Installing Programs

How you install a program depends on where its installation files are located. Most shrink-wrapped programs are installed from a CD or DVD. Windows's *AutoPlay* feature runs the Setup program automatically when you insert the disc into the drive. You also can install programs from the internet or from a network.

To install a program from CD or DVD:

1. Insert the program's installation or setup disc.

   If a security prompt appears, type an administrator password or confirm the action.

2. If the program launches an install wizard, the AutoPlay dialog box will appear, and you can choose to run the wizard (**Figure 6.1**).

   or

   If a program doesn't start to install, check the installation instructions that came with the program (or on the publisher's website). If you can't find instructions, browse through the disc and open the program's setup file, usually named setup.exe or install.exe.

3. Follow the onscreen instructions (**Figure 6.2**).

Figure 6.1 When you insert a program's disc, the AutoPlay dialog box opens; click the option that runs Setup. You may see a vague or puzzling message when you try to install older programs made for Windows 95/98.

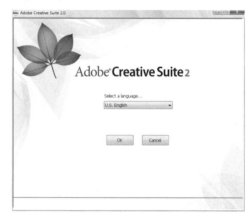

Figure 6.2 This example is the first page of an install wizard for an Adobe package. Install wizards usually make you pick a language, specify a destination folder, accept a license agreement, choose which components to install, and type a serial number or product key from the CD's envelope or registration card.

Installing Programs

Figure 6.3 If you're using the Aero color scheme, a live progress bar appears in the pop-up thumbnail on the taskbar.

✔ Tips

- During lengthy installations, you can switch to other programs and hover your mouse pointer over the install wizard's toolbar button to check its progress (**Figure 6.3**).

- If you're installing an older DOS-based program from a floppy disk, try running it from a command prompt. See "Using the Free Utility Programs" later in this chapter.

- Software publishers create install wizards with third-party programs such as InstallShield, Wise Installer, or Microsoft's Windows Installer, so you'll see those program names in title bars.

continues on next page

Before You Install

Keeps these points in mind before you install a new program:

- ◆ You need Administrator credentials to install programs; see "Setting up User Accounts" in Chapter 17.

- ◆ Your PC's manufacturer may have added software—Microsoft Office or a virus scanner, for example—at the factory. Check the Start > All Programs menu before you install new stuff.

- ◆ Most installations go smoothly, though Windows' security features won't let some poorly designed or malicious programs harm your system by installing outdated drivers or system files that Microsoft knows to be dangerous.

- ◆ If you upgraded to Vista from Windows XP, Windows Setup configured your existing programs to run; you don't have to reinstall them. If an older program doesn't run in Vista, see "Running Older Programs" later in this chapter. If you were a member of XP's Power Users group, which Vista has dropped, you still have the same privileges and can install programs.

- After installation, the program's shortcuts are highlighted in color in the Start > All Programs menu. To turn off high-lighting, right-click the Start button and choose Properties > Customize, uncheck Highlight Newly Installed Programs, and click OK.

- To configure AutoPlay for program discs, choose Start > Control Panel > Hardware and Sound > AutoPlay > Software and Games drop-down list (**Figure 6.4**).

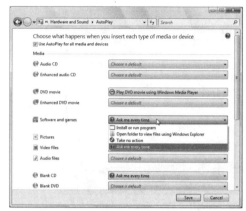

Figure 6.4 The Software and Games drop-down list lets you choose what happens when you insert a program disc. The default setting, Ask Me Every Time, launches the AutoPlay dialog box shown in Figure 6.1.

Who Can Use the Program?

A program installed by you—or any administrator—is available to *all* users by default; its shortcuts appear in everybody's All Programs menu. Sometimes shortcuts end up in your *personal* All Programs menu because you (inadvertently) told Setup to do so or because Setup gave you no choice. Recall from "Using the Start Menu" in Chapter 2 that Windows inspects two folders to build the All Programs menu: one for All Users and another for the logged-on user. To make a program available to everyone (instead of only you), do the following:

1. Choose Start > All Programs.

2. Right-click the item (icon) that you want everyone to be able to access and choose Copy.

3. Right-click the Start button and choose Open All Users.

4. In the folder tree, right-click the Programs folder and choose Paste.

    If a security prompt appears, type an administrator password or confirm the action.

Now the program appears in everyone's All Programs menu. If this method doesn't work, or if a program requires per-user settings, log on to each user account and rerun Setup.

INSTALLING PROGRAMS

Figure 6.5 The Save option is safer because you can scan the downloaded file for viruses if you don't trust the website. It also leaves a copy of the program on your hard disk if you have to reinstall.

The internet is the preferred (sometimes only) distribution method for many software vendors. You can use Internet Explorer (Chapter 14) or any web browser to download thousands of commercial, shareware, demo, and free programs (and updates) from vendors' websites and from independent sites such as www.download.com and www.tucows.com.

To install a program from the internet:

1. In your web browser, click the link to the program.

2. To install the program immediately, click Open or Run (**Figure 6.5**), and follow the onscreen instructions.

    or

    To install the program later, click Save and download the installation file to your computer. (To install the program, double-click the file and follow the onscreen instructions.)

    In either case, if a security prompt appears, type an administrator password or confirm the action.

✔ Tips

- By default, Internet Explorer and other Vista-aware browsers store downloads in the Downloads folder inside your personal folder. You can use the Save As dialog box to pick a different place (**Figure 6.6**).

- Downloaded programs usually are executable (.exe) files, which run when you double-click them and start installation automatically. If the download is a zip archive, extract its files (see "Compressing Files and Folders" in Chapter 5); then look for a read-me file (`readme.txt` or `readme.html`) or double-click the installer program (usually named `setup.exe` or `install.exe`) among the extracted pieces. You can delete these pieces after you install (keep the original zip file if you need it).

Figure 6.6 This dialog box appears if you click Save in Figure 6.5. Your Downloads folder is the best place for downloads—which are easy to "lose" if you're not consistent about where you put them.

If you're on a large network at work or school, your network administrator probably set up an internal webpage with instructions for installing licensed software from the network. If not, you can use Control Panel.

To install a program from a network:

1. Choose Start > Control Panel > Programs > Get Programs.

2. Select a program from the list and click Install.

3. Follow the onscreen instructions.

   If a security prompt appears, type an administrator password or confirm the action.

INSTALLING PROGRAMS

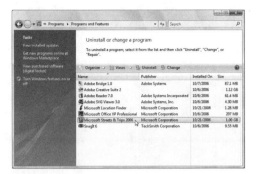

Figure 6.7 The buttons on the toolbar change depending on what uninstall/change/repair options the selected program provides. Big packages like Microsoft Office and Adobe Creative Suite provide the most options.

Removing Programs

When you install a program, it scatters its components all over your folder structure, not just in the Program Files subfolder it creates. Only an unwanted program's uninstall utility can remove it completely. Don't just delete the program's folder; if you do, you'll leave behind shortcuts, support files, hidden folders, registry entries, and other litter on your hard drive.

You can uninstall a program if you no longer use it or if you want to free up space on your hard disk. You also can change the program's configuration by adding or removing certain options. (Some programs don't offer this option, in which case your only choice is to uninstall.)

✔ Tip

- Always exit the program that you're going to remove. If you're using Fast User Switching (see "Logging On and Logging Off" in Chapter 1), make sure that no other logged-on users are using the program.

To uninstall or change a program:

1. Choose Start > Control Panel > Programs > Programs and Features.

2.   Uninstall   To uninstall the program, select the program and then click Uninstall (on the toolbar) (**Figure 6.7**).

   or

     Change   To change or repair the program, click Change or Repair (on the toolbar).

continues on next page

REMOVING PROGRAMS

3. Confirm the removal or change if a dialog box appears.

If a security prompt appears, type an administrator password or confirm the action.

Windows runs the program's uninstall or change utility (which varies by program).

4. Follow any onscreen instructions.

✔ Tips

■ The folder that contained the program may persist after uninstall completes, usually because it contains documents created with the program. Games, for example, often leave keyboard-binding and saved-game files. If you don't need those documents, you can delete the folder and its files safely.

■ Most uninstallers display a progress bar, explain what they're removing or not removing, and tell you whether you must restart your computer to complete the removal.

■ If a program that you want to uninstall isn't listed, look for removal instructions in the program's read-me file (if any) or at the publisher's website. Or search the web for *uninstall* and the program's name. As a last resort, drag the program's folder into the Recycle Bin.

■ You may get a midprocess message asking whether Windows should remove a shared file that other programs may need. Warnings of this type can look a bit dire, but I've always removed them with no ill effects.

Figure 6.8 Some features are grouped in folders, which you can double-click to see. If a check box is partially checked or dark, some of the items inside are turned on and others aren't.

Turning Windows Features On or Off

Some programs and features that are included with Windows must be turned on before you can use them, whereas others, turned on by default, can be turned off if you don't need them.

In earlier versions of Windows, turning off a feature uninstalled it. In Vista, all features remain stored on disk, so you can turn them back on when you want to. Turning off a feature doesn't free hard-disk space.

To turn Windows features on or off:

1. Choose Start > Control Panel > Programs > Turn Windows Features On or Off (in the Programs and Features category).

   If a security prompt appears, type an administrator password or confirm the action.

2. In the list, check or uncheck the boxes to turn features on or off (**Figure 6.8**).

3. Click OK.

✔ Tip

■ To learn about a feature, hover the mouse pointer over it for a pop-up description.

Launching Programs

Windows gives you many ways to launch (open) a program. Even Windows veterans may not know all of them.

To start a program:

◆ Choose Start > All Programs and click the program's icon.

or

Choose Start, type the program's name in the Search box, and then click it in the results list (**Figure 6.9**).

or

On the left side of the Start menu, click the program's icon (if it appears).

or

On the Quick Launch toolbar, click the program's icon (if it appears).

or

Choose Start > Computer > Local Disk (C:) > Program Files. In the program's subfolder, double-click the program's icon (.exe file).

or

Right-click the program's icon and choose Open.

or

Press the keyboard shortcut that you assigned to the program's icon.

or

Press Windows logo key+R, type the program's name, and press Enter (**Figure 6.10**).

You may have to include the full pathname. See "Navigating in Windows Explorer" in Chapter 5.

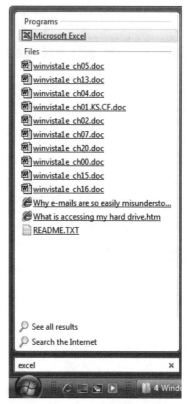

Figure 6.9 You need type only part of a program's name for it to appear in the results list. Windows highlights the most relevant result; if that's the program you're looking for, just press Enter.

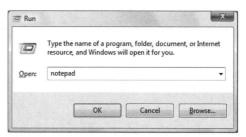

Figure 6.10 The Run dialog box may seem old-fashioned, but for many experienced users and rapid typists, it's the fastest way to open a program or document. Press F4 for a drop-down history of previous commands.

✔ Tips

- You can use any of these methods to open a document with its associated program. If you created the document `stuff.doc` in Microsoft Word, for example, double-click the document's icon to start Word and open that file automatically.

- Most Setup programs put an icon in the All Programs menu or on the desktop. To move these icons, see "Using the Start Menu" in Chapter 2.

- To customize the Quick Launch toolbar, see "Using the Quick Launch Toolbar" in Chapter 2.

- To assign a keyboard shortcut to a shortcut icon, change its Shortcut Key property; see "Managing Shortcuts" in Chapter 2.

- You can open a program or document from a command prompt just as you can from the Run dialog box. See "Using the Free Utility Programs" later in this chapter.

LAUNCHING PROGRAMS

Launching Programs Automatically

The Start > All Programs > Startup folder contains programs that open automatically every time you start Windows. To save yourself a few clicks or keystrokes every time you log on, you can place your own shortcuts to programs or documents in this folder.

To open an item each time you start Windows:

1. Choose Start > All Programs, right-click Startup, and then choose Open (**Figure 6.11**).

   Choose Open All Users (instead of Open) to change the Startup folder that applies to all users, not only yourself.

2. In Windows Explorer or Computer, navigate to the disk, folder, program, or document that you want to open automatically.

3. Right-drag the item to the Startup folder and choose Create Shortcuts Here.

   From now on, the item opens each time you start your computer or log on.

✔ Tips

- For an uncluttered desktop, open startup programs as taskbar buttons rather than as windows. Right-click a Startup shortcut, choose Properties > Shortcut tab, and then choose Minimized from the Run list.

- To identify startup programs, press Windows logo key+R; type `msconfig.exe` and press Enter. (If a security prompt appears, type an administrator password or confirm the action.) You can use the Startup tab's check boxes to isolate startup problems.

Figure 6.11 Your All Users Startup folder probably has a few icons already, put there by programs when they were installed.

Unwelcome Startup Programs

Too many programs add their own shortcuts silently to the All Users Startup folder (or the registry). Many of these programs are unnecessary, slow the boot process, and run invisibly in the background, chewing up processor time. If you know that you can delete or move a Startup shortcut without affecting your system or a program adversely, do so. (You'll want to keep some programs, such as virus scanners.) If you have trouble identifying a startup item, visit www.pacs-portal.co.uk/ startup_index.htm for help.

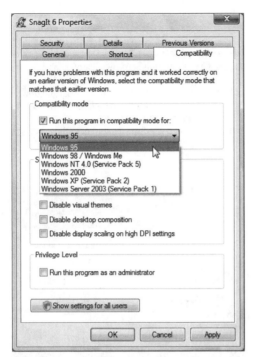

Figure 6.12 Choose the previous version of Windows that the old program was made for.

Running 16-Bit Programs

Windows 3.1 and DOS programs are called *16-bit programs*. Programs written for Windows 95, NT, and later are called *32-bit programs*. The 16-bit programs run slowly because Vista runs them in a leakproof, emulated space called a *virtual machine* that draws on a common memory pool.

To run DOS programs, choose Start > All Programs > Accessories > Command Prompt. See "Using the Free Utility Programs" later in this chapter.

If Vista displays an incompatibility message when you try to install or run a 16-bit program, don't ignore it. Either find a patch (update) or scrap the program.

Running Older Programs

If you're coming to Vista from an earlier Windows version, you probably still need to run your older programs. Vista still can run many of them, even those written for Windows 3.1/95 and DOS, but if it has trouble running a program that used to run fine under your old copy of Windows, you can try changing the compatibility mode.

To run a troublesome older program:

1. Right-click a program's executable (.exe) file or shortcut icon and choose Properties > Compatibility tab (**Figure 6.12**).

2. Change the compatibility settings for the program.

3. Click OK.

   The next time you open the program, Vista tries to run it by using your settings.

✔ Tips

■ If you want to be stepped through the process, use the Program Compatibility wizard: Choose Start > Control Panel > Programs > Use an Older Program with This Version of Windows (in the Programs and Features category).

■ Never try to coerce obsolete hardware-dependent system utilities to run under Vista. Upgrade to the latest version of your virus scanner, backup program, hard-disk partitioning tool, disc burner, or whatever.

■ To run old LucasArts and SCUMM-based adventure games (Monkey Island, Day of the Tentacle, and Sam & Max), try ScummVM (free; www.scummvm.org).

Switching Programs

You'll probably have multiple programs running simultaneously so that you can juggle, say, a word processor, email program, and web browser. You have several techniques for switching programs.

To switch among running programs:

◆ If the program's window is visible in the background, click it. (But click an empty area, not a button or menu, lest you activate it accidentally.)

or

Click the program's taskbar button. (The darkest button indicates the active program.)

or

Hold down Alt, press Tab repeatedly until the desired window is highlighted in the pop-up list, and then release both keys (or click an icon in the list to display that window). This feature is called Alt-tabbing (**Figure 6.13**).

or

Hold down the Windows logo key, press Tab repeatedly until the desired window comes to the front of the stack, and then release both keys (or click any part of any window in the stack to display that window). This feature, new in Vista, is called *Flip 3D* and works only if you're using the Aero color scheme (**Figure 6.14**).

or

Hold down Alt, press Esc repeatedly until the desired program appears, and then release both keys.

Figure 6.13 Alt-tabbing pops up a list of icons representing open windows. If you're using the Aero color scheme, the icons are live previews. Hold down Alt and press Tab repeatedly to highlight a window. If you press and release Alt+Tab quickly, you swap between only two windows instead of cycling through them all.

Figure 6.14 Flip 3D shows a stack of open windows. If you release the Tab key but keep the Windows logo key pressed, you can use the arrow keys or mouse wheel to cycle through open windows.

✔ Tips

■ 🖼 You also can invoke Flip 3D by clicking the Switch Between Windows button on the Quick Launch toolbar (on the taskbar).

■ If you press and release Ctrl+Alt+Tab or Ctrl+Windows logo key+Tab, you can use the arrow keys or Tab to cycle through open windows and then press Enter to activate a window.

■ Flip 3D, Alt+Tab, and Alt+Esc cycle *backward* through programs if you hold down Shift.

■ Alt+Esc—unlike Alt+Tab and Flip 3D—has no pop-up window, doesn't cycle through *minimized* programs, and doesn't swap between two programs. (It simply sends the active program to the bottom of the pile.)

Exiting Programs

When you finish using a program, you should exit (or quit or close) it to get it out of your way and to let Windows reclaim its memory for other use.

To exit a program:

◆ Choose File > Exit (**Figure 6.15**).

or

In Windows Explorer, choose File > Close. (Press Alt if the File menu isn't visible.)

or

Activate the program's window and press Alt+F4.

or

Click the program's close button (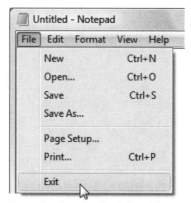).

or

Double-click the program's icon at the left end of the title bar (if visible).

or

Right-click the program's taskbar button and choose Close.

or

Activate the program's window, press Alt+spacebar, and then press C.

✔ Tip

■ Before exiting, the program prompts you to save any unsaved work.

Figure 6.15 Pressing Alt+F4 is quicker than choosing File > Exit.

EXITING PROGRAMS

Killing Unresponsive Programs

Programs that crash/freeze/lock up/hang are said to be "not responding" in Microsoft vernacular; you can move the mouse pointer within the program's window, but the program itself won't respond to clicks or keystrokes. An unresponsive program rarely forces you to restart your computer. Instead, use Task Manager to send the frozen program to its grave.

✔ Tip

■ Before you kill a program, make sure that it's really not responding. Wait a minute or two; Windows may be struggling to allocate extra memory. If you're running a Visual Basic macro in Microsoft Excel or Word, for example, the program may appear frozen while VB has control. Global reformatting or a find-and-replace operation on a long document can keep a word processor hypnotized for minutes. An open dialog box or message box may prevent you from doing anything else in the program; look for one hiding behind another window.

Desperate Measures

If killing an unresponsive program as described doesn't work, you still have these options, in order of preference:

◆ Click the Processes tab in Task Manager, click the program's image name, and then click End Process.

◆ Exit all other programs and log off.

◆ If you can't log off but other users are logged on (via Fast User Switching), right-click another user in Task Manager's Users tab, choose Connect to switch to that user, and then use Task Manager to log off (Disconnect) *yourself.*

◆ If none of these measures works, press your computer's reset button.

To kill an unresponsive program:

1. Right-click an empty area of the taskbar and choose Task Manager.

or

Press Ctrl+Shift+Esc.

or

Press Ctrl+Alt+Delete and click Start Task Manager.

or

Choose Start, type taskmgr in the Search box, and then press Enter.

2. On the Applications tab, select the name of the unresponsive task (**Figure 6.16**).

3. Click End Task.

4. In the dialog box that appears, click End Now or Close the Program (**Figure 6.17**).

✔ Tip

■ As an alternative to killing programs via Task Manager, you can use the tskill command-line program, which allows more control than Task Manager. For usage and syntax, type the command followed by /? or search for *command-line reference* in Help and Support. To use the command prompt, see "Using the Free Utility Programs" later in this chapter.

Figure 6.16 After Windows terminates the program, you can launch it again immediately without repercussions.

KILLING UNRESPONSIVE PROGRAMS

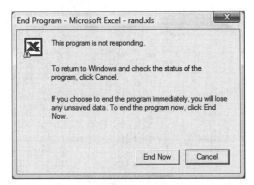

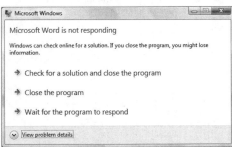

Figure 6.17 Either of these dialog boxes may appear. It may take Windows a few seconds—or minutes—to kill the program.

Figure 6.18 The Start > All Programs > Accessories menu.

Using the Free Utility Programs

The All Programs menu teems with free programs that are part of the standard Windows installation. Some of these programs (such as Internet Explorer and Windows Mail) get their own chapters. But Microsoft also includes useful utility programs, described here.

Most utilities are available in the Start > All Programs > Accessories menu (**Figure 6.18**). Not every utility in the menu is described here; I talk about others elsewhere in this book, where they're relevant.

To get program-specific help for a utility program, use its Help menu (or press F1).

USING THE FREE UTILITY PROGRAMS

Calculator

In Standard mode, Calculator offers add, subtract, square root, invert, and other basic functions. Scientific mode (**Figure 6.19**) adds trigonometric, statistical, logarithmic, and base functions. To operate Calculator, click its buttons with your mouse or press the corresponding keyboard keys. Help > Help Topics gives keyboard shortcuts for Scientific mode.

✔ Tips

- A better calculator is Calc98 (free; www.calculator.org), an engineering, scientific, statistical, and financial calculator.

- On the web, you can type equations in the Google search box and press Enter (see www.google.com/help/features.html#calculator).

Character Map

Character Map (**Figure 6.20**) displays all characters and symbols for a particular font. Use it to copy and paste diacritical marks, currency symbols, copyright signs, and all the other characters that don't appear on your keyboard. To open Character Map, choose Start, type character map in the Search box, and then press Enter.

✔ Tip

- If you're using Microsoft Word, the Insert > Symbol command is faster than using Character Map.

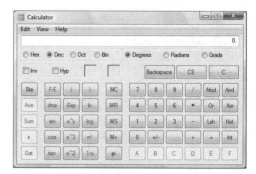

Figure 6.19 Choose View > Scientific to reveal Calculator's geeky secret identity.

Figure 6.20 Here are the characters for the Arial font. Double-click characters to put them in the Characters to Copy text box; then click Copy. Now you can Edit > Paste them into any document. The pop-up tip is for typography experts and programmers: It shows the character's name and hexadecimal code.

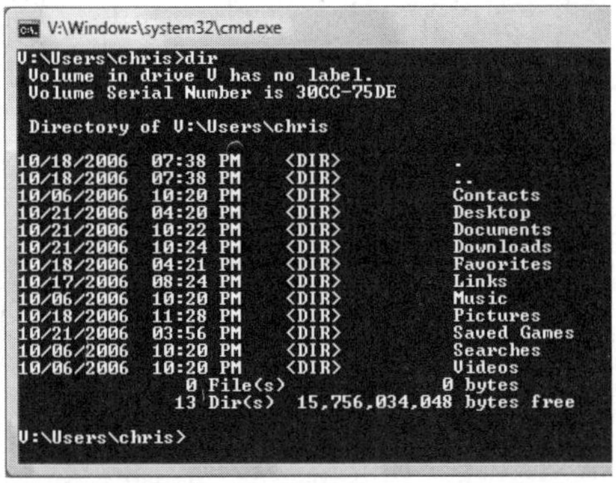

Figure 6.21 To quit Command Prompt, type exit and then press Enter.

Command Prompt

Command Prompt (formerly called DOS Prompt) lets you type commands rather than point and click (**Figure 6.21**). Rapid typists, Unix junkies, and people impatient with Windows safeguards love the command line, but new users find it cryptic and intimidating (experience teaches them to appreciate its efficiency).

Command Prompt is handy for many routine tasks, but it shines when using a graphical interface is impractical. (Network administrators don't add 1,000 user accounts by pointing and clicking, for example.) You also can use Command Prompt to (try to) run your old 16-bit DOS programs and games.

Scores of commands are available; search for *command prompt* and *command-line reference* in Help and Support. The basic commands are cd (or chdir), cls, copy, del, dir, exit, md (or mkdir), more, move, path, rename, rmdir, set, tree, type, and xcopy.

USING THE FREE UTILITY PROGRAMS

✔ Tips

- Command Prompt remembers the commands you've typed. Press the up- and down-arrow keys to review your command history.

- To run a command as an administrator, choose Start and type `command prompt` in the Search box. In the results list, right-click Command Prompt and choose Run As Administrator.

- To customize Command Prompt, right-click its title bar and choose Properties. A few recommendations: On the Options tab, turn on QuickEdit mode, which lets you drag over text and press Enter to copy it to the clipboard. Font tab: Switch the font to Lucida Console, bold, 14-point. Layout tab: Set Window Size to 80 × 40 and Screen Buffer Size to 80 × 1000 (so you can scroll a large results history). Colors tab: Choose black text on a white background. Click OK, and choose to modify the shortcut that started the window.

- To open a command window for a particular folder quickly: In Windows Explorer, hold down Shift, right-click the folder in the file list, and then choose Open Command Window Here.

- A quick way to run a single command— usually to open a program or file—without opening a command window is to use the Run dialog box. Press Windows logo key+R, type the command, and then press Enter. Or instead of typing a command, press F4 for a list of your recent commands, use the arrow keys to choose one, and then press Enter.

Figure 6.22 The Games folder is the central location for games on your computer. Newer Vista-aware games will install their icons in this window. (Older games create their own entries in the Start > All Programs menu.) Click Options (on the toolbar) to set up this folder.

Connect to a Network Projector

This utility lets you give a presentation over a network from any computer (desktop or laptop). The Connect to a Network Projector wizard connects to any available network projector over a wireless or a wired network. You can make a choice from a list of available projectors or enter a projector's network address. If the projector's icon has a small lock, you must enter a password to connect to it. The wizard also lets you choose whether all or part of your desktop appears on the projected image.

After the wizard completes, the Network Presentation dialog box opens. Use it to configure more settings and then minimize it to the taskbar when you give your presentation.

Games

The Start > Games window offers world-class productivity killers Solitaire, FreeCell, and Minesweeper—plus some new ones (**Figure 6.22**).

Meeting Space

Windows Meeting Space (Start > All Programs > Windows Meeting Space) lets you share documents, programs, or your desktop with other people (**Figure 6.23**). It's a peer-to-peer application that sets up an ad hoc network automatically if it can't find an existing one. You can use it in a conference room, a wireless hotspot, or a place where no network exists. With it, you can:

◆ Share your desktop or any program with other meeting participants

◆ Distribute and co-edit documents with other meeting participants

◆ Pass notes to other participants

◆ Connect to a network projector to give a presentation

You can join a meeting that someone else sets up, or you can start a new meeting and invite other people to join it. The first time you open Windows Meeting Space, it prompts you to turn on some services and sign in to People Near Me (which identifies people using computers near you, letting you use peer-to-peer programs).

✔ Tip

■ Windows Meeting Space replaces NetMeeting from earlier Windows versions.

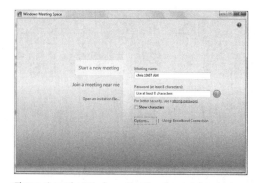

Figure 6.23 The Windows Meeting Space wizard lets you start a new meeting or join an existing one.

Figure 6.24 If you find Notepad too limiting, you can find many excellent shareware editors.

Notepad

Notepad, a bare-bones text editor, is one of the most useful tools in Windows (**Figure 6.24**). Use it to open, create, or edit *text files,* which contain only printable characters—no fonts, formatting, invisible codes, colors, graphics, or any of the clutter usually associated with a word processor. Notepad is the default program for .txt and .log files, but you can use it to view or edit .html files (saved web pages), .ini files (program initialization settings), or any other text-based file types.

✔ Tips

- Notepad does offer a few handy features: Press F5 to insert a time stamp (useful for keeping logs); choose Format > Font to set the display font; or choose File > Page Setup to set headers and footers for printouts.

- Notepad alternatives abound. A few of the better ones are TextPad ($30 U.S.; www.textpad.com), EditPlus ($30 U.S.; www.editplus.com), and NoteTab Pro ($30 U.S.; www.notetab.com).

- If you need an outliner to organize your thoughts, try KeyNote (free; www.tranglos.com/free/index.html).

SourceForge and OpenSource

For lots of free, quality software, browse around SourceForge.net (http://sourceforge.net), a centralized location for software developers to control and manage open-source software projects. Open-source software is free, not privately owned, spyware-free, and dependable. You can even have the source code. For details, go to www.opensource.org.

It's possible to set up your PC completely while spending no money on programs or utilities. Free alternatives to popular commercial products include OpenOffice instead of Microsoft Office, The GIMP for Adobe Photoshop, gzip for WinZip, and AbiWord for Word. Look for them and others at SourceForge, or do a web search.

Paint

Paint is a no-frills image editor with a few drawing, color, and manipulation tools (**Figure 6.25**). Use it to create your own works of art or to view or touch up graphic files that were created in other programs (such as Adobe Photoshop) or that you scanned or downloaded. Paint supports bitmap (.bmp), JPEG, GIF, TIFF, and PNG file formats.

Figure 6.25 The Image menu lets you flip, rotate, and stretch images.

✔ Tip

■ Paint alternatives include Paint Shop Pro ($100 U.S.; www.corel.com), Adobe Photoshop Elements ($90 U.S.; www.adobe.com), Oriens Enhancer ($15 U.S.; www.oriens-solution.com), and The GIMP (free; www.gimp.org).

Windows Ultimate Extras

If you're running the Ultimate edition of Windows Vista, you can download exclusive programs and services from Microsoft. When these Extras are available, they appear in the Windows Ultimate Extras section on the Windows Update page.

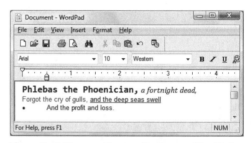

Figure 6.26 Like any other word processor, WordPad lets you apply formatting (italic, justification, colors, fonts, and so on) to text. The Insert > Object command lets you embed images, sounds, movies, charts, spreadsheets, and other objects in your document.

WordPad

WordPad (**Figure 6.26**) is a simple, stripped-down word processor associated with .doc files (unless you've installed Microsoft Word), .rtf files (Rich Text Format), and .wri files (Microsoft Write). You also can use it to edit plain-text files, but Notepad is more appropriate for that task.

✔ Tip

■ WordPad's native file format is RTF (Rich Text Format). If you open a Word file in WordPad, you'll get the raw text mixed with some garbage symbols.

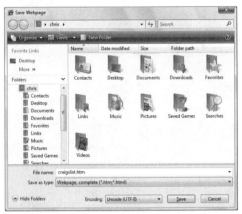

Figure 6.27 The Save dialog box appears the first time you save a file or when you choose File > Save As. The standard Save dialog box (top) expands to show the Navigation pane (bottom) when you click Browse Folders.

Saving Documents

Most programs let you save your work as documents, which you can return to later, print, send to other people, back up, and so on. Documents generally are thought of as being word-processed materials, but here I'm using the word to mean images, spreadsheets, presentations, databases, email, webpages, digital photos, text files, videos, or any other user-created work.

Nearly all programs use Windows' standard Save dialog box. The first time that you save a document, Windows asks you to name it and pick a folder to store it in. (Two files in the same folder can't have the same name.)

To save a document:

1. Choose File > Save.

   or

   To save a copy of a file under a different name or in a different folder, choose File > Save As.

   (Press Alt if the File menu isn't visible.)

2. Click Browse Folders to show the Navigation pane (**Figure 6.27**).

3. Use the address bar or Navigation pane to choose the folder to save the file to (see "Navigating in Windows Explorer" in Chapter 5).

4. In the File Name box, type the name of the file.

   You can use the Cut, Copy, Paste, and Undo keyboard shortcuts (Ctrl+X, Ctrl+C, Ctrl+V, and Ctrl+Z, respectively) while editing. For file-naming rules, see "Naming Files and Folders" in Chapter 5.

continues on next page

5. To save a file in a format other than the program's default (native) format, choose a target format from the Save As Type drop-down list.

This feature lets you, say, save a Word document as text (.txt), Rich Text Format (.rtf), or HTML (.html) so that users without Word can open it in a text editor, WordPad, or a web browser.

6. Click Save.

✔ Tips

■ To bypass step 3, type the filename's full pathname in step 4. See "Navigating in Windows Explorer" in Chapter 5.

■ In the file list, you can click a document to make its name appear in the File Name box; then click Save to overwrite the existing document or edit the name to save a new document. The latter technique saves typing when you're saving similarly named documents.

■ The file list acts like an Explorer window. You can right-click any file or folder to, say, rename or delete it. You even can drag items into and out of this box or use the standard navigation keys.

■ You must close the Save dialog box before you can use another part of the program.

■ Some older programs use the old-style Save dialog box, with Windows XP–style navigation features.

■ You can't save your work in some utility and game programs, such as Calculator and Solitaire.

■ Some programs can autosave your work at a regular time interval that you set. Check the program's Options or Preferences dialog box.

Read-Only Files

You can prevent yourself (and others) from making accidental changes to a file by making it *read-only*. To change a file to read-only, right-click the file and choose Properties > General tab, check Read-Only (or uncheck it to make it *read-write*), and click OK. Read-only files can't be changed, but they can be copied, moved, renamed, or deleted.

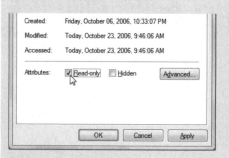

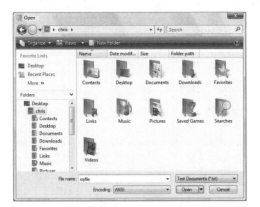

Figure 6.28 The Open dialog box works like the Save dialog box described in the preceding section.

Opening Documents

You have several ways to reopen a document that you've already named and saved.

To open a document:

◆ In the program that created the document, choose File > Open, navigate to the document, and then click Open (**Figure 6.28**). (Press Alt if the File menu isn't visible.)

or

Choose Start, type the document's name in the Search box, and then click it in the results list.

or

In Windows Explorer or on the desktop, double-click the document's icon (or select it and then press Enter).

or

If the document was opened recently, choose it from the Start > Recent Items menu.

or

Press Windows logo key+R, type or paste the document's name and path, and then press Enter.

For details about pathnames, see "Navigating in Windows Explorer" in Chapter 5.

✔ Tips

■ You also can open a document by using any of the techniques described in "Launching Programs" earlier in this chapter.

■ Like the Save dialog box, the Open dialog box must be closed before you can use another part of the program.

■ To open a file that's not associated with a particular program, right-click the file, choose Open With, and then select the name of a program (**Figure 6.29**). See "Associating Documents with Programs" later in this chapter.

■ If you open a document that somebody else already has open, the program usually will warn you or open a *read-only* copy of the document (unless it's a multiuser document such as a database).

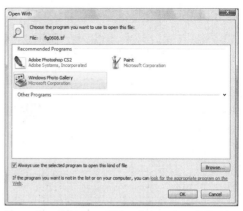

Figure 6.29 If the Open With submenu doesn't list the program that you're looking for, click Choose Default Program to open this dialog box. Click Browse to find the program.

Access Denied

If Windows denies you access when you try to open a file or folder, it may be that:

◆ The file is encrypted. To check whether it's encrypted, right-click the file and choose Properties > General tab > Advanced. If Encrypt Contents to Secure Data is checked, see the person who created the file. If *you* encrypted the file, you might have done so in another user account. See "Encrypting Data" in Chapter 13.

◆ You don't own the folder. To take ownership, right-click the folder and choose Properties > Security tab > Advanced > Owner > Edit. If a security prompt appears, type an administrator password or confirm the action. Click your name or group in the Change Owner To list. If you want to own the files and subfolders too, check Replace Owner on Subcontainers and Objects. Click OK in each open dialog box.

Table 6.1

\multicolumn{2}{l}{**Common File Extensions**}
EXTENSION	DESCRIPTION OR PROGRAM
.ai	Adobe Illustrator
.avi	Windows Media Player
.bmp	Bitmap image
.dll	System file (not a document)
.doc	Microsoft Word (or WordPad)
.exe	Program (not a document)
.gif	GIF image
.htm/.html	Webpage (Internet Explorer)
.indd	Adobe InDesign
.jpg/.jpeg	JPEG image (for photos)
.mdb	Microsoft Access
.pdf	Portable Document Format (Adobe Reader)
.png	PNG image
.ppt	Microsoft PowerPoint
.psd, .pdd	Adobe Photoshop
.qxd	QuarkXPress
.tif	TIFF image
.tmp	Temporary file
.txt	Text file (Notepad)
.wpd	WordPerfect
.xls	Microsoft Excel
.xps	XML Paper Specification (Microsoft XPS Viewer)
.zip	Compressed zip file

Associating Documents with Programs

When you double-click a Word document, Windows launches Word with that document open. Windows knows to launch Word—rather than, say, Paint or Windows Mail—because a document's file type is embedded in its filename, as the (usually three) characters appearing after the name's last dot. These characters, called an *extension* or *file extension,* associate a document with a particular program.

Table 6.1 gives a short list of common extensions; go to `www.filext.com` for a comprehensive list.

Viruses and Extensions

Viruses disguised as innocuous attachments often arrive via email. A virus file with the extension .exe is a program that runs when you double-click it, infecting you. (Some other extensions are dangerous too.) Virus writers will try to trick you into thinking a file is safe by naming it, say, `iloveyou.txt.exe`. If extensions are hidden, you see only `iloveyou.txt`, which appears to be a harmless text file.

Even with extensions showing, the file

`FreeMP3s.txt                    .exe`

will appear to be harmless if the embedded spaces hide the .exe extension in a narrow column.

Microsoft hides extensions by default to make Windows appear friendlier. But even beginners should show extensions for these reasons:

◆ An icon alone can be insufficient to distinguish a file's type (particularly the tiny icons in details and list views).

◆ Extensions impart the types of like-named files quickly (`resume.doc` vs. `resume.txt` vs. `resume.html`, for example) without making you read the Type column in Explorer.

◆ Extensions make it plainer to, say, choose among Photoshop, Paint, Internet Explorer, and Windows Photo Gallery to open .jpg (JPEG) files.

◆ If a newly installed program hijacks an extension's association without asking your permission (both rude and common), you can reassociate the extension with your preferred program.

◆ If you don't learn about extensions, you'll remain mired in beginner status and pester people with trivial problems.

To show file extensions:

1. Choose Start > Control Panel > Appearance and Personalization > Folder Options.

   or

   In a folder window, choose Organize > Folder and Search Options.

   or

   Choose Start, type folder `folder options` in the Search box, and then press Enter.

2. Click the View tab; then, in the Advanced Settings section, uncheck Hide Extensions for Known File Types (**Figure 6.30** and **Figure 6.31**).

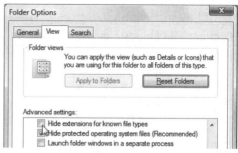

Figure 6.30 Uncheck this box to show file extensions in folder windows, on the desktop, and in dialog boxes.

Figure 6.31 Folder windows that hide (top) and show (bottom) extensions.

Figure 6.32 The Open With dialog box lists programs capable of opening the selected file. Click Browse to pick a program that's not in the list.

To change the program associated with a file extension:

1. In a folder window, select a file having the desired extension.

   or

   Choose Start > Search; then search for a file having the desired extension (see "Searching for Files and Folders" in Chapter 5).

2. Right-click the file and choose Open With > Choose Default Program (**Figure 6.32**).

3. If the program that you want to use to open this type of file is listed, select it.

   or

   If the program isn't listed, click Browse, select the program (.exe) file, and then click Open.

4. Check Always Use the Selected Program to Open This Kind of File.

5. Click OK.

   When you double-click that type of file in the future, the file will open in the program you selected.

ASSOCIATING DOCUMENTS WITH PROGRAMS

✔ Tips

- If you double-click a file with an unknown extension, Windows lets you choose a program or try to look up the extension on Microsoft's website (**Figure 6.33**). You also can visit this website by clicking Look for the Appropriate Program on the Web in the Open With dialog box (refer to Figure 6.32).

- The Details pane in Windows Explorer contains file-type information for the selected file.

- Some file types have multiple extensions (.htm/.html and .jpg/.jpeg, for example). Repeat the association for each form of the extension.

- To scroll through a (long) list of file extensions and set them individually, choose Start > Control Panel > Programs > Default Programs > Associate a File Type or Protocol with a Program (**Figure 6.34**).

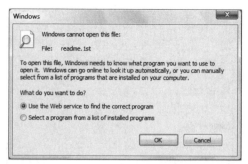

Figure 6.33 This dialog box appears when you double-click a file with an extension that Windows doesn't recognize. A file with an unknown extension (or no extension) often is a text file; try opening it in Notepad before asking Windows to hunt for a program.

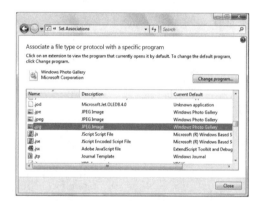

Figure 6.34 To change the default program for an extension, select the extension in the list, click Change Program, and then choose a new program in the Open With dialog box (refer to Figure 6.32).

PRINTING, SCANNING, AND FAXING

Paperless-office propaganda notwithstanding, computer users have felled forests to feed printers and preserve paper trails. In Windows, the operating system handles printing—not individual programs. When you print something in any program, you activate Windows' intermediary printing system, which accepts print jobs from programs and feeds them to the printer. This process, called *background printing*, lets you keep working in your program while your documents print.

Printer installation and configuration are easy. After hardware connection and setup, you can print individual documents with the default settings or override them for special purposes. In this chapter, you'll learn basic printer properties, printing tasks, and a few topics beyond the routine. I'll also describe how to save paper by using your computer to send and receive faxes without a fax machine.

Installing a Printer

A *local printer* attaches directly to your computer through a USB, parallel, or serial port, or via a Bluetooth or wireless signal. Newer printers use USB, Bluetooth, or wireless connections; older ones use parallel or (rarely) serial. You also can use a cableless infrared connection if both your printer and computer (typically a laptop) have infrared lenses. Computers on a network (Chapter 18) can share a *network printer*.

When you attach or connect a printer to your computer, Windows often recognizes the device and searches its extensive collection of built-in drivers to run printers. A *printer driver* is software that lets programs send commands to a particular printer. If your printer isn't in Windows' built-in list, you can use the driver on the CD that came with the printer. If you upgraded from Windows XP, Vista inherited the existing printer driver and settings, and your printer may work fine. In any case, check the printer manufacturer's website for a more recent driver.

✔ Tip

- Installation is trivial for printers that support Plug and Play, which lets Windows detect and configure a connected device automatically. Printers that use USB, Bluetooth, wireless, or infrared connections always support Plug and Play. Parallel connections may support it; serial connections never do. For more details, see Chapter 8.

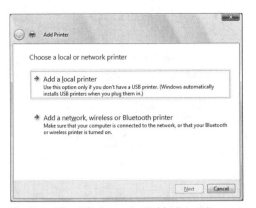

Figure 7.1 When Windows says "Add Printer," it means "Add Printer Driver."

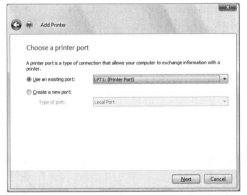

Figure 7.2 For most printer setups, you can accept the default port setting. Windows refers to a parallel port as an *LPT port* and a serial port as a *COM port*.

Read the printer manual before installation. The manufacturer gives directions on how to attach or connect the printer, which Windows will install automatically. The printer also may include a CD to run *before* connection. You can add a printer manually if Windows can't install it, or if you removed it and want to add it again.

To install a local printer:

1. Choose Start > Control Panel > Hardware and Sound > Add a Printer (in the Printers category).

   The Add Printer wizard opens.

2. Choose Add a Local Printer (**Figure 7.1**).

3. On the Choose a Printer Port page, make sure that Use an Existing Port and the recommended printer port are selected; then click Next (**Figure 7.2**).

   In almost all cases, LPT1 (the default) is the correct port.

   continues on next page

INSTALLING A PRINTER

4. On the Install the Printer Driver page, select the manufacturer and model of your printer; then click Next (**Figure 7.3**).

   or

   If your printer model isn't listed and you have the printer installation disc, insert the disc, click Have Disk, and browse to the driver software.

   (If Windows refuses your installation disc, download the current printer driver from the printer manufacturer's website.)

   or

   If your printer isn't listed and you don't have the printer installation disc, click Windows Update and then wait while Windows checks for any available driver software packages. When a new list of manufacturers and printers is displayed, select the appropriate items in each list for your printer.

5. Complete the additional steps in the wizard and click Finish.

   Along the way, you can name the printer (**Figure 7.4**) and print a test page (**Figure 7.5**).

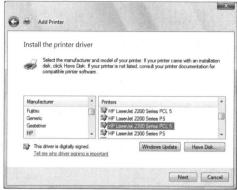

Figure 7.3 Clicking an entry in the Manufacturer list (left) displays Vista's standard drivers for that manufacturer in the Printers list (right). The Windows Update button connects you to Microsoft's website for drivers that were updated since Vista came out (or since the last update).

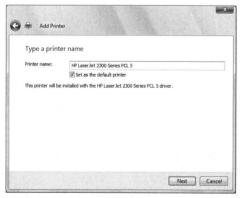

Figure 7.4 Type a name for your printer or accept the default name. Favor names that everyone on your network will recognize. Indicate whether this printer is the one that you'll usually print with (the default).

Figure 7.5 You can print a test page to confirm that your printer is working properly.

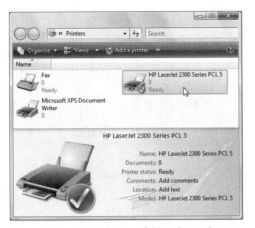

Figure 7.6 To open the Printers folder, choose Start > Control Panel > Hardware and Sound > Printers.

After successful installation, the printer's icon appears in the Printers folder (**Figure 7.6**).

To install a network, wireless, or Bluetooth printer:

1. Make sure that your computer is connected to the network (or that your wireless or Bluetooth printer and adapter are turned on) and that you know the name of the printer you want to add.

 If the name isn't posted on the printer itself, ask the printer owner or your network administrator.

2. Choose Start > Control Panel > Hardware and Sound > Add a Printer (in the Printers category). The Add Printer wizard opens.

3. Choose Add a Network, Wireless or Bluetooth Printer (refer to Figure 7.1).

4. In the list of available printers, select the one that you want to use and then click Next.

 Available printers can include all printers on a network, such as Bluetooth and wireless printers, or printers that are plugged into another computer and shared on the network. If you're on a network domain, only printers for that domain are listed.

 Make sure that you have permission to use these printers before adding them to the computer.

5. Complete the additional steps in the wizard and click Finish.

After successful installation, the printer's icon appears in the Printers folder (refer to Figure 7.6) or the Network folder.

INSTALLING A PRINTER

✔ Tips

- To place a shortcut to the Printers folder in the Start menu, right-click the Start button and choose Properties > Start Menu tab > Customize > check Printers > OK.

- To remove a printer that you no longer use, right-click it in Printers and choose Delete (**Figure 7.7**). You can't remove a printer if you have items in the print queue. Either wait until the items print or cancel all the print jobs. See "Controlling Printouts" later in this chapter.

- A check mark appears on the default printer's icon. To change the default printer, right-click the desired printer in Printers and choose Set As Default Printer (refer to Figure 7.7). This command won't appear if the printer already is the default.

- To rename a printer, right-click it in Printers and choose Rename (refer to Figure 7.7). The default name usually is the manufacturer name and printer model. For a shared printer, you may want to add a bit of text indicating the printer's location and capabilities (color, two-sided printing, and so on).

- For information about installing fonts, see "Managing Fonts" in Chapter 4.

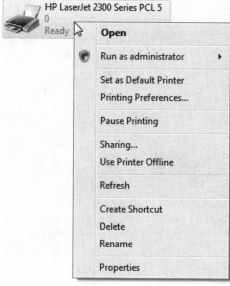

Figure 7.7 Right-click a printer icon to show common printer tasks (many of which are duplicated in the toolbar). Tiles view (shown here) and details view display printer status information.

Microsoft's "PDF Killer"

 In the Printers folder, you'll find a preinstalled icon for XPS Document Writer. *XPS* (XML Paper Specification) is a new Microsoft-developed file format supported in Windows Vista and Microsoft Office 2007. XPS competes with Adobe's Portable Document Format (PDF) as a standard file format for digital documents. Like PDF, XPS renders complex documents faithfully on any platform that supports it without font, layout, viewing, or printing problems.

 Vista has a built-in XPS viewer that opens in Internet Explorer when you double-click an XPS (.xps) file.

To save a document in XPS format, choose File > Print, and choose Microsoft XPS Document Writer in the list of printers. As XPS becomes popular, more programs will let you save to XPS directly in the Save As dialog box.

To encourage wide use of the format, Microsoft sent the XPS specification to an independent standards board and released XPS under a royalty-free we-won't-sue-you license that lets companies freely create XPS readers, writers, and renderers.

Finding Printer Drivers

Go to the manufacturer website For installation and troubleshooting information, go to the printer manufacturer's website: Select the printer in the Printers folder and click Go to the Manufacturer's Website (on the toolbar). You may have to click the chevron (») at the right end of the toolbar to see the command.

If the manufacturer provides no Vista driver for your printer, try the Windows XP driver. If no XP driver exists, try the Windows 2000 driver. No luck? Try a 2000/XP/Vista driver for a different printer from the same manufacturer—but keep it in the family. Inkjet printers can't use laser-printer drivers, for example.

Still no luck? Try *printer emulation*. Check the manual to see whether your printer can mimic a different printer, and use *that* printer's driver. Many non–Hewlett-Packard laser printers can work with HP LaserJet drivers, for example.

The manufacturer's website will have printer-driver installation instructions, but you also can update a driver manually: Right-click a printer in the Printers folder and choose Run As Administrator (refer to Figure 7.7). If a security prompt appears, type an administrator password or confirm the action. Choose Advanced tab > New Driver and complete the steps in the Add Printer Driver wizard.

INSTALLING A PRINTER

Same Printer. Different Purposes.

You can install multiple drivers with different settings for the same physical printer and then switch among these "virtual" printers easily to suit what you're printing. If your printer has two paper trays, create Letterhead and Plain printers; to switch between printing high-resolution graphics and low-res text documents, create 1200 dpi (dots per inch) and 300 dpi printers. Separate Landscape and Portrait printers are popular too.

To create another printer:

1. Install the printer a second time, but under a different name that indicates its purpose (refer to Figure 7.4).

2. After installation, right-click the printer in the Printers folder, choose Printing Preferences (refer to Figure 7.7), and then select the settings appropriate to the printer's role.

3. In the Printers folder, right-click the printer that you use most of the time and choose Set As Default Printer.

From now on, you can choose the appropriate printer in any program's Print dialog box. See "Printing Documents" later in this chapter.

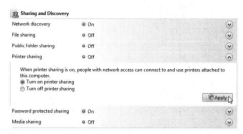

Figure 7.8 Turn on printer sharing to allow others on your network to use the printer connected to your computer.

Figure 7.9 A printer's Sharing tab offers a quick way to turn sharing on or off.

Sharing a Network Printer

You can share a printer attached to your computer with anyone on the same network, as long as the printer is installed on your computer and attached directly with a USB or other type of printer cable. Whoever you choose to share the printer with will be able to use it to print, provided that they can locate your computer on the network.

✔ Tip

- A printer connected directly to a network—rather than attached to a computer—via a network port or wireless connection is available to anyone on the same network, without explicit sharing.

To share a printer attached to your computer:

1. Choose Start > Control Panel > Network and Internet > Network and Sharing Center.

2. Under Printer Sharing, click the arrow button (⊘) to expand the section, click Turn on Printer Sharing, and then click Apply (**Figure 7.8**).

   If a security prompt appears, type an administrator password or confirm the action.

✔ Tip

- To change a printer's sharing options quickly, right-click the printer in the Printers folder and choose Sharing (**Figure 7.9**).

To use a shared printer:

1. Find out the name of the computer that has the shared printer attached to it.

   You can ask someone who uses that computer, or go to the other computer yourself and look it up: Choose Start > Control Panel > System and Maintenance > System (or press Windows logo key+Break) (**Figure 7.10**).

2. Choose Start, and in the Search box, type *computername*, where *computername* is the name of the other computer (for example, \\Office-PC).

3. Press Enter.

4. If Windows finds the computer on the network, a folder for the computer opens; double-click Printers to show the shared printer.

   (If you don't see the printer, ask a person who uses that computer whether the printer is connected, turned on, and shared with other users on the network.)

5. Double-click the printer icon.

   Windows adds the printer to your computer automatically and installs the printer driver.

6. When the process completes, click Next and follow the onscreen instructions.

When you finish, the shared printer appears in your Printers folder. You can select this printer in any program's Print dialog box to print a file.

Table 7.1 shows how a printer's icon reflects its status.

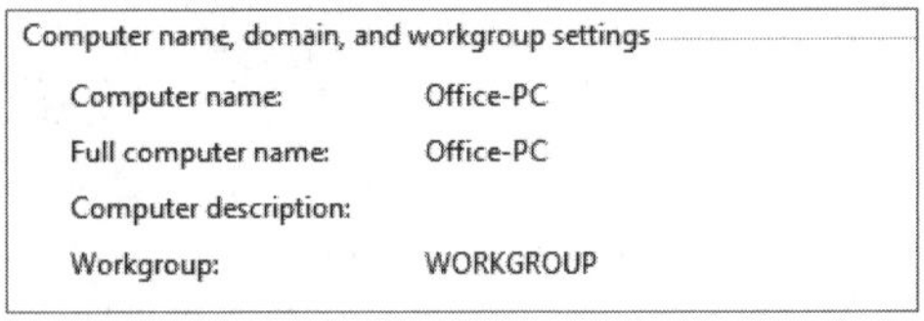

Figure 7.10 The computer's name is listed below Computer Name, Domain, and Workgroup Settings.

Table 7.1

Printer Icons

Icon	Description
	A local printer has a normal printer icon.
	A shared local printer has a small Users symbol.
	A remote printer on the network has a cable below it.
	The default printer has a check mark on it.

✔ Tip

■ When you share a printer connected to your computer, everybody's print jobs go through *your* copy of Windows, draining your system resources. Busy networks use a *print server* to arbitrate print requests. Stand-alone Ethernet or wireless print servers (which require no dedicated PC) cost about $50 to $120 U.S.

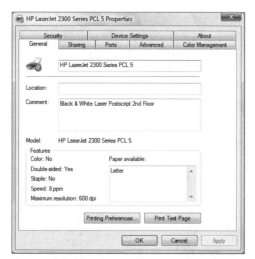

Figure 7.11 If you're sharing a printer, add its location and a few helpful comments for other network users to see.

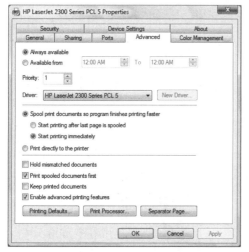

Figure 7.12 With shared printers, separator pages make it easy to find your documents among others at the printer. You can create custom separator pages.

Setting Printer Properties

You can change a printer's default settings through its Properties dialog box. This dialog box varies by printer model because the manufacturer supplies the drivers whose features appear there. Options common to all printers include those in the General and Advanced tabs.

To change a printer's default settings:

1. Choose Start > Control Panel > Hardware and Sound > Printers.

   or

   Choose Start, type `printers` in the Search box, and then press Enter.

2. Right-click a printer and choose Properties.

3. On the following tabs, review or set the printer's default properties:

   General. Change the printer's name, location, or comments. To test the printer, click Print Test Page (**Figure 7.11**).

   Sharing. See "Sharing a Network Printer" earlier in this chapter.

   Ports. Review the printer's port assignment and configuration. You'll rarely want to change these settings.

   Advanced. Change settings such as printer access hours and spooling (queuing) behavior. (*Don't* select Print Directly to the Printer; it turns off background printing.) Click Printing Defaults to view or change the default document properties for all users. Click Separator Page to add or change a separator page that prints between documents (**Figure 7.12**).

continues on next page

SETTING PRINTER PROPERTIES

Device Settings. These options differ by printer model, depending on features (**Figure 7.13**).

About. Review the printer's make and model, driver version numbers, and configuration date and status (**Figure 7.14**).

Security. Review or set the printer's security settings (**Figure 7.15**).

4. Click OK (or Apply).

✔ Tip

■ To set print server properties that affect *all* networked printers, right-click an empty area of the Printers folder and choose Server Properties.

Figure 7.13 Printer-dependent settings affect such things as color, tray selection, fonts, printer memory, and duplex printing.

Figure 7.14 You can compare the versions of the driver files with those of the latest drivers on the printer manufacturer's website.

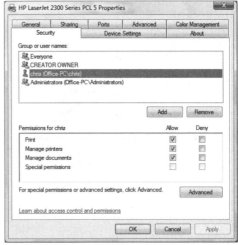

Figure 7.15 You can fine-tune the security settings for groups or individual users.

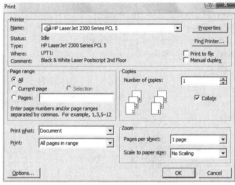

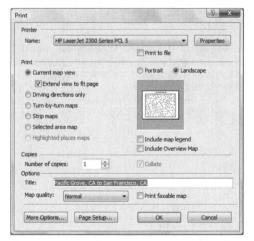

Figure 7.16 Print dialog boxes vary by program and printer model, but you'll find some common settings. Here are Print dialog boxes for Notepad (top), Microsoft Word (middle), and Microsoft Streets & Trips (bottom).

Printing Documents

After your printer is up and running, printing a document is simple.

To print a document:

1. Open the document that you want to print.

2. Choose File > Print, press Ctrl+P, or click the Print button on the toolbar.

3. In the Print dialog box (**Figure 7.16**), select the printer and print options.

   This dialog box varies by printer model and program, but the basic settings are:

   Printer. Choose a local or network printer from the drop-down list or scrolling panel. If you've created several icons for different modes of the same printer, choose among them here.

   Preferences/Properties. Click this to open the Preferences or Properties dialog box (**Figure 7.17**).

continues on next page

Figure 7.17 This dialog box, which varies by printer, lets you specify paper size (for multitray printers), orientation (landscape or portrait), print quality (dots per inch), and so on. These settings apply to the current printout, not to the printer in general.

PRINTING DOCUMENTS

Page Range. Specify which pages of the document to print. The Selection option isn't available if you didn't highlight any text before you opened the Print dialog box.

Copies. Specify the number of copies to print. You'll usually want to turn on collation for multiple copies.

Program-specific settings. Any program can add extra features to the Print dialog box.

4. Click Print or OK (or press Enter).

✔ Tips

■ During printing, a status icon appears in the notification area (**Figure 7.18**).

■ To bypass the Print dialog box and use the default printer and settings to print, click the Print button on the toolbar (**Figure 7.19**).

■ Internet Explorer's Print dialog box lets you print a webpage's frames and links (**Figure 7.20**).

■ You can print a document right from Windows Explorer or the desktop without opening it; right-click the document's icon and choose Print. Or drag a document's icon to a printer in the Printers folder, to a print spooler window, or to a desktop printer shortcut.

■ Most programs have additional print commands in the File menu or a toolbar. Page Setup sets margins, orientation, and other layout options. Print Preview shows how a document will look when you print it.

■ If you have a color printer, see the part about color management in "Configuring the Monitor" in Chapter 4.

■ If you're on a network domain, the Print dialog box has a Find Printer button that you can click to search the network for a particular printer.

Figure 7.18 Point to this icon (without clicking) to see how many print jobs are pending. Right-click it to open the Printers folder. Double-click it for the print queue.

Figure 7.19 The standard Print button on the toolbar (shown here in Microsoft Office) looks like this. This pop-up tip displays the destination printer and keyboard shortcut.

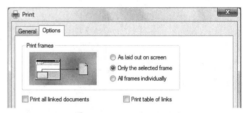

Figure 7.20 Click the Options tab in Internet Explorer's Print dialog box. If a webpage is divided into independent rectangular sections (*frames*), you can print them selectively. You also can print all the linked pages, as well as a table at the end of the printout that lists all the page's links.

Printer Troubleshooting

When you're having printer troubles, you want to determine whether the problem lies with the printer, Windows, or a particular program. Here are some things to check:

♦ Make sure that the printer is plugged in and turned on. Check for snug cable connections on the printer and computer ports.

♦ Remove the paper tray, pop the printer's lid, and check for a jammed paper path.

♦ Streaks of white or gray in printouts mean you're low on toner (ink).

♦ Turn the printer off and on to clear its memory.

♦ Create a file in Notepad, and print it from the command prompt. Choose Start > All Programs > Accessories > Command Prompt; type print *filename.txt* and then press Enter. (Replace *filename.txt* with the name of your homemade text file.) If the file prints, you have a software problem; otherwise, you have a hardware problem.

♦ Consult the printer's manual, and print a test page. (If the page prints, delete and reinstall the printer driver.)

♦ Try Windows' own troubleshooting pages: Choose Start > Help and Support, and search for *troubleshoot printer*.

♦ You may have a malfunctioning printer port (unlikely and somewhat complex).

PRINTING DOCUMENTS

Controlling Printouts

When you print a document, it's intercepted by an intermediary program, called the *print spooler,* on its way to the printer. The print spooler holds your documents (on disk or in memory) until your printer can accept them. The delay is short for text files but can be substantial for large graphics files. The spooler puts each document in a *print queue,* where it waits its turn to be printed. You can change the order of queued documents, pause or resume printing, or cancel specific print jobs. Spooling occurs in the background, so you can keep working in your program—or even quit the program—and documents still print.

To manage the print queue:

1. Choose Start > Control Panel > Hardware and Sound > Printers; then double-click a printer icon.

    or

    Double-click the notification-area printer icon (refer to Figure 7.18).

2. In the print-spooler window, do any of the following (**Figure 7.21**):

    To cancel printing a document, right-click the document name and choose Cancel.

    To cancel printing all documents, choose Printer > Cancel All Documents.

    To pause (or resume) printing a document, right-click the document name and choose Pause (or Resume).

    To pause (or resume) printing all documents, choose Printer > Pause Printing. (Choose it again to resume printing.)

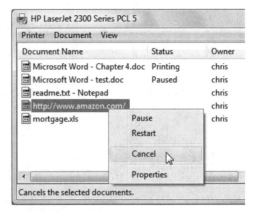

Figure 7.21 The print-spooler window lists the documents waiting to print. The first document is printing, the second one is paused, and I'm about to cancel the fourth one. If you're on a network, by default you can pause, resume, restart, or cancel your own documents but not those of other users.

To add another document to the queue, drag the document's icon from Explorer or the desktop into the print-spooler window.

To rearrange the printing order, right-click a document and choose Properties > General tab; then drag the Priority slider. Higher-priority documents print before lower-priority ones. (You can't reorder the documents by dragging them.)

✔ Tip

■ FinePrint ($50 U.S.; www.fineprint.com) is a printing utility that saves ink, paper, and time by controlsling print jobs. Some of its options: Print multiple pages on one sheet of paper, scale webpages to fit on standard paper sizes, and convert colored text to black and skip graphics (saving ink).

Your Printer Is Lying

Printer manufacturers make money on replacement ink (toner) cartridges like razor manufacturers make money on blades, so be skeptical of your printer's "low ink" warnings, especially with inkjet printers; some multicolor cartridges shut down if even only one color runs out. For laser printers, remove the cartridge and shake it for some extra life.

You have a few money-saving options:

◆ Try the free version of InkSaver (www.inksaver.com) to see whether it saves ink for your printer.

◆ You can buy low-priced inkjet cartridges at Amazon Imaging (www.amazonimaging.com), PrintPal (www.printpal.com), or other online stores. To find discount ink stores, visit www.buyinkcartridges.com.

◆ Don't throw out or return empty laser cartridges; look for a local computer-supplies store that will refill them (or ask an online store).

Be wary of printer-makers that use lockout codes to prevent cartridge refills. Some Hewlett-Packard printers shut down cartridges on a fixed date regardless of whether they're empty—or have even been used.

Scanning and Faxing

Windows Fax and Scan lets you send and receive faxes, fax or email scanned documents, and forward faxes as email attachments from your computer without an actual fax machine (**Figure 7.22**). You'll need a phone line and almost any dial-up modem. Even an old 33.6 Kbps modem can send a multipage fax in a minute or two.

Figure 7.22 Windows Fax and Scan, in fax view.

✔ Tips

■ Fax and Scan is included with only the Business and Ultimate editions of Vista. If you're using a Home edition, you still can scan documents or pictures with Windows Photo Gallery (Chapter 9).

■ Install the modem (a dial-up modem, not a DSL or cable broadband modem) *before* you start the setup process. Make sure that the modem is connected to a phone line and that the phone line is connected to a working jack. Almost all laptops have built-in modems; for desktops, you may have to install one. When you install a modem, Windows usually finds it and installs its drivers automatically. To install a modem manually, choose Start > Control Panel > Hardware and Sound > Phone and Modem Options > Modems tab > Add. You also can use the Modems tab to remove modems and set their properties.

■ You can't use a DSL or cable connection or a digital phone line for faxing.

■ If you don't want to buy a modem or tie up your phone line, consider one of the internet-based fax services listed at http://directory.google.com/Top/Computers/Internet/Internet_Fax/Services.

■ For viewing pictures and faxes, Photo Gallery Viewer, new in Vista, has replaced Windows XP's Windows Picture and Fax Viewer.

PC-Based Faxing Advantages

Faxing through Windows offers these advantages over a traditional fax machine:

◆ Conserves paper

◆ Saves money on paper and fax-machine cartridges

◆ Faxes documents without printing them

◆ Faxes from your computer via the File > Print command

◆ Lets you read incoming faxes onscreen or print them automatically

◆ Lets you manage incoming faxes as you would any other documents: read, save, or delete them, or attach them to email

◆ Generates cleaner, more legible faxes than ones sent via fax machine

SCANNING AND FAXING

To fax documents that aren't computer files, you'll need a scanner. You can connect a *local scanner* directly to your computer, or you can connect to a *network scanner* shared over a network. In both cases, you may need to install a driver or programs for using the scanner on your computer.

To install a local scanner:

◆ Follow the instructions that came with the scanner.

If the scanner has a USB connector (most scanners do), you usually can plug it into your computer, and Windows will install its driver and other software automatically. Some scanners make you install software *before* plugging in the USB connector; others make you turn on the scanner before or during installation.

To install a network scanner:

1. Make sure that your computer is connected to the network and that you know the name of the scanner you want to add.

   If the name isn't posted on the scanner itself, ask the scanner owner or your network administrator.

2. Choose Start > Network.

3. Locate the scanner, right-click it, and then choose Install.

4. Follow the onscreen instructions.

Organizing Scanned Documents

Scanned documents are stored in your Documents folder under Scanned Documents, where you can move or copy them like any other files.

To organize your scanned documents in Fax and Scan, you can create new folders in scan view. In the left pane, right-click a folder name and choose New Folder. To move a scanned document to a folder, right-click the document, choose Move to Folder (refer to Figure 7.24), and then select the target folder

If you use Windows Explorer to create, delete, move, or rename folders and documents in the Scanned Documents folder, the changes won't appear in Fax and Scan until you close and reopen the program, or collapse and expand the folder tree in the left pane in scan view.

✔ Tips

■ To remove a local scanner, unplug it from your computer at any time. To remove scanner drivers, choose Start > Control Panel > System and Maintenance > Device Manager (on the left). If a security prompt appears, type an administrator password or confirm the action. Double-click Imaging Devices, right-click the scanner name, and then choose Uninstall.

■ If Windows doesn't recognize your scanner, use the Scanner and Camera Installation wizard to install its drivers. Make sure that your scanner is connected and turned on; then choose Start > Control Panel > Hardware and Sound > Scanners and Cameras (**Figure 7.23**). Click Refresh if your scanner isn't in the list. If it still isn't listed, click Add Device and follow the onscreen instructions. If a security prompt appears, type an administrator password or confirm the action.

You can scan a document by using the software that came with your scanner or by using Fax and Scan.

To scan by using Fax and Scan:

1. Make sure that your scanner is connected to your computer and turned on.

2. Place a document on the scanner or the scanner's document feeder.

3. Choose Start > All Programs > Windows Fax and Scan (**Figure 7.24**).

4. Choose Scan (at the bottom of the left pane) > New Scan (on the toolbar) > Profile list > Documents.

Figure 7.23 Scanners and Cameras helps you install older scanners and cameras that Windows doesn't recognize.

Figure 7.24 Windows Fax and Scan, in scan view. You can rename, delete, and manage individual scans by using the shortcut menu.

SCANNING AND FAXING

Table 7.2

Image-File Formats	
FORMAT	**DESCRIPTION**
Bitmap	Windows bitmap (.bmp) images tend to be large because this format can't be compressed. BMP is almost always the wrong choice for scanned documents and photos.
JPEG	Joint Photographic Experts Group (.jpg/.jpeg) files are highly compressed and an excellent choice for scanning photos, particularly if you're going to post them on the web. But the JPEG process sacrifices image detail permanently during compression. In most cases, the loss is invisible for onscreen viewing.
PNG	Portable Network Graphics (.png) files, which all modern browsers support, is patent free and license free, and it retains all detail during compression.
TIFF	Tagged Image File Format (.tif) files are compatible with most image-editing programs, even ancient ones. TIFF is a good choice for scanning text documents and grayscale images. TIFF's compression, like PNG's, preserves detail but results in larger files than JPEG. You can scan multiple pages into a single TIFF file; Windows Fax and Scan uses TIFF to send and receive faxes.

5. Change the default settings for scanning a document if desired.

6. Click Preview to see how a document will appear when scanned.

7. Change your scan settings if desired. You can drag the cropping handles to resize the image.

8. Click Scan to scan the document. When the scan completes, Fax and Scan displays the document to view and manage.

✔ Tips

- To configure scanner routing and settings, use the commands in the Tools menu.

- If you're scanning a page with more than one picture, you can save each picture as a separate file by checking Preview or Scan Images As Separate Files.

- To forward scanned documents automatically to an email address or a network folder, choose Tools > Scan Routing.

- Faxes are sent in black and white at a default resolution of 150 × 150 dpi, which any scanner can manage.

- Scanning software usually lets you choose an image format for your scan. **Table 7.2** describes the common formats. If you save an image in the wrong format, you can open it in Paint and save it in another format by choosing File > Save As. To open Paint, choose Start > All Programs > Accessories > Paint.

SCANNING AND FAXING

Before you can send or receive faxes, you must connect to a fax modem (or a fax server on your network) and configure Fax and Scan.

To connect to a fax device for the first time:

1. Choose Start > All Programs > Windows Fax and Scan.

2. Choose Fax (at the bottom of the left pane).

3. Click New Fax (on the toolbar).

4. Follow the onscreen instructions (**Figure 7.25**).

✔ Tip

- To set up your computer to send faxes only, click I'll Choose Later; I Want to Create a Fax Now (**Figure 7.26**).

To configure Fax and Scan:

1. Choose Start > All Programs > Windows Fax and Scan.

2. Choose Fax (at the bottom of the left pane).

3. Choose Tools > Fax Settings.

   If a security prompt appears, type an administrator password or confirm the action.

4. On the General tab, select your fax modem; set it to send, receive, or both; and specify whether you'll answer incoming faxes manually or automatically (**Figure 7.27**).

5. Click More Options.

Figure 7.25 The Fax Setup wizard appears the first time you use Fax and Scan in fax view. To start the wizard manually, choose Tools > Fax Accounts > Add.

Figure 7.26 If you choose the last option here, you'll be able to send faxes but not receive them, and you won't see a security prompt.

Figure 7.27 You can set up Fax and Scan to only send faxes, only receive them, or both.

Figure 7.28 The TSID is mandatory in some cases. This identification information usually appears in the header area of a received fax and serves to identify the sending fax machine. Some fax-routing software depends on TSIDs to determine where to direct incoming faxes. The CSID is displayed on the sending fax machine.

6. Set TSID (Transmitting Subscriber Identification) and CSID (Called Subscriber Identification) to your business name and fax number, and choose whether you want to print or save backup copies of incoming faxes in addition to the ones that Fax and Scan saves automatically in its Inbox (**Figure 7.28**).

7. Click OK to return to the Fax Settings dialog box.

8. On the Tracking tab, specify when and how you want to be notified about the progress of a fax.
   Click Sound Options if you want audio indicators as well as visual ones.

9. On the Advanced tab, set the fax-transmission behavior, including where to store incoming and outgoing faxes, whether to include a cover sheet with outgoing faxes, automatic redialing attempts (for when a fax doesn't go through the first time), and times of day for discount calling.

10. On the Security tab, review or set the security settings for faxing and fax setup.

11. Click OK (or Apply).

✔ Tips

- To set additional options, choose Tools > Options.

- Cover pages help when you fax to big institutions where the fax might be misrouted. Fax and Scan has a few built-in cover pages that work fine, but you can design your own: Choose Tools > Cover Pages. To set the information that cover pages display, choose Tools > Sender Information. The fields all are optional, but include enough for the recipient to contact you if a fax doesn't go through completely.

To send a fax from Fax and Scan:

1. Choose Start > All Programs > Windows Fax and Scan.

2. Choose Fax (at the bottom of the left pane).

3. Click New Fax (on the toolbar).

4. Create a new fax by using the options in the New Fax window; then click Send (**Figure 7.29**).

   The Fax Status Monitor automatically displays the progress of the fax (**Figure 7.30**).

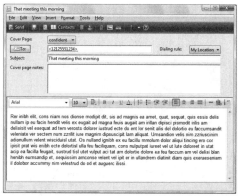

Figure 7.29 The New Fax window offers a complete set of editing, formatting, and other options. Use the toolbar options to attach a file or insert text and pictures from other files to send with your fax.

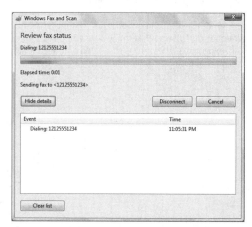

Figure 7.30 Click View Details to see the detailed status of each outgoing fax; click Hide Details if you prefer Windows to do its faxing less conspicuously. A pop-up message appears in the notification area when a fax is sent successfully (or fails).

Figure 7.31 To fax a document by using a program other than Fax and Scan, you "print" the document to a fax printer. A Fax icon appears in the printer list of every program's Print dialog box. The document is converted to a TIFF (.tif) file so that it can be sent as an attachment to a fax.

To send a fax from another program:

1. Open the file that you want to send as a fax.

2. Choose File > Print (or press Ctrl+P).

3. In the Print dialog box, click the Fax icon or choose Fax from the printer list; then click Print or OK, or press Enter (**Figure 7.31**).

   Fax and Scan opens a new fax with your file attached (refer to Figure 7.29).

4. Specify the recipient fax numbers, cover page, and other options in the New Fax window; then click Send.

   The Fax Status Monitor automatically displays the progress of the fax (refer to Figure 7.30).

✔ Tips

■ To send a fax to more than one person, type the recipients' fax numbers in the To box, separated by semicolons (;). To choose recipients from your Windows Contacts folder, click To and then double-click each contact in the list. Make sure that you've saved your recipients' fax numbers in the contact information (see "Managing Your Contacts" in Chapter 15).

■ The Cover Page drop-down list shows the built-in cover pages and any custom pages you've created.

■ If the Dialing Rule drop-down list is set to (None), type the recipient's fax number as it should be dialed. (Parentheses, commas, and hyphens are ignored.) To use a Dialing Rule, choose one from the list or choose New Rule to create one. You also can create dialing rules by choosing Start > Control Panel > Hardware and Sound > Phone and Modem Options > Dialing Rules tab.

■ To attach a document or picture to a fax, drag the file to the New Fax window. Attachments are converted to TIFF images (.tif files) so that they can be received by any fax device. (The original file isn't changed.)

■ If your recipient uses a stand-alone fax machine (one not connected to a computer), each page of your fax—including any attachments—will be printed in order when the fax is received. If the recipient uses Windows Fax and Scan or a similar fax program, your fax will be received as a TIFF (.tif) file that can be viewed onscreen and treated like any other file.

■ To fax or email a scanned file in Fax and Scan, choose Scan (at the bottom of the left pane), and click the file in the list of scanned files. On the toolbar, click Forward As Fax or Forward As Email. To scan a document and attach it to a fax, choose File > New > Fax from Scanner.

■ The Fax printer appears by default in the Printers folder. Choose Start > Control Panel > Hardware and Sound > Printers (**Figure 7.32**).

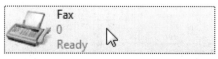

Figure 7.32 Fax appears in every program's Print dialog box because the Printers folder contains a generic fax driver. You can double-click this icon to open Fax and Scan, but there's not much more to do with it than inspect its properties.

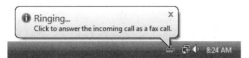

Figure 7.33 If you're expecting a fax, click this message. Fax Monitor (refer to Figure 7.30) appears and downloads the fax. If you're expecting a person to call, just pick up the phone, and this message disappears. If you miss this notification, quickly open Fax and Scan before the phone stops ringing, and in Fax view, click Receive a Fax Now (on the toolbar)

To receive a fax, you must have chosen to receive them in the Fax Setup wizard (refer to Figure 7.26) or checked Allow the Device to Receive Fax Calls in the Fax Settings dialog box (refer to Figure 7.27). Faxes received in Automatic answer mode (best for dedicated fax lines) appear in the Fax and Scan Inbox. Use Manual answer mode if your computer and telephone share a line that you use mostly for talking.

To receive a fax manually:

1. When the phone rings, click the pop-up message in the notification area (**Figure 7.33**).

2. To view the received fax, look in Fax and Scan's Inbox, discussed next.

To manage and view faxes:

1. Choose Start > All Programs > Windows Fax and Scan.

2. Choose Fax (at the bottom of the left pane).

3. In the left pane, expand the Fax folder if necessary.

   Fax contains the following subfolders:

   Incoming contains faxes that you're receiving now.

   Inbox contains faxes that you've received.

   Drafts contains faxes that you're still working on and aren't ready to send.

   Outbox contains faxes that Fax will send later or that failed to go through.

   Sent Items contains faxes that you've sent successfully.

continues on next page

SCANNING AND FAXING

4. Click the folder that you want.

5. In the right pane, click a fax and choose a toolbar command, or right-click it and choose a shortcut-menu command (refer to Figure 7.22).

✔ Tip

- The Preview pane (below the list of faxes in the right pane) shows the first page of the selected fax. To open the fax, double-click it. Use the scroll and zoom controls to view it.

SETTING UP HARDWARE

8

In the broadest sense, *hardware* is your computer and whatever connects to it; everything else is software. Windows generally uses the term to refer to a *peripheral*—nowadays usually called a *device*—which is any part of a computer other than the processor (CPU), motherboard, and memory (RAM and ROM). Your monitor, mouse, keyboard, hard disks, scanner, and printer are devices, as are digital cameras, MP3 players, backup drives, video recorders, external speakers, USB flash drives, and personal digital assistant (PDA) synchronization cradles.

Windows treats any gadget connected to your PC as a device. The software that controls it is called its *device driver* or simply *driver.* A driver mediates communications between a device and Windows.

Connecting Devices to Your Computer

When you install a new device for your computer, you'll either connect it to a port on the front or back of the computer, or insert it into a slot inside the computer case. The port or slot provides the channel that the computer and device use to exchange data.

Ordinarily, there's more to installing a device than just connecting it, but I cover connecting here and the larger process of installing in the next section.

New-computer manuals usually contain diagrams labeling the PC's internal slots and back-panel connectors. Look in the manual for the *motherboard*, also called the *mainboard* or *desktop board* (**Figure 8.1**).

Table 8.1 lists the hardware you need for various tasks.

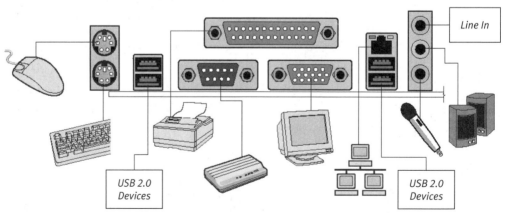

Figure 8.1 Here's an example back-panel diagram from an Intel reference. Your computer manual should have a similar diagram and a diagram of the computer's internal slots.

Line In

USB 2.0 Devices

USB 2.0 Devices

Table 8.1

Hardware Needed for Various Tasks

To	You Need
Rip or burn a disc	For ripping: a CD or DVD drive. For burning: a CD or DVD recorder. See "Burning CDs and DVDs" in Chapter 5 (data discs) and "Ripping CDs to Your Hard Drive" in Chapter 10 (music discs).
Scan documents	A scanner or an all-in-one printer/scanner/fax. See "Scanning and Faxing" in Chapter 7.
Send or receive faxes	A dial-up modem. See "Scanning and Faxing" in Chapter 7.
Transfer photos to your PC	A digital camera and USB cable or a memory-card reader. See "Importing Photos to Your Computer" in Chapter 9.
Transfer video to your PC	A digital video camera and a USB port or IEEE 1394 (FireWire) port. See "Importing Content" in Chapter 11.
Use the internet	For a dial-up connection: a dial-up modem (preferably 56K). For a broadband connection: a DSL or cable modem. Add a router for security. See Chapter 12.
Set up a network	For a wired connection: a network adapter, Ethernet cables, and a switch or hub. For a wireless connection: an 802.11 wireless adapter and an access point. See Chapter 18.
Videoconference	A webcam. (Some digital cameras have webcam mode.)
Listen to audio	A sound card or integrated audio, and speakers or headphones. See "Configuring Sound and Audio Devices" in Chapter 4.
Listen to radio	A radio tuner card.
Watch TV	A TV tuner card.
Input with handwriting	A Tablet PC with a stylus (or a graphics tablet).

Buying Hardware

Windows Vista probably will work with any hardware that worked with Windows XP or 2000, and perhaps with Windows NT, 98, or Me. But if you can't get your hardware to work with Vista—because Vista refuses or doesn't recognize the drivers, and the manufacturer hasn't updated them—you have to buy a new gadget.

Microsoft maintains the Windows Marketplace Tested Products list at http://testedproducts. windowsmarketplace.com. It's a complete reference for hardware (and software) products that have been tested for Windows compatibility. I don't find this list to be all that useful, because just about every product that you can buy today—listed or not—works under Windows. When manufacturers design their products, they're aware that Windows runs on 95% of PCs.

I get hardware-buying advice from www.hardwareguys.com, which makes reliable make-and-model recommendations. The site's authors also have written a few hardware books. For some hardware (like dial-up modems and Ethernet cards), it doesn't much matter what brand you get. For pricier items, do a little research. (For CD/DVD burners, for example, I pay extra for Plextor drives because I've found that they ruin fewer discs.)

External devices

External devices—ones that you can connect without opening your PC's case—plug into *ports* on the computer's front or back panel. **Table 8.2** lists the common PC ports and connections. If your PC doesn't have a particular port, you must install an expansion card to get it.

Table 8.2

Ports and Connections	
PORT	DESCRIPTION
Parallel (DB-25)	A long, narrow, female port with 25 holes along 2 rows. Windows calls it an *LPT port*. If your printer doesn't plug into a USB port, it plugs into this port (usually called a *printer port*). Older backup, tape, CD, and other external drives use this port too. USB connections have replaced parallel connections in newer hardware.
Serial	A short, slightly D-shape male port with 9 pins along 2 rows. Windows calls it a *COM port*. Serial devices are rare nowadays. You might find a serial connector on an old mouse, external modem, or serial printer. USB connections have replaced serial connections.
PS/2	A small, round, female port with six holes. If your mouse and keyboard don't plug into USB ports, they plug into two PS/2 ports. The ports usually are color-coded: purple for keyboards and green for mice. Or look for small pictures of a mouse and a keyboard, each next to its proper port. USB has mostly replaced PS/2.
USB (Universal Serial Bus)	A small, thin, rectangular port that accepts almost all Plug and Play devices: mice, USB flash drives, external drives, scanners, digital cameras, MP3 players, keyboards, printers, Bluetooth adapters, and so on. Most PCs have at least two USB ports, but you can buy an internal or external USB *hub* if you need extra ports. USB ports are *hot-pluggable*, allowing you to connect and disconnect devices without shutting down your PC; Windows automatically loads or unloads the drivers as needed. USB ports can provide power as well as data to the devices they connect. USB 2.0 equipment is much faster than USB 1.1 equipment.
IEEE 1394 (FireWire)	A small, rectangular, very fast port with a tapered (>-shape) plug. These ports are ideal for video, external disk, multiplayer gaming, and network devices. Like USB, IEEE 1394 is Plug and Play–compliant and hot-pluggable, and can provide power to peripherals. You can buy an internal or external hub to add IEEE 1394 ports to your computer.
Video (VGA)	A rectangular, female port with 15 holes along 3 rows. Laptop computers use this port to connect external monitors.
Ethernet (RJ-45)	A jack (which looks like a wide telephone jack) for Ethernet and network connections. If your computer doesn't have an RJ-45 jack, buy a network interface card (NIC) to add one.
Modem (RJ-11)	A ordinary telephone jack that lets you run a telephone line from the wall to your computer for faxing or dial-up internet connections. Laptops, but not desktops, usually have built-in RJ-11 jacks. If you need one, buy a 56K modem card.
Sound	A row of small circular holes for connecting external speakers, headphones, microphones, and audio sources. Most PCs also have built-in sound ports, but adding a good sound card gives you high-quality surround sound.
S-Video	A small, circular, female port for connecting projectors, TVs, and VCRs.
Infrared (IrDA)	A small red lens on laptops that uses line-of-sight infrared light to transfer data from the computer to a similarly equipped device (such as an infrared PDA or printer) without cables.

If you set up your own computer, you're familiar with ports because the monitor, keyboard, mouse, and printer all have cables or adapters that connect to ports. Different shapes for different port types make it hard to plug a cable into the wrong port, but examine the plug and port, and don't force a connection; you'll bend the pins.

To connect an external device:

◆ If the device is hot-pluggable (USB or IEEE 1394), simply plug the device's cable or adapter into the appropriate port.

or

If the device isn't hot-pluggable, turn off the computer and the device, plug the device's cable into the appropriate port, and then turn on the computer and device.

✔ Tips

■ Some PC also have built-in slots for reading digital-camera memory cards.

■ If you want to add both USB and IEEE 1394 ports to your PC, save some money and buy an (internal or external) hub that has them both.

Removing Hardware Safely

A small icon (▣) appears in the notification area when a USB, IEEE 1394, or other hot-pluggable removable-storage device is plugged into your PC. If no data is being transferred between the device and the computer, you can unplug the device at will. Usually, a light on the device or an onscreen warning signals whether data transfer is active. USB flash drives have an activity light that blinks during read–write operations, for example.

If you want to be extra safe when you remove a device (make sure that an external drive's disks have stopped spinning, for example), you can stop the device before unplugging it:

1. Right-click the notification-area icon and choose Safely Remove Hardware.

2. In the dialog box that appears, select the device in the list; then click Stop.

3. Click OK in the confirmation dialog box.

The notification-area icon disappears, and it's safe to unplug the device.

CONNECTING DEVICES TO YOUR COMPUTER

Internal devices

Internal devices are connected inside your PC's case. Storage devices such as CD, DVD, floppy, tape, backup, and hard drives are mounted on stacked shelves, called *bays,* at the front of the case. Printed circuit boards with edge connectors—such as sound cards, video adapters, graphics accelerators, internal modems, Ethernet (network) adapters, and USB hubs—are called *expansion boards* or *cards.* These cards plug into *expansion slots* (or simply *slots*) on the main circuit board (*motherboard*). **Table 8.3** lists the common PC slots. You must open your computer's case to see which slots are empty.

Each type of slot has a different shape and color, so you're unlikely to insert a card into the wrong slot. Inserting a card into a slot takes a little courage and practice. You must seat the card firmly and accurately by using neither too much force nor too little.

Table 8.3

Slots	
SLOT	DESCRIPTION
PCI	A white-cased socket about 3.25 inches (8.25 cm) long, with a white crossbar about three-quarters of the way down the slot. PCI (Peripheral Component Interconnect) slots, developed by Intel but supported by all manufacturers, are the most common type.
PCIe	PCI Express, invented in 2004 by Intel, is based on PCI but is much faster. Vista supports PCIe software and hardware. Over time, PCIe will replace PCI and AGP. Almost all new high-end graphics cards from ATI and NVIDIA use PCIe.
ISA	A black-cased socket about 5.25 inches (13.3 cm) long, with a black crossbar about two-thirds of the way down the slot. Some computers include both ISA (Industry Standard Architecture) slots for older, slower devices and PCI slots for modern ones.
AGP	A brown-cased slot about 3 inches (7.6 cm) long, with a brown crossbar about one-third of the way down the slot. AGP (Accelerated Graphics Port) is based on PCI but gives 3D graphics cards faster access to main memory than PCI. A PC has only one AGP port, occupied by a video card or accelerated graphics card.
PCMCIA (PC Card)	A slot on the side or back of a laptop computer that accepts a metal *PC Card* about the size of a credit card. A PC Card adds a particular feature to a laptop: a modem, Ethernet port, wireless antenna, or extra memory, for example. PC Cards are Plug and Play–compliant and hot-pluggable, and can provide power to peripherals.

✔ Tips

■ Before touching the motherboard or handling a card outside its protective packaging, touch a grounded metal surface (such as the computer case or a pipe) to discharge static electricity.

■ Plugging a card into an expansion slot connects it to the *bus*—the shared collection of hardware conductors that allows computer components to exchange data.

■ PC Cards are hot-pluggable, so you don't have to power down your laptop to insert them.

To connect an expansion card:

1. Shut down Windows, turn off the computer, and unplug the power cord.

2. Remove the computer's cover.

3. Remove the cover plate of an empty slot (to let the card's ports protrude from the computer case).

4. Seat the card in the slot firmly, according to the manufacturer's instructions.

5. Replace the screw that held on the cover plate, tightening it through the hole in the bracket on the back of the card.

6. Replace the cover, reconnect the power cord, and turn on the computer.
   Windows will detect the new card after it starts.

CONNECTING DEVICES TO YOUR COMPUTER

Installing a New Device

Almost all devices made since 1995 are *Plug and Play* (PnP) devices, which means that you can install (plug in) and use (play with) them immediately—no configuration needed. To work properly, Plug and Play requires:

- A Plug and Play–compliant operating system, which Vista is.

- A device that identifies itself to Windows and that lets Windows configure it and install its drivers, which almost all devices do.

- A Plug and Play–compatible system startup chip on the motherboard (called the *BIOS*). Any computer with enough horsepower to run Vista has PnP BIOS.

The port or slot that a device plugs indicates its compatibility:

- All USB, IEEE 1394 (FireWire), Bluetooth, and PCMCIA (PC Card) devices are Plug and Play.

- All but the oldest PCI and parallel devices are Plug and Play.

- No ISA or serial devices are Plug and Play. Most such devices are quite old. If their manufacturers still exist, check their websites for a Windows Vista/XP/2000/NT driver. If there's no such driver, you may be out of luck.

Installing Old Hardware

If you have an old piece of hardware that doesn't support Plug and Play, you can try to install it by using the Add Hardware wizard (a carryover from earlier Windows versions). To start the wizard, choose Start > Control Panel and type *add hardware* in the Search box. In the results list, click Install Drivers for Older Devices with Add Hardware Wizard. If a security prompt appears, type an administrator password or confirm the action. Follow the onscreen instructions.

Welcome to the Add Hardware Wizard

This wizard helps you install driver software to support older devices that do not support Plug-and-Play and which are not automatically recognized by Windows.

You should only use this wizard if you are an advanced user or you have been directed here by technical support.

 If your hardware came with an installation CD, it is recommended that you click Cancel to close this wizard and use the manufacturer's CD to install this hardware.

To continue, click Next.

Installing a New Device

Figure 8.2 When you connect a device, look for pop-up messages in the notification area (top). You might see several such messages, ending with the "success" message (bottom). If you do, you're in luck; the new hardware is ready to use.

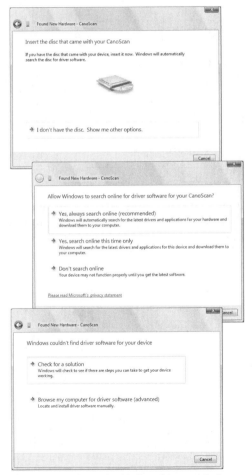

Figure 8.3 Windows tries hard to make your device work. You may see any of these pages when stepping through the Found New Hardware wizard.

Windows stores thousands of drivers on your hard drive and gets more regularly via Windows Update, so Windows usually detects your device when you connect it and installs the proper driver automatically. If Windows doesn't have the right driver, you can install it from either the CD that came with the device or a driver file that you downloaded from the manufacturer's website. The following installation instructions are generic; you should always favor the instructions that came with your device.

To install a new device:

1. Run the device's setup program (if any).

   Many new devices come with a Setup CD that includes driver files. Run this program *before* you connect the device so that Windows can copy the drivers to your hard drive and have them handy for later in the installation.

2. Check the device's installation instructions to determine whether it should be turned on before, during, or after connection and installation.

3. Connect the device to your computer, as described in the preceding section.

   If Windows can install the device driver automatically, you'll be notified that the device is ready to use (**Figure 8.2**). You're done.

   or

   If Windows can't find the right driver, it will prompt you to insert a disc containing driver software for the device. Follow the onscreen instructions (**Figure 8.3**).

✔ Tips

- If Windows can't install your device, you get **Figure 8.4**. Try the manufacturer's website for updated drivers.

- Windows stores drivers in \Windows\System32\DriverStore\FileRepository.

- A downloaded driver usually comes as a self-extracting executable (.exe) file or a compressed (.zip) file that you must decompress before installation. Look for setup instructions on the webpage or, after unzipping, in a read-me file.

- To control how Windows Update finds drivers, choose Start > Control Panel > System and Maintenance > System (or press Windows logo key+Break); then click Advanced System Settings (on the left). If a security prompt appears, type an administrator password or confirm the action. Choose Hardware tab > Windows Update Driver Settings (**Figure 8.5**).

- If, when you plug in a device, AutoPlay opens a program that you don't want to use, choose Start > Control Panel > Hardware and Sound > AutoPlay (**Figure 8.6**).

- To use a game controller with an older game that doesn't recognize it, choose Start > Control Panel > Hardware and Sound > Game Controllers > Advanced.

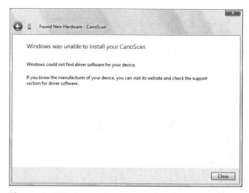

Figure 8.4 Windows gives up.

Figure 8.5 You need an internet connection for Windows Update to check for the latest drivers. See also "Updating Windows" in Chapter 13.

Figure 8.6 If you never want to see the AutoPlay dialog box, choose Take No Action next to the device. To choose an action each time you plug in a device, choose Ask Me Every Time. To have a program open automatically each time, choose the program.

Unsigned Drivers

A *signed driver* is one that has a digital signature to certify that it works properly and hasn't been tampered with since its creation. Driver signing combats the sloppily written, system-destabilizing, third-party drivers that plagued earlier Windows versions. The most stable systems run only signed drivers. When you try to install an *unsigned driver,* Windows displays one of the following messages:

◆ **Windows can't verify the publisher of this driver software.** This driver either lacks a digital signature or has an unverified one. Install this driver only if you trust the source.

◆ **This driver software has been altered.** This driver might contain a virus or malicious software. Don't install it unless it came straight from the manufacturer's CD or website.

◆ **Windows cannot install this driver software.** Windows maintains its own list of drivers that it refuses to install because they are known to cause stability problems. Go to the manufacturer's website, and look for an updated driver.

Driver Information (.inf) Files

When Windows searches for a driver, it's actually looking for an information (.inf) file, which lists the driver files to use and registry entries to make. Windows veterans may recognize that .inf files and initialization (.ini) files are quite similar. But .inf settings are subtler than .ini settings. Never edit an .inf file to try to solve your driver problems.

Hardware setup software can include an .inf file; a .sys file (the actual driver); and subordinate library (.dll), help (.hlp), Control Panel (.cpl), and webpage (.htm) files. Some device drivers are *only* .inf files. A monitor, for example, may be set up by a single .inf file listing the valid resolutions, refresh rates, and other display settings.

Setting up Bluetooth Devices

Bluetooth is a wireless technology that provides short-range (about 30 feet) radio links among desktops, laptops, PDAs, mobile phones, printers, digital cameras, mice, keyboards, and other Bluetooth-equipped devices. It aims to eliminate cable clutter while simplifying communications, sharing, and data synchronization between computers and devices. Bluetooth doesn't need a line-of-sight connection, so you can, say, listen to MP3 music from the laptop in your briefcase on a hands-free headset.

Bluetooth is an open standard (that is, it's not owned by Microsoft or anyone else); see www.bluetooth.com for more information.

To set up a Bluetooth device:

1. Plug the Bluetooth adapter into a USB port on your computer.

2. Turn on the device, and make it *discoverable* (check the device's instructions or the manufacturer's website).

3. Choose Start > Control Panel > Hardware and Sound > Bluetooth Devices.

   If a security prompt appears, type an administrator password or confirm the action.

4. Click Add and follow the onscreen instructions.

   The Add Bluetooth Device wizard finds Bluetooth devices near you.

✔ Tips

- To change the settings of a Bluetooth device, click it in the Bluetooth Devices window and then choose Properties.

- To install a Bluetooth printer, see "Installing a Printer" in Chapter 7.

- To troubleshoot Bluetooth devices, choose Start > Help and Support, type `troubleshoot bluetooth` in the Search box, and then press Enter. In the results list, click Troubleshoot Problems with Bluetooth Enabled Devices.

Bluetooth Passkeys

A *passkey* (or *passcode*) is a number that associates your computer with a Bluetooth device. For security, Bluetooth devices (except mice and a few other exceptions) make you use a passkey to ensure that your computer is connecting to your device and not someone else's nearby.

Passkey exchange (or *pairing*) gets Windows to positively identify the device that you want to connect to. With some devices, you do this by running the Add Bluetooth Device wizard and typing your passkey when prompted. Other devices use a different method; check the device's instructions.

If a passkey is listed in the device's documentation, use that one. If not, the Add Bluetooth Device wizard can generate a passkey for you or let you create your own (up to 16 characters—the longer the better).

Managing Device Drivers

Device Manager is a powerful tool that lets you inspect, manage, and troubleshoot drivers for the hardware already installed on your computer. It lists every device in or attached to your system in an Explorer-like tree (**Figure 8.7**).

To open Device Manager:

◆ Choose Start > Control Panel > System and Maintenance > System > Device Manager (on the left).

   or

   Press Windows logo key+Break and then click Device Manager (on the left).

   or

   Choose Start, type device manager in the Search box, and then press Enter.

   or

   Press Windows logo key+R; type devmgmt.msc and then press Enter.

   If a security prompt appears, type an administrator password or confirm the action.

✔ Tips

■ Choose View > Show Hidden Devices to display legacy (non–Plug and Play) devices.

■ To expand all branches of the Device Manager tree, select the top-level (root) entry and press * (in the numeric keypad).

Figure 8.7 Click a plus (+) symbol to expand a category branch and list all installed devices that fit into that category. Right-click a particular device for a shortcut menu, or double-click it to show its Properties dialog box.

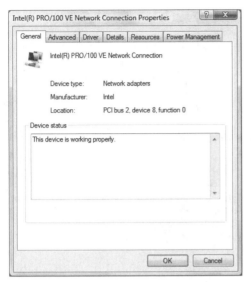

Figure 8.8 The General tab tells you whether a device is working properly.

Figure 8.9 The Driver tab tells you the driver's provider (which, unhelpfully, is its distributor, not its manufacturer), its date and version, and whether it has a signature.

Like any other file, a device driver has properties that determine its behavior.

To show a device's properties:

◆ In Device Manager, right-click the device and choose Properties (refer to Figure 8.7).

or

Double-click the device's name.

The tabs of the Properties dialog box vary by device. The standard ones are:

General shows the name, type, physical location, and status of the device (**Figure 8.8**).

Advanced and **Details** (if they appear) contain device-specific properties.

Driver shows information about the currently installed driver and has buttons that let you manage it (**Figure 8.9**).

Resources lists the system hardware resources (such as interrupts and memory range) that the device uses.

✔ Tip

■ Some devices install their own Control Panel extensions, which let you view or change additional properties.

You can use Device Manager to install a driver that's newer than the current one. But newer doesn't always mean better or more stable. If a driver isn't broken, don't update it unless updating improves things.

To update a device driver:

1. In Device Manager, right-click the device whose driver you want to update and choose Update Driver Software (refer to Figure 8.7).

2. Follow the onscreen instructions (**Figure 8.10**).

✔ Tip

■ Some devices have proprietary update programs that don't support the Update Driver Software wizard.

If a fresh driver causes more problems than it solves (not uncommon for unsigned drivers and prerelease drivers), the driver rollback feature lets you uninstall and replace it with the previous one.

To roll back a device driver:

◆ In Device Manager, right-click the device whose driver you want to roll back and choose Properties > Driver tab > Roll Back Driver (refer to Figure 8.9).

✔ Tips

■ The rollback feature is available only if the driver has been updated since Windows was installed.

■ When you install a prerelease (*beta*) driver, you're helping the software developer. Don't install a beta driver unless it fixes a flaw that's bugging you.

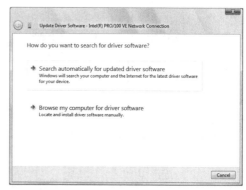

Figure 8.10 You can locate the new driver manually or let the Update Driver Software wizard look for it on your computer and on the internet (if you're connected).

You can remove a driver permanently and erase all the configuration settings for its device. Generally, you uninstall a driver to reclaim system resources after you've removed hardware from your PC. But you can remove a troublesome driver completely, to scrap it or to reinstall it from scratch.

To uninstall a device:

◆ In Device Manager, right-click the device whose driver you want to uninstall and choose Uninstall (refer to Figure 8.7).

✔ Tips

■ You can uninstall a Plug and Play device's driver only if the device is plugged in; otherwise, the driver isn't in memory. To reinstall the driver without unplugging, in Device Manager, choose Action > Scan for Hardware Changes.

■ If Device Manager displays icons for duplicate devices (such as two mice), uninstall *both* of them; then restart your PC. If you uninstall only one device, Windows detects it again when you restart. Click No if Windows asks you to restart after you uninstall the first duplicate; restart manually after removing the second.

Troubleshooting Hardware

If you install and uninstall enough hardware on your system, you're going to have to deal with error messages and system conflicts. When trouble comes, the first step is to review Windows' troubleshooting articles: Choose Start > Help and Support, type troubleshoot in the Search box, and then press Enter. Scan the results list for a topic that pertains to your problem.

No luck? Use Device Manager: Double-click a device to show its Properties dialog box and then click the General tab. If the device isn't working, the Device Status box (refer to Figure 8.8) shows an error message and code. For an explanation of the problem and advice on how to fix it, go to http://support.microsoft.com/?kbid=125174, "Explanation of Error Codes Generated by Device Manager."

If you want to turn off a device without the hassle of removing it, you can disable it. Windows ignores a disabled device's existence and releases the system resources that it uses. You also can disable and enable devices to resolve device conflicts. If two devices are competing for the same resource, disable one of them, restart, and then see whether the other one starts working.

To disable a device:

◆ In Device Manager, right-click the device that you want to disable and choose Disable (refer to Figure 8.7).

A down arrow appears on the disabled device's icon (**Figure 8.11**).

✔ Tip

■ To enable a disabled device, repeat the procedure. (The Disable command becomes the Enable command.)

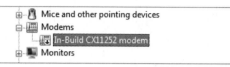

Figure 8.11 A down arrow means that a device isn't working, either because you've disabled it or because it's incompatible with Windows or your PC. Check the Resources and General tabs of the Properties dialog box for an explanation of the problem.

DIGITAL PHOTOS

Windows comes with programs and features
that make it easy to import and organize
digital photos on your computer. Windows
Photo Gallery, new in Vista, copies photos
from your camera to your computer, and lets
you view, organize, find, retouch, print, and
email them. You also can watch and organize
videos in Photo Gallery. In Windows Explorer
(Chapter 5), you can treat photos like any
other files: delete, move, copy, rename, and tag
them. Icons and pop-up tips let you see a
miniature preview of a photo's actual image
without having to open it.

Importing Photos to Your Computer

After connecting your camera to your computer, you can use the Importing Pictures and Videos wizard to import and save pictures on your computer.

Most cameras come with a cable that plugs into your computer's USB port (see "Connecting Devices to Your Computer" in Chapter 8). Windows includes and installs drivers for most camera models, sparing you the chore of manual setup. If your camera is too old (pre-2000) to understand Windows' automated import features, buy an external *memory-card reader* that plugs into a USB port. Insert a memory card into the reader, and Windows treats it like a floppy disk (**Figure 9.1**).

Multislot readers can handle Secure Digital (SD), SmartMedia, CompactFlash, MultiMedia, Memory Stick, xD, and other formats. Some computers—particularly those sold as "multimedia" machines—have built-in slots for memory cards.

Figure 9.1 If you connect a digital camera to your computer, the top icon appears in the Computer window (Start > Computer). If you connect a memory-card reader, the bottom icon appears.

Figure 9.2 A camera's properties include its model, manufacturer, and remaining battery life.

✔ Tips

■ If you have an older camera, you might need to install updated software provided by the camera's manufacturer. Check the manufacturer's website for the latest drivers and installation instructions. (For general information about drivers, see Chapter 8.)

■ If you use a card reader to import your photos, you do so without draining your camera's battery, dealing with connection cables, or installing additional software.

■ You can use a scanner to convert conventional photographs to digital pictures. In Windows Photo Gallery (covered in the next section), choose File > Import from Camera or Scanner. To set up a scanner, see "Scanning and Faxing" in Chapter 7.

■ If you're browsing in Internet Explorer (Chapter 14) and see a photo that you want to save to your computer, right-click it and choose Save Target As. (Every browser has a similar command.)

■ In the Computer window, you can double-click a camera or memory-card icon to browse its files and folders, just as you can for any other storage device. This lets you see your photos before you import them. For information about a camera, right-click its icon and choose Properties (**Figure 9.2**).

To import photos to your computer:

1. Make sure that the memory card is in the camera, connect your camera to your computer with the USB cable, and turn on the camera; if the camera has a special connection mode, switch to it.

   or

   Remove the memory card from your camera and slide it into the card reader.

2. In the AutoPlay dialog box that appears, click Import Pictures Using Windows (**Figure 9.3**).

   Windows finds the photos on your memory card (**Figure 9.4**).

   After Windows finds your photos, it starts the Importing Pictures and Video wizard, which asks whether you want to assign a tag to the photos (**Figure 9.5**).

3. To add a tag, type its name in the Tag These Pictures (Optional) box.

   If the photos don't have any single thing in common, leave the box blank. (You always can add or change tags later; see "Finding Photos" later in this chapter.)

Figure 9.3 Your AutoPlay choices may differ depending on the photo-management software—which may have come with your camera—installed on your computer. Check Always Do This for This Device if you don't want to see this dialog box every time you plug in your camera.

Figure 9.4 This message appears while Windows scans your camera for photos. It's not actually importing yet—just looking.

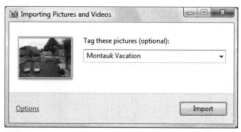

Figure 9.5 A tag is a word or a short phrase that describes the group and makes your photos easier to find and organize. See "To add tags to photos" later in this chapter.

Figure 9.6 You can set the default import options here or in Windows Photo Gallery (see the next section).

Figure 9.7 As Windows imports your photos, you can check Erase After Importing if you want to delete the photos from your memory card after importing finishes, clearing space on the card for new photos. You can click Cancel to stop copying at any time.

Figure 9.8 Windows Photo Gallery opens automatically to display your photos after you import them.

4. *(Optional.)* Click Options if you want to change the import settings; then click OK (**Figure 9.6**).

5. Click Import.

A progress window appears (**Figure 9.7**). After your photos are imported, Windows Photo Gallery opens and displays them (**Figure 9.8**).

✔ Tips

■ By default, Windows saves the imported photos in your Pictures folder (Start > Pictures), in a subfolder named for the current date and the tag you assigned them (if any). Each picture is given a filename that includes the tag and a serial number—for example, `Maui 001.jpg`, `Maui 002.jpg`, and so on.

■ Unlike earlier versions of Windows, Vista doesn't let you choose which photos to import. Instead, Vista detects your newest photos automatically and doesn't import duplicates. If you've already imported all the photos on your camera, Windows displays **Figure 9.9** and stops; otherwise, it imports only the subset of photos that isn't already on your computer. To review and delete imported photos, use Windows Photo Gallery.

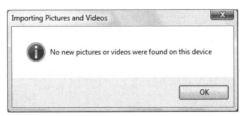

Figure 9.9 Windows won't import copies of photos that you've already imported.

If the AutoPlay dialog box (refer to Figure 9.2) doesn't appear, AutoPlay might be turned off. Instead, you can import your photos by using Windows Photo Gallery, or you can change the AutoPlay options.

To import photos by using Windows Photo Gallery:

1. Choose Start > All Programs > Windows Photo Gallery.

   or

   Choose Start, type photo gallery in the Search box, and then press Enter.

2. Click File (on the toolbar) > Import from Camera or Scanner.

3. In the Import Pictures and Videos dialog box (**Figure 9.10**), choose your camera in the list and click Import.

   The Importing Pictures and Videos wizard starts (refer to Figure 9.5).

4. Follow the onscreen instructions.

Figure 9.10 If your camera or memory card isn't listed, click Refresh.

Figure 9.11 AutoPlay determines what happens when you connect your camera to your computer.

Figure 9.12 This wizard helps you install drivers for older cameras.

To configure AutoPlay:

1. Choose Start > Control Panel > Hardware and Sound > AutoPlay.

or

Choose Start, type autoplay in the Search box, and then press Enter.

2. Scroll to the entry for your camera and choose an action from the drop-down list (**Figure 9.11**):

To import photos automatically without being prompted, choose Import Pictures Using Windows.

To open a folder window showing the photos on the camera's memory card (before importing), choose Open Device to View Files Using Windows Explorer.

To suppress the AutoPlay dialog box, choose Take No Action.

To choose an action each time you plug in the camera, choose Ask Me Every Time.

3. Click Save.

✔ Tips

■ You also can open the AutoPlay window by clicking the AutoPlay link in Figure 9.3 or Figure 9.6.

■ If Windows doesn't recognize your camera, use the Scanner and Camera Installation wizard to install its drivers. Make sure that your camera is connected and turned on; then choose Start > Control Panel > Hardware and Sound > Scanners and Cameras. Click Refresh if your camera isn't in the list. If it still isn't listed, click Add Device, and follow the onscreen instructions (**Figure 9.12**). If a security prompt appears, type an administrator password or confirm the action.

Getting Started with Windows Photo Gallery

You can use Windows Photo Gallery to view, organize, find, retouch, print, and email your photos. It opens automatically after you import a batch of photos, but you can open it at any time.

To open Photo Gallery:

◆ Choose Start > All Programs > Windows Photo Gallery (**Figure 9.13**).

   or

   Choose Start, type photo gallery in the Search box, and then press Enter.

   or

   Double-click an associated image file in Windows Explorer or on the desktop.

✔ Tip

■ Photo Gallery replaces Windows XP's Picture and Fax Viewer.

Figure 9.13 By default, Photo Gallery shows all the photos and videos in your Pictures folder. In general, use Photo Gallery to view, tag, find, print, and email photos; use the Pictures folder to organize your photo folders and files. Changes made in one appear in the other.

Figure 9.14 The Original Pictures setting applies to photos that you edit by using the Fix command (see "Touching up Photos" later in this chapter). If you trash the original, you can't undo your changes and are stuck with the (possibly unsatisfactory) copy. Set this option to Never or to a long period (6 months or 1 year) unless you're short on disk space.

Figure 9.15 To see only the descriptive text in the pop-up tip, without the bulky preview photo, uncheck Show Picture and Video Previews in Tooltips.

To change the default options for Photo Gallery:

1. In Photo Gallery, choose File (on the toolbar) > Options.

2. Click the General tab (**Figure 9.14**), and set the following options:

   Turn on or off the large previews that appear you hover your mouse pointer over a photo (**Figure 9.15**).

   Choose how often to move originals to the Recycle Bin.

   Choose whether Windows checks periodically for updates to Photo Gallery, or click Check for Updates to check now.

   continues on next page

3. Click the Import tab (**Figure 9.16**), and set the following options:

In the Settings For drop-down list, specify whether the options apply to cameras, CDs and DVDs, or scanners.

Click Browse if you want Windows to put imported photos somewhere other than your Pictures folder. (Usually, you don't, for the reasons given later in this section.)

Choose the names that Windows gives the target folder and each photo file. The tag is the text that you assigned in the Importing Pictures and Video wizard (refer to Figure 9.5).

Check or uncheck the other options as desired.

To revert to the factory-installed options, click Restore Defaults.

4. Click OK.

Figure 9.16 You can set import options for cameras, CDs and DVDs, and scanners independently.

Image File Types

Photo Gallery can show photos (and videos) with these file types: BMP, JPEG, JFIF, TIFF, PNG, WDP, ASF, AVI, MPEG, and WMV. The most common file types for photos are JPEG and TIFF (you'll rarely need other types).

JPEG (.jpg/.jpeg) uses compression to create high-quality photos with small file sizes, so they're great for email and web display. When you save a JPEG file in an image-editing program, you can choose the compression level, which trades off file size for image quality. Don't use too high a level; if you do, the image quality will be poor.

TIFF (.tif) files, unlike JPEGs, suffer no loss of quality when you save, so they have enough resolution for, say, printing 8 × 10 enlargements. Unfortunately, they're sometimes too big for email, and web browsers won't display them.

To convert a photo to a different type, open it in Paint (Start > All Programs > Accessories > Paint), choose File > Save As, and then select a type from the Save As Type drop-down list.

Better cameras can save photos in RAW format. RAW files are uncompressed, very large, and professional quality. Each camera manufacturer uses a unique and proprietary RAW file type. (Nikon RAW files end with .nef, for example, and Canon uses .crw or .cr2.) Photo Gallery may be able to display RAW photos, depending on what software updates are installed. RAW editing usually is done in Adobe Photoshop via the Camera Raw plug-in. Some cameras can save RAW files in Digital Negative (.dng) format, a royalty-free and publicly available format designed by Adobe.

The default storage location for photos (and videos) is your Pictures folder and its sub-folders. You can store your them elsewhere, but Pictures is easy to open from the Start menu and Explorer's Navigation pane. It's also where Photo Gallery and most wizards and photo-editing programs assume you will open and save your photos.

To open the Pictures folder:

◆ Choose Start > Pictures (**Figure 9.17**).

or

Choose Start, type `pictures` in the Search box, and then press Enter.

or

In any folder window, click Pictures in the Navigation pane.

✔ Tip

■ If Pictures doesn't appear in your Start menu, right-click Start, choose Properties > Customize, and then choose Display As Link (below Pictures).

Figure 9.17 Windows Photo Gallery and the Pictures folder can do some of the same things. To see a larger view of a picture, click the picture and then click Preview (on the toolbar). You can use other toolbar buttons to print photos, see a slide show, and send photos in email.

Photo Gallery automatically shows all the photos (and videos) in your Pictures folder, but you can add and remove other folders where you store photos. You also can add individual photos without adding an entire folder.

To add a folder to Photo Gallery:

1. In Photo Gallery, choose File (on the toolbar) > Add Folder to Gallery.

2. Click the folder containing the photos that you want to add; then click OK (**Figure 9.18**).

   The folder appears in the Navigation pane, below Folders.

✔ Tips

■  If you double-click a photo file in Windows Explorer, you can add its containing folder to Photo Gallery by clicking Add Folder to Gallery on the toolbar of the preview window.

■ Don't add a top-level or system folder to Photo Gallery. Adding a local disk from the Computer window, for example, makes Photo Gallery look at the entire hard disk and run slowly.

Figure 9.18 Adding a folder to Photo Gallery is convenient if you store some of your photos somewhere other than Pictures.

Figure 9.19 You can't remove a subfolder without removing its top-level folder as well. Here, for example, removing Top-Level Folder also removes its three subfolders. But you can't remove Subfolder 1, 2, or 3 individually without removing all the other subfolders *and* Top-Level Folder.

To add a single photo to Photo Gallery:

1. Open the folder containing the photo that you want to add to Photo Gallery.

2. Open Windows Photo Gallery.

3. Drag the photo from the folder to the Photo Gallery window.

   Windows copies the photo to your Pictures folder and adds it to the gallery.

✔ Tip

■ If you add a file other than a photo or video, it's copied to Pictures but not displayed in Photo Gallery.

Removing a folder from Photo Gallery doesn't delete that folder—just stops Photo Gallery from displaying it. (The folder and its files remain intact on disk.) You can remove folders that you have added but not Photo Gallery's default folders. You can't remove individual photos, either. You can *delete* them, however.

Deleting a photo or folder in Photo Gallery is the same as deleting it in Windows Explorer: It's moved to the Recycle Bin. To delete a photo or folder, right-click it and choose Delete.

To remove a folder from Photo Gallery:

◆ In Photo Gallery, in the Navigation pane, right-click the folder that you want to remove and choose Remove from Gallery (**Figure 9.19**).

Viewing Photos

Windows Photo Gallery is the easiest way to browse and view photos on your computer. By default, Photo Gallery displays all the photos and videos in your Pictures folder unless you've added other folders or photos (see "Getting Started with Windows Photo Gallery" earlier in this chapter).

To see all photos:

◆ In the Navigation pane, click All Pictures and Videos (**Figure 9.20**).

✔ Tip

■ To see only photos that you've imported in the past 30 days, click Recently Imported in Figure 9.20.

To see the photos in a particular folder:

◆ In the Navigation pane, expand Folders and click the desired folder (**Figure 9.21**).

To see a larger preview of a photo thumbnail:

◆ For a medium preview, hover the mouse pointer over a thumbnail (refer to Figure 9.15).

 or

 For a large preview, double-click a thumbnail (or press Enter if the thumbnail is selected) (**Figure 9.22**).

 When you're zoomed in, you can drag any part of the photo to move it around.

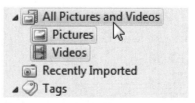

Figure 9.20 To see all photos or all videos, but not both, click either Pictures or Videos.

Figure 9.21 Photo Gallery shows photos in the selected folder and all its subfolders.

Figure 9.22 To return to thumbnail view, click Back to Gallery (on the toolbar) or press Backspace.

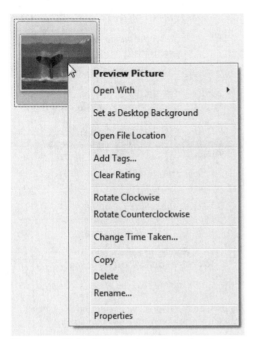

Figure 9.23 Right-clicking a photo shows familiar file commands plus some photo-specific ones. Right-click an empty area to change the details displayed, group or sort photos, or show a table of contents for fast navigation.

✔ Tips

■ A quick way to change the view is to click the menu button to the left of the Search box (below the toolbar).

■ For managing photo files, Photo Gallery has a lot in common with Windows Explorer (Chapter 5). You can click to select individual photos, for example, or Ctrl+click or Shift+click to make multiple selections. Many of the same mouse maneuvers and keyboard shortcuts apply (see "Using Keyboard Shortcuts" later in this chapter). You can right-click a selection or an empty area to display a shortcut menu (**Figure 9.23**).

■ To use a photo as your desktop background, right-click it and choose Set As Desktop Background (refer to Figure 9.23).

■ To use your photos as a screen saver, see "Setting the Screen Saver" in Chapter 4.

■ At the top of every group of photos is a horizontal separator that you can click to select or deselect all the photos in the group. Click the small arrow at the right end of the separator to expand or collapse the group.

continues on next page

VIEWING PHOTOS

■ **Burn** ▾ To burn photos to a data disc, select them and then click Burn > Data Disc (on the toolbar). For details, see "Burning CDs and DVDs" in Chapter 5.

■ **Figure 9.24** describes the controls at the bottom of the Photo Gallery window. When you start a slide show, your screen fills with a self-advancing sequence of photos and video. Before starting the show, select the items that you want to see. (If nothing is selected, the show includes all items in the current view.) The slide-show controls appear when you move your mouse. You also can use the left- and right-arrow keys to move backward and forward, or click the photo itself to advance. To stop the show, click Exit or press Esc.

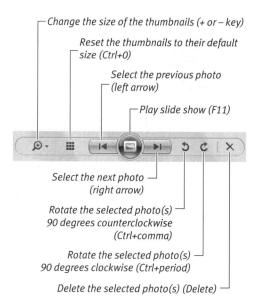

Change the size of the thumbnails (+ or – key)

Reset the thumbnails to their default size (Ctrl+0)

Select the previous photo (left arrow)

Play slide show (F11)

Select the next photo (right arrow)

Rotate the selected photo(s) 90 degrees counterclockwise (Ctrl+comma)

Rotate the selected photo(s) 90 degrees clockwise (Ctrl+period)

Delete the selected photo(s) (Delete)

Figure 9.24 If you forget what a button does, hover your mouse pointer over it for a pop-up tip.

Other Viewers

Windows Photo Gallery is quick and convenient, but if you manage a lot of photos, look into Picasa (free; http:// picasa.google.com), IrfanView (free; www.irfanview.com), ACDSee Photo Manager ($40 U.S.; www.acdsee.com), ThumbsPlus ($50 U.S.; www.cerious.com), or FlipAlbum ($40 U.S.; www.flipalbum.com).

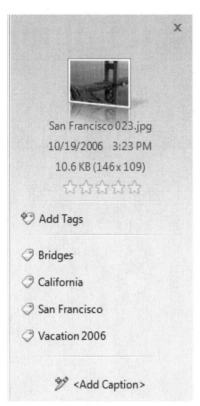

San Francisco 023.jpg

10/19/2006   3:23 PM

10.6 KB (146 x 109)

☆☆☆☆☆

🏷 Add Tags

🏷 Bridges

🏷 California

🏷 San Francisco

🏷 Vacation 2006

🏷 <Add Caption>

Figure 9.25 The Info pane shows a preview, filename, date taken, tags, and other information about the selected photo(s). To close the pane, click the close button in the top-right corner.

Figure 9.26 Your camera labels photos with the date they were taken. The photos taken during the selected period appear in Photo Gallery.

Finding Photos

If you've accumulated thousands of photos on your computer, you can use the search and filtering tools in Windows Photo Gallery to find them individually or in groups with something in common. You can find photos by using the information associated with them, including the file and folder names set during import, tags and other properties that you or Windows assign, and the dates photos were taken.

To see information about photos:

◆   **Info**   Click Info (on the toolbar), or press Ctrl+I or Alt+I.

The Info pane appears on the right side of the window (**Figure 9.25**).

To find photos by date

◆ In the Navigation pane, expand Date Taken, and click a year, month, or day (**Figure 9.26**).

✔ Tip

■ To change the date photos were taken, select one or more photos, and then click the date and time fields in the Info pane (refer to Figure 9.25). You also can right-click a photo or selection and choose Change Time Taken.

Finding photos is easier if you apply tags and ratings to them. Later, you can use the Navigation pane or the Search box to filter the photos by tags or ratings.

Tags are meaningful words and phrases that describe your photos. You may want to create separate tags to represent the location, people, or event represented by each photo.

You had your first chance to apply tags when you imported the photos (refer to Figure 9.5), but you can add more at any time. You can add tags to a single photo or to a bunch of them at the same time. To avoid backlogs, get into the habit of tagging photos immediately after you import them.

To add tags to photos:

1. Select the photos that you want to tag.

   You can tag several photos at the same time. To select adjacent items, click the first item; then Shift+click the last item. To select nonadjacent items, Ctrl+click each item.

2. In the Info pane, click Add Tags (refer to Figure 9.25).

3. Type the tag in the box and press Enter.

   The tag is added to all the selected photos. You can add as many tags as you want.

Figure 9.27 To add an existing tag to a picture, drag one or more pictures to the tag.

Figure 9.28 Nested tags work like folders with subfolders. You can expand and collapse a top-level tag to show or hide its subtags. Click a tag to see all the photos that are tagged with both that tag and any of its nested tags.

✔ Tips

- To delete a tag, right-click it in the Info pane and choose Remove Tag.

- In the Info pane, you also can add a caption (click Add Caption) and give a one- to five-star rating (click a star). To find photos by rating, expand Ratings in the Navigation pane and click a rating. Ctrl+click for multiple ratings.

- After you add a tag to a picture, the tag will be displayed in the Navigation pane (below Tags). To add an existing tag to photos without retyping, drag the photos to the tag in the Navigation pane (**Figure 9.27**).

- You can reorganize a long list of tags by nesting them in related groups. In the Navigation pane, drag a tag that you want to be nested, and drop it on the tag that you want to make the top-level tag (**Figure 9.28**).

- To create a nested tag when typing tags in the Info pane, use a slash (/). Type Animals/Mammals to add the Mammals tag nested below the Animals tag, for example. If the Animals tag doesn't already exist, it's created automatically.

- For general information about tagging, see "Tagging Files" in Chapter 5.

FINDING PHOTOS

To find photos by filename, tag, or caption:

◆ [Search 🔍] Click or tab to the Search box (or press Ctrl+E) and type text. You can type entire words or just the first few letters.

As you type, the photos are filtered to match your text.

✔ Tips

■ To cancel the search, press Esc, backspace over the search text, or click the close button (✖). The window goes back to its unfiltered state.

■ You can type a file extension—such as .jpg, .tif, or .wmv—to limit the results to certain file formats,

■ If your photos have obscure filenames, you can rename them all at the same time. Select the photos that you want to rename, right-click the photos, and then choose Rename. In the Info pane, type a new name in the name box and press Enter. Each photo is given the new name with a different serial number, like this: Paris 2007 (1).jpg, Paris 2007 (2).jpg, and so on.

■ For general information about searching, see "Searching for Files and Folders" in Chapter 5.

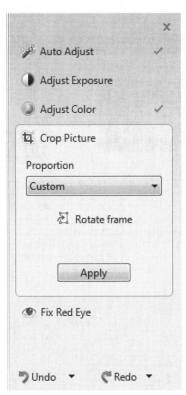

Figure 9.29 Click a button in the Fix pane to expand that section and make adjustments. To compare before-and-after changes, use the Undo and Redo buttons. To cancel all changes, click the triangle on the Undo button and choose Revert to Original (or press Ctrl+R). Photo Gallery keeps the originals for the period set in its Options dialog box (refer to Figure 9.14).

Touching up Photos

Windows Photo Gallery includes a few tools to touch up your photos.

To touch up a photo:

1. Select the photo that you want to touch up.

2. Click Fix (on the toolbar), or press Ctrl+F or Alt+X.

   The photo enlarges, and the Fix pane appears on the right side of the window (**Figure 9.29**).

3. Use the controls to make the following changes:

   Auto Adjust. Automatically optimize the photo's brightness, contrast, and color.

   Adjust Exposure. Manually adjust brightness and contrast.

   Adjust Color. Manually adjust color temperature, tint, and saturation.

   Crop Picture. Trim the photo to remove distracting elements, focus on one part of the scene, or change its proportions.

   Fix Red Eye. Remove the appearance of red eye caused by the flash reflecting off the subject's eyes.

4. To return to thumbnail view, click Back to Gallery (on the toolbar) or press Backspace.

✔ Tip

- You can edit photos in Paint or a third-party image-editing program; see "Using the Free Utility Programs" in Chapter 6.

TOUCHING UP PHOTOS

Printing Photos

If you have an inkjet or dye-sublimation printer, you can use Windows Photo Gallery to print high-quality color photos on special paper. (To install a printer, see Chapter 7.)

To print photos:

1. Select the photos that you want to print.

2. 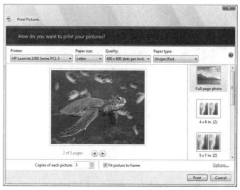 Click Print > Print (on the toolbar) or press Ctrl+P.

3. In the Print Pictures dialog box, select the printer, paper size, print quality, print style, number of copies to print, and other options (**Figure 9.30**).

4. Click Print to start printing.

✔ Tips

■ You also can print photos from the Pictures folder (choose Start > Pictures).

■ If you have a problem or questions about the print settings, click the Help button (●) in the top-right section of the Print Pictures dialog box.

■ Dedicated photo printers usually have built-in memory-card readers and small liquid-crystal display (LCD) screens so that you can print photos without using your computer.

Figure 9.30 The aspect ratio of a digital photo usually doesn't match the printed page, so your photos may have blank borders to ensure that they print in their entirety. Check Fit Picture to Frame to print without any borders (which may cut off parts of the photos).

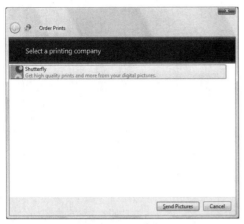

Figure 9.31 Printing companies that have made a deal with Microsoft are listed on this page. Companies may come and go over time.

Ordering Prints Online

Windows Photo Gallery walks you through getting digital photos printed via the internet. You select the photos to be uploaded (copied) to an online photo processor and then enter credit-card and shipping information. Your prints arrive by postal mail in about a week.

To order prints online:

1. Select the photos that you want to order.

2. Click Print > Order Prints (on the toolbar) or press Alt+P, O.

3. On the Select a Printing Company page, select the printing company that you want to use and click Send Pictures (**Figure 9.31**).

4. Follow the onscreen instructions to complete your order.

   The ordering pages vary by print company.

✔ Tips

- Your selected photos are sent to the printing company over the internet. If the photos reside on a camera, CD, USB flash drive, or an external device, don't disconnect or remove it from your computer until the upload completes.

- You also can take your camera's memory card to a camera store, pharmacy, retailer, or other store that offers digital-photo printing services. Some stores have self-serve photo kiosks.

ORDERING PRINTS ONLINE

Emailing Photos

A group of photos to be printed can be too large for emailing. You may have trouble sending photos if your (or your recipient's) ISP or mail service bounces attachments larger than 1 or 2 MB. Even if the transfer is successful, you may overload your recipients' inboxes and annoy them. Windows Photo Gallery solves this problem with image-shrinking tools.

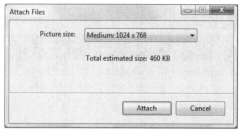

Figure 9.32 Making your photos smaller for email doesn't affect the size or quality of the originals; it simply resizes the email versions.

To email photos:

1. Select the photos that you want to send.

2. Click E-mail (on the toolbar) or press Alt+E.

3. In the Attach Files dialog box, choose a size from the Picture Size drop-down list (**Figure 9.32**).

4. Click Attach.

5. Finish composing the email message and send it (**Figure 9.33**).

✔ Tips

■ If you want to compress photos *without* emailing them, select the icons in the Attach header of the email message (refer to Figure 9.33) and drag them to the desktop or to any folder other than Pictures. Then close the email without saving.

■ Another way to share photos is to upload (copy) them to a photo-sharing website. Anyone you invite can view the photos on the site. Most sites are free, though some will delete your photos if you don't buy prints or gifts by a certain time. Some popular sites are www.flickr.com, www.smugmug.com, www.shutterfly.com, and http://photos.yahoo.com.

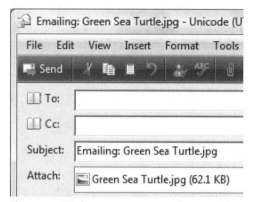

Figure 9.33 Windows opens a new email message in your preferred email program and attaches your photos to the message.

Using Keyboard Shortcuts

Table 9.1 lists the keyboard shortcuts for Windows Photo Gallery. **Table 9.2** lists keyboard shortcuts for watching videos in Photo Gallery.

Table 9.1

Photo Gallery Keyboard Shortcuts	
To	Press
Open the Fix pane	Ctrl+F
Print the selected picture	Ctrl+P
View the selected picture at a larger size	Enter
Open the Info pane	Ctrl+I
Rotate the selected photo(s) 90 degrees clockwise	Ctrl+period (.)
Rotate the selected photo(s) 90 degrees counterclockwise	Ctrl+comma (,)
Rename the selected item	F2
Search for an item	Ctrl+E
Go back	Alt+Left arrow
Go forward	Alt+Right arrow
Make thumbnails bigger	Plus key (+)
Make thumbnails smaller	Minus key (−)
Resize to best fit	Ctrl+B
Select the previous or next item or row	Arrow keys
Go to the previous screen	Page Up
Go to the next screen	Page Down
Select the first item	Home
Select the last item	End
Move the selected item(s) to the Recycle Bin	Delete
Delete the selected item(s) permanently	Shift+Delete
Collapse a node (in Navigation pane)	Left arrow
Expand node (in Navigation pane)	Right arrow

Table 9.2

Photo Gallery Video Keyboard Shortcuts	
To	Press
Move back one frame	J
Pause the playback	K
Move forward one frame	L
Set the start trim point	I
Set the end trim point	O
Split a clip	M
Stop and rewind back to the start trim point	Home
Advance to the next frame	Alt+Right arrow
Go back to the previous frame	Alt+Left arrow
Stop and rewind playback	Ctrl+K
Play from the current location	Ctrl+P
Move the start trim point	Home
Move to the end trim point	End
Seek to nearest split point before the current location	Page Up
Seek to nearest split point after the current location	Page Down

WINDOWS MEDIA PLAYER

10

Windows Media Player:

♦ Plays most of your digital media, including music, videos, CDs, and DVDs

♦ Acts like a digital jukebox that helps you find and organize digital media files

♦ Plays internet radio stations

♦ Rips tracks from audio CDs to your hard drive

♦ Burns music CDs

♦ Downloads songs to portable music players

♦ Lets you buy music and other media online

Windows Media Center

Windows Media Center (Start > All Programs > Windows Media Center), not covered in this book and not available in Vista business editions, is a home-entertainment hub that handles a variety of multimedia content. It can do many of the same things as Windows Media Player, plus it lets you watch live or recorded TV, capture HDTV from cable or satellite TV broadcasts, play on-demand games, listen to FM radio stations, and play digital media anywhere in your home (by using an extender or Xbox 360). It's designed to be viewed on a big screen from a distance of up to 10 feet and controlled by a remote control.

Getting Started with Media Player

Media Player is shown in **Figure 10.1**. You can hover your mouse pointer over any control for a pop-up tip. The interior section changes depending on the tab you've selected; Figure 10.1 shows the Library tab.

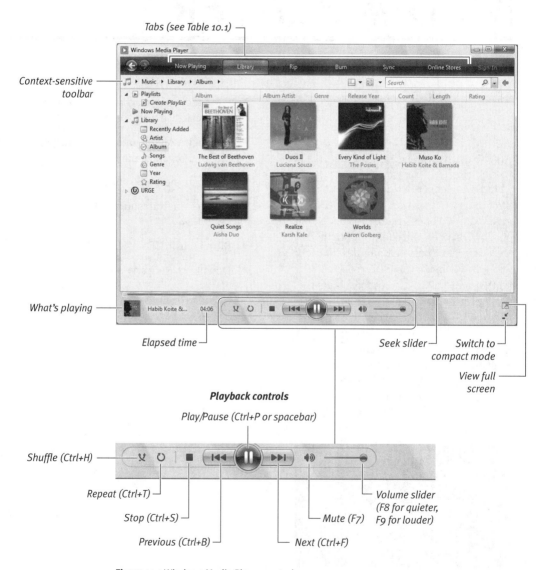

Figure 10.1 Windows Media Player controls.

Table 10.1

Media Player Tabs

Click	To
Now Playing	View a video, visualization, song list, or information about whatever is playing.
Library	Organize media files by using a Explorer-like interface or compile your media files into sets of favorites (playlists).
Rip	Copy (rip) songs from a music CD to your hard drive.
Burn	Create (burn) your own music CDs from the songs stored on your hard drive.
Sync	Transfer music and videos to a portable music or video player.
Online Stores	Visit online stores to browse or buy music, video, radio, audiobooks, and other content.

Figure 10.2 Double-clicking a file with any of the checked extensions opens Media Player. To change a file-type association, see "Associating Documents with Programs" in Chapter 6.

To start Media Player:

◆ Choose Start > All Programs > Windows Media Player.

or

Click the Media Player icon (▶) on the Quick Launch toolbar, located on the taskbar.

or

Double-click any associated media file.

or

Choose Start, type `media player` in the Search box, and then press Enter.

or

Press Windows logo key+R; type `wmplayer` and press Enter.

✔ Tips

■ Naturally, you need speakers or headphones to hear anything. If your computer doesn't have built-in sound support (look for a row of small circular ports), you can buy a sound card (cheap and easy to install). A pricier card plays surround sound and high-definition (HDCD) content. If you're buying speakers, get ones that come with a subwoofer.

■ Click the tabs to show the player's main features. See **Table 10.1** for a summary and later sections for details. As you switch between tabs and views, you can click the Back (Alt+Left arrow) and Forward (Alt+Right arrow) buttons (left of the tabs) to retrace your steps.

■ To see or set the file types that the player opens by default, choose Start > Control Panel > Programs > Default Programs > Set Your Default Programs > Windows Media Player > Choose Defaults for This Program (**Figure 10.2**). Check the box next to a file type to make Media Player its default player or uncheck it to use another player.

To use Media Player menus:

◆ To use a tab menu, click the down arrow on the bottom portion of a tab. You may have to hover the mouse pointer over a tab to make its arrow appear (**Figure 10.3, top**).

or

To show the classic menus as a shortcut menu, right-click an empty area near the tabs or playback controls (or press Alt) (**Figure 10.3, bottom**).

or

To toggle the classic menu bar on and off, press Ctrl+M.

✔ Tips

■ The playback controls shown in Figure 10.1 also are available in the Play menu.

■ Media Player is complex enough to get its own troubleshooting website. Choose Help > Troubleshooting Online. You also can use this menu to check for player updates.

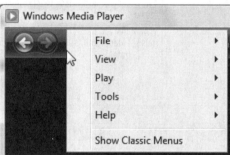

Figure 10.3 Menus keep out of the way until you summon them. The tab menus (top), new in Vista, are preferred, but you can use the classic menus (bottom) at any time.

QuickTime and Real

Media Player doesn't play a few of the most popular media formats: QuickTime (.mov and .qt) and RealMedia (.ra, .rm, .rv, .ram, and .rmvb). To play these files, you can download free players from Apple (www.apple.com/quicktime) and Real (www.real.com). I don't like either player for privacy reasons. Instead, search the web for *"QuickTime Alternative"* and *"Real Alternative"* (include the quotes) for players that are both free and nuisance free.

Figure 10.4 Normally, you'll want to play the music CD. You also can rip tracks to your hard drive (covered later) or open a standard folder window with an icon for each song.

Playing Music CDs

Playing a music CD on your computer isn't too different from playing it on a conventional CD player. You can play music while you're working with other programs.

You can set your CD (or DVD) drive's AutoPlay options to make Windows detect various discs when you insert them.

To play a music CD:

1. Insert a music CD into your computer's CD drive.

2. If Media Player is open already, the CD starts playing automatically.

   or

   If the AutoPlay dialog box appears (**Figure 10.4**), select Play Audio CD.

3. *(Optional)* Click the Now Playing tab to show artist, title, and track information.

✔ Tips

■ Use the playback controls to pause, play, skip or repeat tracks, and so on (refer to Figure 10.1). You can drag the Seek slider to move to a different place within the item that's playing.

■ If the player is minimized, you can use the player toolbar to perform basic play-back functions. To turn on the toolbar, right-click an empty area of the taskbar and choose Toolbars > Windows Media Player (**Figure 10.5**).

■ Media Player plays through the Now Playing playlist (**Figure 10.6**) in order, once, unless you click Shuffle (🔀 or Ctrl+H) to randomize the tracks or Repeat (🔁 or Ctrl+T) to play them forever. If the playlist is hidden, choose Now Playing tab menu > Show List Pane.

■ If your CD doesn't play automatically— or if something else plays—choose the drive that contains the disc from the Now Playing tab menu (refer to Figure 10.3, top).

■ To eject a CD, choose Play > Eject or press Ctrl+J. You also can use this com-mand to open and close the CD tray. If the library's Navigation pane is visible, right-click the disc and choose Eject. (Ctrl+J won't work if you have two or more CD or DVD drives.)

■ If the music skips too much (assuming that your CD is clean and unscratched), try switching to analog playback: Choose Now Playing tab menu > More Options > Devices tab; select your CD drive; click Properties; and then choose Analog (below Playback). If that doesn't work, go back to Digital.

Hide/show visualizations

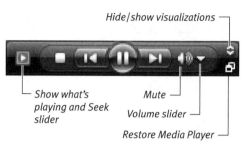

Show what's playing and Seek slider
Mute
Volume slider
Restore Media Player

Figure 10.5 When you've turned on the toolbar and minimized Media Player, the playback controls appear in the taskbar.

Violin Concerto ('L'estate', The Four Seasons)...

Vivaldi: The Four Seasons ▼	✕
Violin Concerto ('La Primavera', The ...	3:24
Violin Concerto ('La Primavera', The ...	2:38
Violin Concerto ('La Primavera', The ...	4:12
Violin Concerto ('L'estate', The Four ...	5:20
Violin Concerto ('L'estate', The Four ...	2:37
Violin Concerto ('L'estate', The Four ...	2:46
Violin Concerto ('L'autunno', The Fo...	4:46
Violin Concerto ('L'autunno', The Fo...	2:37
Violin Concerto ('L'autunno', The Fo...	3:22
Violin Concerto ('L'inverno', The Fou...	3:16
Violin Concerto ('L'inverno', The Fou...	2:26
Violin Concerto ('L'inverno', The Fou...	3:00

Figure 10.6 The playlist lists the CD's track names and durations. Point to a track for pop-up information, or right-click a track for properties and related commands. The drop-down list at the top (labeled with the album name) lets you change the playlist. Point to the album art for album information.

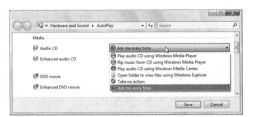

Figure 10.7 You can specify the action that Windows takes when you insert a specific type of disc, thus suppressing dialog boxes like Figure 10.4. Select Ask Me Every Time if you don't want Windows to do the same thing each time. Note that you also can set your DVD Movie action while you're here.

To configure AutoPlay:

1. Choose Start > Control Panel > Hardware and Sound > AutoPlay.

   or

   Choose Start, type `autoplay` in the Search box, and then press Enter.

   or

   Click the AutoPlay link in the AutoPlay dialog box (refer to Figure 10.4).

2. Scroll to an Audio CD entry and choose an action from the drop-down list (**Figure 10.7**).

3. Click Save.

Customizing the Now Playing Tab

The Now Playing tab has several panes that you can use to view visualizations, video, album art, audio and video controls, and the current playlist. **Figure 10.8** shows these panes, and **Table 10.2** describes them.

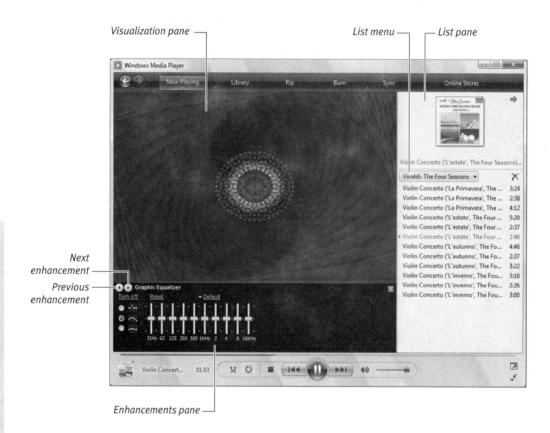

Figure 10.8 Now Playing panes and controls.

Table 10.2

Now Playing Panes	
PANE	DESCRIPTION
Visualization	Displays the current video or visualization that you're playing. If you're playing a video or DVD, rather than music, this pane appears automatically. This pane always appears when the Now Playing tab is active.
Enhancements	Contains several controls that you can use to adjust graphic-equalizer levels, video settings, audio effects, play speed, and the color of Media Player. You also can use this pane to share a streaming media clip with a friend. Figure 10.8 shows the graphic equalizer.
List	Displays the current playlist. For a CD, this pane displays the track names and durations. For a DVD, it displays the title and chapter names.

To show Now Playing:

◆ Click the Now Playing tab.

To show or hide the Now Playing panes:

◆ To toggle the Enhancements pane, choose Now Playing tab menu > Enhancements > Show Enhancements.

or

To toggle the List pane, choose Now Playing tab menu > Show List Pane.

✔ Tips

■ Right-click any pane to show its shortcut menu. In the List pane, right-click a specific item in the playlist.

■ To resize panes, drag the horizontal or vertical lines that separate them. The cursor becomes a double-headed arrow when you hover it over a separator line.

■ If you're connected to the internet, Media Player retrieves CD information and album art automatically. Press F5 to refresh the information in the panes.

CUSTOMIZING THE NOW PLAYING TAB

Viewing Visualizations

Media Player lets you "see" music with *visualizations*—splashes of color and shape that follow the music's beat. The Visualization pane displays the current visualization (refer to Figure 10.8 to see a visualization).

To view a visualization:

1. Play a song.

2. Click the Now Playing tab.

3. Choose Now Playing tab menu > Visualizations.

    or

    Right-click the Visualization pane.

4. Choose a visualization from the submenu or shortcut menu (**Figure 10.9**):

    Info Center View shows album and track details, gleaned from the internet.

    No Visualization blanks the Visualization pane.

    Album Art shows the song's album cover.

    Full Screen fills your screen with a current visualization.

    The other commands choose abstract visualizations.

✔ Tips

■ For full-screen visualizations, click Full Screen (▣), press Alt+Enter, or double-click the visualization. To return to normal, press Esc or repeat any of the full-screen shortcuts.

■ To set options for or remove visualizations, choose Now Playing tab menu > Visualizations > Options > Plug-Ins tab > Visualization (in the Category list) (**Figure 10.10**).

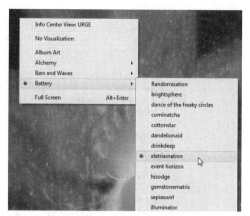

Figure 10.9 Media Player comes with scores of preinstalled visualizations, but you can download more from the internet: Choose Now Playing tab menu > Visualizations > Download Visualizations.

Figure 10.10 Choose a visualization in the right list and click Properties to set its options (if it has any). Click Remove to delete it. You can delete only visualizations that you've downloaded, not preinstalled ones.

Figure 10.11 A preview of the skin appears in the right pane.

Figure 10.12 Media Player in skin mode. You can change skins as often as you like, but you must be in full mode to do so.

- Right-click a skinned player to display its shortcut menu.

Changing Player Appearance with Skins

You can change Media Player's appearance by applying design schemes called *skins*. Each skin offers the basic playback and window controls; other features vary by skin. Play around to see which skin has what.

To apply a skin:

1. Choose View > Skin Chooser (press Alt if the View menu isn't visible).

2. Select a skin from the list (**Figure 10.11**).

3. Click Apply Skin on the toolbar (or press Alt+A).

When you apply a skin, the player's user interface is in *skin mode* (**Figure 10.12**, for example). You can return easily to *full mode*—the default state in which all features are displayed.

To switch modes:

- Press Ctrl+1 for full mode or Ctrl+2 or skin mode.

✔ Tips

- In Skin Chooser, click More Skins on the toolbar (or press Alt+S) to download skins from Microsoft's website.

- To delete a skin from the skins list, select it; then press Delete or click the red *X* in the toolbar. You can't delete the preinstalled skins.

- *Compact mode* shows only the basic controls. To use it, click the Switch to Compact Mode button (⬰) near the bottom-right corner of the player. Click it again for full mode.

- To make the player float over all other windows, choose Tools > Options > Player tab > check Keep the Player on Top of Other Windows > OK.

Shopping Online

If you're connected to the internet, you can use the online stores to buy digital media on the web. Each store is an independent website that offers content for purchase or by subscription.

To shop at an online store:

1. Choose View > Online Stores > Browse All Online Stores (press Alt if the View menu isn't visible).

   or

   Choose Online Stores tab menu > Browse All Online Stores (**Figure 10.13**). The actual text on the tab depends on the current store. It might read *URGE* or *Media Guide*, for example.

2. Click a category to see only the stores that sell the type of content that you're looking for, or click All Services to see all the stores.

3. Click a store and confirm that you want to visit its website.

4. When the store's site appears in the player, follow the store's onscreen instructions.

✔ Tips

■ Content from a store may be available only as long as you're registered with that store, and you won't be able to copy downloaded media files that have DRM (Digital Rights Management) safeguards. Learn about your digital rights at the Electronic Frontier Foundation (EFF) website, www.eff.org.

■ To access your downloaded content, click the Library tab and use the Navigation pane.

Figure 10.13 The online stores that appear on this page have signed a deal with Microsoft. Stores may come and go.

Figure 10.14 The left side of the Internet Radio page has three expandable sections: Featured Stations (starter stations chosen by Microsoft), My Stations, and Recently Played Stations. The right side contains genre links and a search feature.

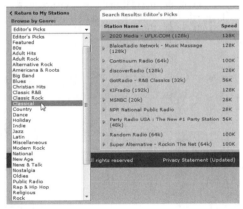

Figure 10.15 You can browse stations around the world by genre. Hidden by the expanded drop-down list are two search boxes that let you find stations by keyword (enter a talk-show host's name, for example) or zip code (U.S. only). Advanced search criteria such as country, language, and call sign also are available.

Listening to Radio Stations

Radio stations around the world stream their signals over the internet. Media Player, an internet connection, and speakers will bring in these stations without a radio, extra software, or extra hardware.

To listen to an internet radio station:

1. Choose View > Online Stores > Media Guide (press Alt if the View menu isn't visible).

   or

   Choose Online Stores tab menu > Media Guide.

   The actual text on the tab depends on the current store. It might read *URGE* or *Media Guide*, for example.

2. When the WindowsMedia.com page appears, click Radio (near the top of the page) and then click Internet Radio.

3. To listen to a featured, preset, or recently played radio station, click the green arrow next to the station's name; then click Play (**Figure 10.14**).

   or

   To find a radio station, click Find More Stations (**Figure 10.15**).

✔ Tips

- To add stations to a preset list to access quickly, click the desired station's name to expand it (refer to Figure 10.14) and then click Add to My Stations. The station is added to the My Stations section of the Internet Radio page.

- The Speed column (visible in Figure 10.15) lists the stations' streaming speeds. Faster means better sound. Don't listen to a 100K station with a dial-up modem.

- To save streaming music to your hard drive, try Super Mp3 Recorder ($30 U.S.; www.supermp3recorder.com).

Ripping CDs to Your Hard Drive

Media Player lets you *rip* (copy) an entire album or selected tracks from a music CD to your hard drive. Each track winds up as a double-clickable file in your Music folder (Start > Music). Disk-based music means no more CD hunts; you can use your CD drive for other things while you play music files. You can organize your tracks into custom playlists, burn them on custom music CDs, or copy them to your portable music player.

Before you copy your first CD, set the default options.

To set options for ripping CDs:

1. Choose Tools > Options > Rip Music tab (press Alt if the Tools menu isn't visible).

   or

   Choose Rip tab menu > More Options > Rip Music tab (**Figure 10.16**).

2. Click Change if you want to store the ripped tracks somewhere other than your Music folder.

3. Click File Name to specify which details to include in the filenames (**Figure 10.17**).

4. Choose a music format from the Format drop-down list.

   Usually, you'll want to create MP3 (.mp3) files rather than Windows Media Audio (.wma) files—Microsoft's proprietary, more compact, and vastly less popular format. If you choose the WMA format, uncheck Copy Protect Music so you can transfer tracks to other computers and portable music players.

Figure 10.16 You almost always want to rip MP3 files. The link at the bottom of this dialog box launches a webpage that compares MP3 and WMA (from Microsoft's point of view).

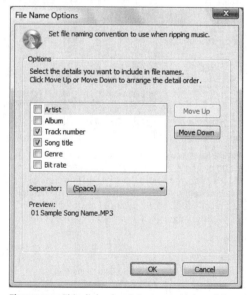

Figure 10.17 This dialog box lets you embed useful information such as the track number, song title, and bit rate in the track's filename.

5. Specify the player's rip behavior for when you insert a blank CD and whether you want to eject the CD when ripping completes.

For more control, uncheck Rip CD When Inserted.

6. Drag the Audio Quality slider to set the bit rate.

Set the slider in the middle of the range for a good sound-quality/file-size trade-off, or experiment with different settings to see what suits your ears.

7. Click OK.

✔ Tips

■ Many of these options also are available on the Rip tab menu.

■ A little hunting around on the internet should find you a way to rip CDs that give you copying troubles.

To rip tracks from a music CD:

1. Make sure that you are connected to the internet.

When connected, the player retrieves CD information from Microsoft's Windows Media database and adds it to the files during ripping. (If the information is wrong or missing, you can add or edit it after ripping).

2. In Media Player, click the Rip tab.

continues on next page

RIPPING CDs TO YOUR HARD DRIVE

3. Insert a music CD into your computer's CD drive.

By default, the player starts ripping the CD automatically when you are in the Rip tab (or switch to it after the CD is inserted).

or

 If you unchecked Rip CD When Inserted in the Options dialog box (refer to Figure 10.16), the player starts playing the CD on insertion (unless you've changed your AutoPlay setting too). You can play and copy tracks at the same time, but click the Stop playback control if you prefer silence while you rip. To start ripping, click Start Rip (or press Alt+S).

4. *(Optional)* As the player begins ripping the CD, uncheck the boxes for the tracks that you don't want to rip (**Figure 10.18**).

or

 Click Stop Rip (or press Alt+S), make your selections, and click Start Rip to restart ripping. (Partially ripped tracks aren't saved.)

By default, Rip appears with all tracks checked or, if you ripped them previously, unchecked. The topmost check box selects or clears all the tracks.

The Rip Status column shows the progress as tracks are copied to your hard drive.

5. When ripping completes, click the Library tab to see and play the tracks (see "Organizing Your Library" later in this chapter).

Figure 10.18 To rename a song, right-click it and choose Edit. (You also can change the artist and composer this way.) This figure shows the player in the middle of ripping an album, so the Start Rip button has changed to Stop Rip.

Name	Artists	Album
♪ 01 True Happiness This Way Lies.mp3		
♪ 02 Love Is Stronger Than Death.mp3		
♪ 03 Dogs of Lust.mp3		
♪ 04 This Is the Night.mp3		
♪ 05 Slow Emotion Replay.mp3		
♪ 06 Helpline Operator.mp3		
♪ 07 Sodium Light Baby.mp3		
♪ 08 Lung Shadows.mp3		
♪ 09 Bluer Than Midnight.mp3		
♪ 10 Lonely Planet.mp3		

Figure 10.19 The ripped songs appear in your Music folder, where you can treat them like any other files. Changes that you make are reflected in the Media Player library.

✔ Tip

■ The selected tracks are copied to your Music folder (unless you changed it in the Options dialog box; refer to Figure 10.16). In Music is a subfolder labeled with the artist's name (or labeled Various Artists). In that folder is a subfolder labeled with the album name. To open Music, choose Start > Music (**Figure 10.19**).

Figure 10.20 In the Navigation pane, expand Library and then click Album. Scroll the right pane to find your newly ripped album.

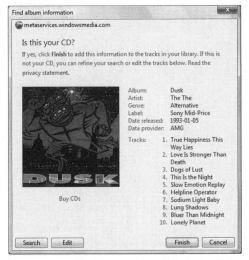

Figure 10.21 Media Player usually will find your CD in its internet database, but if it can't, you can keep trying (using different search criteria each time) or give up and enter the CD information manually.

Sometimes you may be prompted to add missing media information manually after ripping completes.

To add or edit media information after ripping:

1. Connect to the internet.

   If media information is missing because you weren't connected to the internet during ripping, the information usually will appear for the newly ripped tracks soon after you connect. If it doesn't, or if it's wrong, continue with the following steps.

2. Click the Library tab.

3. In the Navigation pane, browse to the album that you just ripped.

4. Right-click the album and choose Find Album Info (**Figure 10.20**).

5. If you get an error message about your privacy settings, choose Rip tab menu > More Options > Privacy tab > check Update Music Files by Retrieving Media Info from the Internet > OK, and then repeat step 4.

6. If the correct album appears in the search results, select it and click Finish; otherwise, click Search to try again using different criteria, or click Edit to add the information manually (**Figure 10.21**).

✔ Tip

- If the song information is correct, but the album art is a generic icon, try finding the art on the internet and copying it (right-click the picture in your web browser and choose Copy). Switch back to Media Player. Then, in the Library tab, right-click the album-art box and choose Paste Album Art.

Organizing Your Library

Over time, your hard drive will become crowded with media files that you've copied or downloaded. Media Player's library is a master list that helps you play and keep track of them. The library lists all the music, videos, and photos on your computer. It's different from the Music, Videos, and Pictures folders because those folders contain actual files, whereas the library contains only links to them, which gives you greater control of how you organize and use the files.

✔ Tip

- Because the library is only a database of links, you can't move it to another computer. (The links would break.) Instead, you'd have to copy all the underlying files (from the Music, Videos, and Pictures folders) to the new machine and rebuild the library by adding items to it.

To show the library:

◆ Click the Library tab (**Figure 10.22**).

The Library tab has many of the same view and navigation controls as Windows Explorer (Chapter 5), so it's easy to change how and which items are displayed.

Navigation pane

Address bar

Details pane

List button

List pane

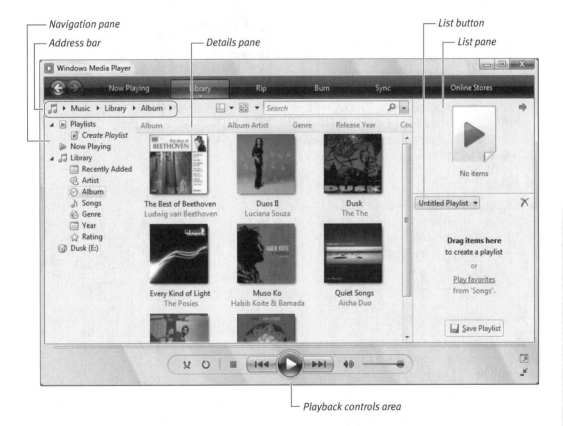

Playback controls area

Figure 10.22 The library uses an Explorer-like display of categories and subcategories. The Navigation pane lets you access your music by artist, album, genre, or other category. The Details pane shows information about the selection in the Navigation pane. You can drag items from the Details pane to the List pane to create a playlist that you want to play, burn, or sync.

ORGANIZING YOUR LIBRARY

To change the library display:

◆ Do any of the following:

To change how items are displayed, click the View Options button (on the toolbar) or press F4.

To show or hide the Navigation or List pane, click the Layout Options button (on the toolbar) and choose one of the Pane commands.

➡ To toggle the List pane, click the List Pane button (at the right end of the toolbar) and then click a pane command.

To change the column headings that are displayed, click the Layout Options button (on the toolbar) and then click Choose Columns.

To change the display category, click the Select a Category button (on the address bar) and choose a category (**Figure 10.23**).

✔ Tip

■ Column headings in the Details pane work like they do in Windows Explorer. To choose which columns appear, right-click a heading and click Choose Columns. To sort by a column, click that column's heading (click it again to reverse the sort). To rearrange columns, drag headings left or right.

It's important that the media information about your media files be correct for the library to be able to organize the files (and for you to be able to find them). Each piece of information is called a *tag*. For music files, the most important tags are title, album, artist, contributing artist, genre, and rating. Your music files are tagged automatically when you rip them or buy them online. The library lets you add or edit tags manually.

Figure 10.23 Each category has several views. After you choose a category, in the Navigation pane, right-click Library and choose Show More Views. These categories also are available in the Library tab menu.

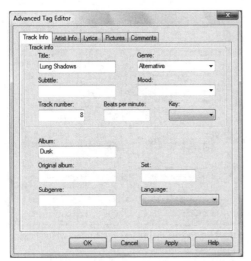

Figure 10.24 The Advanced Tag Editor is the easiest way to edit a music file's many tags. You can find and organize files based on the values of these tags.

✔ Tips

■ To use Find Album Info to tag music files automatically from Microsoft's online database, see "Ripping CDs to Your Hard Drive" earlier in this chapter.

■ Tagging photos is covered in "Finding Photos" in Chapter 9. Tagging files in general is covered in "Tagging Files" in Chapter 5.

To add or edit media information (tags) manually:

◆ In the Details pane, right-click a file's title, artist, or other attribute, and choose Edit. Type a new value and press Enter. (This is easiest in details view.)

or

In the Navigation pane, expand Library and click a view (such as Album, Artist, or Genre). In the Details pane, drag the item(s) with the incorrect tag ("Unknown Album," for example) on top of an item with the correct tag.

or

In the Details pane, right-click a file and choose Advanced Tag Editor. Type new values in the boxes and click OK (**Figure 10.24**).

✔ Tip

■ To prevent media information from being overwritten, choose Library tab menu > More Options > Library tab > check Retrieve Additional Information from Internet > select Only Add Missing Information > OK. (This is the default setting.)

Before you can create playlists, burn CDs, or copy files to portable music players, you must add (to the library) links to digital media files. The following files become part of the library automatically:

◆ CDs ripped to your hard drive

◆ Media files that you play on your computer or on the internet (but not those on removable storage, such as CDs, DVDs, USB flash drives, or shared network folders)

◆ Media files downloaded from online stores

◆ Music, video, and picture files from your personal folders and other folders that the library monitors

You can add links to other media files by changing which folders the library monitors.

To add items to your library:

1. Choose Library tab menu > Add to Library (or press F3).

   The Add to Library dialog box opens (**Figure 10.25**).

2. Select My Personal Folders to monitor the media files stored in your Music, Pictures, and Videos folders, as well as files in the public Music, Pictures, and Video folders that everyone with a user account can access.

   or

   Select My Folders and Those of Others That I Can Access to monitor the same folders as My Personal Folders, as well as the shared Music, Pictures, and Videos folders of other users.

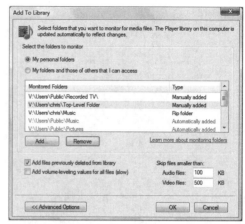

Figure 10.25 This dialog box determines which links appear in the library.

3. Click Advanced Options and do any of the following:

▲ To monitor more folders, click Add and choose a folder.

▲ To stop monitoring a folder that you added, select the folder and click Remove.

▲ To stop monitoring a folder that was added automatically, select the folder and click Ignore.

▲ To specify whether the player should add files previously deleted from the library, check or uncheck Add Files Previously Deleted from Library.

▲ To prevent files that are smaller than a certain size from being added to the library, enter size limits in the Audio Files and Video Files boxes.

4. Click OK.

✔ Tips

■ To share a personal folder, right-click its icon in Windows Explorer and choose Share. In Media Player, sharing is available via Library menu tab > Media Sharing. See also "Sharing Files" in Chapter 18.

■ To specify whether media files are added automatically to the library when played, choose Library tab menu > More Options > Player tab > check or uncheck Add Media Files to Library When Played > OK.

■ The Now Playing tab lists the item that's playing currently, even if that item hasn't been added to the library.

ORGANIZING YOUR LIBRARY

In your library, you can delete links to files and playlists on your computer. When you delete a link, the file or playlist that it's linked to isn't deleted unless you choose to do so.

To delete items from your library:

1. In the library, right-click the item to delete and choose Delete.

   You can delete several items at the same time. To select adjacent items, click the first item; then Shift+click the last item. To select nonadjacent items, Ctrl+click each item. Right-click the selected items and choose Delete.

2. If prompted, choose whether to delete only the link or delete the file on your hard drive as well (to land in the Recycle Bin) (**Figure 10.26**).

✔ Tip

■ To remove a portable device from the library, disconnect the device from your computer. Then, in the Navigation pane, right-click the device and choose End Sync Partnership.

You can search for library items and then play the ones that meet your search criteria or add them to a playlist. Search on media information (tags) or use the wildcard characters * (to represent any group of zero or more characters) and ? (to represent any single character).

To search for items in your library:

1. On the address bar, choose the category that you want to search (refer to Figure 10.23).

Figure 10.26 If you previously checked Don't Show This Message Again, and you want to get this dialog box back, choose Library tab menu > More Options > Library tab > check Delete Files from Computer When Deleted from Library.

2. `Search 🔍` Click or tab to the Search box (or press Ctrl+E) and type text. You can type entire words or just the first few letters.

As you type, matches are displayed in the Details pane.

✔ Tips

- To cancel the search, press Esc, backspace over the search text, or click the close button (✖). The tab goes back to its normal state.

- Help for advanced searches is available: Choose Start > Help and Support, type windows media advanced searches in the Search box, and then press Enter. In the results list, click How Do I Perform Advanced Searches in Windows Media Player?

- For general information about searching, see "Searching for Files and Folders" in Chapter 5.

- To find music from the same album, in the List pane, right-click a song and choose Find in Library.

- To find where a file is stored, right-click it and choose Open File Location.

- To see only files added in the past 30 days, in the Navigation pane, click Recently Added.

- To find files that you downloaded from an online store, in the Navigation pane, right-click Library and choose Show More Views > Online Stores.

Privacy and Security

Media Player relies on the internet to get information about the music and DVDs that you play. You also can use the player to shop at online stores and share your library with other users. All these third-party interactions can expose information about yourself that you'd rather keep private.

The relevant options are on the Privacy tab and the Security tab in the Tools > Options dialog box. (Press Alt if the Tools menu isn't visible.) You should inspect the options, changing them if necessary to suit your preferences. For a description of each option, click Read the Privacy/Security Statement Online in the tabs.

ORGANIZING YOUR LIBRARY

Working with Playlists

A *playlist* is a list of media files that you want to watch or listen to. Media Player generates a temporary playlist automatically when you play a CD (refer to Figure 10.6), but you also can create your own playlists that group any mix of songs and videos in the order in which you want them to be played. You can create a playlist that includes tracks from various CDs, for example. Classical-music fans use playlists to compare the same piece performed by different artists. You also can use playlists to burn your own CDs or copy files to portable music players.

Media player offers regular playlists and auto playlists. *Regular playlists* don't change unless you manually add or remove items. An *auto playlist* is compiled automatically, based on criteria that you specify (songs rated four stars or higher, for example). Auto playlists are updated each time you open them, based on the current contents of the library.

✔ Tips

- You can add any audio, video, or photo file that the player recognizes to a playlist. Nonfiles, such as CDs and DVDs, can't be added.

- Playlist files are saved by default in the Playlists folder in your Music folder (Start > Music).

- Media Player plays through a playlist in order, once, unless you click Shuffle (❎ or Ctrl+H) to randomize the tracks or Repeat (◯ or Ctrl+T) to play them forever.

- If you burn an audio or data CD, the playlist items are burned to the CD, but the playlist file isn't. When you sync a playlist to a portable device, both the playlist file and its items are copied to the device.

Figure 10.27 Save the playlist in M3U format if you're going to share it with others.

Figure 10.28 To play a playlist, double-click it, or right-click it and choose Play. Use the playback controls to pause, play, skip or repeat tracks, and so on (refer to Figure 10.1).

To create a regular playlist:

1. If you need to clear the List pane before creating the playlist, click the Clear List Pane button.

2. Drag items from the Details pane in the library to the List pane to add them to the new playlist.

   You can select several items at the same time. To select adjacent items, click the first item; then Shift+click the last item. To select nonadjacent items, Ctrl+click each item.

3. To reorder items, drag them up or down in the List pane.

4. Click Save Playlist (at the bottom of the List pane) or press Alt+S.

5. Type the playlist name and press Enter.

   By default, the playlist is saved as a .wpl file. To save as a (more popular) .m3u or .asx file, click the List button (at the top of the playlist) and choose Save Playlist As (**Figure 10.27**).

6. To see the new playlist, expand Playlists in the Navigation pane (**Figure 10.28**).

✔ Tips

- To create a new empty playlist quickly, press Ctrl+N.

- To create a playlist of favorite items, turn on Library tab menu > Add Favorites to List When Dragging. When you drag a category (such as an Album or Genre) from the Details pane to the List pane, only the songs with the highest user and auto ratings are added to the new playlist. To add favorites one time only, right-click a category in the Details pane and choose Add To > "Untitled Playlist" (Favorites Only).

To edit a regular playlist:

1. Expand Playlists in the Navigation pane (refer to Figure 10.28).

2.  Right-click a playlist and choose Edit in List Pane (or select it and click the Edit in List Pane button in the Details pane).

3. Click the List button (at the top of the playlist) or right-click any item; then use the menus to edit the list (**Figure 10.29**).

    You can select several items at the same time. To select adjacent items, click the first item; then Shift+click the last item. To select nonadjacent items, Ctrl+click each item.

4. Click Save Playlist (at the bottom of the List pane) or press Alt+S.

Figure 10.29 The playlist menus let you add, remove, shuffle, sort, reorder, and rate items. You also can reorder items by dragging them up or down the list.

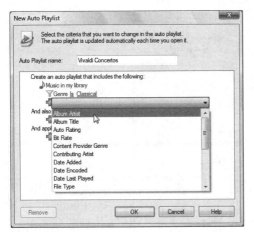

Figure 10.30 You can specify multiple filters for items to be included in (or excluded from) an auto playlist. Media Player updates the list automatically each time you open it.

Figure 10.31 Auto playlists are distinguished from regular playlists by a slightly different icon containing a curved arrow.

To create an auto playlist:

1. Choose Library tab menu > Create Auto Playlist.

2. In the New Auto Playlist dialog box, type the name of the new auto playlist.

3. Specify criteria for the items in the auto playlist (**Figure 10.30**).

   To remove a criterion, select it and click Remove.

4. Click OK.

5. To see the new playlist, expand Playlists in the Navigation pane (**Figure 10.31**).

✔ Tips

■ To edit an auto playlist, right-click it in Figure 10.31 and choose Edit.

■ To save an auto playlist as a regular playlist, clear the List pane (click the red X); right-click the auto playlist in Figure 10.31 and choose Add to "Untitled Playlist"; then click Save Playlist (at the bottom of the List pane) and type a name for the playlist. The playlist no longer autoupdates after conversion.

WORKING WITH PLAYLISTS

Burning Music CDs

If your computer has a CD (or DVD) recorder, you can copy—or *burn*—songs to a writeable disc to create custom music CDs. The Burn tab in Media Player lets you burn a mix of songs from your library to a blank CD-R or CD-RW, which will play in a standard CD player.

✔ Tips

■ You can't burn live streams, such as radio stations.

■ Before you burn, you can set options for CD burning: Choose Burn tab menu > More Options > Burn tab (**Figure 10.32**).

■ This section covers *music* CDs. To burn *data* CDs or DVDs, see "Burning CDs and DVDs" in Chapter 5. To burn multimedia DVDs with video, photos, and audio, use DVD Maker (Start > All Programs > Windows DVD Maker). See also "Publishing a Movie" in Chapter 11.

To burn a music CD:

1. Click the Burn tab.

2. Choose Burn tab menu > Audio CD.

3. Insert a blank CD-R or CD-RW into your CD burner.

   A blank disc is required. If you insert a rewriteable disc (CD-RW) that has files on it, you can erase it by right-clicking the drive in the Navigation pane and choosing Erase Disc.

4. If you have multiple burners, and the one that you want to use isn't selected, click Next Drive in the List pane above the playlist.

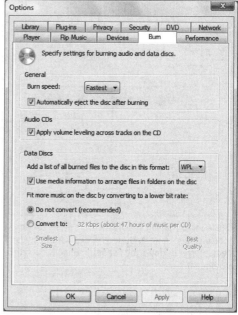

Figure 10.32 It's usually unnecessary to adjust the default options. The bottom section applies only to data discs (not music discs). Some of these options also are available in the Burn tab menu.

Burning Problems

CD burners are so cranky and skittish that you should close all other programs, leave your PC alone, and not stomp around until Media Player ejects the completed CD. If you still get music files that skip and pop, try slowing the burn speed (refer to Figure 10.32).

To make an exact duplicate of a CD, try Nero Ultra Edition ($80 U.S.; www.nero.com), Roxio Easy Media Creator ($80 U.S.; www.roxio.com), or Exact Audio Copy (free; www.exactaudiocopy.de). If you're recording from vinyl LPs, try Wave Corrector ($39 U.S.; www.wavecor.co.uk).

5. If you need to clear the List pane before building a burn list, click the Clear List Pane button.

6. Drag items (playlists, individual songs, albums, and so on) from the Navigation and Details panes to the List pane to build a burn list.

If a song isn't in your library, you can drag it to the List pane from Windows Explorer (or right-click it and choose Add to Burn List).

7. Drag items up or down the burn list to their desired positions in the burning order.

The player calculates how many minutes and seconds of empty space remain on the CD after you add each song to the burn list.

8. If you've added too many songs, right-click items and choose Remove From List until everything fits.

(Account for the player's inserting 2 seconds between songs when burning.)

9. Click Start Burn (or press Alt+S).

The process takes a bit of time and disk space. You can check the progress in the burn list.

Syncing with a Portable Music Player

If you're like most people, your portable player is an Apple iPod. To sync your music between it and your computer, use iTunes, not Media Player. Download a free copy at www.apple.com/itunes/download.

If you have a different player—such as a Rio, Nomad, iRiver, Sansa, or Zune—you can use the software that came with the player or the Sync tab of Media Player. For instructions on using the Sync tab, choose Start > Help and Support and then search for *media player sync*.

BURNING MUSIC CDS

Playing DVDs

If you have a DVD drive, you can use Media Player to watch DVD movies.

✔ Tips

- To access the DVD menu and special features, right-click the movie picture and choose DVD Features > Root Menu. Other DVD commands are available in the View and Play menus (press Alt if these menus aren't visible).

- To turn on parental controls for DVDs, choose Now Playing tab menu > More Options > DVD tab > Change (**Figure 10.33**). See also "Setting Parental Controls" in Chapter 13.

- Media Player also can play VCDs (video CDs).

To play a DVD:

1. Insert a DVD into your computer's DVD drive.

2. Depending on the DVD Movie setting in AutoPlay (refer to Figure 10.7), Media Player opens automatically or offers to do so.

    If not, open Media Player; then choose the drive that contains the DVD from the Now Playing tab menu.

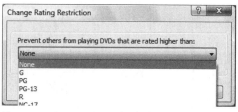

Figure 10.33 You can prevent people with non-Administrator accounts from playing DVDs based on the movie's rating. Not all DVDs support this feature.

DVD Decoders

DVD playback requires a software *decoder.* If you bought your system with Windows and a DVD drive installed, you probably can play any DVD on your PC as is. If you don't have a compatible decoder installed, Media Player will display an error message. Click Web Help in the message to learn how to download the decoder.

I never use Media Player for DVD movies. A better player—one that plays just about everything everywhere, without error messages—is VLC media player (free; www.videolan.org/vlc). VLC also won't force you to watch the intros, coming attractions, ads, and FBI warnings that you have to sit through when you watch a DVD on a conventional player or Windows Media Player.

PLAYING DVDs

Table 10.3

DVD Keyboard Shortcuts	
To	Press
Play/pause	Ctrl+P or spacebar
Stop	Ctrl+S
Rewind	Ctrl+Shift+B
Fast-forward	Ctrl+Shift+F
Previous/next chapter	Ctrl+B/Ctrl+F
Quieter/louder	F8/F9
Mute	F7
Eject	Ctrl+J
Play fast	Ctrl+Shift+G
Play normal	Ctrl+Shift+N
Play slow	Ctrl+Shift+S
Toggle captions and subtitles	Ctrl+Shift+C

3. In the List pane on the right, click a DVD title or chapter name, if appropriate.

If the pane is hidden, choose Now Playing tab menu > Show List Pane.

4. To enlarge the picture to fill the screen, click Full Screen (⬀), press Alt+Enter, or double-click the movie.

To return to normal, press Esc or repeat any of the full-screen shortcuts (**Figure 10.34**).

You can control playback with the onscreen controls or the keyboard shortcuts listed in **Table 10.3**.

Figure 10.34 In full-screen mode, the playback controls appear automatically when you move the mouse and disappear after the mouse is idle for a few seconds. To control playback, you can right-click the movie or use the keyboard shortcuts listed in Table 10.3. The playlist (on the right) divides the movie into discrete "chapters"; double-click a chapter to jump to a particular scene.

PLAYING DVDS

Using Keyboard Shortcuts

Table 10.4 lists Media Player's keyboard shortcuts. Table 10.3 in the preceding section also contains some keyboard shortcuts.

Table 10.4

Media Player Keyboard Shortcuts

To	Press
Zoom to 50%	Alt+1
Zoom to 100%	Alt+2
Zoom to 200%	Alt+3
Display video in full screen	Alt+Enter or F11
Revisit recent views	Alt+Left arrow or Alt+Right arrow
Switch to full mode	Ctrl+1
Switch to skin mode	Ctrl+2
Revisit the most recent library views	Ctrl+7, Ctrl+8, or Ctrl+9
Search for an item	Ctrl+E
Shuffle the playlist	Ctrl+H
Eject the CD or DVD	Ctrl+J
Toggle the classic menu bar (full mode)	Ctrl+M
Create a new playlist	Ctrl+N
Open a file	Ctrl+O
Repeat the playlist	Ctrl+T
Specify a URL or path to a file	Ctrl+U
Close or stop playing a file	Ctrl+W
Rate the playing item from 0 to 5 stars	Ctrl+Windows logo key+[0–5]
Return to full mode from full screen	Esc
Get help	F1
Edit media information on a selected item in the library	F2
Add media files to the library	F3
Cycle view options in the Details pane	F4
Refresh information in the panes	F5
Increase/decrease the size of album art	F6/Shift+F6
Show the classic menu bar	F10
Quit Media Player	Alt+F

WINDOWS MOVIE MAKER

Windows Movie Maker lets you transfer audio and video to your computer from a digital video camera, web camera, or other digital source and use that as raw material for your own movies. You can combine footage, still photos, music tracks, videos, voice-over narratives, and other media files. Then you can edit; add titles, video transitions, and special effects; and save the result as a stand-alone file in Windows Media Audio/Video (.wmv) format. Your movie is ready to play or to share with friends and enemies via email, web, DVD, or CD.

✔ Tips

- Video editing is a computer-intensive activity that requires at least a 2 GHz processor, 1 GB of RAM, and a fast hard disk (7200 rpm or better) with a lot of free space.

- If Movie Maker doesn't meet your needs, try a video editor from Adobe, Avid, or Pinnacle.

Getting Started with Movie Maker

Like all video-editing software, Movie Maker is a complex program; making a movie isn't a simple matter of opening, editing, saving, and closing a document. Before you work with Movie Maker, you'll need to explore the interface and grasp a few concepts. **Figure 11.1** shows Movie Maker's main sections, which are described in **Table 11.1.** You can point (without clicking) to any Movie Maker control for a pop-up tip.

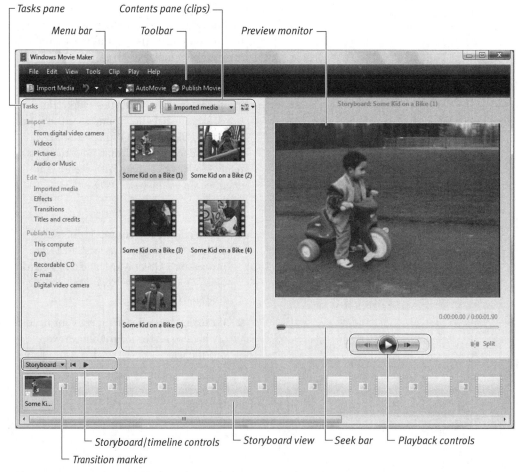

Figure 11.1 Movie Maker is divided into three main horizontal sections: the menu bar and toolbar, the panes, and the storyboard/timeline.

Table 11.1

Movie Maker Sections

FEATURE	DESCRIPTION
Tasks pane	Lists common moviemaking tasks, such as importing video, editing a movie, adding effects, and saving or sending a movie.
Collections pane	(Not shown) Displays your collections in an Explorer-like tree. A collection is a container of video clips, audio clips, and pictures that you've imported. Each clip is a smaller continuous segment of audio and video. (Not everything in a collection must appear in a final movie.) See "Organizing Your Clips" later in this chapter.
Contents pane	Displays the clips that are contained in the selected collection, including all the video, audio, pictures, transitions, and effects that you can add to the storyboard/timeline to include in your movie.
Storyboard view	Displays the sequence of the clips in your project and lets you rearrange them easily. This view also lets you see any transitions or effects that you've added.
Timeline view	(Not shown) Lets you review or modify the timing of clips in your project. You can zoom in or out on project details, record narration, add background music, adjust audio levels, and trim unwanted portions of a clip (among other things). See "Editing a Project" later in this chapter.
Preview monitor	Plays individual clips or an entire project. Use this feature to preview your project before saving it as a movie.

To start Movie Maker:

◆ Choose Start > All Programs > Windows Movie Maker.

or

Choose Start, type `movie maker` in the search box, and then press Enter.

or

Press Windows logo key+R; type `moviemk` and press Enter.

✔ Tips

■ You can't display the Tasks pane and the Collections pane, or storyboard view and timeline view, at the same time. Use the View menu or toolbar buttons to show, hide, or toggle panes and views.

■ Right-click any section (or specific item in a section) to show its shortcut menu.

■ To resize sections, drag the horizontal or vertical lines that separate them. The cursor becomes a double-headed arrow when you hover it over a separator line.

■ Choose Tools > Options to change Movie Maker's default settings.

■ For a list of keyboard shortcuts, choose Start > Help and Support and search for *movie maker keyboard shortcuts*.

GETTING STARTED WITH MOVIE MAKE

Importing Content

You edit and create movies with Movie Maker by using footage transferred from camera to computer.

To import digital video:

1. Connect your digital video camera to your computer (see the sidebar in this section).

2. Choose File > Import from Digital Video Camera (or press Ctrl+R).

   or

   In the Tasks pane, below Import, click From Digital Video Camera.

3. Follow the onscreen instructions.

   The wizard lets you choose a device, video settings, and what to import. You can import:

   ▲ The entire video from a tape in a digital video (DV) camera

   ▲ Parts of video from a tape in a DV camera

   ▲ Live video

   Movie Maker imports the content into a new collection with the same name as the specified video file.

✔ Tips

■ For help choosing video settings, choose Start > Help and Support and search for *import videotape*.

■ Copy-protected tapes may show up as onscreen garbage.

Your movie can combine footage that you've imported from your video camera with audio clips, still photos, and other video files that you've downloaded from the internet, copied from CDs, transferred from a digital camera, or scanned into your computer.

To import existing video, audio, and pictures:

1. Choose File > Import Media Items (or press Ctrl+I).

   or

   [Import Media] Click Import Media (on the toolbar).

   or

   In the Tasks pane, below Import, click the link for the type of file that you want to import (Videos, Pictures, or Audio or Music).

2. In the Import Media Items dialog box, locate the file that you want to import.

   You can import these types of files:

   Video files – .asf, .avi, .m1v, .mp2, .mp2v, .mpe, .mpeg, .mpg, .mpv2, .wm, .wmv

   Audio files – .aif, .aifc, .aiff .asf, .au, .mp2, .mp3, .mpa, .snd, .wav, .wma

   Picture files – .bmp, .dib, .emf, .gif, .jfif, .jpe, .jpeg, .jpg, .png, .tif, .tiff, .wmf

   For a description of each file type, go to http://support.microsoft.com/?kbid=31 6992, "Windows Media Player Multimedia File Formats."

continues on next page

3. Select the file you want to import.

You also can import several files at the same time. To select adjacent items, click the first item; then Shift+click the last item. To select nonadjacent items, Ctrl+click each item.

4. Click Import.

New clips appear in the Contents pane (**Figure 11.2**).

✔ Tips

- After you import a video, you can have Movie Maker separate it automatically into smaller, more manageable clips. Each new clip starts when there's a substantial change from one frame of the video to the next. If the source video is from a DV camera, clips are based on the time stamps as well. To create clips, select the video in the Contents pane and choose Tools > Create Clips (or right-click the video and choose Create Clips).

- Imported files actually remain in their original locations. Movie Maker doesn't create copies; instead, a clip in the Contents pane is a shortcut that points to the source file. If you move, rename, or delete a source file after you import it, you'll break the link. Movie Maker may try to find moved or renamed files, but sometimes, you'll have to import them again.

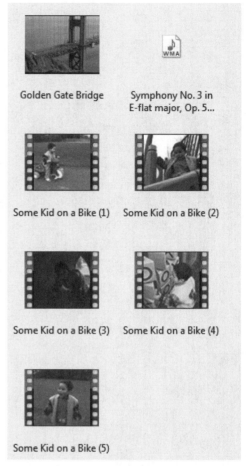

Golden Gate Bridge Symphony No. 3 in E-flat major, Op. 5...

Some Kid on a Bike (1) Some Kid on a Bike (2)

Some Kid on a Bike (3) Some Kid on a Bike (4)

Some Kid on a Bike (5)

Figure 11.2 Imported clips appear as thumbnails in the Contents pane. Icons indicate the clip type: The top-left clip is a still photo, the top-right clip is an audio file, and the bottom five clips are videos. The five video clips actually come from a single file; I used the Create Clips command to divide the video into smaller segments, so they're ready to edit.

Connecting a Video Camera to Your Computer

A variety of hardware capture devices can transfer content to your computer from your digital video devices. These are only guidelines about connecting; specific configuration will depend on your hardware. See Chapter 8 for tips on installing hardware.

Digital video camera. Connect a DV camera (which uses MiniDV, MICROMV, or Digital8 tapes) to your computer's USB or IEEE 1394 (FireWire) port. An IEEE 1394 port is preferred. If your computer didn't come with one of these ports, you can buy and install a card that provides it. These connections transfer high-quality content very quickly because they're designed to transmit digital data like your camera's audio and video information.

Use the cable that came with your camera to connect the camera's DV-out port to the IEEE 1394 port. The cable transfers both audio and video. Many digital cameras also have analog outputs, which you can connect to a video capture card to transfer video and audio to your computer, but converting the signal from digital to analog and back again will degrade picture and sound quality.

Web camera. A webcam connects to a USB port, to an IEEE 1394 port, or (if it's a video composite camera) to a video capture card. A laptop may have a webcam built into the lid. Some webcams have a built-in microphone for capturing audio too.

Analog camera or VCR. You can't import video from these devices by using Movie Maker. Instead, install an analog video capture card on your computer to get extra video and probably audio ports. Connect a VCR or analog camcorder (which uses VHS, 8mm, or Hi8 tapes) to the card. For video capture, you can connect your camera's video line-out port to the card's video line-in port. For audio capture, you could then connect the left and right audio lines (usually, through RCA-style single-channel connectors to a 3.5mm stereo plug Y-adapter) to the line-in port on a sound card or a video capture card with audio ports.

If both your camera and video capture card have *S-Video* connectors, you can attach those connectors to record video while the attached audio connectors capture sound. Use the software that came with the card to import the video.

Audio only. Use a stand-alone microphone connected to a sound card's line-in port, a built-in line-in port, or a USB port.

TV. You can capture video from TV if you have a TV tuner card installed on your computer.

Organizing Your Clips

After importing clips, you can organize them in *collections*—Explorer-like folder hierarchies (**Figure 11.3**). A collection doesn't apply to any specific movie project; you can use it many times over in different movies.

To create a collection:

1. If the Collections pane is hidden, choose View > Collections.

2. In the Collections pane, right-click the collection folder where you want to add the collection and choose New Collection Folder (refer to Figure 11.3).

3. Type a name and press Enter.

✔ Tip

■ Right-click a collection to rename or remove it. Removing a collection or clip deletes only links; source files remain in their original locations on disk.

To store a clip in a particular collection folder, just drag the clip's icon from the Contents pane to the folder. You can sort the clips in the Contents pane.

To arrange clips:

1. In the Collections pane, click the collection folder that contains the clips you want to arrange.

   The clips appear in the Contents pane.

2. To change how much detail is displayed, choose View > Details or View > Thumbnails.

3. Choose View > Arrange Icons By; then choose a property (**Figure 11.4**).

Figure 11.3 Here's a reasonable way to organize clips in a collection hierarchy. Alternatively, you can organize your clips by event rather than by clip type. If you have only a few clips, you can stick them all in one collection folder.

Figure 11.4 You also can arrange clips via the shortcut menu; just right-click an empty area of the Contents pane. (You can't drag and drop clips in this pane to reorder them.)

Figure 11.5 You can specify values for different properties (except Duration, which is preset) and use Windows Explorer to search for specific projects or organize them according to title, author, and so on.

Creating a Project

Your works in progress in Movie Maker are stored in *projects*. A project (.mswmm) file isn't an end-result movie but a framework containing arrangement and timing information for audio and video clips, transitions, effects, and titles that you've added to the storyboard/timeline. Project files also have properties that you can define and use to organize your projects.

You open and save existing projects with the usual Open, Save, and Save As commands in the toolbar or File menu.

To create a new project:

◆ Choose File > New Project.

✔ Tips

■ You can have only one project open at a time.

■ Project files are saved by default in your Videos folder (choose View > Windows Photo Gallery).

■ Movie Maker opens by default with a blank, untitled project. If you'd rather start editing where you left off, choose Tools > Options > General tab; then check Open Last Project on Startup.

To view a project's properties:

◆ Choose File > Project Properties (**Figure 11.5**).

✔ Tips

■ The properties that you enter become part of the project file *and* of your final, saved movie. Don't enter any information in the Project Properties dialog box that you don't want others to see.

■ To view an individual clip's properties (such as duration, source file, and bit rate), right-click the clip and choose Properties.

Editing a Project

Now the good part. To begin editing your project, you add imported video, audio, or pictures to the storyboard/timeline. The storyboard/timeline clips become the contents of your project and future movie.

Both the storyboard and the timeline display your work in progress, but from different perspectives. The storyboard shows the sequence of clips (**Figure 11.6**), whereas the timeline shows their timing (**Figure 11.7**).

You can preview your entire project or a particular clip in the preview monitor.

To switch between storyboard and timeline view:

◆ Press Ctrl+T (or choose View > Storyboard or View > Timeline).

or

Storyboard ▾ Click the Storyboard/Timeline menu button.

✔ Tips

■ Timeline time is displayed as hours: minutes:seconds.hundredths of a second (h:mm:ss.ss).

■ Some editing tasks can be performed in both storyboard and timeline views; others, in only one view.

Figure 11.6 Use the storyboard to look at the sequence of clips in your project and rearrange them, if necessary. You can preview all the clips and see any effects or transitions that you've added. Audio clips aren't displayed on the storyboard, but they are in the timeline.

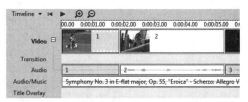

Figure 11.7 Use the timeline to review or modify the timing of clips; use its buttons to rewind, play, zoom in or out, record narration, or adjust audio levels. Click the small + icon next to the Video track to expand it and display Transition and Audio tracks.

Timeline Tracks

Each timeline track (refer to Figure 11.7) shows specific items that you've added to a project:

Video. Shows video clips, pictures, and titles. If you add effects to a clip, a small star icon appears on that clip.

Transition. Shows transitions between clips.

Audio. Shows the audio that's included in any video clips.

Audio/Music. Shows audio clips that aren't part of the video track, such as narration and background music.

Title Overlay. Shows any titles or credits.

EDITING A PROJECT

To add a clip to a project:

1. In the Collections pane, click the collection that contains the clip that you want to add to your project.

2. In the Contents pane, click the clip that you want to add (or Ctrl+click or Shift+click to select multiple clips).

3. Drag the clip (or multiple clips) onto the storyboard/timeline in whatever order you like, or choose Clip > Add to Storyboard/Timeline (Ctrl+D).

✔ Tips

■ To rearrange your clips, just drag them to a different location on the storyboard/ timeline. You also can move or duplicate clips with the usual Cut, Copy, and Paste commands in the Edit menu.

■ To move a clip only slightly, select it; then choose Clip > Nudge Left/Right or press Ctrl+Shift+B/N (timeline view only).

■ To remove a clip from the storyboard/ timeline, right-click it and choose Remove (or select it and press Delete). To remove all clips, press Ctrl+Delete or choose Edit > Clear Storyboard/Timeline.

■ If the timeline's clips become too cramped or too spread out, you can zoom to change the level of detail displayed. From the View menu, choose Zoom In, Zoom Out, or Zoom to Fit (or press Page Down, Page Up, or F9, respectively).

EDITING A PROJECT

To preview a project or clip:

◆ To preview a project, choose Play > Play Storyboard/Timeline (or press Ctrl+W).

or

To preview a clip, select the clip and choose Play > Play Clip (or press K).

✔ Tips

■ The Play menu and the preview monitor's playback controls let you play the current selection continuously or frame by frame.

■ Press Alt+Enter to preview in full-screen mode. Press Esc (or Alt+Enter again) to go back to normal.

Movie Maker's AutoMovie feature creates a movie quickly and automatically based on the selected clips or collection.

To create a movie automatically:

1. Select a collection in the Collections pane or multiple clips in the Contents pane.

2. Choose Tools > AutoMovie.

3. Select an AutoMovie editing style.

4. If desired, click the More Options links to enter a movie title and select audio or background music (**Figure 11.8**).

5. Click Create AutoMovie.

✔ Tip

■ After you create an AutoMovie, you can save it with the Publish Movie wizard or make further edits, just as you would when creating a project and movie manually.

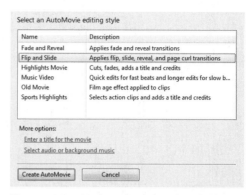

Figure 11.8 AutoMovie analyzes the selected video, audio, and picture clips, and combines them to make one movie based on the automatic editing style that you choose.

Editing Clips

You have several ways to edit the clips that you've arranged on the storyboard/timeline.

You can *split* an audio or video clip into smaller, more manageable clips. By splitting a clip, you can, say, insert a transition or title into the middle.

To split a clip:

1. In the Contents pane or on the storyboard/timeline, select the clip that you want to split.

2. Press the spacebar to play the clip; then press the spacebar again to pause at the point at which you want to split the clip.

   or

   On the preview monitor, move the Seek bar to the point at which you want to split the clip, or click the Previous Frame and Next Frame playback controls for precise movements.

3. Choose Clip > Split (or press M).

Conversely, you *combine* an audio or video clip that's divided into small clips. You can combine only contiguous clips. (The second clip's start time immediately follows the first clip's end time.)

To combine a split clip:

1. In the Contents pane or on the storyboard/timeline, hold down the Ctrl key; then select two or more contiguous clips that you want to combine.

2. Choose Clip > Combine (or press N).

You can *trim* a clip to hide its unwanted parts. By trimming an audio or video clip, you edit its starting and ending points, therefore editing its length. Trimmed content isn't removed but merely hidden from the movie's audience.

To trim a clip:

1. Choose View > Timeline.

2. Select the clip that you want to trim.

3. Drag the trim handles to set the start and end trim points (**Figure 11.9**).

✔ Tips

- For precise trimming, use the preview monitor's playback controls to pause at a trim point; then use the Clip menu's Trim commands.

- To clear trim points, select the trimmed clip on the timeline and choose Clip > Clear Trim Points (or press U).

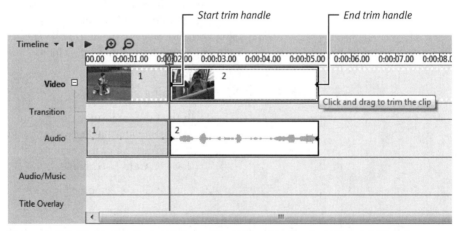

Figure 11.9 Drag the trim handles to set start and end trim points. The start trim point determines when the clip will begin to play; the end trim point determines when the clip will stop playing.

EDITING CLIPS

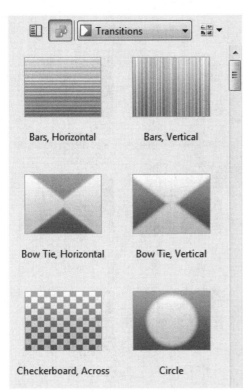

Figure 11.10 Several transitions appear in the Contents pane. Double-click a transition to test it in the monitor.

Figure 11.11 The box between these clips shows a checkerboard transition, which plays before the first clip ends and while the other clip starts to play. In timeline view, you can drag the transition's left edge to change its duration. The starred boxes in each clip's bottom-left corner indicate effects. You can right-click a transition or effect to remove it.

Adding Visual Content

You can embroider your movies with transitions, effects, and titles and credits.

A *transition* controls how your movie plays from one video clip or picture to the next.

To add a transition:

1. Choose Tools > Transitions (**Figure 11.10**).

2. In storyboard view, drag a transition to the transition marker between two video clips or pictures (**Figure 11.11**).

   or

   In timeline view, drag a transition between two clips on the Video track.

An *effect* is a special effect that determines how a video clip, picture, or title appears in a movie. The effect lasts for the clip's entire duration.

To add an effect:

1. Choose Tools > Effects (**Figure 11.12**).

2. In storyboard view, drag an effect to a clip's effects box (refer to Figure 11.11).

   or

   In timeline view, drag an effect to the Video track.

Titles and credits add text-based information, such as a movie title or your name, to a movie. You can add multiple titles to a track at different points in a movie. The titles overlay the video.

To add a title or credit:

1. Choose Tools > Title and Credits.

2. In the pane that appears, select where you want to add text.

3. Type the text.

   Use the More Options link to tailor the text's appearance.

4. Click Add Title.

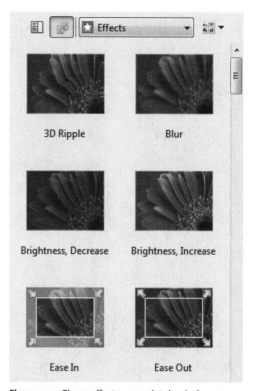

Figure 11.12 These effects are maintained when you split, cut, copy, or move a video clip or picture. You can add multiple effects to each clip.

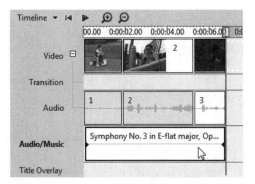

Figure 11.13 You can drag an audio clip left or right to adjust its position in the movie or drag the clip's left or right edge to trim its length. (The Audio track—above the Audio/Music track—holds the *video's* audio track.) You can add video clips to the Audio/Music track if you want the audio, but not the video, to play in your movie.

Adding Audio Tracks

If you've imported music or audio files, you can add them to your movie as background music or sounds.

If you have a microphone connected to your computer, you can add audio narration to video clips. Your narration is synchronized with the video automatically, so the narration describes the action in your movie as it plays.

To add audio:

1. Choose View > Timeline.

2. In the Collections pane, click the collection that contains the audio clip you want to add to your project.

3. Drag the clip from the Contents pane to the timeline's Audio/Music track (**Figure 11.13**).

To narrate the timeline:

1. Choose View > Timeline.

2. Move the timeline's playback indicator (the square with a vertical line; refer to Figure 11.13) to an empty point on the Audio/Music track where you want to begin your audio narration.

3. Choose Tools > Narrate Timeline (**Figure 11.14**).

4. Click Start Narration; then speak into the microphone to narrate the movie as it progresses.

5. Click Stop Narration.

6. Save the file.

✔ Tips

- You can record audio clips in Sound Recorder and import them into your project. To start Sound Recorder, choose Start > All Programs > Accessories > Sound Recorder (**Figure 11.15**). A much better sound editor, however, is Audacity (free; http://audacity.sourceforge.net).

- Right-click an audio clip to adjust its volume levels or to remove it.

Figure 11.14 Click Show Options to set additional recording options. If the Limit Narration box is unchecked, you can keep talking past the end of the movie.

Figure 11.15 Sound Recorder is a free Windows program. Click the Help button for instructions.

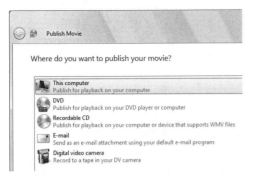

Figure 11.16 The Publish Movie wizard simplifies and automates the process of assembling your clips and compressing digital video to create movies.

Figure 11.17 You can launch and use DVD Maker independently of Movie Maker. Choose Start > All Programs > Windows DVD Maker.

Publishing a Movie

Now you're ready to use the Publish Movie wizard to save your final project as an actual movie. The wizard lets you choose among destinations: You can store the movie on your computer, burn it on a DVD or CD, send it as an email attachment, or record it to a tape in your DV camera. The wizard's pages vary by the destination.

To publish a movie:

1. Choose File > Publish Movie (or press Ctrl+P).

2. Select where you want to publish your movie (**Figure 11.16**); then click Next.

3. Follow the onscreen instructions.

✔ Tips

■ Movies are saved in Windows Media Audio/Video (.wmv) format. You can watch them in Windows Media Player, Internet Explorer, Windows Photo Gallery, or any media player that can play .wmv files.

■ You also can start the wizard from the Publish To section of the Tasks pane.

■ If you choose to burn a DVD in Figure 11.16, Movie Maker opens Windows DVD Maker, new in Vista (**Figure 11.17**). DVD Maker is a wizard that helps you create DVDs with video, photos, and audio. Click the Help button (❷) for instructions. (See also "Burning CDs and DVDs" in Chapter 5.)

Connecting to the Internet

After you finish using your computer to write memos, create spreadsheets, and cook books, you can connect to the internet to browse the web, pirate music, flirt with strangers, send email, and chat online. Windows' Connect to the Internet wizard simplifies connections.

As an individual, you can't connect to the internet directly. You must pay a go-between *internet service provider (ISP)* and rely on it to provide setup instructions, turn on your service, equip and maintain dependable connections, and help you when things go wrong.

In this chapter, you'll learn about connection types and how to connect. Subsequent chapters show you how to armor your computer against outside attacks, browse the web, send email, and chat after you're hooked up.

Understanding Connection Types

First, you can skip this chapter if:

◆ **You upgraded from Windows XP and had internet access.** Windows Setup preserved the configuration; your Vista connection should work fine.

◆ **You want to transfer internet connection settings from another computer.** Use Windows Easy Transfer; see "Transferring Existing Files and Settings" in the appendix.

◆ **Your computer is on a local area network (LAN) at work or school.** You have internet access through the network. Ask your network administrator about connection details.

◆ **You want to share an internet connection provided by another computer.** Use Internet Connection Sharing (or a router); see "Sharing an Internet Connection" in Chapter 18.

If you're not in any of these situations, you can set up your own internet connection by using:

◆ A *dial-up connection* through an analog modem over ordinary phone lines

◆ A high-speed *broadband connection* such as DSL or cable

◆ A *wireless connection* through a wireless router or wireless network, or a hotspot

For any connection type, you'll need an account with an ISP. If you don't have one already, ask a friend or colleague to recommend one; find an online computer and go to **www.dslreports.com**; or look in your local phone directory under, say, *Computers— Online Services*. Internet junkies use traditional ISPs, which provide direct, unsanitized internet access. Some beginners like online services like America Online (AOL) or the Microsoft Network (MSN) because they're easy to use and set up, and they have their own little nonhostile online communities. After you've signed up, see "Connecting to the Internet" later in this chapter.

Dial-up

Each time you connect to the internet via dial-up, your analog modem dials your ISP over a standard phone line. (If you have only one line, callers can't reach you while you're online.) Dial-up connections are slow compared with broadband, but they're a good choice for frequent travelers, because big ISPs provide local access numbers over large geographic areas. In some areas, dial-up is your only choice. Dial-up service costs upward of $7 U.S. a month for unlimited access (plus your cost for the calls).

You need an analog modem for a dial-up connection. Plug the telephone cable from your wall jack into the modem's Line (not Phone) jack. If you have to run your modem and a phone off the same line at the same jack, run a second cable from the modem's Phone jack to the telephone's Line jack. If your computer didn't come with a built-in modem, buy a 56 Kbps model and install it (see Chapter 8).

Broadband

Broadband (DSL and cable) connections are:

◆ *Fast.* Broadband modems are 10 to 50 times faster than dial-up modems.

◆ *Persistent.* Broadband connections are always on. No dialing is involved.

◆ *Easy to set up.* Sometimes a technician comes to your home to install and configure everything; otherwise, your ISP will mail you a kit with equipment and setup instructions.

◆ *Cheaper (maybe).* Broadband service costs upward of $15 a month for unlimited access (plus one-time setup and equipment costs ranging from zero to a few hundred dollars). Dial-up's monthly fee is cheaper, but with broadband, you don't need to pay for a second phone line for internet access or for the extra connect time needed for big downloads.

DSL (Digital Subscriber Line) uses a DSL modem to operate over a standard phone line without interfering with normal voice calls. For some areas, DSL is available only if you're no more than 3 miles from a phone-company central office. (The closer you are, the faster the connection speed.) For other areas, you can be outside the 3-mile limit.

Cable uses a cable modem to operate over a cable TV line (coaxial cable). If you're wired for cable TV, you can get a connection through your cable company. Cable speed can drop precipitously when too many people in your area use the system.

Before you set up a broadband connection, make sure that there's a cable running from your computer's Ethernet (network) port to a DSL modem, a cable modem, or a network jack. The correct lights on the modem must be lit. (Typically, you want to see four steady green lights, but refer to the documentation.)

Next, check the setup instructions or ask your ISP or network administrator whether you have a static IP address or a dynamic IP address (for Point-to-Point Protocol over Ethernet, or PPPoE, connections). An *IP address* identifies your computer uniquely on the internet.

A *static* (or *fixed*) IP address stays the same every time you connect. In a PPPoE connection, the IP address changes each time. Unlike a static IP connection, PPPoE requires a user name and password; the IP address must be initiated *(leased)* each time you reconnect to the internet. For some ISPs, your connection hardware can handle reconnection; for others, you have to initiate it yourself, as with a dial-up connection.

Most connections are PPPoE. ISPs usually make groups of static IP addresses available only to business customers at extra cost, if at all.

Use the Connect to the Internet wizard to set up a PPPoE connection. Static connections are set up differently.

Wireless

Wireless isn't a really connection type but a network type—a way to use an existing broadband connection. For a wireless connection, you need a wireless router or wireless network (see "Understanding Network Types" in Chapter 18). Or you can connect through a *hotspot*—a public place (such as a café, airport, hotel, or sometimes even an entire town) with a wireless network. Many workplaces have secured hotspots throughout the floor or building. If you're at a friend's house, you can connect through his wireless network, provided that he gives you the security key.

Other connection types

Other connection types include satellite and ISDN (an older, slower sort-of-DSL). If your connection doesn't fit neatly into a particular category, your setup still may be similar to those described in the following section. In any case, your ISP will provide equipment, instructions, and possibly an on-site technician.

Figure 12.1 Network Connections lists your current internet and network connections. Type descriptive connection names when you're prompted; the names appear as icon labels in this window.

Figure 12.2 These connection types are described in "Understanding Connection Types" earlier in this chapter.

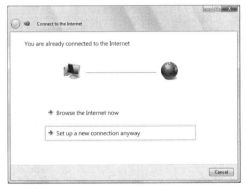

Figure 12.3 If you're connected already, this page appears instead of Figure 12.2. You still can create a new connection.

Connecting to the Internet

The Connect to the Internet wizard guides you through the steps of setting up an internet connection. The setup pages vary by connection type.

✔ Tips

■ Before you start, look in the Network Connections window for existing connections: Choose Start > Control Panel > Network and Internet > Network and Sharing Center > Manage Network Connections (on the left) (**Figure 12.1**).

■ Always favor your ISP's own instructions over the generic instructions given here.

■ Set up a firewall and secure your computer as soon as you're connected; see Chapter 13.

To connect to the internet:

1. Choose Start > Control Panel > Network and Internet > Network and Sharing Center > Set up a Connection or Network (on the left) > Connect to the Internet > Next.

or

If Welcome Center is open (see "Using Welcome Center" in Chapter 1), click the Connect to the Internet icon; then click Connect to the Internet in the top pane.

2. Click your connection type (**Figure 12.2**).

or

If a connection already exists, and you want to set up another one, click Set up a New Connection Anyway (**Figure 12.3**); select No, Create a New Connection; and then click Next. Figure 12.2 will appear; click your connection type.

continues on next page

3. Follow the onscreen instructions.

For dial-up connections, enter the local access telephone number, user name, and password that your ISP gave you (**Figure 12.4**).

For broadband (PPPoE) connections, the data-entry page is similar to Figure 12.4, but no local access number is needed.

For wireless connections, choose your wireless network (**Figure 12.5**). If the network is secured, type the password (**Figure 12.6**).

4. For dial-up and broadband connections, in Figure 12.4, check Allow Other People to Use This Connection to let all logged-on users use this connection; uncheck it if you don't want to share the connection.

5. On the last page of the wizard, click Connect to test the connection.

If the wizard can't connect, it gives you a chance to retry connecting, diagnose the problem, or create the connection anyway.

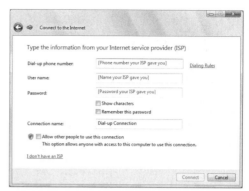

Figure 12.4 If you're a traveler with multiple dial-up connections on your laptop, use connection names like *AOL (New York)* or *ATT (San Francisco)*.

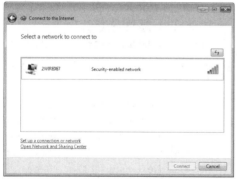

Figure 12.5 Depending on where you are, you may see ten or more in-range wireless networks in this list. Each list entry tells you whether the network is secured and gives its signal strength. (In the case of hotspots, you can move for a better signal.) To update the list, click Refresh (⟳).

Figure 12.6 This page appears when you try to connect to a secured wireless network, for which you need a password. Ask whoever set up the network.

CONNECTING TO THE INTERNET

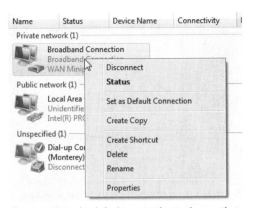

Figure 12.7 Set the default connection to the one that you use most often. A check mark appears on the default's icon.

✔ Tips

- For every new connection, an icon appears in Network Connections (refer to Figure 12.1). The newest connection becomes the default. To change the default, right-click the desired connection and choose Set As Default Connection (**Figure 12.7**). If a security prompt appears, type an administrator password or confirm the action.

- If you're disconnected, and you use a program that requires an internet connection (a web browser, for example), Windows displays a dialog box to let you connect. To connect manually, double-click a connection in Network Connections (**Figure 12.8**). If you double-click an active connection, you get its status (**Figure 12.9**).

continues on next page

Figure 12.8 This dialog box appears when you start a connection.

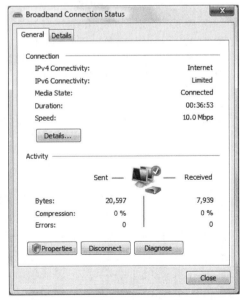

Figure 12.9 A connection's Status dialog box provides details about a connection, including how long you've been connected, how much you've downloaded or uploaded, and (on the Details tab) the IP address.

- To suppress the Connect dialog box (refer to Figure 12.8), right-click the connection and choose Properties > Options tab > uncheck Prompt for Name and Password, Certificate, Etc.

- To have Windows connect automatically when needed, choose Start > Control Panel > Network and Internet > Internet Options > Connections tab > check Always Dial My Default Connection.

- To add alternative numbers to a dial-up connection, right-click it and choose Properties > General tab > Alternates.

- To create another connection quickly, right-click an existing connection and choose Create Copy; then right-click the new icon and edit its properties.

- Network and Sharing Center is the main hub for network and internet connections and activities. Choose Start > Control Panel > Network and Internet > Network and Sharing Center (**Figure 12.10**).

- Hover your pointer over the Network icon in the notification area for a quick look at your current connections. Clicking the icon shows the same information plus a few links to related windows (**Figure 12.11**). Right-click the icon for even more commands.

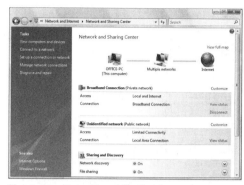

Figure 12.10 Network and Sharing Center shows an overview of your network and internet connections. The links in the left pane take you to related activities.

Figure 12.11 If the Network icon doesn't appear, right-click an empty area of the notification area and choose Properties > Notification Area tab > Network > OK.

Troubleshooting Tools

Windows includes a few tools that let you inspect and troubleshoot your internet and network connections.

Try Help first: Choose Start > Help and Support and search for *troubleshoot internet connection.*

The following command-line commands are faster and more useful than almost anything else in the graphical interface: ipconfig, netsh, netstat, pathping, ping, and tracert. Also try 3d Traceroute (free; www.d3tr.com).

To determine your actual internet connection speed (as opposed to what your ISP tells you), go to www.testmyspeed.com or http://speedtest.dslreports.com.

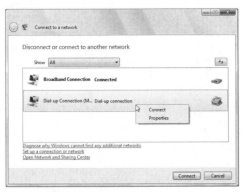

Figure 12.12 Right-click any connection to connect or disconnect, check its status, or see and change its properties. To access this window from Network and Sharing Center (refer to Figure 12.10), click Connect to a Network (in the left pane) or choose Start > Connect To.

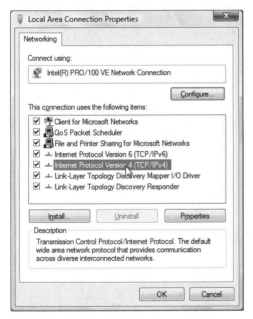

Figure 12.13 TCP/IP is the standard protocol for computer communications over the internet.

- Click Connect or Disconnect in Figure 12.11 for a quick way to review and control all your connections (**Figure 12.12**).

- When you close your browser or other internet program, a dial-up connection doesn't hang up automatically; it ties up your phone line until disconnected. By default, Windows disconnects automatically after 20 minutes of inactivity. To change this period, right-click the dial-up icon (refer to Figure 12.12) and choose Properties > Options tab; then select a time limit from the Idle Time Before Hanging Up list.

To set up a static IP connection:

1. Choose Start > Control Panel > Network and Internet > Network and Sharing Center > Manage Network Connections (in the left pane) (refer to Figure 12.10).

2. Right-click the Local Area Connection icon and choose Properties.

   If a security prompt appears, type an administrator password or confirm the action.

3. On the Networking tab, double-click Internet Protocol Version 4 (TCP/IPv4) in the connections list (**Figure 12.13**).

continues on next page

4. On the General tab, select Use the Following IP Address, select Use the Following DNS Server Addresses, and then type your IP addresses (**Figure 12.14**).

5. Click OK in each open dialog box.

✔ Tips

■ If you're using IPv6, repeat the procedure, but double-click Internet Protocol Version 6 (TCP/IPv6) in step 3.

■ If you have a static IP connection, and Windows ever prompts you to connect, choose Start > Control Panel > Network and Internet > Internet Options > Connections tab > check Never Dial a Connection.

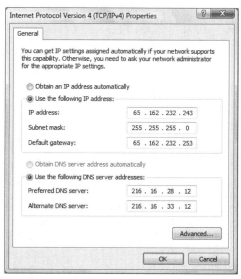

Figure 12.14 Your ISP may have sent you your static IP addresses, but you can type these settings while you've got your DSL provider, cable company, or network administrator on the phone.

Why Dynamic IP Addresses?

Dynamic IP addresses are more complicated than static ones, but they're needed because of the IP-address shortage. About 4.3 billion addresses exist (ranging from 0.0.0.0 to 255.255.255.255), but along with the growing number of networked computers, IP-aware cell phones and consumer toys, car navigation systems, shipping containers, and other devices are swallowing them up.

The problem with static addresses is that once an IP address is allocated to a particular computer or device, it's off the market—even when that machine is offline. With dynamic addresses, an online machine asks the server, "Got an IP address I can use temporarily?", and the server replies, "Take this one while you're here." It's a technically more difficult but more efficient use of a scarce resource.

SECURITY
AND PRIVACY

Computer security is no longer an after-thought, and a three-pronged defense will protect you from most attacks:

Firewall. A firewall is a secure boundary between your computer (or network) and the internet, protecting you against external threats such as crackers and malicious programs.

Software updates. Windows Update monitors the Microsoft website for new security patches, updates, bug fixes, and hardware drivers, which it downloads and installs promptly.

Malware protection. Malicious software, or malware, includes viruses and spyware. Antivirus and antispyware programs find and remove malware from your hard drives, down-loaded files, and email attachments. Most malware programs include an autoupdate feature to counter emerging threats.

This chapter also covers parental controls and encryption. Other security measures, such as User Account Control (Chapter 17), are covered where they're relevant.

"Hackers"

When computer insiders call someone a *hacker*, it's not an insult. Though the term is pejorative in the mainstream press and common usage, it actually acknowledges the person's advanced computer skills and ethos. Hackers generally aren't malicious, though some practice "electronic civil disobedience" to, say, expose flaws in electronic voting machines. In fact, hackers who discover security holes often report them quietly to software makers to be fixed before becoming common knowledge.

Cracker is the correct term for someone who breaks into systems to steal data and passwords, cause trouble, or make money.

For more information, search for *"hacker vs. cracker"* on the web. Look especially at Eric S. Raymond's *The Jargon File* (http://catb.org/jargon/html).

Checking Your Security Status

Windows Security Center is a one-stop Control Panel program for checking the status of your firewall, automatic updates, antivirus and antispyware software, and other security essentials on your computer. When something's amiss, a Security Center warning message appears in the notification area (**Figure 13.1**). This message and icon appear (or sometimes only the icon does) if Security Center thinks that your computer has insufficient protection, or if it doesn't recognize the firewall and antivirus software that you're using.

Figure 13.1 A message like this means that your computer's security settings need attention.

✔ Tip

- If you're on a network domain, you may not be able to use Security Center if your network administrator manages your security settings.

To open Security Center:

◆ Click the Security Center icon (⊗) or pop-up message, if it appears.

or

Choose Start > Control Panel > Security > Security Center.

or

Choose Start, type `security center` in the Search box, and then press Enter.

or

Press Windows logo key+R; type `wscui.cpl` and press Enter.

If a security prompt appears, type an administrator password or confirm the action.

Security Center (**Figure 13.2**) has a dashboard of indicator "lights" for your computer's firewall, updates, malware, and other components. For each item, a green bar and green light labeled On mean that everything is OK. Otherwise, you'll see a yellow or red bar and light labeled Off, Check Settings, Not Found, Not Monitored, or Out of Date. Click one of the headings to expand that section and to learn what the problem is and what to do about it. Security Center offers a status report and provides links to the relevant help screens, online resources, and Control Panel programs that you'll need to fix things.

Security status reports

Open individual security programs

Open the Microsoft security webpage in a browser

Change Security Center alert options

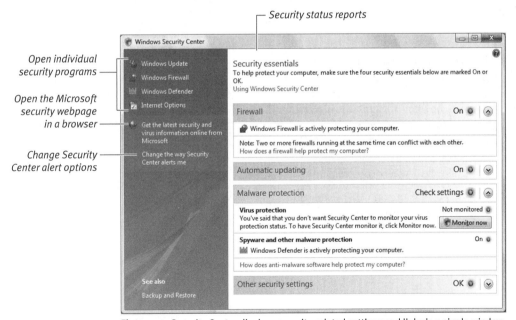

Figure 13.2 Security Center displays security-related settings and links in a single window.

If you don't want to be bothered with alerts, you can turn them off. You might want to do this if Security Center doesn't recognize your firewall or antimalware program, usually because you're using a third-party program that came out before Vista was released (look for an update).

To turn on or off Security Center alerts:

1. In Security Center, click Change the Way Security Center Alerts Me (in the left pane).

If a security prompt appears, type an administrator password or confirm the action.

2. Click the alert option that you want (**Figure 13.3**).

3. Click OK.

✔ Tips

■ Microsoft Baseline Security Analyzer is a little-known but excellent tool that scans your computer for security holes and suggests how to fix them. Download it for free at www.microsoft.com/technet/ security/tools/mbsahome.mspx. Its diagnoses contain some technical language but make clear where the problems lie.

■ A good general site on web privacy and security is www.junkbusters.com.

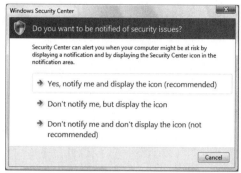

Figure 13.3 Security Center monitoring continues silently even if you switch off the alert notifications and icons.

Viruses and Spyware

Malicious software (malware) comes in two broad categories: viruses and spyware. They can resemble each other—they're both installed without your knowledge or consent and make your system unstable—but have some important differences.

A *virus* is a program that infects your computer. The type of attack depends on the skill and intent of the virus writer. A virus can erase or corrupt files, steal your personal data, spread other viruses, email copies of itself to people in your address list, chew up memory to slow or halt your system, install a backdoor that lets remote attackers log on to your computer, turn your computer into a *zombie* that sends spam without your knowledge . . . or only display a practical-joke screen. A virus often arrives as an innocent-looking email attachment with an executable file extension such as .exe, .scr, .bat, or .pif (see "Associating Documents with Programs" in Chapter 6).

Viruses have specialized variants. A *worm* is a self-replicating virus that spreads quickly over a network. A *Trojan horse* is a destructive program disguised as legitimate or enticing software, or even as a logon screen. (A file named `sexy.exe` or `FreeMP3s.bat` probably is dangerous.) Trojans don't replicate themselves like worms, but they can be just as destructive. A *dialer* uses your modem to make calls to premium-rate telephone numbers (at, say, $20 per minute).

Spyware (or *adware*) relies on people's credulity or ignorance—children are a favorite target—to download and install it. Trickery or bait often are part of the repertoire. If a pop-up window that looks like a legitimate Windows dialog box appears when you're browsing, don't click an Agree, OK, or Close button; that might trigger a spyware installer. Instead, always click the red close button ( ) or press Alt+F4 in this situation.

Other programs, such as the popular Kazaa and BearShare file-swapping programs, promise free music or software but also install spyware surreptitiously. Some spyware exploits security flaws in Internet Explorer to install itself when you simply *visit* a website (usually a pornographic or "Free Stuff!" site—you'll learn to recognize them); it's not unusual for these *drive-by downloads* to install dozens of spyware programs on your PC in a single visit.

Like those of viruses, spyware's effects depend on the creator's intent. Spyware can report your browsing habits to third parties, hijack your browser's home page, redirect your web searches, inundate you with ads (even when you're offline), steal online-store affiliate commissions, or plant a new barnaclelike toolbar in your browser. You also may notice system slowdowns and instability, but these are only side effects; spyware's aim is profit, not destruction.

CHECKING YOUR SECURITY STATUS

Using a Firewall

A *firewall* is a piece of software or hardware that helps screen out crackers and viruses that try to reach your computer over the internet. It's the most important security component on your PC or network; attackers can compromise your computer easily if you don't have one. Always turn on a firewall *before* you connect to the internet, no matter how you connect. It's no exaggeration to say that unprotected computers often are compromised minutes after going online.

Windows provides Windows Firewall for free, but you have choices:

Router (hardware). A router is a small box that distributes the signal from your modem (DSL, cable, or dial-up) to the computers on your network (**Figure 13.4**). A router has a built-in firewall and appears to the outside world to be a computer without programs and hard drives to attack or infect; it's the safest type of firewall, because it protects your entire network and is always on. Even if you're not on a network, you can put a router between your PC and your modem. (Chapter 18 covers routers in more detail.)

If you're on a network, a router won't protect you from *other* computers on the network if one of them becomes infected because someone downloaded a virus. For that kind of protection, you'll need a software firewall on your individual computer. Also, laptop users will want a software firewall so that they don't have to lug around a router. If all you need is a router, turn off the Windows (software) firewall, ignoring the dire warning that appears.

Figure 13.4 This Linksys firewall router is popular for home and small-office networks. Other brand-name router makers include 3Com, D-Link, NETGEAR, Belkin, SMC, and Microsoft.

USING A FIREWALL

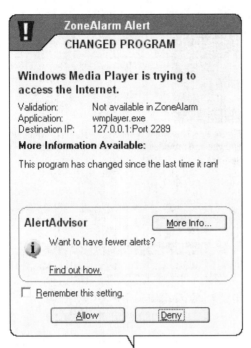

Figure 13.5 This personal firewall, ZoneAlarm (free; www.zonealarm.com), asks you whether you want to allow or forbid a program to access the internet from your computer. (It might surprise you how many programs try this.) Check Remember This Setting to always allow or always deny a program access, suppressing this dialog box for that program.

Third-party firewall (software). You can use a non-Microsoft firewall instead of Windows' built-in one. You can find lots of free and for-pay software firewalls on the web by searching for *personal firewall* or by visiting www.firewallguide.com/software. Popular ones include ZoneAlarm, BlackICE, Norton, Sunbelt Kerio, Kaspersky, and F-Secure. Personal firewalls block inbound and outbound traffic. Blocking outbound traffic selectively can stop spyware and viruses on an already-infected PC from sending your personal information out. Every time that a program (*any* program) tries to access the internet, the firewall intercepts it and asks for your approval (**Figure 13.5**).

Security Center recognizes popular third-party firewalls and turns off its own firewall automatically. (Don't run two software firewalls at the same time; you might not be able to get online.) If Security Center doesn't know your firewall, turn off Windows Firewall manually—and look for a post-Vista update of your firewall.

Windows Firewall (software). Windows Firewall is available in Control Panel and turned on by default with the safest settings chosen.

To turn on or off Windows Firewall:

1. Choose Start > Control Panel > Security > Windows Firewall.

    or

    In Security Center, click the Windows Firewall link (in the left pane).

    or

    Choose Start, type `windows firewall` in the Search box, and then select Windows Firewall in the results list.

    or

    Press Windows logo key+R; type `firewall.cpl` and press Enter.

2. Click Turn Windows Firewall On or Off (in the left pane; **Figure 13.6**).

    If a security prompt appears, type an administrator password or confirm the action.

3. Click On or Off; then click OK (**Figure 13.7**).

✔ Tips

■ You can check Block All Incoming Connections (refer to Figure 13.7) to block *all* unsolicited incoming traffic, even traffic that normally would be permitted by an exception (described next). Use this extra-secure mode when you connect to a public wireless hotspot in a café, airport, or hotel, or when a virus is spreading over your network.

■ A very secure way to protect yourself from wireless hotspot hazards is HotSpotVPN ($8.88 per month U.S.; `www.hotspotvpn.com`).

Figure 13.6 This window shows the status of Windows Firewall and provides links for changing the default settings.

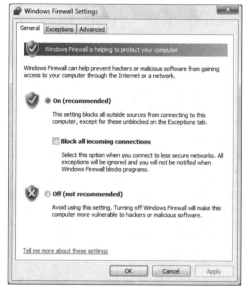

Figure 13.7 In general, the only reason to switch off Windows Firewall is if you've installed a third-party firewall. (Windows Firewall turns itself off automatically if you install a Vista-aware firewall.)

Figure 13.8 Online gamers see this dialog box often. You'll never see it on a public or network PC on which the administrator has blocked *all* exceptions.

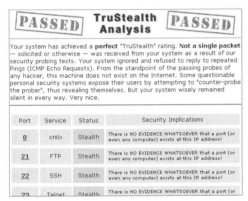

Figure 13.9 A sterling security report for a firewalled computer.

Traffic flows in and out of your computer through *ports*—small, authorized doors in the firewall. (These ports aren't the same as the hardware ports that you connect devices to.) A port number identifies each port uniquely, and certain ports handle only a specific type of traffic. Port 80 is used for HTTP (web) traffic, for example. Other ports allow instant messages, printer sharing, and so on. (You can find others by searching the web for *"well-known ports"*.)

Windows Firewall leaves some ports open by default (File and Printer Sharing and your local network connections, for example) but blocks most of them to incoming traffic, so when a new program wants to get online, the firewall displays a dialog box asking you whether it's OK (**Figure 13.8**). Click:

◆ **Unblock** if you recognize the program name. The firewall opens the relevant listening port for this connection and future incoming connections. If a security prompt appears, type an administrator password or confirm the action.

◆ **Keep Blocking** if you don't know which program the firewall is asking about, or if you know it but don't want it phoning home. The program might not work properly if it can't accept incoming traffic (desirable in some cases).

✔ Tip

■ To test your computer for online vulnerabilities, go to www.grc.com and navigate to the ShieldsUP! page; then run the tests (**Figure 13.9**). (The tests take some reading and clicking to find.) This website also contains a lot of useful internet security information, as well as free and for-pay software.

Common sense applies to opening ports: Open one only when you really need it, never unblock a program that you don't recognize, and close a port when you no longer need it. But sometimes you'll change your mind about a program or will be tricked into unblocking a hostile program named to fool you. Windows Firewall lets you create *exceptions* for these programs and manage them manually.

To configure programs and ports:

1. Open Windows Firewall.

2. Click Allow a Program Through Windows Firewall (in the left pane; refer to Figure 13.6).

   If a security prompt appears, type an administrator password or confirm the action.

3. On the Exceptions tab of the Windows Firewall Settings dialog box (**Figure 13.10**), do any of the following:

   ▲ To open or close ports for specific programs, check or uncheck the boxes.

   ▲ To add a program, click Add Program; then select it in the list or browse to it.

   ▲ To delete a program, select it in the list; then click Delete. (You can't delete the preconfigured programs.)

   ▲ To open an individual port by number, click Add Port; then type the port name (any name) and number, and select a protocol. (Windows assumes that you're geeky enough to know the port number and protocol or that you read it in the program's documentation.)

   If you're adding a program or port, you can click Change Scope to change the set of computers that can use this port.

4. Click OK in each open dialog box.

Figure 13.10 The Exceptions tab lists every program that's been granted an open port in the firewall.

✔ Tips

■ Adding a program is preferable to opening a specific port because it's easier to do, you don't need to know which port number to use, and the firewall is open only while the program is waiting to receive the connection.

■ To protect or unprotect individual internet and network connections, or to restore the firewall's default settings, click the Advanced tab in the Windows Firewall Settings dialog box (refer to Figure 13.10).

USING A FIREWALL

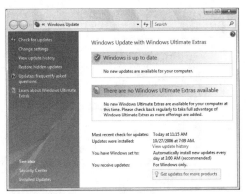

Figure 13.11 This window shows the status of Windows Update and provides links that let you control and view updates.

Updating Windows

Microsoft publishes patches, bug fixes, and other improvements on its website. These changes include minor additions to the Windows feature set, upgrades to the free programs, and driver updates. The most important changes are those designated *critical updates* or *hotfixes,* which plug security holes or fix stability problems. Periodically, Microsoft combines new fixes and previously released ones into a package called a *Service Pack* (SP). Never wait for an SP to install updates, particularly critical updates (which appear with alarming regularity).

You can use Windows Update to choose how and when updates are installed on your computer. By default, Windows Update is set to the most secure option: Automatic, which checks Microsoft's website regularly for important fixes and, if they're available, downloads and installs them automatically. Security Center objects to any other setting and alerts you with a Not Automatic or Off message if you choose something weaker than Automatic.

To set up Windows Update:

1. Choose Start > Control Panel > Security > Windows Update.

   or

   In Security Center, click the Windows Update link (in the left pane).

   or

   Choose Start, type windows update in the Search box, and then press Enter.

2. Do one of the following (**Figure 13.11**):

   ▲ To check for updates now, click Check for Updates.

   continues on next page

▲ To change when and how updates are applied, click Change Settings, choose among the options described in **Table 13.1**, and then click OK (**Figure 13.12**). If a security prompt appears, type an administrator password or confirm the action.

▲ To review the updates installed to date, click View Update History (**Figure 13.13**).

▲ To see or install updates that you previously declined to install, click Restore Hidden Updates.

Figure 13.12 Windows can download and install updates without your intervention (first option), ask for your permission (second or third options), or leave everything for you to do manually (fourth option).

Table 13.1

Windows Update Options

Option	Description
Install Updates Automatically (Recommended)	This set-it-and-forget-it option downloads and installs all patches automatically, according to the schedule you choose. This option is appropriate if you have an always-on internet connection (DSL or cable). If you miss an update because you're offline, it'll catch up with you when you go back on.
Download Updates but Let Me Choose Whether to Install Them	The download happens in the background, silently and without interfering with anything that you might be downloading yourself. After download, Windows alerts you to get your permission to install the update. This option lets you research the patch before you install it; try Google or www.annoyances.org to see whether it's giving people trouble.
Check for Updates but Let Me Choose Whether to Download and Install Them	Windows alerts you when it detects an update on the Microsoft website. With your permission, it downloads and installs it in separate steps. This option is a good choice for on-the-go laptop users.
Never Check for Updates (Not Recommended)	No updates occur. Choose this option if you want to update Windows manually (by clicking Check for Updates) or if you're on a network domain and you update from a network server rather than from Microsoft directly.
Recommended Updates	Uncheck this box if you want Windows Update to download and install only critical updates, and omit less important (but often useful) "recommended updates."

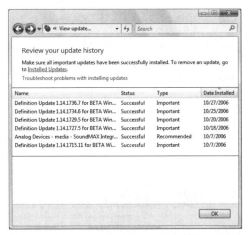

Figure 13.13 You can *un*install an update if it's causing problems. Click Installed Updates in this window, or choose Start > Control Panel > Programs > Programs and Features > View Installed Updates.

✔ Tips

■ Try Help if you're having a problem updating: Choose Start > Help and Support, and search for *troubleshoot updates*.

■ If you ignore Windows Update when it's ready to install an update and try to shut down, a shield appears on the Power button in the Start menu (see "Logging On and Logging Off" in Chapter 1). Clicking this button ends your session, installs the updates, and then shuts down your computer.

Updating Device Drivers

Windows Update can provide new device drivers for your PC's hardware. Unlike the other types of updates, this one should be approached skeptically, because Windows Update has a habit of recommending the wrong drivers for some hardware.

I recommend that you install drivers for only Microsoft-branded hardware, such as mice, keyboards, and game controllers. For other products, download drivers from the manufacturers' websites directly. And don't be surprised if the sites don't offer an updated driver; it means only that Windows Update guessed wrong about your equipment.

If Windows Update installed a driver, and your device stopped working, you can roll back; see "Managing Device Drivers" in Chapter 8.

Defending Against Viruses and Spyware

Security Center helps protect your computer against viruses and spyware (called malicious software, or malware) by checking whether your computer is using up-to-date antivirus and antispyware programs (**Figure 13.14**).

Viruses

Windows doesn't provide an antivirus program. If you want one (see the "Is Antivirus Software Necessary?" sidebar), you'll have to install your own. If it's Vista-aware, Security Center will find it, monitor it, and respond with a green On light when happy. If it's not Vista-aware, click Show Me My Available Options in Figure 13.14 and choose a monitoring option (**Figure 13.15**). (To show this link, you may have to click the Monitor Now button in the Malware Protection section of Security Center; refer to Figure 13.2.)

Figure 13.14 If an antimalware program is turned off or out of date, Security Center tells you here and posts an alert in the notification area.

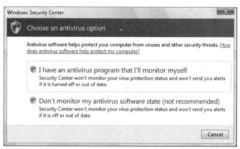

Figure 13.15 Both these options are identical as far as Windows is concerned. The "Not Recommended" option is just Microsoft's way of reminding you to install an antivirus program.

Is Antivirus Software Necessary?

No. Plenty of people—including me—use no virus protection and don't get infected. I don't like antivirus programs because they display chronic Chicken Little warnings that interfere with my workflow, program installations, and routine internet transactions.

If you think that you have a virus, run an antivirus program to eradicate it. The 24/7 protection that continuously running antivirus programs promise is cold comfort.

The best way to avoid viruses is to *behave* safely: Use hardware and software firewalls, keep Windows updated, use a Standard (not Administrator) account for everyday use, delete executable or risky email attachments (even from friends), browse with Mozilla Firefox instead of Internet Explorer, use an aggressive spam filter, learn to recognize untrustworthy websites and email, and use open-source software whenever possible (try www.sourceforge.net and www.freshmeat.net).

Also, ignore virus myths, publicity stunts, hoaxes, chain letters, and hysteria. Take a look at some back issues of Crypt Newsletter (http://sun.soci.niu.edu/~crypt).

To get Microsoft's recommendations for antivirus programs, click Find a Program in Figure 13.14. This launches your browser to show a list of programs at Microsoft's website.

Spyware

Windows Defender (**Figure 13.16**), new in Vista, protects your computer against spyware infections. You can use real-time (always-on) protection and manual (on-demand) scanning.

To open Windows Defender:

◆ Choose Start > Control Panel > Security > Windows Defender.

or

In Security Center, click the Windows Defender link (in the left pane).

or

Choose Start, type `windows defender` in the Search box, and then press Enter.

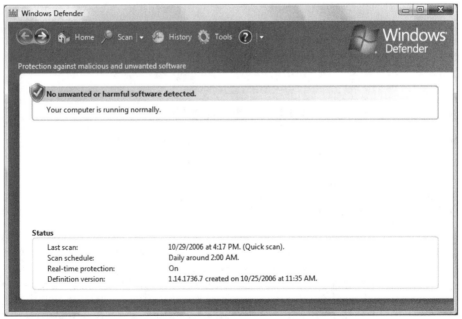

Figure 13.16 Spyware can try to install itself secretly any time you're connected to the internet, or possibly when you install some programs from a CD, DVD, or other removable media.

By default, Defender is turned on and alerts you when spyware tries to self-install, run, or change important Windows settings.

Defender uses color-coded severity levels for alerts: Severe, High, Medium, Low, and Not Yet Classified. Depending on the alert level, you can choose one of the actions in **Table 13.2** to apply to the software. For Severe and High, remove the software immediately. For Medium, consider removing or quarantining it if you don't trust the publisher. For Low and Not Yet Classified, the software is probably benign, but it's your call. If software tries to change a system setting, Defender asks you to permit or deny the change.

Table 13.2

Windows Defender Actions	
ACTION	DESCRIPTION
Ignore	Allows the software to be installed or run. If the software still is running during the next scan, or if it tries to change security-related settings, Defender alerts you again.
Quarantine	Moves the software to another location on your computer and prevents it from running until you restore or delete it. To view and manage these items, choose Tools > Quarantined Items.
Remove	Deletes the software permanently.
Always Allow	Adds the software to the Allowed Items list and lets it run. Defender stops alerting you about the software. Choose this option only if you trust the software and the software publisher. To move and manage this list, choose Tools > Allowed Items.

Is DRM Software a Virus?

Almost all antivirus programs are worthless. Security experts (real ones) know this, but it's the elephant in the living room that no one talks about.

In 2005, for example, Sony distributed a nasty program called a *rootkit* on its music CDs. This rootkit installed itself secretly with the purpose of preventing music copying. It was nominally digital rights management (DRM) software, but what it really did was leave PCs vulnerable to attacks.

Almost no antivirus program removed the rootkit until the whole sorry mess went public; some vendors apparently were appeasing Sony. For details, see Bruce Schneier's article "Sony's DRM Rootkit: The Real Story" (www.schneier.com/blog/archives/2005/11/sonys_drm_rootk.html).

When I need antivirus software, I try Kaspersky (www.kaspersky.com) and F-Secure (www.f-secure.com) first. I never bother with Norton or McAfee.

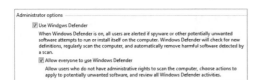

Figure 13.17 You can uncheck the bottom box to prevent nonadministrators from using Defender.

Figure 13.18 Use a custom scan if you think that spyware has infected a specific area of your computer.

To turn Windows Defender on or off:

1. Choose Tools > Options.

2. Under Administrator Options, check or uncheck Use Windows Defender (**Figure 13.17**).

   If a security prompt appears, type an administrator password or confirm the action.

3. Click Save.

By default, Defender checks for new spyware definitions and regularly scans your hard disks for spyware, removing any that it finds. You can run a quick, full, or custom scan manually at any time.

To run a scan:

◆ To run a quick scan, click Scan.

   or

   To run a full system scan, click the down arrow next to the Scan button and choose Full Scan.

   or

   To run a custom scan, click the down arrow next to the Scan button and choose Custom Scan. Click Select, choose the drives and folders that you want to check (**Figure 13.18**), click OK, and then click Scan Now.

   If a security prompt appears, type an administrator password or confirm the action.

DEFENDING AGAINST VIRUSES AND SPYWARE

Defender's default options are safe and unintrusive, but you can customize them to change:

◆ Whether and how often automatic scans take place

◆ Actions to display or apply for a specific alert levels

◆ The aspects of Windows that real-time protection monitors

◆ Advanced options

To set Windows Defender options:

1. Choose Tools > Options (**Figure 13.19**).

2. Set the desired options.

3. Click Save.

   If a security prompt appears, type an administrator password or confirm the action.

✔ Tips

■ To see (or clear) the history of your Windows Defender activities, click History (on the toolbar).

■ Defender offers access to the online Microsoft SpyNet community to help you see how other people respond to software that has not yet been classified for risks. To join, choose Tools > Microsoft SpyNet and follow the onscreen instructions.

■ You can use the Software Explorer tool to see detailed information about software that is currently running on your computer, including programs that run automatically at startup. Choose Tools > Software Explorer (**Figure 13.20**).

Figure 13.19 You can set dozens of options in Windows Defender.

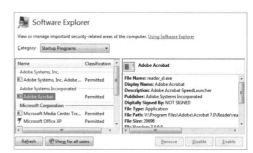

Figure 13.20 Use the Category list to monitor startup programs, currently running programs, network-connected programs, or low-level networking and communication (Winsock) services.

Antispyware Resources

You're most likely to pick up spyware when you download free file-sharing *(peer-to-peer)*, shopping, animated-buddy, weather, toolbar, or search utilities. The home sites of some utilities swear that they're spyware free, but they define "spyware" very narrowly.

PC Pitstop publishes a regularly updated "Top 25 Spyware and Adware" list at www.pcpitstop.com/spycheck/top25.asp. Before you visit a suspect website, check it out at www.siteadvisor.com or www.stopbadware.org.

Spyware is very difficult to remove without a spyware cleaner (and sometimes with one), so do a little research before you download a suspicious program. Search the Web for the program name and *"spyware"*. A *kazaa spyware* search, for example, yields more than 3 million hits. Some sites that list clean freeware are www.nonags.com, www.pricelessware.org, www.onlythebestfreeware.com, and www.majorgeeks.com.

Some spyware-laden programs fraudulently promise to *remove* spyware. Spyware Warrior (www.spywarewarrior.com) publishes a list of such products (click the Rogue/Suspect Anti-Spyware link). Other worthwhile sites are www.benedelman.org and www.spywareinfo.com.

No spyware cleaner can detect every spyware program, so use a second cleaner in tandem. Try Ad-Aware SE Personal Edition (free; www.lavasoftusa.com), Spybot Search & Destroy (free; www.safer-networking.org), or Spy Sweeper ($30 U.S.; www.webroot.com).

DEFENDING AGAINST VIRUSES AND SPYWARE

Setting Parental Controls

Parental Controls, new in Vista (Home and Ultimate editions only), lets you manage how your children (or anyone) can use the computer. You can set limits on web access, logon hours, games played, and programs run.

Before you start, set up a standard user account for each child, and log on yourself as an administrator. Parental Controls can be applied only to standard users, not administrators. To create accounts, see "Setting up User Accounts" in Chapter 17.

To set up Parental Controls:

1. Choose Start > Control Panel > Security > Parental Controls.

   or

   Choose Start, type parental controls in the Search box, and then press Enter.

   If a security prompt appears, type an administrator password or confirm the action.

2. Click the Standard user account to which you want to apply parental controls (**Figure 13.21**).

3. Under Parental Controls, select On, Enforce Current Settings (**Figure 13.22**).

Figure 13.21 If you haven't set up Standard accounts for your kids, this screen provides links to the User Accounts tool.

Figure 13.22 The settings apply only to the indicated user account. You can apply different parental controls to each child individually.

Table 13.3

Parental Control Settings

SETTING	DESCRIPTION
Windows Vista Web Filter	Specifies which websites your children can and can't visit. You can create a custom Allow list or Block list. You also can block websites based on their content (pornography, drugs, hate speech, and so on), but this filter isn't dependable. You can disable downloads too.
Time Limits	Specifies, in a 24 x 7 grid, the times when your children can and can't log on. If they're already logged on during a blocked time, they'll be logged off automatically.
Games	Specifies whether any game-playing is allowed and, if so, which game ratings (Mature, Teen, Everyone, and so on) are permitted. You also can limit specific games.
Allow or Block Specific Programs	Specify whether all installed programs can be run or only the ones you choose.

4. Adjust the individual settings that you want to control (**Table 13.3**).

5. Click OK.

✔ Tips

■ When your child is logged on, he can click a notification-area icon (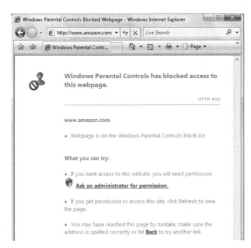) to see which restrictions you've applied.

■ When Parental Controls blocks access to a webpage or game, it displays a "You've been blocked" message (**Figure 13.23**).

■ You can use activity reports to check your child's online comings and goings. In Figure 13.21, click the account of whoever you want to spy on. Under Activity Reporting, select On, Collect Information About Computer Usage (refer to Figure 13.22). To see the reports, go back to the same page and click View Activity Reports.

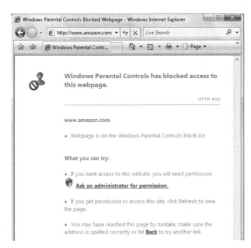

Figure 13.23 Your child can click a link to request permission for access to that webpage or program. You can allow access by entering your account information.

SETTING PARENTAL CONTROLS

Encrypting Data

Encryption is one of the strongest ways to secure your sensitive documents and personal information. When you encrypt files, Windows' Encrypting File System (EFS) scrambles them so that only you can read them, providing an extra measure of protection for user accounts (Chapter 17). EFS is transparent: Encrypted file and folder icons change color, but otherwise, you open, edit, and save them in the usual way.

✔ Tips

- EFS isn't available in Vista Home editions, but see the "Stronger Encryption Tools" sidebar.

- EFS works on only NTFS-formatted hard drives, not FAT or FAT32. To check a drive, choose Start > Computer, right-click a drive icon, and choose Properties > General tab. The File System entry should be NTFS.

- NTFS-compressed files can't be EFS-encrypted (but you *can* encrypt zipped folders). See "Compressing Files and Folders" in Chapter 5.

- You can't encrypt system files, such as those in the Windows folder.

To encrypt a file or folder:

1. In Windows Explorer, right-click the file or folder that you want to encrypt and choose Properties > General tab > Advanced.

    If the Advanced button is missing, the selected file or folder isn't on an NTFS drive.

2. Check Encrypt Contents to Secure Data (**Figure 13.24**).

3. Click OK in each open dialog box.

Figure 13.24 If you've selected a folder to encrypt, Windows responds with a Confirm Attribute Change message box, asking you whether you want to encrypt just that folder or everything that it contains too.

Figure 13.25 Generally, you should encrypt folders and all their contents so that it's easier to track what's encrypted and what's not.

Stronger Encryption Tools

EFS isn't all that safe, because an administrator can use a Group Policy "backdoor" to recover your encrypted data. For better protection, use a stand-alone encryption tool such as TrueCrypt (free; www.truecrypt.org).

Before you pick a tool, read Matt Curtin's "Snake Oil Warning Signs: Encryption Software to Avoid" (www.interhack.net/people/cmcurtin/snake-oil-faq.html). And try Bruce Schneier's free monthly Crypto-Gram newsletter (www.counterpane.com/crypto-gram.html). After encrypting files, paranoids should flush RAM and shred the swap file so that enemies can't lift passwords and keys with forensic tools.

A simple alternative to encrypting files is hiding them. (You can't steal what you can't find.) Try Hide Folders ($30 U.S.; www.fspro.net), Magic Folders ($25 U.S.; www.pc-magic.com), or bProtected ($20 U.S.; www.clasys.com).

✔ Tips

■ If you encrypt only a folder, EFS won't encrypt any files currently in the folder, but it will encrypt any new files that you copy, move, or create within the folder.

■ If you encrypt a file in an unencrypted folder, Windows displays an Encryption Warning dialog box that lets you choose whether to encrypt only the file or both the file and its parent folder (**Figure 13.25**).

■ EFS encrypts any file or folder that you move into an encrypted folder but won't decrypt one that you drag *out* unless you decrypt it manually by unchecking the Encrypt box in Figure 13.24, drag it to a FAT or FAT32 drive, or transmit it via email or network. (Lesson: Don't keep encrypted material on shared network drives; other users can read it without your account password.)

■ When you decrypt a folder, Windows asks whether you want all files and sub-folders within the folder to be decrypted as well. If you choose to decrypt the folder only, the encrypted files and folders within the decrypted folder remain encrypted. But EFS won't encrypt new files and folder that you copy, move, or create within the decrypted folder.

■ To display encrypted files and folders in a different color in Windows Explorer, choose Organize > Folder and Search Options > View tab > check Show Encrypted or Compressed NTFS Files in Color > OK. Consider *not* coloring encrypted files so that onlookers won't know that you're using EFS.

ENCRYPTING DATA

14

INTERNET EXPLORER

After your internet connection is working (Chapter 12), use Internet Explorer (IE) to browse the web. If you've used IE before, turn the page; otherwise, here's a 30-second tutorial:

◆ The *internet* is a global network that connects millions of computers. Unlike online services like AOL, the internet is decentralized—by design. You can use to it exchange data, news, opinions, ideas, and things (you can buy or sell almost anything on it).

◆ The *World Wide Web,* or simply *web,* is a way of viewing and sharing information over the internet via specially formatted documents—*webpages*—that support text, graphics, sounds, video, and links to other webpages. A *website* is a group of related webpages.

◆ A *web browser* is an application that locates and displays webpages, and downloads files to your hard drive.

✔ Tip

■ The web is a *portion* of the internet. (The terms are not synonyms.) The internet contains not only the web, but also channels for email and newsgroups (Chapter 15), as well as instant messages (Chapter 16).

Mozilla Firefox

IE is popular because it's included with Windows, but Mozilla Firefox (free; www.mozilla.org/products/firefox) is a better browser, even accounting for IE 7's new features. Firefox is smaller, faster, simpler, more secure, and updated more frequently. You can customize it with easily installed extensions (free add-ons) that include a Google toolbar, Adobe Flash–animation suppressor, banner-ad killer, weather-forecast display, and hundreds more. One of its best features finds webpage text as you type, with no need for a Find dialog box.

Firefox can import and export IE settings and bookmarks. Also, it has an extension that opens a webpage in IE in case it doesn't display or work properly in Firefox (which happens occasionally).

Getting Started with Internet Explorer

Figure 14.1 shows Internet Explorer's main controls. You can point (without clicking) to any control for a pop-up tip. The important part of IE is not the program itself but the webpages and resources that it gives you access to. You'll spend most of your browsing time working within the web itself—reading, searching, scrolling, clicking links, filling out forms, downloading files—rather than using IE's controls and menus.

To start Internet Explorer:

◆ Choose Start > Internet Explorer (or Start > All Programs > Internet Explorer).

or

Click the Internet Explorer icon (🅔) on the Quick Launch toolbar, located on the taskbar.

or

Double-click an internet shortcut.

or

Choose Start, type `internet explorer` in the Search box, and then press Enter.

or

Press Windows logo key+R; type `iexplore` and press Enter.

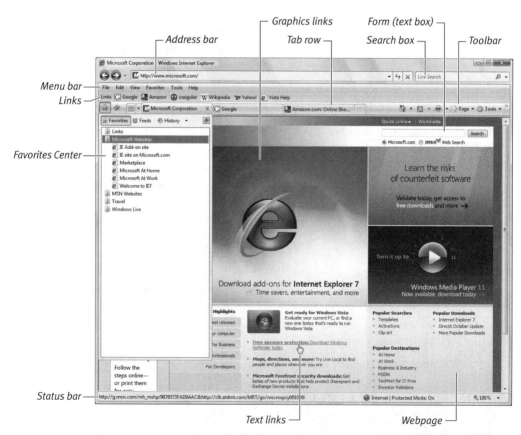

Figure 14.1 Internet Explorer's main panel shows a webpage (Microsoft's home page, in this case).

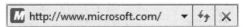

Figure 14.2 The address bar displays the address (URL) of the current webpage. Type a new address to go to a different page.

Figure 14.3 (Left to right) Back button, Forward button, and Recent Pages menu.

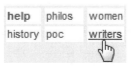

Figure 14.4 Links take you to a new webpage (or another place on the same page).

| help | philos | women |
| history | poc | writers |

human genome project

Figure 14.5 Type keywords in the Search box and press Enter to search the web.

Navigating the Web

You have a few ways to move among webpages:

◆ Type a web address (URL) (**Figure 14.2**).

◆ Click a navigation button (**Figure 14.3**).

◆ Click a *link,* or *hyperlink* (**Figure 14.4**).

◆ Search for a webpage on a specific topic (**Figure 14.5**).

URLs

A *URL* (Uniform Resource Locator) is a case-insensitive address that identifies a webpage uniquely. The URL for Microsoft's home page, for example, is `http://www.microsoft.com`. The transmission standard for all webpages is `http://`, so you don't type it (IE fills it in for you). The rest of the address specifies the web server and the webpage's location on it. Some URLs don't need the `www.`; others require additional dot-separated elements.

The server name's last part (called the *top-level domain,* or *TLD*) usually tells you about the website's owner or country. `.com` is a business, `.gov` is a government, `.edu` is a school, and `.org` is a not-for-profit organization, for example. `.uk` is a United Kingdom site; `.ca` is a Canadian site, and so on. For a list of TLDs, see `www.iana.org/domain-names.htm`.

Like your own documents, webpage files are organized in folder trees on the server, so a long URL (`www.microsoft.com/windows/support`, for example) works like a pathname. Complicated URLs that contain ?, =, and & symbols are pages created on the fly in response to a query.

Note that URLs use forward slashes, not backslashes as in Windows pathnames.

By the way, articulate each letter: *U–R–L.* Don't say *earl.*

✔ Tips

- Text links typically are underlined blue phrases (or they were until web designers decided to be artists). Pictures and buttons also can be links. Some links sprout a menu when you point to them. If links are hard to spot at first, watch your pointer; wherever it turns from an arrow into a finger-pointing hand (👆), you've discovered a link.

- **Tools ▾** To show or hide the menu bar, status bar, Links, and other parts of the IE interface, use the Tools menu (on the toolbar). To set which buttons appear on the toolbar itself, choose Tools (Alt+O) > Toolbars > Customize (**Figure 14.6**). If you don't show the menu bar permanently, you can always summon it by pressing Alt.

- To visit a page on a particular website, go to the site's home page; then use *the site's* search and navigation tools to find your target. **Table 14.1** lists a few sites to get you started.

- If an error message ("Cannot find server" or "The page cannot be displayed") appears instead of a webpage, you may have mistyped the URL, or the webpage may have been moved.

- The status bar shows IE's progress ("Waiting for . . ." or "Done") and displays the target URL of any link that you point to.

- Press Alt+L to show IE's Help menu.

Figure 14.6 To lock the toolbar (and other bars) after you've made changes, choose Tools > Toolbars > Lock the Toolbars.

Table 14.1

Website Sampler	
TOPIC	SITE
Auctions	www.ebay.com
Blogging	www.blogger.com
Classifieds	www.craigslist.org
Dating	www.match.com
Encyclopedia	www.wikipedia.org
Everything	www.yahoo.com
File sharing	www.torrentspy.com
Great books	www.bartleby.com
Internet security	www.cert.org
Jobs	www.monster.com
Legal	www.nolo.com
Maps	http://maps.google.com
Movie reviews	www.rottentomatoes.com
Movies	www.imdb.com
Open source	http://sourceforge.net
Photo galleries	www.flickr.com
Search	www.google.com
Shareware	www.download.com
Shopping	www.amazon.com
Socializing	www.myspace.com
Tech terms	www.webopedia.com
Travel	www.travelzoo.com
Videos	www.youtube.com
Weather (U.S.)	www.weather.gov
Web design	www.useit.com

To visit a webpage by typing a URL:

1. Click the address bar (or press Alt+D).

2. Type or paste the URL and press Enter.

✔ Tips

- If you type a URL in the *Windows* Explorer address bar, it launches IE with that webpage. If you type a pathname (C:\Users\John\Documents, for example) in the *IE* address bar, Windows Explorer goes to that location.

- The address bar autocompletes—that is, proposes a list of matching sites that you've visited recently. Keep typing or use the down-arrow key to select a match; then press Enter. To show or hide the address list manually, press F4.

- Typing shortcut: To visit a .com site, type only the business name; then press Ctrl+Enter. IE adds the http://www. and .com bits automatically. (Even without this shortcut, IE adds http:// if you don't.)

- When you're editing a URL, Ctrl+Left arrow or Ctrl+Right arrow jump back or forward to the URL's next logical break (dot or slash).

NAVIGATING THE WEB

To visit a webpage via navigation buttons or links:

◆ Click a link in a webpage, email message, or document.

or

To revisit pages that you've seen recently, click Back (Backspace or Alt+Left arrow), Forward (Alt+Right arrow), or Recent Pages (**Figure 14.7**).

or

History ▾ To return to a page you've visited in the past few weeks, choose Tools > Toolbars > History (or press Ctrl+Shift+H); then click a link on the History bar (**Figure 14.8**).

or

To go to a bookmarked page, choose it from the Favorites Center (press Alt+C); see "Bookmarking Pages" later in this chapter.

✔ Tips

■ To stop downloading a page, click Stop (✖) at the right end of the address bar (or press Esc).

■ To reload a stale or incomplete page, click Refresh (↻) at the right end of the address bar (or press F5). But Refresh decides for itself what and what not to fetch from the web server; Ctrl+Refresh forces a reload of everything and may bring you newer content.

■ To erase your browsing history, choose Tools > Internet Options > General tab > Delete (below Browsing History) > Delete History > Yes > Close. To change the number of days that pages are saved in the History list, click Settings (below Browsing History) (**Figure 14.9**).

Figure 14.7 Click the Recent Pages button to jump back or forward several pages.

Figure 14.8 The History bar is an organized list of pages that you've visited recently. Click a calendar icon to list the websites visited during that period; then click a website icon to view each page visited within that site. To sort or search the history, click the History button. To delete or copy a link, right-click it.

Figure 14.9 If you don't want people peeking at the sites you've visited, after you clear your history, set Days to Keep Pages in History to zero, thus covering your tracks and disabling the History feature.

Figure 14.10 If no search providers besides Live Search are listed in this menu, choose Find More Providers to add them. After you've added a few, choose Change Search Defaults to specify the default provider.

To search for a webpage:

1. Click in the Search box (or press Ctrl+E).

2. Type one or more keywords and press Enter, or press Alt+Enter to display the results in a new tab.

   IE responds with a list of links, ordered by relevance.

3. Click any result link to visit the page.

✔ Tips

■ By default, the Search box uses Live Search (Windows' search engine; www.live.com). To use a different search provider, click the Search Options button to the right of the search box and then select a different provider (**Figure 14.10**). The search is repeated with the new provider. Note that some providers are general search engines (Google and Yahoo, for example) and others search only within a specific website (Amazon and eBay).

■ If the cursor is in the Search box, press Ctrl+Down arrow to open the provider menu.

■ To search directly from the address bar, press Alt+D; type go, find, or ?, followed by a space and a search phrase; and then press Enter.

■ After you go to a webpage, press Ctrl+F to search for specific text on that page.

continues on next page

NAVIGATING THE WEB

- You can increase the accuracy of your searches by adding operators that fine-tune your keywords. Use the minus sign (–) before a keyword, for example (with no intervening space), to exclude pages with that term. The search text *aspen -tree* finds pages that contain *aspen* but not *tree*. Use quotes to find exact phrases: *"aspen tree"* finds pages with those two words adjacent in the text. Google's operators, for example, are described at www.google.com/help/refinesearch.html. Many operators are common to all major search engines, but check the search engine's help pages for idiosyncrasies.

- Beware of advertisements posing as "sponsored links" interlaced with results. Reputable search engines color-code paid links or set them apart from legitimate results.

Search Engines

Search engines index billions of webpages and put them at your fingertips. Google (www.google.com) is best for all-around searching, but you may prefer other engines for specialized searches or if Google doesn't do what you want. (No one engine knows about every webpage.)

Each engine has a different spin on analyzing and organizing relevant links. Search engines rank pages by using proprietary (and competing) "relevance" formulas; Google's is called PageRank, for example. You can find search-engine recommendations, news, tips—and about everything else you'd want to know about the subject—at http://searchenginewatch.com.

You can move around a webpage by using scroll bars, but it's faster to use keyboard shortcuts or the mouse wheel. Almost all web scrolling is up/down; some pages or large images will make you scroll left/right.

To move around a webpage:

◆ To scroll up or down incrementally (or line by line), press the up- or down-arrow key or spin the mouse wheel.

or

To scroll up or down by a windowful, press Page Up or Page Down.

or

To scroll to the beginning or end, press Home or End.

or

To move the cursor forward or back through webpage items, the address bar, and the History Center, press Tab or Shift+Tab.

If a link is selected, press Enter to activate it.

✔ Tip

■ If the insertion point isn't blinking in a text box or the address bar, press the spacebar or Shift+spacebar to scroll down or up.

.comBAT

When you search for information about health, science, weather, scholarly disciplines, government services, high culture, charitable causes, not-for-profits, news, and religion (not shopping, sports, or celebrities), favor .org, .gov, .edu, and other noncommercial domains over .com sites. A comparison should convince you: Visit www.weather.gov (the U.S. government's National Weather Service site) and www.weather.com (The Weather Channel's commercial site), and behold:

◆ The NWS site loads quickly, has no ads, shows only weather information, uses graphics sparingly and effectively, plants no cookies, has an obvious search function, and shows a clear map of nationwide weather and warnings.

◆ The Weather Channel site greets you with a pop-up ad; has banner ads that occupy substantial screen real estate; plays Flash animations; is inundated with sales pitches, self-promotion, and slow-loading images; plants a cookie; and has one tiny weather map.

The site operator, for example, can help you. To search for, say, philosophy pages at only educational sites, use the query philosophy site:edu. To search at only United Kingdom academic sites, use philosophy site:ac.uk.

NAVIGATING THE WEB

Using Tabs

Tabbed browsing, new in IE 7, lets you open multiple webpages in a single browser window. You can open webpages or links in new tabs and switch among them by clicking a tab. If you have many tabs open, you can use Quick Tabs to switch easily or save them as a group to open all at the same time in the future.

To open a tab:

◆ To open a new blank tab, click the New Tab button in the tab row (or press Ctrl+T) (**Figure 14.11**).

   or

   To open a new tab when you follow a link on a webpage, press Ctrl as you click the link (or right-click the link and choose Open in New Tab). If you have a mouse with a wheel, click a link with the wheel to open a new tab.

✔ Tips

■ To reorder tabs, drag them left or right in the tab row.

■ To open a new IE window, press Ctrl+N.

Figure 14.11 The New Tab button is at the right end of the tab row. You also can right-click a tab and choose New Tab.

USING TABS

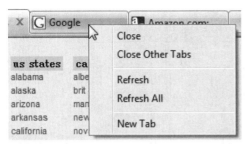

Figure 14.12 The shortcut menu lets you close any tab (not just the active one).

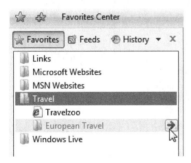

Figure 14.13 You can save the current set of tabs as a group to open in tandem at any time.

Figure 14.14 All the webpages in the group will open in separate tabs.

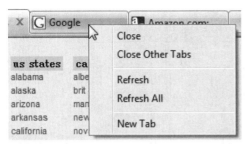

Figure 14.15 You can reopen the same tabs automatically the next time you start IE.

To close a tab:

◆ To close the active (frontmost) tab, click the close button on the tab (⊠, visible in Figure 14.11).You also can press Ctrl+W to close the tab, but if it's the only open tab, IE will close too.

or

To close any tab, right-click the tab and choose Close (**Figure 14.12**). If you have a mouse with a wheel, click a tab with the wheel to close it.

or

To close all tabs but one, right-click the tab that you want to keep open and choose Close Other Tabs (refer to Figure 14.12).

To save a group of tabs:

1. Click the Add to Favorites button (⬚) and choose Add Tab Group to Favorites.

2. Type a name for the group, select the folder that you want the group to be stored in, and then click Add (**Figure 14.13**).

To open a saved group of tabs:

1. Click the Favorites Center button (⬚); then click the Favorites button (or press Ctrl+I).

2. Navigate to the folder that contains the tab group you want to open and click the arrow to the right of the folder name (**Figure 14.14**).

✔ Tip

■ You can reopen the current set of tabs the next time you start IE. When you close IE and are prompted whether to close all tabs, click Show Options, check Open These the Next Time I Use Internet Explorer, and then click Close Tabs (**Figure 14.15**).

USING TABS

To see all open tabs at the same time:

◆  Click the Quick Tabs button (or press Ctrl+Q) (**Figure 14.16**).

✔ Tips

■ To close the Quick Tabs view, click the Quick Tabs button again. The last webpage that you viewed will be displayed.

■ Click the arrow next to the Quick Tabs button to see a menu of open webpages.

To configure tabbed browsing:

◆ Choose Tools > Internet Options > General tab > Settings (below Tabs) (**Figure 14.17**).

Table 14.2 shows keyboard shortcuts for tabbed browsing.

Figure 14.16 Quick Tabs shows all your open webpages on one screen. Click the thumbnail that you want to view. You also can click the close button in the top-right corner of a thumbnail to close that page.

Table 14.2

Tab Keyboard Shortcuts

To	Press
Open links in a new tab in the background	Ctrl+click
Open links in a new tab in the foreground	Ctrl+Shift+click
Open a new tab in the foreground	Ctrl+T (or double-click an empty area of the tab row)
Switch among tabs	Ctrl+Tab or Ctrl+Shift+Tab
Close the current tab (or IE when there are no open tabs)	Ctrl+W or Alt+F4
Open a new tab in the foreground from the address bar	Alt+Enter
Switch to a specific tab number	Ctrl+n (where n is a number between 1 and 8)
Switch to the last tab	Ctrl+9
Close other tabs	Ctrl+Alt+F4
Open Quick Tabs (thumbnail view)	Ctrl+Q
Open a link in a tab with a wheel mouse	Click the link with the mouse wheel
Close a tab with a wheel mouse	Click the tab with the mouse wheel

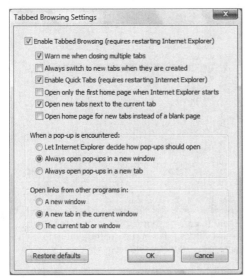

Figure 14.17 You can change the default behavior of tabs, including whether pop-ups are displayed in a new window or on a new tab. You can even turn off tabbed browsing if you want to go back to the old one-webpage-per-window display.

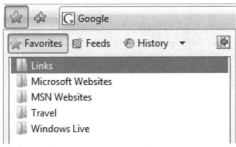

Figure 14.18 To pin the Favorites Center so that it's always open, click the Pin button (🔲) in the top-right corner. (The Pin button turns into a close button.)

Figure 14.19 The new favorite will appear in the folder you specify in Figure 14.18.

Bookmarking Pages

You can keep track of webpages that you like and open them quickly in the future.

⭐ Favorites   You can add a page to your Favorites list (**Figure 14.18**). Any time you want to open that page, click the Favorites Center button (⭐), click Favorites (or press Ctrl+I), and then click the shortcut.

To add a page to your Favorites list:

1. Go to the page that you want to add.

2. Click the Add to Favorites button (⭐) and choose Add to Favorites (or press Ctrl+D) (**Figure 14.19**).

3. Type a new name for the favorite, if you like.

4. Click Create In to choose the folder (or create a new folder) to store the favorite in.

5. Click Add.

✔ Tips

- To open Favorites Center by using the keyboard, press Alt+C. To open Add to Favorites, press Alt+Z. Press Ctrl+Shift+I/H/J to toggle the Favorites/History/Feeds list.

- As your Favorites list grows, you can organize your bookmarks into folders: Click Add to Favorites (⊛) and choose Organize Favorites (or press Ctrl+B) (**Figure 14.20**). It's easier, however, to work in the Favorites folder directly. In Windows Explorer, navigate to C:\Users*username*\Favorites and use it like any other folder (see Chapter 5).

You can add a few pages that you visit often to the Links bar for one-click access.

To add a page to your Links bar:

1. Go to the page that you want to add.

2. Drag the page icon from the address bar to Links (**Figure 14.21**).

Figure 14.20 Drag shortcuts up or down to organize the list. Click a list item and use the buttons to rename it, delete it, or stick it in a folder.

Figure 14.21 You can drag a link to the Links folder in your Favorites list. If the Links bar is hidden, choose Tools > Toolbars > Links. Right-click a link to rename it, delete it, or see its properties. Drag links around the Links bar to rearrange them.

Figure 14.22 You can use the active page or set of pages as your home page, or add the active page to the existing set.

Your *home page* appears when IE first opens or when you click the Home button (or press Alt+Home). It can be a single page or a set of pages.

To set your home page:

1. Open your desired home page(s) in a tab or tabs.

2. Click the arrow to the right of the Home button and choose Add or Change Home Page (**Figure 14.22**).

3. Select an option and click Yes.

✔ Tip

- Choose Tools > Internet Options > General tab > Home Page section to reset the home page to the default (the one used when IE was first installed) or use a blank home page (handy if you work offline).

Bookmark Tools

The Import/Export Wizard lets you import and export your bookmarks (and cookies) to other browsers or files. In IE, click the Add to Favorites button (📑), choose Import and Export, and then follow the onscreen instructions.

AM-DeadLink (free; http://aignes.com/deadlink.htm) scans your bookmarks for dead links and duplicate links, and lets you delete them.

BookmarkBridge (free; http://bookmarkbridge.sourceforge.net) lets you synchronize and share your bookmarks among all your browsers.

BOOKMARKING PAGES

Blocking Pop-Up Windows

Pop-up and *pop-under ads* are separate windows that appear uninvited above or beneath your browser window. When you visit a webpage and the taskbar starts sprouting new buttons, you have pop-unders. Kill this pestilence with IE's Pop-Up Blocker. It's on by default, but you can turn it off or customize its settings to let certain pop-ups through. Pop-ups are useful in some circumstances, such as showing small help windows, seating diagrams for concert halls or airplanes, and larger versions of thumbnail images.

To block pop-up windows:

◆ Choose Tools > Pop-Up Blocker > Turn on Pop-Up Blocker.

   From now on, when IE blocks a pop-up, the Information bar appears with a "Pop-up blocked" message (**Figure 14.23**).

To see a blocked pop-up:

1. Click the Information bar when it notifies you that a pop-up has been blocked (**Figure 14.24**).

2. Click Temporarily Allow Pop-Ups.

Figure 14.23 The Information bar appears near the top of the browser window to alert you when IE blocks a pop-up window or a download file that might not be safe.

Figure 14.24 Click the Information bar to reveal a menu of pop-up customization options.

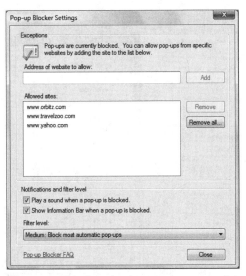

Figure 14.25 This dialog box lets you manage your list of approved sites. You also can turn off the "blocked pop-up" sound, suppress the Information bar, and adjust the pop-up filter's aggressiveness.

To allow pop-ups from a specific website:

1. Choose Tools > Pop-Up Blocker > Pop-Up Blocker Settings (**Figure 14.25**).

2. In the Address of Website to Allow box, type the address (URL) of the website that you want to see pop-ups from; then click Add.

Use the Remove and Remove All buttons to delete previously added sites.

✔ Tips

■ If you've installed the Google Toolbar (or other third-party utility) to block pop-ups, you can turn off the IE blocker: Choose Tools > Pop-Up Blocker > Turn off Pop-Up Blocker.

■ Pop-Up Blocker doesn't block pop-ups that appear when you click a link . . . unless you've chosen the High filter level (refer to the bottom of Figure 14.25). To see pop-ups when you have this setting turned on, hold down the Ctrl key while the webpage loads.

Unblockable Pop-Ups

Some reasons why you still may see pop-ups when Pop-Up Blocker is turned on:

◆ The site is in your Allowed Sites list (refer to Figure 14.25).

◆ The ad designer found a way to circumvent Microsoft's blocking method. (Nothing you can do here.)

◆ You have spyware. Remove it. See "Defending Against Viruses and Spyware" in Chapter 13.

◆ It's a window with animated content that Pop-Up Blocker doesn't block.

◆ It's a website in the Local Intranet or Trusted Sites web-content zone. Choose Tools > Internet Options > Security tab; click the zone that you want to block pop-ups from; click Sites; in the Websites box, click the website for which you want to block pop-ups; and then click Remove.

BLOCKING POP-UP WINDOWS

Browsing Tips

This section contains tips for browsing the web and using Internet Explorer's features.

Using shortcut menus. Right-click toolbars, tabs, favorites, shortcuts, links, or images to select commands quickly (**Figure 14.26**).

Using keyboard shortcuts. For a complete list of IE's keyboard shortcuts, choose Help (Alt+L) > Contents and Index, and search for *internet explorer keyboard shortcuts*.

Navigating frames. Some webpages are divided into independent rectangular sections called *frames* (**Figure 14.27**). Press F6 to cycle forward through frames or Shift+F6 to cycle backward.

Changing text size, font, and color. To change the size of text displayed in webpages, choose a relative size from the Page > Text Size submenu. To change the text's typeface or link colors, choose Tools > Internet Options > General tab; then click the Fonts or Colors button. Some rude webpages won't let you change text properties. To override this restriction, click Accessibility on the same tab.

Zooming. Zoom, new in IE 7, lets you enlarge or reduce the view of a webpage. Unlike changing text size, zoom enlarges or reduces everything on the page, including images and some controls. You can zoom from 10% to 1000%. Use the Change Zoom Level button or menu in the bottom-right corner. If you have a mouse wheel, hold down Ctrl and spin the wheel to zoom. Or press Ctrl+plus (zoom in), Ctrl+minus (zoom out), or Ctrl+0 (zoom to 100%).

Full-screen browsing. Press F11 to toggle between full-screen and normal view. In full-screen view, the address bar and toolbars will autohide until you move the pointer to the top edge of the screen.

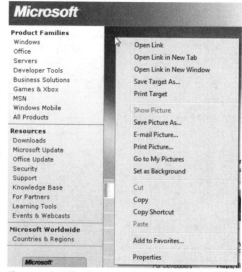

Figure 14.26 This shortcut menu appears when you right-click an image link. Note that you can save a copy of a web image on your own disk.

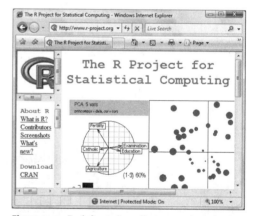

Figure 14.27 Each frame is really a separate webpage. The three sets of scroll bars show that this page has three frames. On some pages, frame boundaries are invisible.

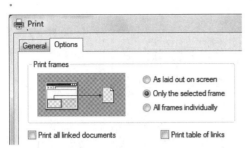

Figure 14.28 The Print dialog box's Options tab lets you print a webpage's frames and links. Be sure to click the desired frame before you print.

Figure 14.29 This site has two feeds (top). Subscribing to feeds adds them to Favorites Center (bottom). A feed can have the same content as the source webpage, but it's formatted differently.

Printing webpages. To preview a webpage before printing, click the arrow next to the Print button to show the Print menu, choose Print Preview, and then use the toolbars to view each page to be printed. To set margins, headers, footers, and other printing options, choose Print > Page Setup (or press Alt+U while you're in Print Preview). To print a webpage, choose Print > Print or press Ctrl+P (**Figure 14.28**). To bypass the Print dialog box and print immediately, click the Print button (not the arrow).

Saving pages. To save a webpage on your hard drive, choose Page > Save As. From the Save As Type drop-down list, choose Web Archive, Single File (*.mht) to save the page as a single file. If you want to edit the page rather than simply view it, use one of the other options to save the page as a group of files or save only parts of the page. To open the saved webpage, double-click it or, in IE, choose File > Open or press Ctrl+O. (Press Alt if the File menu isn't visible.) To specify how Windows treats saved webpages, see Table 5.3 in Chapter 5.

Using RSS feeds. An *RSS feed* is frequently updated free content published by a website. RSS feeds are common for news sites and blogs, but they also can be used to distribute photos, video, and audio (the latter is called *podcasting*). When a website has a feed, the Feeds button (🔊) on the toolbar, new in IE 7, turns from gray to orange and plays a sound. Click the icon to see the feed and, if you want, subscribe to have the feed sent to your computer automatically. When you click the Subscribe button (🔶), the feed is added automatically to the Feeds section of Favorites Center. Press Ctrl+Shift+J to toggle Feeds quickly (**Figure 14.29**).

BROWSING TIPS

Foiling phishers. Online *phishing* (pronounced *fishing*) tries to trick you into revealing financial data through an email message or website. A phishing scam starts with a legitimate-looking email from a bank, credit-card company, or online store arriving in your inbox. The message directs you to a fraudulent (but also legitimate-looking) website where the phishers hope you'll enter your personal data, account numbers, passwords . . . you get the picture.

Phishing Filter (Tools > Phishing Filter), new in IE 7, helps detect phishing websites and warns you with color-coded alerts in the address bar when you visit a known or suspected one. You can check sites manually or automatically and report suspected sites to Microsoft. For more information, choose Start > Help and Support, and search for *phishing*.

Covering your tracks. New in IE 7, the Delete Browsing History dialog box lets you delete your temporary files, cookies, webpage history, saved passwords, and form information in one place. Choose Tools > Delete Browsing History (**Figure 14.30**).

Removing banner advertisements. The Pop-Up Blocker stops pop-up ads, but that still leaves *banner ads*—rectangular "billboards" at the edges of a page. You can remove them with a third-party filter such as Privoxy (free; www.privoxy.org) or, better, by modifying your hosts file; see www.everythingisnt.com/hosts.html or http://pgl.yoyo.org/adservers (**Figure 14.31**).

Figure 14.30 Delete selected categories or everything at the same time.

Figure 14.31 The same page with (top) and without (bottom) banner ads.

Figure 14.32 Click the Custom Level button to specify individual security settings for add-ons, downloads, scripting, and more. Or choose a preset group of settings. The High option provides the safest way to browse but may inactivate some websites.

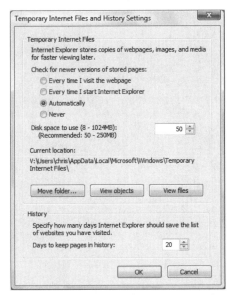

Figure 14.33 Increase the Disk Space to Use setting (the size of the cache folder) so that revisited pages load faster. If IE displays stale pages from the cache instead of fresh ones from the web, select an option that makes IE check for newer versions more frequently than Automatically.

Using graphics features. Right-click a picture to save it, email it, print it, or use it as a desktop background (refer to Figure 14.26). IE resizes large images automatically to fit in your browser window. To always see images in the original size, choose Tools > Internet Options > Advanced tab > uncheck Enable Automatic Image Resizing. While you're there, you can set other image options in the Multimedia category. For faster browsing with *no* graphics, uncheck Show Pictures. (To see a particular picture, right-click it and choose Show Picture.)

Setting security options. IE's Tools > Internet Options > Security tab features help prevent intruders from seeing your personal information, such as credit-card numbers that you enter when shopping online. Security features also can protect your PC from unsafe software (**Figure 14.32**).

Managing temporary files. When you visit a page, IE stores, or *caches* (say "cashes"), temporary internet files on your hard disk. These files speed the display of pages that you visit frequently or already have seen, because IE can open them from your hard disk instead of from the web server. To view or manage these files, choose Tools > Internet Options > General tab > Settings (below Browsing History) (**Figure 14.33**). Change the disk space to decrease or increase the cache size (a browsing-speed/disk-space trade-off). To delete existing cache files, click Delete Files in the Delete Browsing History dialog box (refer to Figure 14.30).

Managing cookies and privacy. *Cookies* are messages given to IE by websites and stored in text files on your hard disk. A cookie's main purpose is to identify you and possibly prepare customized webpages for you. When you enter shopping preferences and personal information at, say, Amazon.com, that information is stored in a cookie, which Amazon can read when you return. (Other sites can't read the Amazon cookie.)

Most cookies are innocuous and spare you from having to fill out forms repeatedly, but some sites and advertisers use *tracking cookies* to record your browsing history. To control how IE handles cookies, choose Tools > Internet Options > Privacy tab (**Figure 14.34**). To delete existing cookies, click Delete Cookies in the Delete Browsing History dialog box (refer to Figure 14.30).

Using Content Advisor and Parental Controls. IE's Content Advisor (Tools > Internet Options > Content tab > Content Advisor section > Enable) purportedly filters material (sex, violence, nudity, language) that you may find offensive or may not want your kids to see. Don't bother—Content Advisor and all programs that make similar claims are 21st-century snake oil. They invariably filter legitimate topics (such as breast cancer) and let offensive stuff through. You're better off using Parental Controls, on the same tab; see "Setting Parental Controls" in Chapter 13.

Surfing anonymously. Surfing the web exposes certain information about you, including (possibly) your IP address, rough geographic location, browsing history, clipboard contents, cache contents, and machine name. To surf anonymously, try Tor (free; http://tor.eff.org), Anonymous Surfing ($30 U.S.; www.anonymizer.com), the-Cloak (free; www.the-cloak.com), or JAP (free; http://anon.inf.tu-dresden.de/index_en.html).

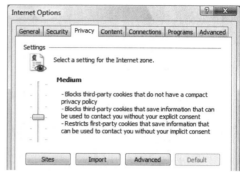

Figure 14.34 The more paranoid you are, the higher you should drag this slider. Tip: Always block third-party cookies, which come from spying advertisers. Click Sites to specify websites that are always or never allowed to use cookies, regardless of your privacy-policy setting. Click Advanced to override automatic cookie handling.

Figure 14.35 AutoComplete shows a list of suggested matches based on the previous entries you've typed. For security, uncheck User Names and Passwords on Forms.

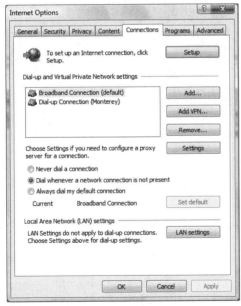

Figure 14.36 Configure your existing internet connections or create a new one on this page.

These services are called *anonymous proxy servers*. Your browser doesn't visit a site directly. Instead, it tells the proxy server which site to visit and deliver back with no direct contact from you. The price of anonymity is slower surfing as you're relayed through a chain of servers and, for some sites, oddly displayed text and graphics.

Using AutoComplete. AutoComplete not only works in the address bar, but also can autocomplete forms (text boxes), user names, and passwords. To turn AutoComplete on or off, choose Tools > Internet Options > Content tab > Settings (below AutoComplete) (**Figure 14.35**).

Managing internet connections. To display and manage your internet connections (Chapter 12), choose Tools > Internet Options > Connections tab (**Figure 14.36**).

Setting the default browser. A newly installed browser usually assumes default-browser status. To reinstate IE, choose Tools > Internet Options > Programs tab > Make Default. To be warned of future hijackings, check Tell Me If Internet Explorer Is Not the Default Browser. You also can click Set Programs to set the defaults for other internet programs, such as email. Alternatively, you can pick your default browser via the Start menu: Right-click the Start button, choose Properties > Customize, and then select a browser from the Show on Start Menu list.

Cutting, copying, and pasting. You can copy (but not cut, of course) selected text and images from webpages and paste them into other programs by using the usual Edit-menu commands or keyboard shortcuts.

Downloading files. When you click a link to a file that you can download to your computer, IE displays **Figure 14.37.** Click Save, specify a download location on your hard drive, and then click Save to start the download. When the download completes (**Figure 14.38**), you can move, double-click, or rename the new file.

Viewing HTML. Webpages are created with *HTML* (Hypertext Markup Language). To view a page's source HTML, choose Page > View Source.

Using Java applets. The *Java virtual machine* (JVM) or *Java run-time environment* (JRE) is a useful add-on that may be missing from IE. The JVM or JRE runs many stock tickers, games, and other complex web programs, called *applets*. IE should prompt you when it encounters an applet, but you can get the JVM at `http://java.sun.com`. If you're having trouble, visit `www.microsoft.com/mscorp/java`.

Bypassing site registration. Some sites, such as `www.nytimes.com`, require you to register before you can read their content. Registration usually means handing over your location and email address so that the site can compile marketing and demographic databases. Like most people, you can simply enter fake details, but that's still a waste of time. Instead, use BugMeNot (free; `www.bugmenot.com`) to bypass logging on to websites that make registration compulsory.

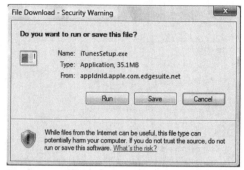

Figure 14.37 To bypass this dialog box, right-click a download link and choose Save Target As.

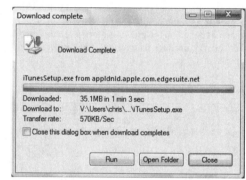

Figure 14.38 When the download completes, click Open Folder to open a window containing the downloaded file.

Figure 14.39 If you think that an add-on has been causing trouble or crashes, turn it off. From the Show drop-down list, choose Add-Ons That Have Been Used by Internet Explorer; click an entry in the Name column; then click Disable. Keep an eye on the Publisher column for mysterious, and possibly untrustworthy, companies.

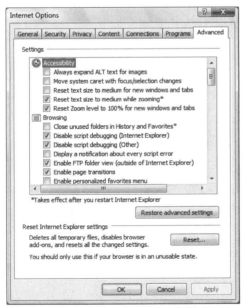

Figure 14.40 Dozens of settings are available to make browsing faster, stop animations, strengthen security, and so on.

Getting add-ons. For webpages with video, sounds, and animation, you need free plug-in programs called *add-ons*. Popular add-ons include QuickTime (video), Adobe Flash and Shockwave (animations), and Adobe Reader (documents). When a website tries to install a plug-in, ActiveX control, or toolbar, IE will warn you with the pop-up Information bar (refer to Figure 14.23) or a dialog box. Allow installation only if you trust the source.

To manage add-ons, choose Tools > Manage Add-Ons > Enable or Disable Add-Ons. The Manage Add-Ons dialog box (**Figure 14.39**) lets you see where add-ons came from (usually), turn them on and off individually, and delete them.

To get more free and for-pay add-ons, choose Tools > Manage Add-Ons > Find More Add-Ons. If you think that an add-on is causing your trouble, you can open IE without them: Choose Start > All Programs > Accessories > System Tools > Internet Explorer (No Add-Ons).

Setting other options. IE has a slew of other options that you can change to suit your preferences; choose Tools > Internet Options > Advanced tab (**Figure 14.40**).

Email, Contacts, and Calendars

Email is a fast, convenient, and cheap way to exchange written messages and files over the internet. Windows Mail (which replaces Outlook Express) lets you send and receive email, as well as read *newsgroups* (internet discussion forums). You can communicate with anyone who has an email account. Your recipient doesn't have to have Windows Mail, or even Windows, to read and reply to your messages; any email program can talk to any other one.

You can't use Windows Mail to manage your email with any of the web-based (HTTP) mail services (Hotmail and free Yahoo accounts, for example).

This chapter also covers Windows Contacts and Windows Calendar—both new in Vista—for managing your contacts and for creating and sharing personal schedules, respectively.

✔ Tip

- The bigger brother of Windows Mail is Outlook, in the Microsoft Office suite. Outlook is a complex program that manages your email, schedule, meetings, contacts, and more.

Other Email Programs

A few other (and better) email programs are available. Trying an alternative doesn't lock you into it; email programs can import one another's messages and account settings.

Eudora (free; www.eudora.com) existed before Outlook and Windows Mail, is still going strong, and is still the choice of serious emailers. It has all sorts of features that you won't find elsewhere. Eudora was commercial software but became open source in 2007.

Thunderbird (free; www.mozilla.com/thunderbird) is from the same folks who brought you the Mozilla Firefox browser. It has enough features to compete with Outlook as well as Windows Mail, and it's updated more frequently.

Getting Started with Windows Mail

Figure 15.1 shows Windows Mail's main panes and controls. If your copy of Windows Mail doesn't look like the pictured one, it's configured differently; choose View > Layout to show, hide, customize, or rearrange the panes. To resize panes, drag the horizontal or vertical lines that separate them.

To start Windows Mail:

◆ Choose Start > Windows Mail (or Start > All Programs > Windows Mail).

or

Choose Start, type `windows mail` in the Search box, and then press Enter.

or

Press Windows logo key+R; type `winmail` and press Enter.

Figure 15.1 The parts of Windows Mail. Click a message name in the Message list to make the message itself appear in the Preview pane. You can delete the "Welcome to Windows Mail" message from Microsoft; it didn't arrive via the internet.

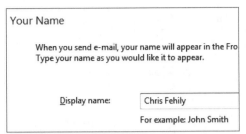

Figure 15.2 This name appears in the From header of email that you send. Don't type something cute or clever; people or spam filters may mistake your messages for junk mail.

Figure 15.3 A email address has two parts. To the left of the *at* symbol (@) is the *alias*, which you choose; to the right is the *domain*, which depends on your ISP.

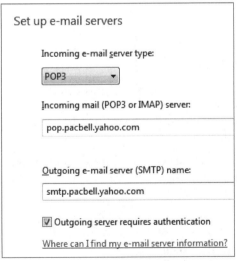

Figure 15.4 Your ISP provider will tell you the server type and server names, which will look something like this.

Setting up an Email Account

Before you set up an email account, you must connect to the internet (Chapter 12). If you upgraded from Windows XP or used Windows Easy Transfer, your email settings may be in place already, and you can skip this section. Otherwise, use the wizard that appears the first time you start Windows Mail. (If it doesn't appear, choose Tools > Accounts > Add > E-Mail Account.) The wizard helps you enter the addresses (provided by your ISP or network administrator) that let Windows Mail find your electronic mailbox.

To set up an email account:

1. If the Account Type page appears, choose E-Mail Account and click Next.

2. On the Your Name page, type your display name (**Figure 15.2**) and click Next.

3. On the Internet E-Mail Address page, type the email address that you chose when you signed up with your ISP (**Figure 15.3**) and click Next.

4. On the Set up E-Mail Servers page, type the information that your ISP provided about its mail servers (see the "Email Protocols" sidebar) (**Figure 15.4**) and click Next.

continues on next page

5. On the Internet Mail Logon page, type your logon name and password, check Remember Password to avoid being prompted for it each time you check your mail (**Figure 15.5**), and then click Next.

6. On the Congratulations page, click Finish to create the account.

(Optional) Uncheck the Download box if you don't want Windows Mail to get your email from the mail server yet; you can always get it later.

Now you should be able to send and receive email.

Figure 15.5 If you and someone else share a Windows logon account but have separate email accounts, uncheck Remember Password if you don't want the other person to be able to read your email.

✔ Tips

- If you have multiple email accounts, choose Tools > Accounts > Add > E-Mail Account. The wizard appears, ready to accept another account. You also can use the Accounts dialog box to edit, delete, import, and export existing accounts.

- For computers with separate user accounts (Chapter 17), each user must create his own email account when logged on.

Email Protocols

Mail servers are networked computers that manage your mailbox. ISP server administrators limit the number and size of messages that you can send or receive, as well as how much space is available in your mailbox. A server handles *incoming* messages by using one of three standards, or *protocols* (your ISP can tell you which protocol it uses):

◆ A *POP3* server (the most common type) transfers your messages to your hard drive before you read them and then deletes its server copies. You save, manage, delete, and back up messages yourself.

◆ An *IMAP* server lets you read, delete, and search your messages while they're still on the server. Then you can choose which messages to download to your hard drive. If your server mailbox reaches its capacity, incoming messages bounce back to their senders.

◆ An *HTTP* server, such as Hotmail and other web-based email providers, lets you send, receive, and manage your email with any web browser. Windows Mail no longer supports HTTP mail.

SMTP servers handle *outgoing* messages.

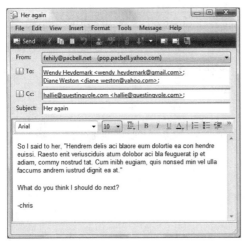

Figure 15.6 The two sections of a message are the *headers* (top), which contain information about the message, and the *body* (bottom), which contains the message itself. Each message window contains its own menu bar and toolbar.

Sending Email

After you've set up your email account, you can compose a message and send it.

To compose and send a message:

1. Choose Message > New Message (or press Ctrl+N).

   or

   Click Create Mail on the toolbar.

   A new message window appears (**Figure 15.6**).

2. Type the recipient's email address in the To box.

   The box autocompletes—that is, proposes a list of matching addresses that you've typed recently. Keep typing or use the arrow keys to select a match; then press Enter.

   To send the message to more than one person, separate the addresses with semicolons (;).

   Mail recognizes and autoexpands names that you've entered in Windows Contacts (see "Managing Your Contacts" later in this chapter). Type all or part of a contact name and press Tab to jump to the Cc box, or press the semicolon to stay in the To box and type another address.

3. To send a copy of the message to other recipients, type additional email addresses in the Cc box, pressing Tab when you're finished.

   The address box autocompletes, and the recognized contacts autoexpand as before.

   Cc (carbon-copy) recipients receive the same message as To recipients, but Cc lets them know that you sent them the message as a courtesy and that you're not expecting them to reply.

continues on next page

4. Type the message's topic in the Subject box and press Tab.

Recipients appreciate a descriptive subject rather than, say, "Hi," which makes your mail look like junk.

5. Type the text of your message.

You can use cut, copy, paste, undo, and all the standard editing techniques.

6. [Send] Click Send on the toolbar (or press Alt+S).

Your computer sends the message over the internet, first connecting to it if necessary.

✔ Tips

■ To attach a file to a message, click Attach on the toolbar, locate the file, and then click Open. Or drag files from Windows Explorer to the message window (**Figure 15.7**). Or right-click the file and choose Send To > Mail Recipient (thereby creating a new message).

■ ISPs limit attached-file sizes to a few megabytes, and many email programs block executable attachments, so zip your files before attaching them (see "Compressing Files and Folders" in Chapter 5). If you attach a photo, Windows automatically gives you a chance to shrink it. See also "Receiving Attachments" later in this chapter.

■ To embed (rather than attach) an image in a message, choose Format > Rich Text (HTML) while in the message body; then choose Insert > Picture, browse to the image to insert, and click Open. Your recipient won't have to open a viewing program to see the picture.

Figure 15.7 Attached files appear in the Attach header. To remove a file from the outgoing message, right-click its icon and choose Remove.

SENDING EMAIL

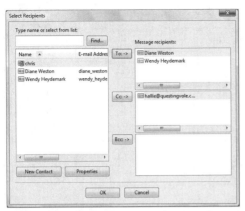

Figure 15.8 Click the To or Cc button (both visible in Figure 15.7) to open this dialog box. You can specify your recipients by pointing and clicking rather than typing.

- Names that you add to your contacts list (choose Tools > Windows Contacts, press Ctrl+Shift+B, or click Contacts on the toolbar) appear in the Select Recipients dialog box (**Figure 15.8**). To add the sender of a message to your contacts list quickly, right-click the message in the Message list and choose Add Sender to Contacts.

- Click Spelling on the toolbar (or press F7) to spell-check your message.

- A *signature* is a distinctive bit of text— usually, your choice of contact information, a quotation, or something flippant— added at the bottom of outgoing messages. To create signatures, choose Tools > Options > Signatures tab > New and type a signature in the Edit Signature box. Click New again if you want to create multiple signatures. You can add a signature to all messages by checking Add Signatures to All Outgoing Messages in this dialog box or to individual messages by choosing Insert > Signature in the message window.

- The Bcc (blind carbon copy) header is hidden by default. To show it, choose View > All Headers in the message window. Bcc recipients receive the same message as To and Cc recipients, but secretly, without the other recipients knowing. If you send, say, a joke or announcement to many recipients, it's polite to put them all in the Bcc list; then no one has to scroll through the long list of To or Cc names that appears at the top of the message, and individual email addresses aren't revealed to the entire list.

continues on next page

SENDING EMAIL

- To save an incomplete message in the Drafts folder, choose File > Save (or press Ctrl+S), and finish composing it later.

- To keep a copy of all outgoing messages, choose Tools > Options > Send tab > check Save Copy of Sent Messages in the "Sent Items" Folder.

- If you've defined multiple email accounts and want to send from an account other than the current one, choose the account that you want to use from the From drop-down list in the message window.

- Windows Mail has scores of options. To see or change them, choose Tools > Options (**Figure 15.9**). Many options are self-explanatory, but you can click the Help button () in the top-right corner for help with each tab.

- In Outlook Express, you could send instant messages; in Windows Mail, you can't. See Chapter 16 instead.

- Try Help if you're having trouble setting up an account or sending or receiving mail: Choose Start > Help and Support, and search for *troubleshoot windows mail.*

Figure 15.9 Most tabs have buttons that open even more dialog boxes.

Plain Text or HTML?

You can format your message body as plain text or HTML. Plain-text messages contain only unadorned text without italics, boldface, colors, custom font sizes, and so on. HTML—the language used to format webpages—permits fancy formatting. In general, use plain text because:

- Some older email programs (especially in Unix) can't read HTML formatting.

- Amateurish HTML formatting irritates recipients.

- Most junk email (spam) uses HTML formatting. *Your* HTML messages may be caught by filtering software and routed—unread—to the recipient's trash.

- HTML formatting is inconsistent across programs. What looks good on your screen might look bad on your recipient's.

- Extra formatting increases download and display times.

To change the default format for all new messages, choose Tools > Options > Send tab > Mail Sending Format section, select HTML or Plain Text, and then click OK.

No matter what the default format, you can switch it for individual messages: In the message window, choose Format > Plain Text or Format > Rich Text (HTML). Choosing HTML activates the HTML toolbar, which contains buttons for styles, formatting, hyperlinks, and so on. Choosing Plain Text brings up a warning that certain embellishments, such as images, won't be possible.

SENDING EMAIL

Reading Email

When you open Windows Mail, it retrieves (downloads) your messages automatically from your ISP's mail server. If you keep Windows Mail running, it checks for new mail every 30 minutes, but you can change the interval or check on demand.

To check now for new messages:

◆ **Send/Receive** Click Send/Receive on the toolbar (or press Ctrl+M).

✔ Tips

■ The preceding method receives messages *and* sends any messages in your Outbox. To receive only, choose Tools > Send and Receive > Receive All, or click the small arrow on the Send/Receive button and choose Receive All (**Figure 15.10**).

■ If you've defined several email accounts, you don't have to check them all. To turn off an account, choose Tools > Accounts, double-click the account in the list, and then uncheck Include This Account When Receiving Mail or Synchronizing. To check a disabled account occasionally, choose its name at the bottom of the Send/Receive menu (refer to Figure 15.10).

■ To change the mail-retrieval interval, choose Tools > Options > General tab and change the time period for Check for New Messages Every __ Minute(s) (refer to Figure 15.9).

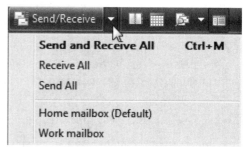

Figure 15.10 Click the arrow to the right of the Send/Receive button to reveal a drop-down list, where you can choose to send messages, receive them, or both. To check an individual email account (rather than all of them), click its name at the bottom of the list.

Figure 15.11 The names of new (unread) messages appear in bold in the Message list (on the right). Folders (on the left) containing new messages appear in bold, too, along with the number of unread messages in each folder.

Figure 15.12 You'll get spam eventually. Practicing safe email (posting disguised addresses in newsgroups, for example) only delays it. Spammers scour the web for email addresses, and nothing stops ISPs (yours or your recipients') from selling your address. Eventually, you'll end up on a spammer's list—and soon thereafter, on hundreds of them.

Newly arrived messages land in your Inbox (**Figure 15.11**) unless they're redirected by rules (see "Applying Message Rules" later in this chapter). Arrivals display an icon in the notification area (📫) and play a sound.

When you open Windows Mail, you may see **Figure 15.12**. Mail automatically redirects spam—unsolicited commercial email—to the Junk E-Mail folder. Junk E-Mail filtering, new in Windows Mail, keeps spam out of your Inbox and is turned on by default. Inspect the Junk E-Mail folder occasionally to make sure that Mail didn't put any legitimate messages in there. To configure spam filtering, choose Tools > Junk E-Mail Options. Mail also filters messages with suspected phishing links; see "Browsing Tips" in Chapter 14. To learn more about spam, visit http://spam.abuse.net or the websites listed at www.google.com/Top/Computers/ Internet/Abuse/Spam.

To read messages:

1. Click Inbox (or another folder) in the Folders list.

2. To view a message in the Preview pane, click the message in the Message list.

   or

   To view a message in a separate window, double-click the message in the Message list.

3. To move back or forward through messages, press Ctrl+<, Ctrl+>, or (in preview mode) the up- or down-arrow key.

   or

   To view the next *unread* message, press Ctrl+U.

READING EMAIL

✔ Tips

■ To view all of a message's information, right-click it in the message list and choose Properties, or press Alt+Enter in a message window.

■ To switch a message's read/unread status manually, right-click the message and choose Mark As Unread or Mark As Read.

■ To read, send, and manage messages from any browser, anywhere, visit a POP3-access website such as www.mail2web.com. Your ISP also may provide a webpage that lets you manage your mail in a browser.

■ To hide read messages, choose View > Current View > Hide Read Messages, or click the Views bar (to the right of the toolbar) and choose Hide Read Messages. To customize and save views, use the Customize and Define commands in the View > Current View submenu. Your new views appear in the Views bar.

■ The Message list behaves like Windows Explorer in details view. Choose View > Columns to choose which columns to display. To resize a column, drag its heading's right edge left or right (or double-click the right edge to autosize the column). To reorder columns, drag the headings left or right. To sort by a column, click its heading; click again to reverse the order.

Organizing Your Messages

Use the Folders list (refer to Figure 15.1) to organize your messages. It contains the following folders initially (but you can create new ones):

Inbox holds mail that you've received.

Outbox holds mail that you've written but haven't sent.

Sent Items holds copies of messages that you've sent.

Deleted Items holds received mail that you've deleted.

Drafts holds mail that you're working on but aren't ready to send.

Junk E-Mail holds messages that Mail thinks are spam.

The Folders list acts like a normal Windows Explorer tree. Click a folder to see what's in it. Choose File > New > Folder (Ctrl+Shift+E) to create a new folder. Right-click a folder that you've created to rename or delete it. To file a message, drag it from the Message list to a folder icon, or right-click it and choose Move to Folder or Copy to Folder. To save a message in a Windows Explorer folder, choose File > Save As.

After you've read a message, you can print it, delete it, reply to it, forward it (that is, pass it on to a third person), or file it in a folder (see the "Organizing Your Messages" sidebar). You can process a message that's displayed in the Preview pane or one that's open in a separate window. The Search box, new in Windows Mail, lets you find messages instantly based on their header and body contents.

To print, delete, forward, or file multiple messages simultaneously, Ctrl+click each message to select it. (Ctrl+clicking again deselects it.) To select a group of contiguous messages, click the first message and then Shift+click the last.

To print a message:

◆   Select a message and click Print on the toolbar (or press Ctrl+P).

To delete a message:

1.   Select a message and click Delete on the toolbar (or press Delete). Deleted messages aren't erased but are placed in the Deleted Items folder.

2. To erase all deleted messages permanently, choose Edit > Empty Deleted Items Folder.

   or

   To erase a specific deleted message permanently, select it in the Deleted Items folder and press Delete.

   or

   To erase all deleted messages permanently and automatically when you quit Windows Mail, choose Tools > Options > Advanced tab > Maintenance button > check Empty Messages from the Deleted Items Folder on Exit.

3. To rescue a deleted message, drag it from Deleted Items to another folder.

To reply to a message:

1.  **Reply** To reply to only the sender, select a message and click Reply on the toolbar (or press Ctrl+R) (**Figure 15.13**).

   or

   Reply All To reply to everyone in the To and Cc lines (for group discussions), select a message and click Reply All on the toolbar (or press Ctrl+Shift+R).

2. Type a response to the message.

3. **Send** Click Send on the toolbar (or press Alt+S).

To forward a message:

1. **Forward** Select a message and click Forward on the toolbar (or press Ctrl+F).

   A new message opens, containing the original message's text.

2. Type the email addresses of the recipients (see "Sending Email" earlier in this chapter).

3. Edit the subject line or original message, or add your own comments, if you want.

4. **Send** Click Send on the toolbar (or press Alt+S).

Figure 15.13 A preaddressed reply opens with Re: (regarding) added to the subject line and the original message's text (which you can edit, cut, or commingle with your own comments) in the body. To turn off the original-text feature, choose Tools > Options > Send tab > uncheck Include Message in Reply.

To find a message:

1. In the Folder list, click the folder that you want to search.

2. `Search` 🔎 Click the Search box (or press Ctrl+E) and type text.

   You can type entire words or just the first few letters, including email addresses.

   As you type, the messages are filtered to match your text based on their header and body content.

3. Stop typing when you see the message you want, and double-click the message to open it.

   or

   To cancel the search, press Esc, backspace over the search text, or click the close button (✖).

   The list goes back to its unfiltered state.

✔ Tips

- For general information about the Search box, see "Searching for Files and Folders" in Chapter 5.

- To search by a particular field or date, choose Edit > Find > Message (or press Ctrl+Shift+F).

- When you receive an important message, you can *flag* it for later reference. Select a message and choose Message > Flag Message, or click the flag column next to the message. A small red flag appears (refer to Figure 15.11). You can click a flag icon to remove it or click the flag-column header to sort flagged messages together.

continues on next page

READING EMAIL

- Message headers contain detailed information about who sent a message and the path it took. Windows Mail hides headers, which is fine for everyday use, but you can reveal them if you're curious or want to troubleshoot messages that bounce back to you. In the message window, choose File > Properties > Details tab.

- If your mailbox fills up, and your friends complain that their messages to you are bouncing back, choose Tools > Accounts, click the relevant account, and then choose Properties > Advanced tab. If Leave a Copy of Messages on Server is checked, check Remove from Server After __ Days, and change 5 (the default) to 1 or 2.

- By default, the Preview pane (refer to Figure 15.1) marks messages as read whether or not you've actually read them. To turn off the Preview pane, choose View > Layout > uncheck Show Preview Pane. If you want to keep the Preview pane but not mark messages as read, choose Tools > Options > Read tab > uncheck Mark Message Read After Displaying for __ Seconds.

READING EMAIL

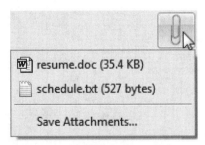

Figure 15.14 If the selected message has a file attached, a paper-clip icon appears at the right end of the Preview pane header. Click the icon for a shortcut menu and choose the name of the attached file to open (in Microsoft Word, Windows Photo Gallery, Microsoft Excel, or whatever), or choose Save Attachments to save it to your hard drive.

Figure 15.15 After you've saved an attachment on your hard drive, you can delete the message it came with.

Receiving Attachments

If someone has sent a you a file, a paper-clip icon appears next to the message name in the Message list (refer to the top message in Figure 15.11). Windows Mail stores an attachment with its message in a single, specially encoded mail file. You can open an attachment from the mail file or save it separately as a normal file on your hard drive. (To send attachments, see the Tips in "Sending Email" earlier in this chapter.)

To open an attachment:

◆ In the Preview pane, click the paper-clip icon in the header and choose the file-name (**Figure 15.14**).

   or

   At the top of the message window, double-click the file icon in the Attach header (refer to Figure 15.7).

To save an attachment:

1. In the Preview pane, click the paper-clip icon in the header and choose Save Attachments (refer to Figure 15.14).

   or

   Select the message and choose File > Save Attachments.

2. Select a folder for the file and click Save (**Figure 15.15**).

Attachment Manager is a background security program that handles email attachments and internet downloads. Attachment Manager is part of Windows, but Windows Mail, Windows Live Messenger, and Internet Explorer (and possibly other programs) use it.

To combat email-borne viruses, Windows Mail blocks attachments with high-risk extensions because you could infect your computer if you open them. The extensions include common ones such as .exe and .bat; the "Risky File Types" sidebar has a complete list. In the message window or Preview pane header, you'll see a warning strip letting you know that the file has been blocked. You can unblock the file if you're sure that it isn't dangerous.

Figure 15.16 Uncheck the Always Ask box if you don't want to be bothered by future security warnings.

To unblock and open a blocked attachment:

1. Choose Tools > Options > Security tab > uncheck Do Not Allow Attachments to Be Saved or Opened That Could Potentially Be a Virus > OK.

2. Save the attachment to your hard drive (as described in "To save an attachment" earlier in this section).

3. In Windows Explorer or on the desktop, double-click the file.

4. If an Open File - Security Warning dialog box appears, click Run (**Figure 15.16**). The file opens normally.

Risky File Types

.ade, .adp, .app, .asp, .bas, .bat, .cer, .chm, .cmd, .com, .cpl, .crt, .csh, .exe, .fxp, .hlp, .hta, .inf, .ins, .isp, .its, .js, .jse, .ksh, .lnk, .mad, .maf, .mag, .mam, .maq, .mar, .mas, .mat, .mau, .mav, .maw, .mda, .mdb, .mde, .mdt, .mdw, .mdz, .msc, .msi, .msp, .mst, .ops, .pcd, .pif, .prf, .prg, .pst, .reg, .scf, .scr, .sct, .shb, .shs, .tmp, .url, .vb, .vbe, .vbs, .vsmacros, .vss, .vst, .vsw, .ws, .wsc, .wsf, .wsh

RECEIVING ATTACHMENTS

✔ Tips

■ Instead of completing steps 3 and 4, you can right-click the file and choose Properties. The Properties dialog box that appears contains an Unblock button. Clicking it is the same as unchecking the Always Ask box in Figure 15.16, and it removes the Unblock button from future Properties dialog boxes.

■ Even attachments from friends are risky because a self-forwarding virus may have picked your name out of a friend's contacts list.

■ To remove viruses, see "Defending Against Viruses and Spyware" in Chapter 13. Virus scanners can check your incoming and outgoing messages automatically.

Blocked Pictures

Windows Mail also blocks graphics in HTML-format email—not attached graphic files, but *references* to graphics that sit on a web server somewhere. When you open such a message, Windows Mail won't fetch the image from the server, because most of these images come from spammers trying to confirm (and sell) your email address. To download images and see them in the message, click the Some Pictures Have Been Blocked warning strip that appears in the message header. To turn off this feature, choose Tools > Options > Security tab > uncheck Block Images and Other External Content in HTML E-Mail. You might want to disable this feature if you get a lot of email containing photos from online dating sites.

RECEIVING ATTACHMENTS

Applying Message Rules

Windows Mail lets you define *message rules* that answer, redirect, or delete incoming messages automatically, based on subject, sender, message text, size, or other criteria.

To set up message rules:

1. Choose Tools > Messages Rules > Mail > New (**Figure 15.17**).

2. In the top section, specify selection criteria for messages.

   To look for messages from a certain person, for example, check Where the From Line Contains People.

3. In the second section, specify what happens to messages that meet the selection criteria.

   You can define complex rule systems that move, copy, delete, reply to, forward, flag, ignore, or highlight messages automatically.

4. In the third section, click underlined phrases to specify which people, words, or values the message rules apply to (**Figure 15.18**).

5. In the bottom text box, type the rule's name; then click OK (**Figure 15.19**).

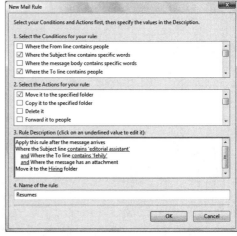

Figure 15.17 This rule, named Resumes, moves a message to my Hiring folder if the message is addressed to *fehily* directly, contains *editorial assistant* in the Subject line, and has an attachment (presumably, a résumé).

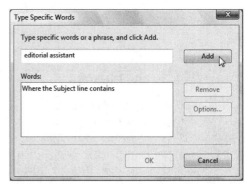

Figure 15.18 Enter the values to watch for in the dialog box that appears when you click an underlined phrase.

APPLYING MESSAGE RULES

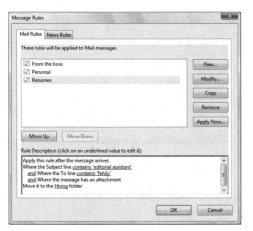

Figure 15.19 All the rules that you've created appear in this dialog box. Select a rule to see what it does, or double-click it to edit it. Use the Move Up and Move Down buttons to change the order in which rules run.

✔ Tips

■ Don't expect to get all your rules right the first time. Windows Mail applies the rules in the Message Rules dialog box from top to bottom. You may find that an earlier rule contradicts a later one or that legitimate messages are deleted inadvertently. After creating a new rule, watch how it's applied as new mail arrives.

■ To create a rule based on a selected message, choose Message > Create Rule from Message.

■ Message rules apply to all active email accounts.

Using Newsgroups

The internet's uncensored anarchy is evident in the tens of thousands of online forums, called *newsgroups* (or *Usenet*), that cover almost every conceivable interest. A newsgroup consists of messages and follow-up posts, which are (supposed to be) related to the original message's subject line. A message and its follow-ups are called a *thread*. To view and post newsgroup messages, use Windows Mail as a *newsreader*.

Setting up a news account is similar to setting up an email account.

To set up and use a newsgroup account:

1. Choose Tools > Accounts > Add > Newsgroup Account.

2. Follow the onscreen instructions and click Finish when you're done (**Figure 15.20**).

3. When you're prompted to subscribe to newsgroups, choose one of the Show Available Newsgroups options.

   You may have to wait a few seconds or minutes for the list to populate.

4. In the Newsgroup Subscriptions dialog box that appears, click a newsgroup account (in the left pane), and type a term of interest in the text box.

   The newsgroups are filtered to match your text (**Figure 15.21**).

   To summon Newsgroup Subscriptions at any time, choose Tools > Newsgroups (or press Ctrl+W).

5. When you find an interesting newsgroup, select it and click Subscribe.

   An icon appears near the newsgroup name.

Figure 15.20 Get your user name, password, and NNTP news-server address from your ISP. If your ISP doesn't provide access to newsgroups, try www.newsguy.com, www.easynews.com, or www.mailgate.org.

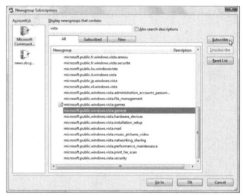

Figure 15.21 A newsgroup name is a series of dot-separated words that indicates the newsgroup's topic in increasingly narrow categories, such as microsoft.public.windows.vista.games. The Microsoft Communities newsgroups, shown here, are installed by default.

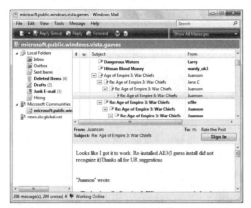

Figure 15.22 Lurk on a newsgroup before participating. Asking recently answered (or dumb) questions irritates people and marks you as a fool.

6. When you finish subscribing to newsgroups, click OK.

   The new newsgroups appear in the Folders list, below the news-server name.

7. In the Folders list, click a newsgroup name to download its recent threads (**Figure 15.22**).

8. Click (or double-click) a header in the Message list to read the message.

   Reply to or post newsgroup messages as you would normal email. Note the Reply (to individuals) and Reply Group (for public posts) toolbar buttons.

✔ Tips

■ The Search box lets you find newsgroup messages instantly based on their header and body contents; see "To find a message" in "Reading Email" earlier in this chapter.

■ Usenet, home of newsgroups, is one of the oldest parts of the internet and is encrusted with etiquette and rules, some of which may seem silly. They're not. Before you post extensively to a newsgroup, observe it silently *(lurk)* for a few days to test the waters.

■ Learn the ropes by joining and reading news.answers and news.announce.newusers. Find out what *crossposting* is and how not to do it.

■ Usenet, like instant messaging, will gobble your life if you dive into it. Don't plan on joining more than three or four newsgroups, but if you do, make yourself cut back to what really interests you.

■ If you join a newsgroup, find and read its *FAQ* (frequently asked questions) file, which may answer your questions before you ask the group.

Managing Your Contacts

Windows Contacts, new in Vista (and replacing Address Book), stores information about people and organizations so you can send them email quickly. You also can combine multiple contacts into contact groups so you can send email to many people at the same time.

To open Windows Contacts:

◆ Choose Start > All Programs > Windows Contacts (**Figure 15.23**).

or

Choose Start, type windows contacts in the Search box, and then press Enter.

or

Press Windows logo key+R; type contacts and press Enter.

To add a contact:

1. Click New Contact or New Contact Group (on the toolbar).

2. Fill out the information in the Properties dialog box (**Figure 15.24**).

3. Click OK.

✔ Tips

■ Treat contacts and groups like any other files. Double-click to edit or right-click to delete, rename, print, send email, and so on.

■ To find a contact, type one or more keywords in the Search box (top-right corner of the window).

■ The Import and Export commands (on the toolbar) let you work with contacts in other formats, such as CSV (comma-separated values), vCard (VCF file), Windows Address Book (Outlook Express files), and LDIF (LDAP server).

Figure 15.23 Contacts (.contact files) and contact groups (.group files) are stored in the Contacts folder inside your personal folder. Because your contacts are stored centrally and not tied to Windows Mail, other programs are free to use them.

Figure 15.24 To add a photo to a contact, click the picture icon on the Name and E-Mail tab. You can add multiple email addresses to each contact and designate one Preferred.

Creating a Personal Calendar

Windows Calendar, new in Vista, manages your appointments and tasks. Your calendar is private by default, but you can publish it to share with others or subscribe to calendars that others have published. If you've used Microsoft Outlook's scheduling features, you're already familiar with how Calendar works.

To open Windows Calendar:

◆ Choose Start > All Programs > Windows Calendar (**Figure 15.25**).

or

Choose Start, type `windows calendar` in the Search box, and then press Enter.

or

Press Windows logo key+R; type `wincal` and press Enter.

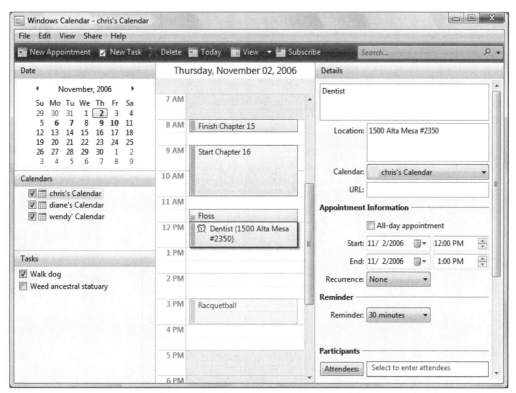

Figure 15.25 Appointments and tasks are color-coded so you can distinguish other people's schedules when they appear on the same calendar. When you make an appointment with someone (that is, click Attendees in the bottom-right corner), Calendar looks that person up in Windows Contacts.

✔ Tips

- Calendar's main functions are on the toolbar, where you can create and delete tasks and appointments, change the time period displayed, and subscribe to other people's calendars. You also can use the menus or right-click individual calendars, tasks, and appointments or empty areas of the various panes. To share your calendar, choose Share > Publish.

- To find an appointment or task, type one or more keywords in the Search box (top-right corner).

- To change Calendar's default settings, choose File > Options.

WINDOWS LIVE MESSENGER

Windows Live Messenger (formerly Windows Messenger, and MSN Messenger before that) is instant gratification for those of you impatient with email delays. Messenger lets you *chat* privately with other people on the internet—one or several at a time—by typing live comments in a small window. This communications channel, called *instant messaging* or *IM,* also is the idea behind AOL Instant Messenger, Yahoo Messenger, ICQ, and Google Talk. Unfortunately, whoever you want to chat with must use the same messaging network that you do, so if you chat with a lot of friends, it's not unusual to have two or three of these programs on your computer.

To get around this limit, use Trillian (free; www.ceruleanstudios.com), Gaim (free; http://gaim.sourceforge.net), or Mercury Messenger (free; www.mercury.to), which let you chat on several IM networks at the same time (and without advertisements).

Besides chatting or even while you're chatting, you can monitor your email, exchange files, have a teleconference, and make free voice calls.

Setting up Messenger

Windows Live Messenger isn't included with Windows. You have to download it from Microsoft.

To download and install Windows Live Messenger:

1. Choose Start > All Programs > Windows Live Messenger Download.

   A web browser opens to the Messenger download page.

2. Click the download link (**Figure 16.1**).

3. If a File Download - Security Warning dialog box appears, click Save.

4. In the Save As dialog box, choose a target folder for the download and click Save.

5. When the download completes, click Open Folder in the Download Complete dialog box (**Figure 16.2**).

6. Double-click the download file.

   If an Open File - Security Warning dialog box appears, click Run.

7. Follow the onscreen instruction in the Windows Live Messenger Setup wizard, choosing the features and settings that you want (**Figure 16.3**).

   If a security prompt appears, type an administrator password or confirm the action.

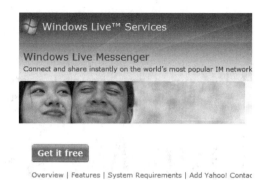

Figure 16.1 In this version of the Messenger page, the download link is labeled Get It Free.

Figure 16.2 If this dialog box disappears when the download completes, use Windows Explorer to open the target folder.

Figure 16.3 You can uncheck all these features if you want only a basic Messenger setup.

Figure 16.4 The Messenger sign-in page.

When Setup completes, it:

◆ Plants Messenger icons (▣) on the Quick Launch toolbar and the notification area

◆ Adds a Windows Live Messenger entry to the Start > All Programs menu

◆ Opens the Messenger sign-in page (**Figure 16.4**)

✔ Tip

■ To use Messenger, you need an internet connection (Chapter 12). A broadband (DSL or cable) connection is ideal, but a 28K or 56K dial-up connection is adequate for chat.

Signing in to Messenger

You need a Windows Live ID to run Messenger, even to chat within your local area network. Your Live ID is Microsoft's way of identifying you uniquely on the internet. It's free and requires only a (real) email address. If you don't have one, click Get a New Account at the bottom of the Messenger sign-in page (refer to Figure 16.4) and follow the instructions on the webpage that opens (**Figure 16.5**). Your Live ID password doesn't have to be the same as your Windows password.

If Messenger doesn't sign you in automatically when you go online, you must do so manually. When you're finished using Messenger, sign out.

When you sign in for the first time, you might see a Windows Security Alert (**Figure 16.6**). Click Unblock to punch a hole in your firewall that Messenger can communicate through. If a security prompt appears, type an administrator password or confirm the action.

Figure 16.5 Windows Live ID replaces (actually, renames) the .NET Passport you needed for previous versions of Messenger. Microsoft prefers that you use a Windows Live (Hotmail) email address, but you can use your own address in most cases. If you sign up for a Hotmail account, you can manage your email in Messenger or at www.hotmail.com.

Figure 16.6 Click Unblock to create an exception in Windows Firewall; see "Using a Firewall" in Chapter 13. If you're using a different firewall, add msnmsgr.exe to the firewall's list of allowed programs.

Figure 16.7 The Messenger icon appears whether or not you're online and signed in. The left icon indicates that you're offline; the right one means you're online and signed in.

Figure 16.8 The main Messenger window.

To open Messenger and sign in:

1. Choose Start > All Programs > Windows Live Messenger.

   or

   Click the Messenger icon (🎇) in the Quick Launch toolbar.

   or

   Double-click the Messenger icon in the notification area (**Figure 16.7**).

   or

   Choose Start, type `messenger` in the Search box, and then select Windows Live Messenger in the results list.

   or

   Press Windows logo key+R; type `msnmsgr` and press Enter.

2. On the sign-in page (refer to Figure 16.4), type your Windows Live ID email address and password.

3. To sign in automatically in the future, select the check boxes below the Password box.

   Don't check these boxes on public PCs or a PC on which your user account is shared.

4. Click Sign In to go online (**Figure 16.8**).

To sign out:

◆ Choose File > Sign Out (press Alt if the File menu isn't visible).

   or

   Right-click the Messenger notification-area icon and choose Sign Out.

   Signing out doesn't break your internet connection or close Messenger. When you sign out, you'll appear offline to others, but you'll still be online.

✔ Tips

■ To return to manual sign-in, sign out and uncheck the auto-sign-in boxes.

■ The Windows Live Today window that appears alongside Messenger is mostly gossip, ads, and fake news. To never see it again, check the box in the bottom-left corner.

■ To stop Messenger from starting automatically, choose Tools > Options > General section > uncheck Automatically Run Windows Live Messenger When I Log on to Windows (below Sign In). You can start Messenger manually from the Start menu.

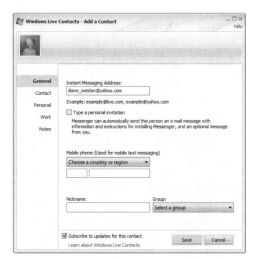

Figure 16.9 To keep contact information current, check Subscribe to Updates for This Contact (at the bottom). To learn more about this feature, click Learn About Windows Live Contacts.

Creating a Contacts List

To send instant messages, you need a list of contacts who have Live ID accounts and Messenger (or MSN Messenger) installed.

To add a contact:

1. In the main Messenger window, at the top of your contacts list, click the Add a Contact button.

2. Type the instant-messaging address in the space provided (**Figure 16.9**).

3. If your contact doesn't have Windows Live Messenger, check Type a Personal Invitation and type your message in the space that appears below it.

4. In the Contact, Personal, Work, and Notes sections, add any additional information, such as a nickname or birthday.

5. Click Save.

   Contacts are listed in the main window.

✔ Tips

■ To edit, delete, or block a contact, right-click the contact in the list or use the Contacts menu (press Alt if the Contacts menu isn't visible). To rearrange the contacts list, use the Sort, Filter, and View commands in the Contacts menu.

■ To search for your contacts, click inside the Find a Contact or Number box at the top of the main window and start typing. Matching contacts appear in the list. To cancel the search, press Esc, backspace over the search text, or click the clear button ( ).

■ To save your contacts in a file so that you can import them on other computers, choose Contacts > Save Instant Messaging Contacts. The Import command is in the same menu.

■ You can create and edit groups to make finding contacts easy. Contacts can be members of more than one group. Use the Group commands in the Contacts menu.

CREATING A CONTACTS LIST

Using Messenger

This section contains instructions and tips for using the features of Windows Live Messenger.

Getting help. Messenger help isn't part of Windows Help and Support; it's at the Messenger website. Choose Help > Help Topics. You also can hover your mouse pointer over any Messenger control for a pop-up tip.

Using the notification-area menu. If Messenger is closed, right-click its notification-area icon to sign in or out quickly, open or exit Messenger, change your chat status, or send an instant message.

Changing the default settings. Choose Tools > Options in the main window or a conversation window to change Messenger's default settings.

Sending an instant message. To send an instant message:

1. Choose Actions > Send an Instant Message.

2. Click a contact or group, or enter an email address, and then click OK.

3. In the conversation window that opens, type your message and click Send.

If the person replies, you're chatting. You can cut, copy, paste, undo, and use all the standard editing techniques. The conversation's transcript rolls down the top box, identifying each message's speaker. Close the conversation window when you're done chatting or leave it open to continue the conversation later. (You remain signed in to Messenger when you close a conversation window.)

Sending another type of message. Choose Actions > Send Other to send an email, a message to a mobile device, a message to an MSN Direct device, a wink, or a single file.

Showing the menu bars. To show the menu bar in the main window or a conversation window, press Alt or click Show Menu (⬛) on the title bar. To show the menu bar permanently, choose Show Menu > Show Menu Bar. (Click Show Menu again to hide the menu bar.) To toggle toolbars in a conversation window, choose Tools > Show Toolbars.

Keeping Messenger in sight. To make the main window or a conversation window remain in front of all other windows unless minimized, choose Tools > Always on Top.

Changing fonts. Change the font or color of your messages to distinguish them from the other person's messages. In the main window, choose Tools > Options > Message section > Change Font, or in a conversation window, choose Edit > Change Font. Both of you will see the change (assuming that you have similar fonts installed). You can't change the other person's font in your window, but you can change text size with the Tools > Text Size submenu.

Adding other chatters. To add more people to a chat, in a conversation window, choose Actions > Invite a Contact to Join This Conversation; then double-click the name of an online contact.

Cold-shouldering someone. To block somebody from chatting with you:

◆ In a conversation window with the person you want to block, choose Actions > Block or click Block on the toolbar.

or

In the main window, right-click a contact's name and choose Block Contact.

or

In any window, choose Tools > Options > Privacy tab; then click the victim's name and add it to the Block list.

Among veteran chatters, blocking can be a mild to significant insult, depending on circumstances. To unblock someone, repeat the Block command (Block toggles to Unblock) or move the person back to the Allow list.

Ignoring people. If you step away from your computer or don't want to be bothered, broadcast your status by using the File > My Status submenu in the main window. (Choose Busy, Be Right Back, Away, Appear Offline, and so on.) You also can change your status by right-clicking the Messenger icon in the notification area.

Expressing your feelings. On the toolbar near the bottom of a conversation window is a drop-down list of smiley-face icons. You can insert these *emoticons* into your messages to indicate how the message should be interpreted (that is, your mood—embarrassment, anger, surprise, delight, whatever). Emoticons may be annoying, but they help prevent misunderstandings if your correspondent has no sense of irony. Messenger converts common text emoticons to graphic ones automatically; type :) to make a smiley face (🙂), for example. To turn off autoconversion, choose Tools > Options > Messages section > uncheck Show Emoticons and Show Custom Emoticons.

Sending winks. You can send a wink to express your mood. A *wink* is an animated greeting that you can send to your contacts. Choose Tools > My Winks, choose a wink, and click Send. Click Get More Winks to download more winks.

Saving conversations. To save a transcript of your chat on disk, in a conversation window, choose File > Save As. To preserve the transcript's colors and fonts, save as an RTF file; to save only the text, save as a text file.

Customizing your display settings. Choose Tools > Options > Messages section; then define how you want the Messenger window to appear and how you want Messenger to respond when you receive messages from others.

Playing sounds and showing alerts.
Messenger can play a sound during certain events, such as when contacts sign in or send you a message. Choose Tools > Options > Alerts and Sounds section. Below Sounds, uncheck the boxes for silence or check them for event-triggered sounds. To change a sound, choose an event and click Browse. (For information about sounds, see "Configuring Sound and Audio Devices" in Chapter 4.) Below Alerts in the same section, you can control the display of visual notifications for various events.

Rearranging the tabs. Choose Tools > Options > Tabs section, and use the Up and Down buttons to reorder the tabs in the main window. Click Restore Defaults to go back to the original order.

Displaying personal information.
Choose Tools > Options > Personal section to set what information others see about you when you send them messages.

Putting a background in your message.
Choose Tools > My Backgrounds and choose a background for your messages. Click Browse to choose other backgrounds on your computer or click Get More Backgrounds to download more.

Changing your display picture. Choose Tools > Change Display Picture to change or create the display picture for your message window.

Setting security options. Choose Tools > Options > Security section to make a messaging session a little safer. You may want to change some of these options when you use a public computer.

Seeing which contacts lists you're on.
Choose Tools > Options > Privacy section. Below Contact Lists, click View to see a list of people who have added you to their contacts list. If you want to be alerted each time someone adds you, check the nearby Alert Me box.

Checking your connection. Choose Tools > Options > Connection section. Click Refresh to update your display and view current information, such as signal strength, account name, and connection type. To test or change connection settings, click Advanced Settings. To troubleshoot a connection, click Start (if available).

Sending and receiving email. In the main window, right-click a contact and choose Send Other > E-Mail to open your email program with a preaddressed message to the contact. To check your email, click the E-Mail Inbox button (⊡ ⊚).

Sharing or transferring files. You can share files with your contacts by using Sharing Folders, or you can transfer one file at a time. Sharing Folders lets you share the same files with more than one contact and update the content automatically. To share a file:

1. Choose Tools > Options > Sharing Folders section.

2. Check both check boxes below Sharing Folders.

3. Add contacts to or remove contacts from the Sharing Folders list to set whether they can access shared files.

4. Click OK.

USING MESSENGER

Now you can drag the file from your file folder onto the contact in the main window (or onto the message area of a conversation window). Click the Sharing Folders button (🖼) in the main window to add files, pause sharing, or view the activity logs of files that you've shared.

To send a single file, choose Actions > Send Other > Send a Single File. To set transfer options, choose Tools > Options > File Transfer section. Here, you also can choose where to save files that you receive.

Sharing games and activities. You and your contacts can share music, games, and applications; collaborate on a project by using a whiteboard; and more. You also can provide assistance to a friend by using Remote Assistance. From the Actions menu, choose Start an Activity, Play a Game, or Request Remote Assistance; then follow the onscreen instructions.

Sending, saving, or playing a voice clip. If you have a microphone, you can send a voice clip, which will appear in your contact's conversation window and play automatically. To send a voice clip, click and hold the Voice Clip button (🗭) in a conversation window (or press and hold F2), say your message, and then release the button. To save a clip, drag it from the conversation window onto your desktop or into a folder window. To forward or recycle a clip, drag it to other conversations. Press Esc or click Play/Stop to stop a clip during playback.

To stop voice clips from playing automatically, choose Tools > Options > Messages section > uncheck Play Voice Clips Automatically When They Are Received.

To set up your microphone and speakers, choose Tools > Audio and Video Setup.

Making video calls, sending your webcam, or viewing a contact's webcam. To add video to your conversations, use the Actions > Video submenu in the main window or a conversation window. To set up your webcam, choose Tools > Webcam Settings.

Making a telephone call. To make free internet phone calls via Windows Live Call, choose Actions > Call in the main window (or click 🕾) and call a contact's computer, a contact's phone, or any other phone. A phone dialer appears for the latter two options.

MANAGING USER ACCOUNTS

Windows is a true multiple-user OS that lets several people use one PC without intruding on—or even viewing—one another's files, settings, and tastes. To start a Windows session, you log on to your *user account,* which gives you personalized access to the system. You, like each user, have your own desktop, Start menu, personal folder, Control Panel settings, email account, internet details (favorites, history, feeds, cookies, and cached webpages), program settings, permissions, network connections, and other odds and ends. Your private files, folders, and preferences are stored on the Windows drive in \Users*username,* which lets Windows personalize your desktop each time that you log on.

In this chapter, you'll learn to create, edit, and delete user accounts as an administrator. If you're a standard user who's not called on to administer, you still can change your account password and picture.

Workgroup vs. Domain

The type of network (Chapter 18) that you're on determines how you administer accounts.

A *workgroup* is a simple home or small-business network whose computers each maintain separate user accounts and security settings. These informal networks exist primarily to help users share printers, folders, files, and other resources. User accounts don't float around the network; you need a separate account on each networked PC to access its files.

A *domain* is a large, business-oriented, centrally administered network. Files can reside on local hard disks or on a network *server* that distributes files across the network. Centralized user accounts let you log on to any domain computer. Vista Home editions support only workgroups. The Business and Ultimate editions support both workgroups and domains.

Setting up User Accounts

Use Control Panel's User Accounts program to create, change, and delete accounts. Your computer will have at least one account: yours. It might have other accounts if you upgraded from Windows XP. If your PC is new, its manufacturer may have created a predefined account named, say, Owner. See "Logging On and Logging Off" in Chapter 1.

To open User Accounts:

◆ Choose Start > Control Panel > User Accounts and Family Safety > User Accounts (**Figure 17.1**).

or

If you're on a network domain, choose Start > Control Panel > User Accounts > User Accounts.

To create an account:

1. In User Accounts, click Manage Another Account (refer to Figure 17.1).

    If a security prompt appears, type an administrator password or confirm the action.

    A list of accounts appears (**Figure 17.2**).

2. Click Create a New Account.

Figure 17.1 User Accounts opens to your account and shows links to account-management tasks.

Figure 17.2 This page lists everyone who has a user account.

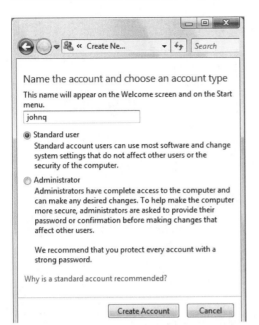

Figure 17.3 Best practice: Don't use spaces in a user name for easy typing in programs and command-line tools. Capitalization doesn't matter, but favor only lowercase letters. Most punctuation is forbidden. Use a short name that will fit easily in messages and dialog boxes.

3. Type a user name and select an account type (see the "Account Types" sidebar; **Figure 17.3**).

4. Click Create Account.

The new account will appear in the account-management window (refer to Figure 17.2).

✔ Tip

■ To create an account if you're on a network domain, in User Accounts, click Manage User Accounts, click Add, and then follow the onscreen instructions. The new account works only for the computer that you're using; it doesn't roam on the domain.

Account Types

An *account type* defines a user's *privileges*—rights to perform specific tasks. The account type appears below each user's name.

An *Administrator* account has sweeping systemwide rights to create, change, and delete user accounts and passwords; access all files (including other users' files); and install programs and hardware. Many of the settings described in this book require administrative privileges, which you should grant to few users besides yourself. Windows must have at least one Administrator account, and if you installed Windows or maintain it, this is *your* account type.

If you're not an administrator, you have an everyday *Standard* account. You can change your own password, picture, desktop theme, and Start menu; change some Control Panel settings (you can't change the system time, for example); and access files in your personal folder (everyone else's files are off limits) and the Public folder (which Windows creates automatically under the Users folder as a shared location for all users).

Windows also comes with a no-password *Guest* account that has about the same privileges as a Standard account. This account, intended for visitors, is turned off by default and should stay that way.

After creating a user account, you edit it to set up its other information. You can change a user account's details, such as its password and picture, at any time after creating it.

To edit an account:

1. In User Accounts, click Manage Another Account (refer to Figure 17.1).

   If a security prompt appears, type an administrator password or confirm the action.

   A list of accounts appears (refer to Figure 17.2).

2. Click the account that you want to change.

3. In the page that appears (**Figure 17.4**), choose among these options:

   Change the Account Name. Type a new user name, which will appear in the Welcome screen, Start menu, and User Accounts window.

   Change the Password. Type (and retype) a password (capitalization counts) and optional logon hint to remind you of a forgotten password (**Figure 17.5**).

   Remove the Password. If the account has a password, you can remove it. (In most situations, you should password-protect every account.)

Figure 17.4 Administrators have full access to all accounts. Standard users see about the same options, but if they don't have an administrator password, they can change only their account password and picture.

Figure 17.5 For advice on creating a password, click How to Create a Strong Password.

Choose a new picture for wendy's account

wendy
Administrator
Password protected

The picture you choose will appear on the Welcome screen and on the Start menu.

Browse for more pictures...

Change Picture   Cancel

Figure 17.6 Click Browse for More Pictures to post your own picture, automatically scaled to fit. To open User Accounts for your account quickly (refer to Figure 17.4), click your Start-menu picture.

Change the Picture. Change the picture associated with you in the Welcome screen, Start menu, and User Accounts window (**Figure 17.6**). (The picture doesn't appear if you're a domain member or if you use the classic Start menu.)

Set up Parental Controls. See "Setting Parental Controls" in Chapter 13.

Change the Account Type. Change an Administrator account to a Standard account, or vice versa. See the "Account Types" sidebar and Figure 17.3.

Delete the Account. See "To delete an account" later in this section.

Manage Another Account. Choose another account to edit after you're finished with this one.

✔ Tips

■ To edit an account if you're on a network domain, in User Accounts, click Manage User Accounts. On the Users tab, under Users for This Computer, click the user account name and then click Properties.

■ If you provide a password hint, use one that's meaningful to only you, because everyone who uses your PC can see it on the Welcome screen.

■ If an administrator removes or changes the password of another user (of any account type), the secondary passwords stored in that user's account for certain websites, network files and folders, encrypted files, and so on *are lost*, thus preventing someone unscrupulous from, say, cleaning out a bank account courtesy of a password memorized by a browser.

If you're worried that you'll forget your password and draw a blank on your password hint, create a *password reset disk* to recover it. You must create it now, before you actually need it. Keep the disk safe; anyone can use it to change your password. (An administrator always can reset your forgotten password, but a reset wipes your secondary passwords, as described in the preceding tip.)

To create a password reset disk:

1. In User Accounts (refer to Figure 17.1), click Create a Password Reset Disk (in the left pane).

    The Forgotten Password wizard opens (**Figure 17.7**).

2. Follow the onscreen instructions.

    You'll need a formatted floppy disk.

    If you mistype a password in future logons, Windows displays a message that the password is wrong. Close the message and click Reset Password. Insert your password reset disk and follow the steps in the Password Reset wizard. You don't need to make a new password reset disk after you're logged on; reuse the old one.

You, as an administrator, can delete any account that's not logged on. (Press Ctrl+Shift+Esc and click the Users tab to see who's logged on.) You can't delete the account that you're logged on to or the last Administrator account. A deleted account is gone forever, along with its settings and secondary passwords. If you create a new account with the same name and password, Windows considers it to be a different account.

Welcome to the Forgotten Password Wizard

This wizard helps you create a "password reset" disk. If you forget the password for this user account and are unable to log on, you can use this disk to create a new password.

Note: No matter how many times you change your password, you only need to create this disk once.

Warning: Anyone can use this disk to reset the password, and therefore have access to this account.

To continue, click Next.

Figure 17.7 You can have only one password reset disk for each account. If you make a new one, the old one becomes unusable.

Figure 17.8 If you click Keep Files, Windows saves documents and media files but not email or settings.

Figure 17.9 This dialog box, courtesy of User Account Control, appears when you try to install a program as a standard user. To continue, type the password for one of the listed Administrator accounts (only one appears here) and click OK. If you're logged on as an administrator, you'll see a similar dialog box, only you won't have to enter a password.

To delete an account:

1. In User Accounts, click Manage Another Account (refer to Figure 17.1).

   If a security prompt appears, type an administrator password or confirm the action.

   A list of accounts appears (refer to Figure 17.2).

2. Click the account that you want to delete.

3. Click Delete the Account (refer to Figure 17.4).

4. Click Keep Files to save the user's desktop and personal files on your desktop in a folder named after the deleted user (**Figure 17.8**).

   or

   Click Delete Files to erase the user's files.

5. Click Delete Account.

✔ Tips

- For information about sharing files and folders with other users, see "Sharing Files" in Chapter 18.

- Manage accounts only through User Accounts. Don't tinker with accounts directly in the Users folder.

- For security reasons, consider using a Standard account for everyday use and an Administrator account for special occasions. If you're logged on as a standard user and try to install a program that requires administrator privileges, **Figure 17.9** appears to let you install it as an administrator.

continues on next page

SETTING UP USER ACCOUNTS

- Power users prefer the old-style User Accounts dialog box to manage accounts. It's hidden in Vista. To open it, press Windows logo key+R; type `control userpasswords2` and press Enter (**Figure 17.10**). If a security prompt appears, type an administrator password or confirm the action.

- Upon graduation to advanced user management, you'll use the Local Users and Groups console (**Figure 17.11**). Click the Advanced tab in Figure 17.10 and then click the Advanced button (or press Windows logo key+R; type `lusrmgr.msc` and press Enter). If a security prompt appears, type an administrator password or confirm the action.

With this console, you can create and manage users and groups. *Groups* are named collections of users that transcend the Administrator/Standard account types and give you great flexibility in fine-tuning file and folder permissions. It's also here that you can manage the built-in, no-password, hidden Administrator account that's used in emergencies (like recovering after a bad crash).

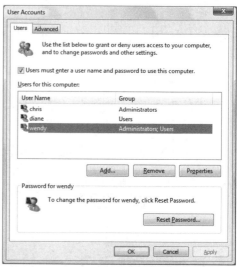

Figure 17.10 This dialog box is more powerful and direct than Control Panel's User Accounts. You can create, edit, and delete accounts without slogging through a wizard. Click the Advanced tab for more options.

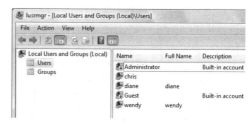

Figure 17.11 Despite its austere appearance, this tool offers power and flexibility. Double-click an account name to set advanced options, for example.

Disabling Accounts

One thing Local Users and Groups lets you do that User Accounts doesn't is disable accounts temporarily, which may be preferable to deleting them in some cases. A disabled account's files and settings aren't touched; they just become unavailable to the user.

To disable an account, double-click the user in the list (refer to Figure 17.11). In the Properties dialog box, on the General tab, check Account Is Disabled. That user won't be able to log on until you enable the account again.

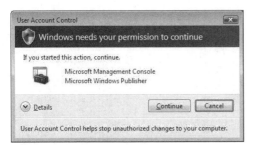

Figure 17.12 UAC helps stop unauthorized changes to your computer by asking you for permission or an administrator password before doing something that affects your computer's operation or changes settings for other users.

Table 17.1

UAC Messages

ICON	MESSAGE AND DESCRIPTION
	Windows needs your permission to continue. A Windows function or program that can affect other users wants to start.
	A program needs your permission to continue. A program that's not part of Windows wants to start. It has a valid digital signature indicating its name and its publisher, which helps ensure that the program is what it claims to be.
	An unidentified program wants access to your computer. A program without a digital signature wants to start. Many older, legitimate programs lack signatures. Run the program if you trust the source. You can trust the original CD or the publisher's website, for example.
	This program has been blocked. An administrator has specifically blocked this program from starting. Contact an administrator to unblock it.

Using User Account Control

Microsoft's security-minded answer to years of viruses and spyware is User Account Control (UAC), new in Vista. If you've used Windows for even a little while, you've seen a UAC dialog box like Figure 17.9 or **Figure 17.12**.

Some of the actions that UAC intercepts might seem trivial to you at first, but they're chosen sensibly. By verifying actions before they start, UAC can stop malware from installing or making changes.

Table 17.1 describes the different UAC dialog boxes, each of which has its own shield icon, color, and message. In each case, check the name of the action or program in the dialog box to make sure that it's the one you want to run.

✔ Tips

■ You can turn off UAC. In User Accounts (refer to Figure 17.1), click Turn User Account Control On or Off. If a security prompt appears, type an administrator password or confirm the action. Uncheck Use User Account Control (UAC) to Help Protect Your Computer and then click OK. You must restart your computer (now or later) for the change to take effect.

■ Best security practice: Log on with a Standard account most of the time. You can surf the web, send email, and use a word processor, all without an Administrator account. When you perform an administrative task, you don't have to switch to an Administrator account; UAC will prompt you for permission or an administrator password.

Managing User Profiles

A *user profile* contains an account's personal settings that Windows uses to configure the desktop each time the user logs on. Each user's settings, network connections, and so on are saved in \Users*username*. Windows also has a default profile that defines settings for newly created accounts. (The default profile is a hidden folder in Users.) To change this starting point, change the desktop, Start menu, favorites, and theme of a normal account (your own, perhaps) to what you want the new default to be; then complete the following steps.

To change the default user profile:

1. In Windows Explorer, choose Organize > Folder and Search Options > View tab, select Show Hidden Files and Folders, and then click OK.

2. Choose Start > Control Panel > System and Maintenance > System > Advanced System Settings (in the left pane) > Settings (below User Profiles) (**Figure 17.13**).

   If a security prompt appears, type an administrator password or confirm the action.

3. Select the account whose settings you want to copy and click Copy To.

   The Copy To dialog box opens.

4. Click Browse and navigate to \Users\Default on the drive that contains Windows.

5. Click OK in each open dialog box.

6. In Explorer, rehide hidden files.

✔ Tip

- A *roaming user profile*, which your network administrator creates, is available every time you log on to any computer on a network domain.

Figure 17.13 The (hidden) Default profile determines what a newly created user sees on the desktop. Use the User Profiles dialog box to change the default appearance by copying other profile settings to the Default profile.

MANAGING USER PROFILES

SETTING UP
A SMALL NETWORK

You create a *network* when you connect two or more computers to exchange data or share equipment. Cheap hardware and simpler configurations have made networks common in homes and small businesses. Setup is no longer a bad experience, thanks to Windows' setup tools and wizards (but the hassle of buying and installing network hardware remains). You can add computers running Windows XP to your network too.

Networks let you:

Share files. You can designate disks, folders, and files as shared network resources.

Share printers and devices. Any computer on the network can use a printer connected to another network computer. Ditto for backup devices, scanners, and other devices.

Share an internet connection. You can set up an internet connection on one computer and let every computer on the network share that connection.

Workgroups and Domains

This chapter describes how to set up a simple *workgroup* network (also called a *peer-to-peer* network), appropriate for ten or fewer computers, in all Vista editions. The Business and Ultimate (but not Home) editions also support *domain* networks for large organizations. A full-time geek (or department) sets up and administers a domain, which can have thousands of users. Ordinary users can set up and administer their own workgroup but not a domain. In this chapter, I cover domain file-sharing but not setup.

To join an existing domain, see the "Domain Logons" sidebar in "Logging On and Logging Off" in Chapter 1.

Understanding Network Types

Before you can set up Windows' network software, you must install and configure network hardware. Your choice of network depends on your budget, the proximity of the computers to be networked, and your inclination to lay cable.

✔ Tip

■ A geographically limited network that spans a small area (typically, a building or two) is called a *local area network (LAN)*.

Ethernet (802.3)

The most popular network standard, *Ethernet*, is cheap, fast, and reliable, and it imposes few limits on where the networked PCs are placed in your home or office. To create an Ethernet network, you'll need three components along with your PCs (**Figure 18.1**):

Network adapter. Each computer must have a *network adapter* (about $15 U.S.) that provides a physical connection to the network. An adapter has an *RJ-45 jack* that you connect an Ethernet cable to. If you have an older computer that didn't come with a built-in Ethernet jack, you can buy a *network interface card,* or *NIC* (a PCI expansion card that you open your computer to install), or an external network adapter that plugs into a USB port. For laptops, plug in a PC Card (about $30) that provides an Ethernet jack. All newer NICs are Plug and Play.

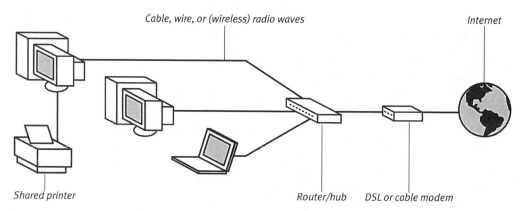

Cable, wire, or (wireless) radio waves

Internet

Shared printer

Router/hub

DSL or cable modem

Figure 18.1 A typical network, in which three computers share a printer and a broadband internet connection.

UNDERSTANDING NETWORK TYPES

For installation tips, see "Connecting Devices to Your Computer" in Chapter 8.

Ethernet cables. The cables used in Ethernet networks are a little thicker than telephone cables, and the *RJ-45 connectors* at each end are wider than ordinary phone (RJ-11) connectors. You can buy Ethernet cables—called *10BaseT, 100BaseT, CAT5, CAT5e, CAT6,* or *twisted-pair* cables—with preattached connectors ($5 to $50, depending on length). For custom lengths, you (or someone at the store) can cut the cable off a spool and attach the connectors. Or you can join two lengths by using an RJ-45 female/female coupler. A connection's length shouldn't exceed 100 meters (328 feet).

If you're drilling through walls to lay cable, consider hiring a professional cable installer (or using a wireless network).

Hub. On an Ethernet network, you connect each cable from a PC's network adapter to a central connection point called a *hub* (about $30)—a small box with a row of five to eight or more jacks (called *ports*) that accept RJ-45 connectors. Small green lights on the hub glow or flicker to signal an active connection. Computers communicate through the hub, so there's no direct connection between any two PCs.

One port, labeled *Uplink,* connects to a router, broadband modem, or another hub to expand the network. The other ports are numbered, but it doesn't matter which port you plug which cable into. You also can connect shared devices, such as printers, to the hub.

If you have an internet connection, use a *router/hub* instead of an ordinary hub to share the connection, as described later in this chapter.

Wireless (802.11)

Wireless networks are versatile and don't require cables. The wireless standard is called *Wi-Fi* or 802.11 (say *eight-oh-two-eleven*).

To set up a wireless network, install a wireless network adapter (about $60) in each PC. Most laptops have a built-in wireless adapter. To make sure, choose Start > Control Panel > Network and Internet > Network and Sharing Center > Manage Network Connections. For desktops, the adapter has a small antenna that sticks out the back of the computer to transmit and receive radio waves over a range of about 150 feet (through walls). To share a broadband internet connection, you need a *base station* or *access point* (about $100).

To stop neighbors or passersby from stealing your internet bandwidth and eavesdropping, turn on the password or encryption option—usually labeled *WPA* or *WPA2.* (Don't use *WEP,* an older and easily broken protocol.) Position the router or access point near the center of your house rather than near a window or outside wall. Also, change the default service set identifier (SSID) to stop your network from overlapping with other wireless networks using the same SSID.

UNDERSTANDING NETWORK TYPES

Wireless equipment comes in one of three flavors: 802.11*a*, 802.11*b*, or 802.11*g*. These three protocols vary by compatibility, band, range, and speed. If you're not interested in the details, buy only *g* equipment and stop reading. Otherwise, here are a few things to know about *a*, *b*, and *g* gear:

◆ *a* and *g* are about five times faster than *b* (54 Mbps versus 11 Mbps).

◆ *b* and *g* have a greater range than *a* (150 feet versus 60 feet).

◆ *b* and *g* work in the 2.4 GHz band and are subject to interference from pipes, weather, microwave ovens, 2.4 GHz cordless phones, and Bluetooth devices. (*a* works in the 5 GHz band.)

◆ *g* is backward-compatible with *b*. You can mix a *b* card with a *g* base station, and vice versa.

◆ *a* isn't compatible with *b* or *g* unless the equipment is labeled dual-band or tri-mode.

◆ *a* hasn't been adopted widely because of the popularity of *b* and *g*.

◆ Faster wireless equipment doesn't make your internet connection faster. (The modem is the bottleneck.)

◆ A wireless network is compatible with an Apple AirPort (802.11b) or AirPort Extreme (802.11g) network.

◆ The next standard, 802.11*n*, is due for approval in 2007 and offers greater throughput and increased range over 802.11a/b/g.

◆ The Wi-Fi Alliance (www.wi-fi.org) is a trade organization that tests and certifies equipment compliance with the 802.11 standards.

Telephone lines (HomePNA)

Network equipment certified by the *Home Phoneline Networking Alliance*, or *HomePNA*, uses your existing phone wires to connect computers. HomePNA networks don't interfere with other wire communications. You can use standard telephones, dial-up modems, DSL or cable modems, faxes, and answering machines simultaneously with HomePNA, because even though the devices use the same telephone wires, they occupy different frequency bands. These networks don't require a hub; instead, you plug your HomePNA network adapter (about $70) into the nearest phone jack. For more information, see www.homepna.org.

Electrical outlets (HomePlug)

Network equipment certified by the *HomePlug Powerline Alliance* uses the existing electrical wiring in your home to connect computers. Unlike phone jacks, power outlets are available in almost every room, ready to pull double duty as power sources and network ports.

A HomePlug network is easy to set up; you simply plug your HomePlug network adapter (about $100) into the nearest power outlet. The network range is about 1,000 feet, including the length that the wires travel in your walls. For more information, see www.homeplug.org.

UNDERSTANDING NETWORK TYPES

IEEE 1394 (FireWire)

You can form a simple network if your computers all have IEEE 1394 (FireWire) jacks, which usually are used to capture video from a digital video camera. (You can buy a 1394 card to get these jacks; see "Connecting Devices to Your Computer" in Chapter 8.) Just hook together the computers with 6-pin-to-6-pin IEEE 1394 cables (about $20). There's no need to buy a hub or router. Each computer should have two free 1394 ports so that you can form a chain.

The computers have to be close; 1394 cables can't be more than 15 feet (4.5 meters) long. And you can't use this arrangement to share a printer or DSL/cable modem. 1394 also is sometimes called i.Link or Lynx.

Crossover cable

If your network has only two computers that are close together, you can connect them with a *crossover cable* (about $10), which runs directly between the two PCs' Ethernet jacks. This no-hassle network saves you the cost of a hub and works exactly like a "real" Ethernet network. (If you expand the network to three computers, you must buy a hub.)

✔ Tips

■ Network speeds are measured in *megabits per second (Mbps)*. 10 Mbps, called *10BaseT* or *Ethernet*, is adequate for most homes and small businesses. Most new hubs and adapters handle both 10BaseT and *100BaseT* or *Fast Ethernet* (100 Mbps) on the same network; look for the label *10/100* or *dual speed*. Pricier *Gigabit Ethernet* (1000 Mbps) equipment also is available. Wireless, HomePNA, and HomePlug speeds are comparable to 10BaseT. (Network speed doesn't affect internet-connection speed; DSL and cable modems are 10 to 20 times slower than 10BaseT.)

■ Brand-name network equipment manufacturers include 3Com, Belkin, D-Link, Linksys, Microsoft, Motorola, Netgear, and SMC. No-name hardware is cheaper, but the few dollars extra that you pay for a name brand get you phone and web support, better documentation, and regularly updated drivers.

UNDERSTANDING NETWORK TYPES

Sharing an Internet Connection

To share one internet connection with every computer on a network, you have two options:

Install a router. A *router*—also called a *residential gateway* by Microsoft—is a small box with one jack that connects to a hub and another jack that connects to a DSL, cable, or dial-up modem. A *router/hub* (about $70) doubles as a hub, sharing the modem's bandwidth among multiple Ethernet ports that the network PCs connect to. A slightly more expensive *router/switch* is faster than a router/hub and should be used when you're passing lots of data around the network (when playing network games or sharing music, for example).

You're better off using a router than dealing with the limits of ICS (described next). A router is easy to install and configure, uses little power, lets any PC go online at any time, and has a built-in firewall. To the outside world, a router appears to be a computer, but one without programs and hard drives to attack or infect.

Use Internet Connection Sharing (ICS). ICS is a built-in Windows feature that acts like a software router. It's free but difficult to configure. You must designate one computer as the *host,* or *gateway,* PC through which all internet traffic passes. For broadband connections, the host PC must have *two* Ethernet adapters: one that connects to the DSL or cable modem and one that connects to a hub. If the host PC is turned off, the other PCs—called *clients*—can't go online.

Like a router, ICS works best with a high-speed internet connection, but a dial-up modem works acceptably.

ICS Setup

Some setup tips for Internet Connection Sharing:

◆ Make sure that the host PC can go online before you enable ICS.

◆ The client PCs can be running pre-Vista Windows versions (except Windows 95/3.*x*).

◆ Turn on the host PC before turning on the client PCs. Turning off the host kills all client internet connections.

◆ To enable ICS on the host, choose Start > Control Panel > Network and Internet > Network and Sharing Center > Manage Network Connections. Right-click the connection that you want to share and choose Properties > Sharing tab > check Allow Other Network Users to Connect Through This Computer's Internet Connection. Check the other boxes, if desired. (The Sharing tab isn't available if you have only one network connection.)

◆ When you enable ICS, your LAN connection gets a new static IP address. For instructions on reestablishing the TCP/IP connections between the host and clients, click Using ICS on the Sharing tab described in the preceding tip.

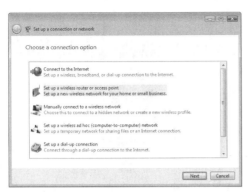

Figure 18.2 If your network is wireless, run the Set up a Wireless Router or Access Point wizard on the computer attached to the router. The wizard walks you through the process of adding other computers and devices to the network. For details on adding devices, search for the Help and Support topic *Add a device or computer to a network*.

Setting up a Network

After you've decided what type of network you want and bought the necessary hardware, you're ready to set up the network.

To set up a network:

1. Install network adapters in any computers that need them, according to the manufacturer's instructions (see "Understanding Network Types" earlier in this chapter).

2. *(Optional)* Set up an internet connection (see Chapter 12).

   A network doesn't need an internet connection, but most networks have one.

   To share an existing internet connection on the network, see "Sharing an Internet Connection" earlier in this chapter.

2. Connect the computers.

   The connections depend on the type of network adapters, modem, internet connection, and internet sharing.

3. Turn on all computers and devices (such as printers) that you want to be part of your network.

   If your network is wired (Ethernet or HomePNA, for example), Windows will set it up automatically, and it should be ready to use.

   or

   If your network is wireless, choose Start > Control Panel > Network and Internet > Network and Sharing Center > Set up a Connection or Network (in the left pane) > Set up a Wireless Router or Access Point (**Figure 18.2**).

   continues on next page

SETTING UP A NETWORK

The wizard saves your network settings to a USB flash drive, which you insert into each computer or device that you want to add to the wireless network. (You still can use the wizard even if you don't have a USB flash drive, but it's tedious.)

4. Test your network to make sure that all the computers and devices are connected and working properly.

On each network computer, choose Start > Network. (On computers running Windows XP, choose Start > My Network Places.) You should be able to see icons for the computer you are on and for all the other computers and devices that you have added to the network (**Figure 18.3**). Icons for network printers won't appear until you turn on Printer Sharing; see "Managing a Network" later in this chapter.

Figure 18.3 This simple Ethernet network has two computers and a router (and a shared printer not visible at this level). Here, the Network folder shows tiles view, grouped by category; switch to details view if you want to see more information about each computer and device.

Finding Missing Network Computers

If computers on the network are missing from the Network folder (refer to Figure 18.3), try these solutions to common problems.

◆ On each computer, choose Start > Connect To and connect to the network.

◆ On each computer, choose Start > Control Panel > Network and Internet > Network and Sharing Center. If Network Discovery is off, click the arrow button (⌄) to expand the section, select Turn on Network Discovery, and then click Apply. If a security prompt appears, type an administrator password or confirm the action.

◆ Right-click the Network icon (▤) in the notification area of the taskbar and choose Diagnose and Repair.

◆ Make sure all the computers are turned on and connected.

◆ Make sure that your hub, switch, or router is plugged in and turned on, and that all network adapters are firmly seated and cables are firmly connected to their jacks and ports. Use Device Manager to make sure that each network adapter is working properly (see "Managing Device Drivers" in Chapter 8).

◆ For other solutions, search for the Help and Support topic *Troubleshooting network problems*.

Figure 18.4 The name of each computer (here, Office-PC) appears in the Network folder (refer to Figure 18.3) and in other network tools and windows.

Figure 18.5 If you change the name of a workgroup on any computer, you also have to change the workgroup name (to match the new name) on each networked computer that you want to include in the new workgroup.

When you set up a network, Windows creates a workgroup and gives it a name automatically. You can join an existing workgroup on a network or create a new one. You also can change the name of the computer.

To rename a computer, join an existing workgroup, or create a new workgroup:

1. Choose Start > Control Panel > System and Maintenance > System > Change Settings (**Figure 18.4**).

   If a security prompt appears, type an administrator password or confirm the action.

2. On the Computer Name tab, click Change.

3. Type a new name for the computer, if desired (**Figure 18.5**).

4. In the Member Of section, select Workgroup.

5. Type the name of an existing workgroup that you want to join.

   or

   Type the name of the new workgroup that you want to create.

6. Click OK in each open dialog box.

✔ Tips

- To change the computer and workgroup name on a network computer running Windows XP, choose Start > Control Panel > Performance and Maintenance > System > Change Settings.

- The Network folder (refer to Figure 18.3) behaves like any other folder window, as described in Chapter 5. Double-click items to open or explore them, just as though you were working in your Computer folder or a Windows Explorer window. You can see the contents of other people's shared disks, folders, and files (see "Sharing Files" later in this chapter). You can move and copy items between network computers or rename, delete, select, sort, group, tag, search for, view properties of, and manipulate them just as you would items on your local drive. (Beware: If you delete a shared item on another computer, the item bypasses the Recycle Bin and disappears forever.) To navigate the network in the Folders list, expand the Network branch of the tree (**Figure 18.6**).

- In applications, shared files are available via the standard File > Open and File > Save As dialog boxes. File > Save saves a file in its original network location; to save a local copy on your hard disk, choose File > Save As.

Figure 18.6 The Network folder shows what's available to you over the network. Here, I'm logged on to OFFICE-PC, and I've expanded LAPTOP-PC to get to Wendy's travel folder (under Users\wendy\Documents), which she has shared. Also, note the shared network printer visible below OFFICE-PC.

Figure 18.7 Mapping a shared network item lets you refer to it by a drive letter, the same way you refer to your local A or C drive.

UNC Names

The *Uniform Naming Convention (UNC)* is a system of naming network files, folders, and other shared resources so that an item's address identifies it uniquely on the network. UNC uses the following format:

`\\server\resource_pathname`

server is a computer name (refer to Figure 18.4) or an IP address; *resource_pathname* is a standard pathname (see "Navigating in Windows Explorer" in Chapter 5). Some example UNCs for a folder, file, and printer are:

`\\yangtze\budget\2003\qtr2`

`\\nile\books\mynovel\chap1.doc`

`\\thames\HPcolor`

To view a shared item quickly, type its UNC name in an address bar or in the Run dialog box (press Windows logo key+R).

- You can *map* (assign) a shared disk or folder to a drive letter so that you can access the item via Start > Computer or the Open or Save As dialog box. In a folder window, choose Tools > Map Network Drive (press Alt if the Tools menu isn't visible). Then select a drive letter, browse for an item or type its Uniform Naming Convention (UNC) name, check Reconnect at Logon, and click Finish (**Figure 18.7**). The new "drive" appears in your Folders tree. To kill the mapping, choose Tools > Disconnect Network Drive.

- To connect a laptop to an Ethernet network, plug one end of an Ethernet cable into the laptop and the other end into the hub, switch, or router. To connect to a wireless network, choose Start > Connect To and select the network in the list. If the network is secured, type the password.

- You also can set up a wireless *ad hoc network*, which is a temporary connection between computers and devices used to, say, share files, play multiplayer games, or share an internet connection. Choose Start > Connect To > Set up a Connection or Network > Set up an Ad Hoc (Computer-to-Computer) Network. Click Next and follow the steps in the wizard.

- You can use command-line tools to get network information. The most useful are `hostname`, `ipconfig`, `net`, `netstat`, `ping`, and `tracer`.Type each command following by a space and /? for usage and syntax. To open the command window, choose Start > All Programs > Accessories > Command Prompt.

Managing a Network

Network and Sharing Center (**Figure 18.8**), new in Vista, is a dashboard for managing your network and viewing its status in real time (useful when you're having setup or connection problems). It also has links to Windows' other networking tools and wizards.

To open Network and Sharing Center:

◆ Choose Start > Control Panel > Network and Internet > Network and Sharing Center.

or

Right-click the Network icon (🖳) in the notification area of the taskbar and choose Network and Sharing Center.

✔ Tip

■ If the Network icon is hidden, right-click an empty area of the taskbar and choose Properties > Notification Area tab > check Network > OK.

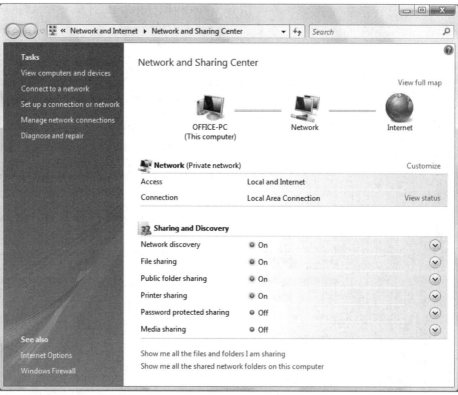

Figure 18.8 Network and Sharing Center lets you see whether your computer is connected to your network or the internet, the type of connection, and what level of access you have to other computers and devices on the network.

MANAGING A NETWORK

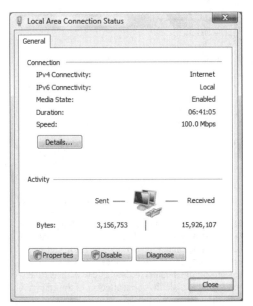

Figure 18.9 The Status dialog box shows the dead-or-alive state of the network and statistics on maximum speed, connection duration, and bytes uploaded and downloaded. Click Details for the IP address or Properties for more-advanced settings.

Figure 18.10 You also can choose a new name and icon for your network, which will appear in Network and Sharing Center and on network maps (useful if you have multiple networks).

To see the current status of a network connection:

◆ In Network and Sharing Center, click View Status (**Figure 18.9**).

You chose a network location (Home, Work, or Public Place) the first time that you connected to a network, letting Windows know which firewall and security settings to use when you connect:

◆ **Home and Work locations.** Windows assumes that you trust the people and devices on the network, so it turns on *network discovery,* which lets you see other computers and devices on a network, and allows other network users to see your computer. You also can access shared files and devices on other computers, and other people can access files and devices on your computer that you've shared.

◆ **Public Place locations.** Windows keeps your PC invisible to the other computers around you (at a café, for example) by turning off network discovery.

If you're a traveling laptop user who connects to networks at home, school, work, airports, and coffee shops, you can change the network location based on where you are.

To change the network location:

1. In Network and Sharing Center, click Customize (**Figure 18.10**).

2. Select Public (for Public Place networks) or Private (for Home or Work networks).

   If a security prompt appears, type an administrator password or confirm the action.

3. Click Next and then click Close.

You can control how your computer is seen and shared on the network by setting options in Network and Sharing Center.

To configure the network connection settings:

◆ In Network and Sharing Center, turn on or off the settings below Sharing and Discovery (**Figure 18.11**).

If a security prompt appears, type an administrator password or confirm the action.

✔ Tips

■ Most of the network settings are covered elsewhere in this book. Network discovery is described earlier in this section. File sharing and Public folder sharing are covered in "Sharing Files" later in this chapter. For printer sharing, see "Sharing a Network Printer" in Chapter 7. The media folders—Pictures, Music, and Videos—are covered in chapters 9, 10, and 11, respectively.

■ The network map at the top of Network and Sharing Center is live and interactive (**Figure 18.12**). Click (or right-click) your computer to open the Computer folder, for example. Click another computer on the network to bring up its shared devices and folders. Click a network icon to show the Network folder (refer to Figure 18.3). Click Internet to open a web browser.

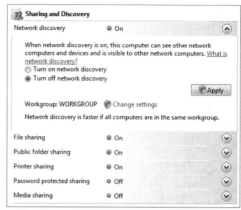

Figure 18.11 To expand or collapse a section, click the On/Off light or the arrow button (ⓥ). Each section contains an explanation of the setting; the setting's options; a button to apply changes; and in some cases, links to change related settings and to display Help topics that explain the consequences of the change.

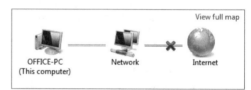

Figure 18.12 The X means that this network has lost its internet connection. Click the X to have Windows try to diagnose and solve the problem, or look for an unplugged cable or switched-off modem or router. Click View Full Map to see a detailed map, with icons for all the computers on the network, connections, router, switch, and so on.

If you don't want your computer to be on a network, you can disconnect it without unplugging cables.

To disconnect from a network:

1. In Network and Sharing Center, click Manage Network Connections (in the left pane).

2. In the Network Connections folder, right-click the connection that you want to disconnect from and choose Disconnect or Disable.

   If a security prompt appears, type an administrator password or confirm the action.

✔ Tip

■ If you disable a LAN connection, the network adapter is disabled until you reconnect.

MANAGING A NETWORK

Sharing Files

Windows gives you two ways to share disks, folders, and files: Public folder sharing and any-folder sharing. Either method lets you share with someone using your computer or another computer on the same network.

The Public folder

The easiest way to share files and folders is to put them in the Public folder. Everyone with a user account and password on your computer can access the Public folder, but you decide whether people on the network can access it. You can't choose *who* on the network can access it. You must grant access either to everyone on the network or to no one. You can set the permission level, however, by choosing whether those who have network access can only open files or also change and create them.

Other Ways to Share

Ways to share files that don't make you share from specific folders:

◆ Removable media (floppies, CDs, DVDs, portable hard disks, flash-memory cards, and USB flash drives)

◆ Email attachments (see "Sending Email" in Chapter 15)

◆ Instant messaging (see "Using Messenger" in Chapter 16)

◆ Photo-sharing websites (see "Emailing Photos" in Chapter 9)

◆ Ad hoc network (see the Tips in "Setting up a Network" earlier in this chapter)

◆ Windows Meeting Space (see "Using the Free Utility Programs" in Chapter 6)

Figure 18.13 Copy or move whichever files you want to share to the Public folder or one of its subfolders, which help you organize shared files by content type. You have to place the files themselves; shortcuts won't work.

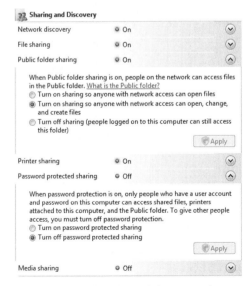

Figure 18.14 To control the level of access to the Public folder, use the Public Folder Sharing option. To control who can access the Public folder, set the Password Protected Sharing option.

Use the Public folder if you want to able to see everything you've shared just by looking in one place, separate from your personal folders (Documents, Music, Pictures, and so on), or if you want to set sharing permissions for everyone on your network rather than individual users.

To open the Public folder:

◆ Choose Start > Documents, and in the Navigation pane, click Public (**Figure 18.13**).

✔ Tips

■ By default, network access to the Public folder is turned off. Use Network and Sharing Center to control access to it (**Figure 18.14**).

■ Password-protected sharing doesn't work if you're on a network domain, limiting access to the Public folder to only those people with password-protected accounts on your computer.

Any-folder sharing

Using the Public folder can be inefficient. If you're sharing hundreds of photos, for example, it's wasteful to store copies in both your (unshared) Pictures folder and your Public folder. If you create or update files frequently, it's cumbersome to keep copying them to your Public folder.

Use any-folder sharing to share files and folders directly from the location where they're stored (typically, in your Documents, Pictures, or Music folder). You can set sharing permissions for individual users rather than for everyone on your network, giving some people more or less access (or no access).

To share files from any folder on your computer:

1. In a folder window, locate the folder with the files that you want to share.

2. Select one or more files or folders that you want to share and click Share on the toolbar (or right-click and choose Share).

3. In the File Sharing dialog box (**Figure 18.15**), do one of the following:

   ▲ If your computer is on a domain or workgroup, type the name of the person you want to share files with and click Add.

   ▲ If your computer is on a domain, click the arrow to the right of the text box and choose Find. Type the name of the person you want to share files with, click Check Names, and then click OK.

   ▲ If your computer is on a domain, click the arrow to the right of the text box, choose Everyone to share the files with everyone on your network, and then click Add.

   ▲ If your computer is on a workgroup, click the arrow to the right of the text box, choose the person's name in the list, and then click Add.

   ▲ If your computer is on a workgroup, and you don't see the name of the person you want to share files with in the list, click the arrow to the right of the text box and choose Create a New User to create a new account for the person.

   The name of the person or group that you selected appears in the list of people you want to share files with.

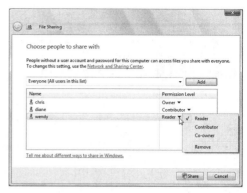

Figure 18.15 If you're sharing a file instead of a folder, there's no option to set the permission level to Contributor. You also can choose Remove to stop sharing with someone.

Figure 18.16 This dialog box lets you tell people that they can access your shared files.

4. In the Permission Level column, click the arrow for that person or group and choose one of the following sharing permissions:

▲ **Reader** restricts the person or group to viewing files in the shared folder.

▲ **Contributor** lets the person or group view all files, add files, and change or delete the files that they add.

▲ **Co-Owner** lets the person or group view, change, add, and delete files in the shared folder,

5. Click Share.

If a security prompt appears, type an administrator password or confirm the action.

6. After you receive confirmation that your folder is shared (**Figure 18.16**), you can notify the people that you're sharing with and send them a link to access the files.

Do one of the following:

▲ Click **Email** to open a Windows Mail message automatically with the link to your shared files.

▲ Click **Copy** (or right-click the shared item in the list and choose Copy Link) if you want to paste the link into an email message manually (if you don't use Windows Mail).

▲ Click **Done** if you don't want to send an email message.

SHARING FILES

✔ Tips

-  A small indicator appears in the bottom-left corner of the icon of shared files and folders.

- Make sure that File Sharing is turned on in Network and Sharing Center (refer to Figure 18.14).

- To see what you're sharing, click Show Me All the Files I Am Sharing in the File Sharing confirmation dialog box (refer to Figure 18.16) or in Network and Sharing Center (refer to Figure 18.8).

- A *share name* makes it easy for someone to find a shared folder on your computer. Right-click a folder that you've already shared and choose Properties > Sharing tab > Advanced Sharing (**Figure 18.17**). If a security prompt appears, type an administrator password or confirm the action.

- To share an entire hard disk, choose Start > Computer, right-click the disk, and choose Properties > Sharing tab > Advanced Sharing.

- You can't share encrypted files and folders (see "Encrypting Data" in Chapter 13).

Figure 18.17 On the Sharing tab, click the Share button to start sharing, stop sharing, or change the existing sharing permissions. Or click Advanced Sharing for more-complex administrator-level sharing options.

19

WORKING REMOTELY

Remote Connections

Windows' remote-access features come in two flavors: remote networking (direct dialing and VPN) and remote control (Remote Desktop).

Remote networking lets your local PC access remote-PC or network resources over a modem or internet link. If you double-click a Microsoft Word file that resides on the remote PC, for example, the file is transmitted to your local PC and opens in your *local* copy of Word. If you have no copy of Word on your local PC, Word is transmitted, too—which would take days over dial-up. The moral: Avoid running programs that reside only on the remote PC, especially for slow connections.

Remote control doesn't have this problem; *all* work is done on the remote PC. If you double-click that same Word file, the remote PC's copy of Word opens. Only keystrokes, mouse gestures, and desktop images are transmitted between the two PCs. Depending on your connection speed, refresh of the remote desktop may be slow on your local screen.

Windows gives you several ways to connect to a computer remotely. If you're a business traveler on the road or a late sleeper working from home, for example, you can connect from your laptop or home PC (the *local computer*) to the unattended, distant machine (the *remote computer* or *host computer*) in your office to access its files and resources.

In this chapter, you'll learn three preferred remote-access techniques:

◆ Traditional **direct dialing** connects to a faraway computer via phone lines, racking up toll charges.

◆ **Virtual private networking (VPN)** lets you connect to a workplace network via the internet, avoiding long-distance charges.

◆ **Remote Desktop** lets you control a remote computer, whose desktop appears on your local PC's screen just as though you were sitting at the remote PC's keyboard.

This chapter also covers features especially for traveling laptop users.

Dialing Direct

A wizard takes you through the steps of creating a dial-up (modem-to-modem) connection.

To set up a dial-up connection:

1. Choose Start > Control Panel > Network and Internet > Network and Sharing Center > Set up a Connection or Network (in the left pane).

2. Select Connect to a Workplace and click Next (**Figure 19.1**).

3. If you have an existing dial-up connection, select No, Create a New Connection and click Next; otherwise, skip this step.

4. Click Dial Directly and follow the onscreen instructions.

   Along the way, you're asked for the phone number, destination name (for the icon label), user name, password, and (optional) domain. You can get this information from your network administrator.

5. To connect, choose Start > Connect To; then right-click the dial-up connection in the list and choose Connect.

   or

   To disconnect, right-click the dial-up connection in the Connect To window and choose Disconnect (**Figure 19.2**).

✔ Tips

- To manage all your connections in one place, click Manage Network Connections in Network and Sharing Center.

- To configure your modem, choose Start > Hardware and Sound > Phone and Modem Options.

Figure 19.1 This window launches various wizards for creating connections on your computer.

Figure 19.2 If you're already connected, right-click to disconnect. The shortcut menu also lets you reconfigure the connection and see the status of an active connection.

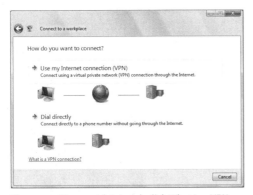

Figure 19.3 For a quick tutorial, click What Is a VPN Connection?

Connecting to a Virtual Private Network Server

A *virtual private network (VPN)* lets you connect from your PC to a network securely and privately by using the internet as a conduit. VPNs overcome direct dialing's twin evils: slow speeds and high costs.

To set up a VPN connection:

1. Choose Start > Control Panel > Network and Internet > Network and Sharing Center > Set up a Connection or Network (in the left pane).

2. Select Connect to a Workplace and click Next (refer to Figure 19.1).

3. If you have an existing dial-up connection, select No, Create a New Connection and click Next; otherwise, skip this step.

4. Click Use My Internet Connection (VPN) and follow the onscreen instructions (**Figure 19.3**).

   Along the way, you're asked for the internet address, destination name (for the icon label), user name, password, and (optional) domain. You can get this information from your network administrator.

5. To connect, choose Start > Connect To; then right-click the VPN connection in the list and choose Connect.

   or

   To disconnect, right-click the VPN connection in the Connect To window and choose Disconnect (refer to Figure 19.2).

✔ Tip

■ To manage all your connections in one place, click Manage Network Connections in Network and Sharing Center.

CONNECTING TO A VPN SERVER

Controlling a Computer with Remote Desktop

Remote Desktop lets you connect to a remote computer and use it as though you were sitting in front of it. Much more than a simple direct-dial or VPN connection, Remote Desktop lets you control the remote PC's full desktop, with its Start menu, taskbar, icons, documents, and programs. Programs run on the remote computer, and only the keyboard input, mouse input, and display output are transmitted over the connection. The *remote computer* is the PC that you want to control from afar. The *local* (or *client*) *computer* is the one that you'll be sitting at, driving the remote PC.

To set up a remote computer:

1. Choose Start > Control Panel > System and Maintenance > System (or press Windows logo key+Break) > Remote Settings (in the left pane).

   If a security prompt appears, type an administrator password or confirm the action.

Remote Desktop Requirements

You can access a computer running Windows from another computer running Windows that's connected to the same network or to the internet. To connect to the remote computer:

◆ That computer must be turned on.

◆ It must have a network connection.

◆ Remote Desktop must be enabled.

◆ You must have network access to it. (This could be through the internet.)

◆ You must have permission to connect. (For permission to connect, you must be in the list of users.)

You can't use Remote Desktop to connect to computers running the Home editions of Windows Vista and XP, though you can create outgoing connections from those editions. (XP Pro works with incoming and outgoing connections.)

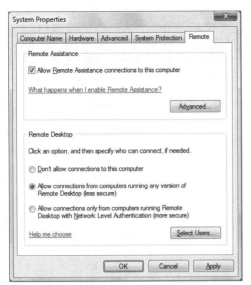

Figure 19.4 Select the second or third Remote Desktop option to let other users control this computer remotely.

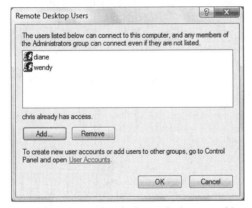

Figure 19.5 Don't add anybody you don't trust to this list. For security reasons, only users with password-protected accounts can make a Remote Desktop connection.

2. On the Remote tab, select the one of the options below Remote Desktop (**Figure 19.4**).

3. Click Select Users (**Figure 19.5**).

   If you are enabling Remote Desktop for your current user account, your name is added to the list of remote users automatically, and you can skip the next two steps.

4. Click Add.

5. In the Select Users dialog box, do the following:

   To search for a different location, click Locations.

   or

   In Enter the Object Names to Select, type the name of the user that you want to add and click Check Names.

6. Click OK in the open dialog boxes.

   Now the remote computer listens for incoming Remote Desktop connection requests.

To connect to a remote desktop:

1. Connect to the internet normally.

   Skip this step if the remote PC is on your local area network.

2. Choose Start > All Programs > Accessories > Remote Desktop Connection.

   The Remote Desktop Connection dialog box appears.

3. Click Options to expand the dialog box, if necessary; then change the settings as desired for this remote session (**Figure 19.6**).

4. Click Connect.

5. Enter your credentials for the remote computer.

   You can type the remote computer's network name, IP address, or registered DNS name. Type your name and password (and domain, if necessary) exactly as you would if you were logging on to the remote PC in person.

6. Click OK.

   Your screen goes black momentarily; then the remote PC's desktop fills the screen, hiding *your* desktop and taskbar (**Figure 19.7**).

   Now you can operate the distant PC as though you were sitting in front of it. All your actions—running programs, printing, sending email, installing drivers, whatever—happen on the remote PC.

   Anyone looking at the remote PC in person sees a Welcome screen or an Unlock Computer screen; that person can't see what you're doing.

Figure 19.6 You can configure Remote Desktop before you connect. You may want to try a remote session or two before adjusting the default settings. If you connect regularly to multiple PCs by using different settings, you can save each group of settings as an .rdp file to open in future sessions. Logon credentials aren't saved in the file.

Minimize—Reduces the remote
desktop to a taskbar button on
your own desktop

Restore—Displays the remote
desktop in a floating, resizable
window on your own desktop

Pushpin—Locks this title bar in place
or makes it hide automatically —

Close—Disconnects the remote
PC but doesn't log off

Figure 19.7 A full-screen remote desktop shows a title bar at the screen's top edge, letting you switch between your own desktop and the remote desktop. The title bar retracts from view unless you lock it or move your pointer to the top edge.

CONTROLLING A COMPUTER W/REMOTE DESKTOP

✔ Tips

- If you have trouble connecting, search Help and Support for the topics *Remote Desktop connection: frequently asked questions* and *Troubleshoot Remote Desktop problems*. Be sure to check that the Windows Firewall exception for Remote Desktop is turned on (see "Using a Firewall" in Chapter 13).

- Clicking Restore (refer to Figure 19.7) puts the remote desktop in a floating, resizable window on your local desktop (**Figure 19.8**).

- You can use the standard cut, copy, and paste commands to transfer text, graphics, and files between the two PCs. If both desktops are visible (as in Figure 19.8), you can drag between local and remote windows.

- Clicking the close button (refer to Figure 19.7) disconnects the remote PC but doesn't log it off; it leaves your documents open and programs running, as though you had used Fast User Switching (see "Logging On and Logging Off" in Chapter 1). To pick up where you left off, reconnect via Remote Desktop or log on in person at the remote PC. To log off the remote PC, choose Log Off from *its* Start menu, not yours.

- To shut down the remote PC, choose Start > Windows Security remotely; then use the security screen to shut down, restart, log off, hibernate, lock the computer, and so on. (The Windows Security command appears only when you're connected remotely.)

Figure 19.8 Click Restore to show your own desktop. To return to full-screen view, click Maximize in the remote window's title bar.

Logon Conflicts

If someone else already is logged on to the remote PC that you're connecting to, Windows warns you and asks whether you want to continue. If you do, the other person gets the chance to accept or reject your connection and must respond within 30 seconds or be disconnected automatically. Fortunately, that user remains logged on, loses no work, and can resume the session later, just as in Fast User Switching.

If someone logs on to the remote PC in person while *you're* connected, the situation is opposite: You get the chance to accept or reject the connection within 30 seconds. If you disconnect your remote session (by choice or automatically), you remain logged on and lose no work; you can reconnect after the other party logs off.

Table 19.1

Keyboard Shortcuts

LOCAL DESKTOP SHORTCUT	REMOTE DESKTOP SHORTCUT	DESCRIPTION
Alt+Tab	Alt+Page Up	Switches among programs
Alt+Shift+Tab	Alt+Page Down	Switches among programs in reverse order
Alt+Esc	Alt+Insert	Cycles through programs in the order in which they were started
Ctrl+Esc	Alt+Home	Opens the Start menu
Ctrl+Alt+Delete	Ctrl+Alt+End	Displays Task Manager or, for domains, the Windows Security dialog box
N/A	Ctrl+Alt+Break	Switches the remote desktop between a window and full screen
N/A	Alt+Delete	Displays the active window's control menu

- If the Remote Desktop window is maximized (refer to Figure 19.7), the standard Windows keyboard shortcuts apply to the *remote* computer. Alt+Tab, for example, switches between programs on the distant PC, not your local one. But if the Remote Desktop window is active and floating on your desktop (refer to Figure 19.8), those same shortcuts apply to the *local* PC. (Alt+Tab will switch between locally running programs.)

  Fortunately, keyboard junkies can use the standard shortcuts in the first column of **Table 19.1** to control the *local* desktop and the second-column shortcuts to perform the equivalent function on an active, floating Remote Desktop window.

- You can use Remote Desktop to let someone connect to your PC to give you technical help, much like Remote Assistance (Chapter 3), except that you don't have to be present at your PC to accept the connection.

- Remote Desktop alternatives: Ultr@VNC (free; `http://ultravnc.sourceforge.net`) is a more versatile remote-control program. To find commercial products, search the web for *remote control software*. Some popular products are CoSession, Laplink, and pcAnywhere. Read reviews first; these programs vary in ease of setup, connection options, and response time.

CONTROLLING A COMPUTER W/REMOTE DESKTOP

Making Network Files and Folders Available Offline

Offline Files is designed for travelers who work with a laptop computer that's often disconnected from the network. When you make a file or folder available offline, Windows makes a temporary copy of it on your laptop; you can work with this copy as you would the original. When you reconnect to the network, Windows *synchronizes* your laptop documents with the network originals so that you have up-to-date versions in both places. Offline Files isn't available in Vista Home editions.

To turn on offline files:

◆ Choose Start > Control Panel > Network and Internet > Offline Files > General tab > Enable Offline Files > OK (**Figure 19.9**).

If a security prompt appears, type an administrator password or confirm the action.

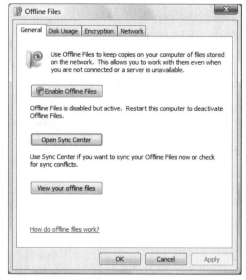

Figure 19.9 If you work with offline files in many different folders, click View Your Offline Files to see them all without opening each folder individually. You can use the other tabs to limit disk space for offline files, encrypt offline files, or work offline automatically if your network connection is slow.

To make a file or folder available offline:

1. Choose Start > Network (on your laptop) and locate the network file or folder that you want to make available offline.

2. Right-click the file or folder and choose Always Available Offline.

The next time that you try to access the file or folder, you'll be able to open it even if the network version is unavailable.

✔ Tips

■ **Documents** You open offline files as though you were working with them online. A small indicator in the icon's bottom-left corner reminds you that you're working offline.

■ You *must* log off or shut down to effect synchronization. If you simply disconnect from the network, Windows won't have time to synchronize files.

■ Synchronization is at Windows' discretion by default. To synchronize manually when you're connected to the network, choose Start > All Programs > Accessories > Sync Center; select Offline Files and then click Sync (on the toolbar).

■ To make an item *un*available offline, right-click it; then choose Always Available Offline again to uncheck it.

■ I've covered only the basics here. For details, search Help and Support for *offline files*.

Using Laptop Utilities

Sync Center and Windows Mobility Center, both new in Vista, are designed especially for laptop users.

Sync Center. Sync, short for *synchronization,* keeps two or more versions of the same file stored in different locations matched with each other. If you add, change, or delete a file in one location, Windows can add, change, or delete the same file in the other locations that you choose to sync with, whenever you choose to sync.

Sync Center (Start > All Programs > Accessories > Sync Center) lets you keep information in sync between your computer and offline files (covered in the preceding section), programs that support Sync Center, and mobile devices (plugged-in or wireless music players, digital cameras, and mobile phones). Search Help and Support for *sync center.*

Windows Mobility Center. Mobility Center (**Figure 19.10**) lets you adjust your laptop settings in a central location. To open Mobility Center (on laptops only), choose Start > Control Panel > Mobile PC > Windows Mobility Center, or press Windows logo key+X. You also can click the battery icon (▣) on the taskbar and choose Windows Mobility Center.

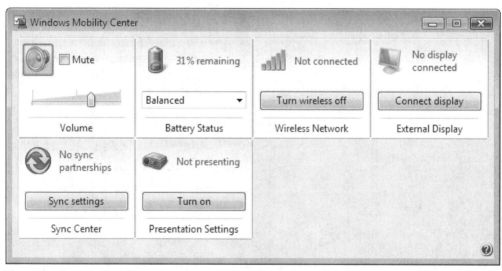

Figure 19.10 You can adjust the speaker volume, check the status of your wireless network connection, and change the power plan, for example.

MAINTENANCE & TROUBLESHOOTING 20

Periodic checkups and routine maintenance will keep your system running smoothly. In this chapter, you'll learn how to use Windows tools to monitor your PC's health and:

◆ Manage your hard disks

◆ Schedule tasks

◆ View or edit the registry

◆ Restore your PC to a previous working condition

◆ Back up your files

◆ Recover from a crash

✔ Tip

■ Search for *troubleshoot* in Windows Help and Support to see a list of topics designed to help you identify and resolve hardware, software, and networking problems.

Getting System Information

System Information compiles and reports information about your PC's hardware, drivers, system resources, and internet settings. This overview saves you from visiting scores of Control Panel dialog boxes to see how your PC is configured. You can find information quickly to give to a techie who's trouble-shooting your system.

To display system data:

1. Choose Start > All Programs > Accessories > System Tools > System Information.

2. Use the Explorer-like tree to display information in the various categories (**Figure 20.1**):

   Hardware Resources displays hardware settings, such as IRQs and memory addresses. The Conflicts/Sharing view identifies devices that are sharing resources or are in conflict.

   Components displays Windows config-uration information for device drivers, as well as networking and multimedia software.

   Software Environment displays a snapshot of the software loaded into computer memory. Use this information to see whether a process is still running or to check version information.

Figure 20.1 To find system data, type search text in the Find What box at the bottom of the window, check the appropriate search-option boxes, and then click Find.

✔ Tips

- To get system information for a different computer on your network, choose View > Remote Computer.

- To save system data in a System Information file—which you can archive or email to a techie to open in his copy of System Information—choose File > Save. To save system data in a text file, choose File > Export.

- File > Print produces a 50-page printout. It makes more sense to export the data to a text file and print your choice of sec-tions in Notepad.

GETTING SYSTEM INFORMATION

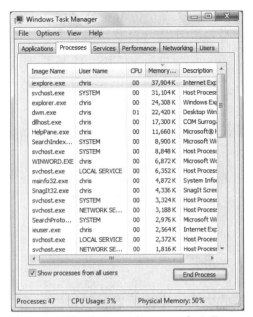

Figure 20.2 This tab shows all programs (including background tasks) running on your PC. Click a column header to sort by that column. This display is sorted by memory use.

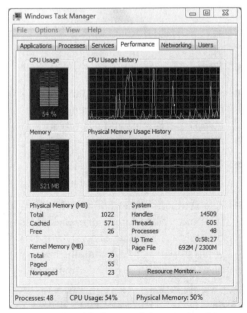

Figure 20.3 This tab shows real-time graphs of the load on your CPU and physical memory.

Managing Tasks

Task Manager is one of the most useful tools in Windows. It displays running programs, background processes, performance statistics, network activity, and user information. It also can shut down misbehaving programs.

To start Task Manager:

1. Right-click an empty area of the taskbar and choose Task Manager (or press Ctrl+Shift+Esc).

2. Click any of the following tabs:

   Applications for a list of foreground applications and the status of each one. See also "Killing Unresponsive Programs" in Chapter 6.

   Processes for a list of all programs running on your computer, including background programs and those shown on the Applications tab (**Figure 20.2**).

   Services for a list of programs that run in the background to support other programs.

   Performance for real-time graphs and statistics that show your system's performance (**Figure 20.3**).

   Networking is similar to the Performance tab except that it shows real-time graphs of network traffic.

   Users displays logged-on users and the status of each one. See "Logging On and Logging Off" in Chapter 1.

✔ Tips

- Use the Options and View menus to select preferences. These menus' commands change depending on the selected tab.

- Choose Options > Always on Top to make Task Manager float over all other windows.

- You can right-click an entry in the Applications, Processes, Services, or Users tab for a shortcut menu.

- If you're curious about a process, go to www.processid.com/processes.html.

MANAGING TASKS

Cleaning up a Disk

Over time, your hard disk will accumulate temporary files, stale components, recycled junk, and space-wasters that you can remove safely. Use Disk Cleanup to reclaim disk space if you're running out of room.

To remove unneeded files:

1. Choose Start > All Programs > Accessories > System Tools > Disk Cleanup.

   or

   Choose Start > Computer, right-click a disk, and choose Properties > General tab > Disk Cleanup.

   or

   Press Windows logo key+R; type `cleanmgr` and press Enter.

2. Select whether you want to clean up only your own files or those of all users.

   If a security prompt appears, type an administrator password or confirm the action.

3. In the Disk Cleanup dialog box, check the boxes of the files that you want to delete (**Figure 20.4**).

   The right column shows how much space you can make available. The text below the list box describes the selected option.

4. Click OK.

Figure 20.4 Disk Cleanup searches your drive and then shows you temporary files, internet cache files, and unnecessary program files that you can delete safely.

✔ Tips

■ The More Options tab contains other cleanup tools that let you remove installed programs and all but your most recent System Restore restore point.

■ Avoid deleting Downloaded Program Files, which often are useful add-ons.

■ The Temporary Files option deletes only temporary files more than a week old, so the right column may show 0 KB even if your temporary folder contains many files. To clean out this folder manually, close all programs; press Windows logo key+R; type %temp% and press Enter; and then delete the files in the folder window that appears.

Figure 20.5 Defragmentation takes between a few minutes and a few hours to finish, depending on the size and degree of fragmentation of your hard disk. While you're here, you can change whether and when Disk Defragmenter runs automatically.

Defragmenting a Disk

When a file grows, it won't fit back into its original disk location and becomes physically fragmented into noncontiguous pieces on the disk. As more files become fragmented, Windows has to retrieve the chopped-up pieces and reassemble them, which impairs the disk's performance and reliability. Disk Defragmenter consolidates fragmented files, making both files and free space contiguous. Large blocks of available space make it less likely that new files will be fragmented. Disk Defragmenter runs on a schedule, but you can defragment manually.

To defragment a disk:

1. Exit all programs, turn off antivirus software, and then run Disk Cleanup (see "Cleaning up a Disk" earlier in this chapter).

2. Choose Start > All Programs > Accessories > System Tools > Disk Defragmenter.

   or

   Choose Start > Computer, right-click a disk, and choose Properties > Tools tab > Defragment Now.

   or

   Press Windows logo key+R; type `dfrgui` and press Enter.

   If a security prompt appears, type an administrator password or confirm the action.

3. Click Defragment Now (**Figure 20.5**). You can cancel at any time.

✔ Tips

■ You still can use your computer during defragmentation, but the process is delicate. It's less risky to do nothing until defragmentation completes.

■ A better defragmenter is Diskeeper ($30 U.S.; www.diskeeper.com).

Checking for Disk Errors

Improper shutdowns—usually caused by power outages, mechanical problems, or system crashes (blue screens)—may create defects on disk surfaces. These errors can cause numerous problems, such as random crashes, data corruption, or the inability to save or open files. Check Disk scans the disk surface for errors and fixes any that it finds.

To detect and repair disk errors:

1. Exit all programs.

2. Choose Start > Computer, right-click a disk, and choose Properties > Tools tab > Check Now (**Figure 20.6**).

   If a security prompt appears, type an administrator password or confirm the action.

3. Check or uncheck the following boxes:

   Automatically Fix File System Errors. Check this box to make Windows repair any errors it finds; if it's unchecked, errors are merely reported, not fixed. If the disk is in use, or if you're checking the system disk (the one with Windows on it), you'll see **Figure 20.7**; click Schedule Disk Check to defer the scan until the next time you restart your PC.

   Scan for and Attempt Recovery of Bad Sectors. Check this box to make Windows recover readable files and folders it finds in the disk's defective sections, and move them elsewhere on the disk. This option fixes errors as well, even if the other option is unchecked. Unrepairable sections are locked out of available storage.

4. Click Start to begin the checking process.

   The progress bar indicates the phase Check Disk is in. When all phases are complete, a dialog box tells you how things turned out.

Figure 20.6 Check Disk usually completes in less than a minute.

Figure 20.7 This message appears if the disk is in use. Check Disk runs the next time you restart your system. The disk won't be available for other tasks during the check.

✔ Tip

■ The best protection against disk dings from power fluctuation is an Uninterruptible Power Supply (UPS). See "Conserving Power" in Chapter 4.

Figure 20.8 Drive Management is a cog in the larger machine named Computer Management, which groups many tools described elsewhere in this book. Click a tool in the left pane's console tree to open it.

Managing Disks

Disk Management lets you inspect and manage hard disks. On new hardware, you can initialize a disk and create or format partitions. You also can assess a disk's health, assign drive letters, format, and do related tasks.

To open Disk Management:

1. Choose Start > Control Panel > System and Maintenance > Administrative Tools > Computer Management; then click Disk Management in the left pane (**Figure 20.8**).

   or

   In the Start menu, right-click Computer; choose Manage and then click Disk Management in the left pane.

   or

   Press Windows logo key+R; type `diskmgmt.msc` and press Enter.

   If a security prompt appears, type an administrator password or confirm the action.

2. Right-click any disk or partition for a list of commands, or use the View menu to specify how disks are displayed.

Partitions

A *partition,* or *volume,* is a portion of a physical disk that functions as though it were a separate disk. After you create a partition, you must format it and assign it a drive letter before you can store data on it. Every hard disk has one partition, but you can create several on one disk, mainly to:

◆ Separate files and folders from the operating system, keeping your personal documents safe if an OS upgrade turns ugly

◆ Create dual-boot systems with multiple OSes

Unfortunately, Disk Management erases a hard disk before partitioning it, which makes it suitable for only blank or new disks. To create or resize partitions without erasing, try PartitionMagic ($70 U.S.; *www.partitionmagic.com/partitionmagic*) or Partition Manager ($50 U.S.; *www.partition-manager.com*).

MANAGING DISKS

Scheduling Tasks

Periodic maintenance and backups aren't useful unless they actually occur periodically—and human memory often fails here. Task Scheduler schedules automated tasks that perform actions at a specific time or when a certain event occurs.

Task Scheduler can open programs, send email, and show pop-up messages. In some cases, it's adequate simply to open a program or remind yourself of something on schedule, but for true automation you should use command-line commands that run to completion without your intervention.

A *command name* is a program's filename as typed at a command prompt (choose Start > All Programs > Accessories > Command Prompt). Disk Defragmenter's command name is `defrag`, and Backup's is `wbadmin`, for example. *Command-line options,* or *switches,* are space-separated parameters—prefixed by the - or / character—that follow the command name and control that command's behavior.

Search for the Help and Support topic *Command-line reference for IT pros* and click the link for the command-line reference to find commands, their switches, and examples (**Figure 20.9**).

✔ Tips

- To run a command-line program as an administrator, choose Start and type `command prompt` in the Search box. In the results list, right-click Command Prompt and choose Run As Administrator.

- You can place multiple command-line commands in a text file with a .bat extension and run this *batch file* as a single task instead of running each command individually.

Defrag

Locates and consolidates fragmented boot files, data files, and folders on local volumes.

Syntax
defrag *volume*

defrag *volume* [**/a**]

defrag *volume* [**/a**] [**/v**]

defrag *volume* [**/v**]

defrag *volume* [**/f**]

↑ Top of page

Parameters

volume : The drive letter or a mount point of the volume to be defragmented.

/a : Analyzes the volume and displays a summary of the analysis report.

/v : Displays the complete analysis and defragmentation reports.

When used in combination with **/a**, displays only the analysis report. When used alone, displays both the analysis and defragmentation reports.

/f : Forces defragmentation of the volume regardless of whether it needs to be defragmented.

/? : Displays help at the command prompt.

Figure 20.9 The description of the `defrag` command and its command-line options. The command `defrag C: /f` defragments your C drive, for example.

Figure 20.10 If you use a specific program on a regular basis, you can use Task Scheduler to create a task that opens the program for you automatically according to the schedule you choose.

To schedule a task:

1. Choose Start > All Programs > Accessories > System Tools > Task Scheduler (**Figure 20.10**).

   If a security prompt appears, type an administrator password or confirm the action.

2. In the right pane, below Actions, click Create Basic Task.

   Follow the steps in the Create Basic Task wizard. When you finish, the task will run according to schedule, even if somebody else (or nobody) is logged on.

✔ Tips

- Task Scheduler is fairly complex. For help, choose Help > Help Topics. (Task Scheduler help isn't available in Windows Help and Support.)

- The center pane in Task Scheduler lists tasks that have run (and whether they completed successfully) and have yet to run.

- Click the taskbar clock to confirm that your system date and time are accurate. Task Scheduler relies on this information.

- Command-prompt junkies can use the at command instead of Task Scheduler.

SCHEDULING TASKS

Editing the Registry

Windows stores its configuration information in a large database called the *registry*, containing information about all hardware, software, and drivers. Windows references this information and updates it quietly and continually. Editing it incorrectly can damage your system severely. Lots of books, magazines, and websites, however, offer useful tips that involve registry changes. As long as you have precise instructions, editing the registry is easy; it's common even for beginners.

To edit the registry:

1. Press Windows logo key+R; type `regedit` and press Enter.

   If a security prompt appears, type an administrator password or confirm the action.

   Registry Editor opens.

2. In the left pane, use the Explorer-like tree to navigate to the desired folder (**Figure 20.11**).

3. Double-click an entry (called a *key*) in the right pane, edit its value (**Figure 20.12**), and then click OK.

✔ Tips

■ To back up the registry before you edit it, choose File > Export.

■ Visit www.winguides.com/registry and www.annoyances.org for registry tricks.

■ To learn about the registry, read http://support.microsoft.com/?kbid=25 6986, "Description of the Microsoft Windows Registry."

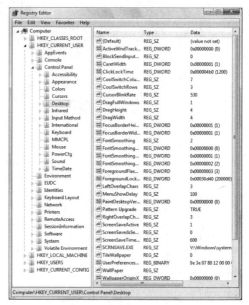

Figure 20.11 Windows stores its configuration information in a database (the registry). Registry Editor organizes the data in tree format.

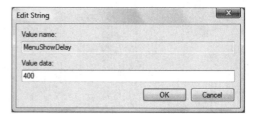

Figure 20.12 Double-click a registry key to edit it.

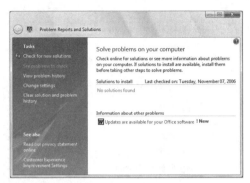

Figure 20.13 Problem Reports and Solutions, new in Vista, searches Microsoft's online database of problems reported by others to try to help you with your own.

Reporting and Solving Problems

When you have hardware or software problems—a program stops working or responding, for example—Windows creates a problem report so you can check online with Microsoft for a solution. You can use Problem Reports and Solutions (**Figure 20.13**) to check for solutions automatically, or you can check manually at any time.

To check online for solutions:

1. Choose Start > Control Panel > System and Maintenance > Problem Reports and Solutions.

2. To check automatically, click Change Settings (in the left pane), select Check for Solutions Automatically (Recommended), and then click OK.

   or

   To check manually (now), select Check for New Solutions (in the left pane).

   When a problems occurs, Windows notifies you of steps that you can take to prevent or solve the problem, or tells you that Microsoft needs more information to find or create a solution (usually because your problem is new, complex, or caused by a bug that the company is fixing).

✔ Tips

- To choose which information to send to Microsoft when a problem occurs, click Advanced Settings on the Change Settings page.

- Some problems and solutions can be viewed and fixed only by an administrator.

- Problem Reports and Solutions replaces Dr. Watson, the system-failure tool in earlier Windows versions.

Boosting Memory

ReadyBoost, new in Vista, can use storage space on USB flash drives and other flash-memory devices to speed your computer. ReadyBoost uses only fast flash memory. (If your device contains both slow and fast memory, only the fast is used.)

Set ReadyBoost memory to one to three times the amount of physical memory (RAM) installed in your computer. If your computer has 512 MB of RAM, and you plug in a 4 GB USB flash drive, set aside between 512 MB and 1.5 GB of that drive for the best performance boost.

To use flash memory to speed your computer:

1. Insert a USB flash drive or other flash-memory device.

2. When the AutoPlay dialog box appears, click Speed up My System (**Figure 20.14**).

3. Select Use This Device and choose how much memory to use for system speed (**Figure 20.15**).

4. Click OK.

Figure 20.14 If the AutoPlay dialog box doesn't appear, use the ReadyBoost tab in the device's Properties dialog box: Choose Start > Computer, right-click the device, and choose Properties. Or you can turn on AutoPlay: Choose Start > Control Panel > Hardware and Sound > AutoPlay.

Figure 20.15 Use the slider to choose an amount one to three times the amount of your physical memory. To see how much physical memory you have, press Ctrl+Shift+Esc to open Task Manager and then click the Performance tab.

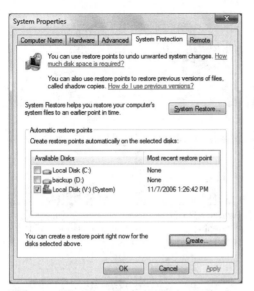

Figure 20.16 Restore points are created every day automatically and just before significant system events, such as the installation of a program or device driver. You can turn off System Restore by unchecking all the boxes below Available Disks (which erases existing restore points).

Restoring Your System

If your system becomes persistently unstable—thanks to an incompatible program, faulty driver, or bad system setting, or for no apparent reason—use System Restore to return Windows to its previous working state without risk to your personal files.

System Restore uses a feature called System Protection to create and save restore points regularly on your computer. These restore points contain snapshots of the system files, registry, and settings that Windows needs to work properly. You also can create restore points manually. Note that System Restore protects only Windows *system* files; use Backup and Restore Center (described later in this chapter) to protect your personal files.

To configure System Restore:

1. Choose Start > Control Panel > System and Maintenance > System (or press Windows logo key+Break).

2. Click Advanced System Settings (in the left pane) > System Protection tab (**Figure 20.16**).

   If a security prompt appears, type an administrator password or confirm the action.

3. Below Automatic Restore Points, use the check boxes to select the disks for which you want System Restore to create restore points automatically.

4. To create a restore point now for the selected disks, click Create, type a description for the restore point (something like `Before video driver update`), and then click Create in the System Protection dialog box.

5. Click OK (or Apply).

When your PC behaves badly, you can return Windows to one of the restore points that System Restore, or you, created. But do so only as a last resort. Remember, if a driver upgrade doesn't work out, you can roll back *just* the driver rather than your entire system (see "Managing Device Drivers" in Chapter 8). Similarly, you can uninstall a suspect program (see "Removing Programs" in Chapter 6).

To restore system files and settings:

1. Save your work and close all programs.

2. Choose Start > All Programs > Accessories > System Tools > System Restore (**Figure 20.17**).

   or

   Click System Restore in the System Protection tab of the System Properties dialog box (refer to Figure 20.16).

   If a security prompt appears, type an administrator password or confirm the action.

3. Click Next.

4. Select the restore point that you want to use and click Next (**Figure 20.18**).

5. Click Finish.

   Your computer restarts in its previous state. Check the system to see whether it's running correctly.

Figure 20.17 If no restore points exist, you'll see a different page explaining how to create them and configure System Restore.

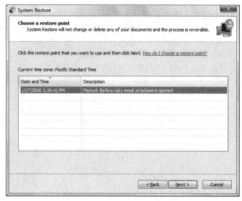

Figure 20.18 All restore points are time-stamped. Pick the one just before things went bad. You always can roll back farther if that one doesn't work.

✔ Tips

■ If restoring the system didn't fix your problem (or made it worse), you can repeat the process and choose a restore point farther back in the past. Or you can undo the restoration: Open System Restore, click Undo System Restore, click Next, review your choices, and then click Finish.

■ System Restore requires at least 300 MB of free disk space and uses up to 15 percent of the disk. (Older restore points are deleted to make room for new ones.) When a disk runs low on space, System Restore turns itself off silently, losing that disk's restore points. It turns itself back on when you free enough space.

■ You can't rely on System Restore to protect you from viruses. By the time you discover the infection, it may have spread to other files that System Restore doesn't touch, in which case rolling back does you no good. Use an antivirus program instead (see "Defending Against Viruses and Spyware" in Chapter 13).

RESTORING YOUR SYSTEM

Backing up Your Files

The love that you shower on your hard drive isn't requited. Eventually it will betray you and fail catastrophically, taking your data with it. Make backup copies of your work. Copies protect you against misbehaving hardware and software, accidental deletions, and virus attacks. They also let you archive finished projects for remote storage.

You'll worry less if you schedule regular, automatic backups. How often you back up—daily, weekly, or monthly—should depend on how often you update or create files and on the pain involved in re-creating them. You also can back up manually between automatic backups.

✔ Tips

- You can't set up automatic backups in Vista Home Basic edition; however, Windows will remind you periodically to back up your files.

- If you store your files on a network server at work, you don't need to back them up. Your network administrator does it for you.

- If your disk fails, and you have no backup, try to recover with SpinRite ($90 U.S.; www.spinrite.com). You also can hire a data recovery service (quite expensive).

Backup Locations

You *can* back up to:

- ◆ Hard disks (internal and external)
- ◆ Other removable disks
- ◆ Network locations
- ◆ Writeable CDs and DVDs
- ◆ USB flash drives

You *can't* back up to:

- ◆ Windows system or boot disks
- ◆ Non-NTFS, -FAT, or -UDF drives
- ◆ The same disk that you're backing up (you can't back up drive C to drive C, for example)
- ◆ Tape drives

Never back up to a different partition on the same physical hard drive, because if the drive fails, all partitions go with it.

To back up files:

1. Choose Start > Control Panel > System and Maintenance > Backup and Restore Center (**Figure 20.19**).

2. Click Back up Files and follow the steps in the wizard.

If a security prompt appears, type an administrator password or confirm the action.

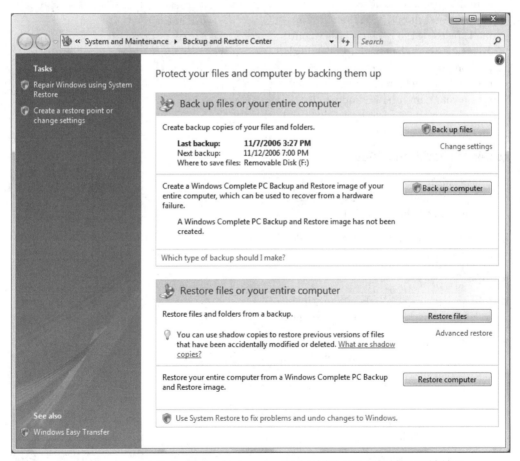

Figure 20.19 Backup and Restore Center lets you back up an entire hard disk or specified files and folders periodically. Wizards walk you through the process of backing up your files or restoring backed-up files when disaster strikes.

✔ Tips

■ Only the last saved version of each file is backed up, so any files that you change during backup will need to be backed up the next time.

■ To change automatic backup settings, click Change Settings (below Back up Files).

■ Windows Complete PC Backup and Restore creates a backup copy of your entire computer (a snapshot of your programs, system settings, and files), which you can restore if your PC dies. Though a complete backup includes your personal files, you still should back them up separately by using the Back up Files wizard. To create a complete backup, click Back up Computer (refer to Figure 20.19). Create a complete image when you first set up your computer and update it every 6 months. This feature isn't included in Vista Home editions.

To restore backed-up files:

1. Choose Start > Control Panel > System and Maintenance > Backup and Restore Center (refer to Figure 20.19).

2. Click Restore Files and follow the steps in the wizard.

✔ Tips

■ Restore backups regularly to a test folder to confirm that they're working properly.

■ To restore a backup made on another computer, click Advanced Restore (below Restore Files).

Files Omitted from Backups

The following files aren't included in backups:

◆ System files

◆ Program files

◆ Files in the Recycle Bin

◆ Files on FAT-formatted drives

◆ Temporary files

◆ Web-based email not on a hard drive

◆ EFS-encrypted files (see "Encrypting Data" in Chapter 13)

◆ User profile settings

Real-Life Backups

Serious backer-uppers use third-party programs and have multiple backup strategies. Some popular backup schemes are:

◆ **Traditional backup.** Copies selected files on a regular schedule to a target such as an external drive or network server.

◆ **Zip archives.** Copies selected files to a compressed zip file to be stored on an external drive or network server.

◆ **Online backup service.** Copies selected files over an internet connection to a remote server. (Go to http://mozy.com for 2 GB of free online backup space.)

◆ **Cloning.** Creates an exact byte-for-byte replica of your hard drive on a different physical drive.

◆ **Rollback.** Maintains copies of files so that you can roll back to earlier versions.

You can find backup-software articles and reviews on the web. For starters, see http://db.tidbits.com/getbits.acgi?tbart=07912 and http://en.wikipedia.org/wiki/Backup.

Don't store your only backup on the same premises as the original, lest a fire destroy both. One tactic: Keep daily backups in a fireproof box purchased from an office-supply store; then make weekly trips to a safe-deposit box to swap your penultimate backup with the latest one.

The poor man's online backup system uses free high-capacity email accounts. (A Google Gmail account, for example, has a few GB of storage.) With WinZip or PKZip, create an encrypted zip archive of backup files and email it to yourself. Let it sit on the mail server until your next backup. Or use GMail Drive (free; www.viksoe.dk/code/gmail.htm) to turn your Gmail account into a virtual drive for backup storage.

If you have an iPod or other portable music player, you can back up to that too; it's really just an external disk or flash drive.

BACKING UP YOUR FILES

Recovering After a Crash

If a faulty driver or program keeps Windows from booting—perhaps greeting you with a black screen—you can use a boot option to recover.

To choose a boot option:

1. Remove all floppies, CDs, DVDs, and USB flash drives, and restart your computer.

2. When the computer startup messages finish (and before the Windows logo appears), tap the F8 key repeatedly until the Advanced Options menu appears (**Figure 20.20**).

   If you have a dual-boot system, use the arrow keys to select the OS that you need; then press F8.

3. Use the arrow keys to select a boot option; then press Enter.

Table 20.1 lists the most appropriate boot options.

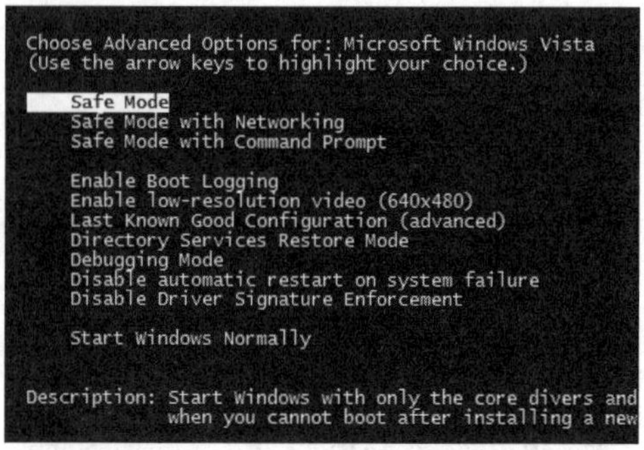

```
Choose Advanced Options for: Microsoft Windows Vista
(Use the arrow keys to highlight your choice.)

    Safe Mode
    Safe Mode with Networking
    Safe Mode with Command Prompt

    Enable Boot Logging
    Enable low-resolution video (640x480)
    Last Known Good Configuration (advanced)
    Directory Services Restore Mode
    Debugging Mode
    Disable automatic restart on system failure
    Disable Driver Signature Enforcement

    Start Windows Normally

Description: Start Windows with only the core divers and
            when you cannot boot after installing a new
```

Figure 20.20 If Windows won't boot, this screen gives you a chance to recover.

Table 20.1

Boot Options	
OPTION	DESCRIPTION
Safe Mode	Starts Windows with only its fundamental files, drivers, and components. Only your mouse, keyboard, monitor, and disk drives will work. A generic video driver makes everything appear in jaggy 640 x 480 screen resolution. Safe mode lets you run most essential configuration and troubleshooting tools, including Device Manager, System Restore, Registry Editor, Backup, Services, and Help and Support. You can uninstall a program or driver that you suspect is causing the problems.
Safe Mode with Networking	Offers the same functions as safe mode, plus access to your network connections. Use this mode if you need files or drivers from another PC on the network. This mode won't work for laptops that connect via a PC Card network adapter; PC Card drivers are disabled in safe mode.
Safe Mode with Command Prompt	Loads the same set of services as safe mode but displays only the command prompt instead of the Windows graphical interface. This mode is for command-line geeks only.
Enable Boot Logging	Creates a file, ntbtlog.txt, that lists all drivers installed during startup.
Enable Low-Resolution Video (640 x 480)	Starts the PC with the safe-mode VGA driver but doesn't invoke any *other* part of safe mode. Use this option to boot past a bogus video driver.
Last Known Good Configuration (Advanced)	Starts the PC by using the registry information and drivers that were in effect the last time your PC was working, effectively undoing the changes that caused the problems. (This is the old Windows 2000 system rollback option; System Restore is preferable, because it restores OS system files too.)
Disable Automatic Restart on System Failure	Stops Windows from restarting automatically when an error occurs. Choose this option if you're stuck in a loop where Windows fails, restarts, fails . . .
Start Windows Normally	Starts Windows in the usual way.

INSTALLING WINDOWS VISTA

If your PC came with Windows Vista installed, you may be able to use it for the life of the machine without ever referring to this appendix. But if you're upgrading to Vista, this appendix will show you how to install your new operating system. Tinkerers and hobbyists will find useful information here too; a clean Windows installation is the last word in restoring the speed of a computer that has grown slow with accumulated software glitches, partially uninstalled programs, and other baggage.

Getting Ready to Install Windows Vista

This section describes the preparations to make before you install Vista. Some steps are only for those of you upgrading from a previous Windows version.

Check system requirements

Windows Vista has two levels of system requirements: Vista Capable and Premium Ready. Machines that are only Vista Capable can run Vista but won't display the new Aero user interface (see "Setting the Window Color and Color Scheme" in Chapter 4).

A Windows Vista Capable PC includes at least:

◆ 800 MHz processor

◆ 512 MB of system memory (RAM)

◆ DirectX 9–capable graphics processor

A Windows Vista Premium Ready PC includes at least:

◆ 1 GHz 32-bit (x86) or 64-bit (x64) processor

◆ 1 GB of system memory (RAM)

◆ Support for DirectX 9 graphics with a WDDM driver, 128 MB of graphics memory (minimum), Pixel Shader 2.0, and 32 bits per pixel

◆ 40 GB hard drive with 15 GB free space

◆ DVD-ROM drive

◆ Audio output capability

◆ Internet access capability

Figure A.1 Upgrade Advisor tells you whether your PC can run Vista and recommends an edition (Home Basic, Home Premium, Business, or Ultimate).

Figure A.2 Click the Task List tab in the report and print it. This list tells you what you need to do to make your hardware, programs, and drivers Vista ready.

If these requirements seem tame, keep in mind that they're minimal. Running Vista on a PC that's barely Vista Capable probably would be intolerable. And you'll need better than Premium Ready if you're going to edit digital video, do scientific calculations, or play network games or Half-Life. If you're upgrading a PC to run Vista, don't skimp on RAM. Lots of memory and a fast hard disk can compensate for a slowish processor.

Check system compatibility

Upgrade Advisor tells you about potential problems that your computer may have if you upgrade to Windows Vista. Upgrade Advisor checks the system and generates an action list for you. You can download Upgrade Advisor from www.microsoft.com/ windowsvista/getready/upgradeadvisor/ default.mspx. Install and run it. This wizard-like program scans your system and tells you whether your computer can run Vista and what you need to do before you install (**Figure A.1** and **Figure A.2**).

Back up your files

Back up your files just before installation by using your usual backup medium (such as another hard drive, CD/DVD burner, USB flash drive, network location, second PC, or web-based backup service). See also "Transferring Existing Files and Settings" later in this appendix.

Turn off your antivirus program

If you're upgrading to Vista, update your antivirus program and then turn it off, lest it interpret Vista as a harmful infestation.

Connect to the internet

If you're upgrading to Vista, make sure that your internet connection is working so that you can get the latest security and driver updates that Microsoft has released since it published the Vista disc. The installer will download and apply these updates. If you don't update during installation, you can do it later via Windows Update (see "Updating Windows" in Chapter 13).

If you're doing a clean install, you can use Windows Easy Transfer to transfer your internet connection settings from your old OS to Vista (see "Transferring Existing Files and Settings" later in this appendix). If you're worried, you can gather your connection settings beforehand and write them down. Your ISP's website will have information, such as access telephone numbers; customer service has a record of your account user name and password, if you've mislaid them. While you're at it, you may want to write down or back up your user names and passwords for websites that you visit regularly.

Plug in and switch on devices

Make sure that devices, such as your printer or scanner, are attached to your computer and powered up so that Windows can detect them during installation.

Get network settings

You'll need your computer name if your computer is connected to a network. If you're using Windows XP, choose Start, right-click My Computer, choose Properties, and then click the Computer Name tab.

You also will need:

◆ The name of your workgroup or domain

◆ If you're on a domain, your domain user name and password

◆ An IP address, if your network doesn't have a DHCP or WINS server

To connect to a workgroup after you install, see Chapter 18. If you're on a domain, see the "Domain Logons" sidebar in "Logging On and Logging Off" in Chapter 1.

Find your product key

You can find your Vista product key stuck on the side of your computer or on the installation disc holder inside the Windows package. It looks like this:

✔ Tips

■ Vista uses the NTFS file system only; you can't use the FAT or FAT32 file system. If you upgrade a Windows XP computer that uses FAT, it's converted to NTFS, which might affect some older programs.

■ You can't uninstall Vista to revert to your previous operating system. To use your old OS again, you must reinstall it.

■ You can't boot a Vista drive off a DOS floppy disk. Boot off the Vista disc.

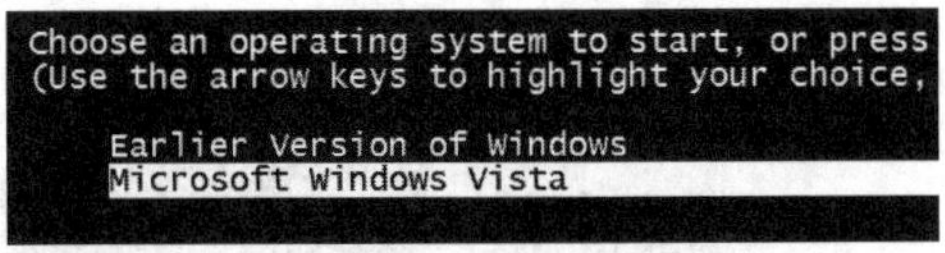

```
Choose an operating system to start, or press
(Use the arrow keys to highlight your choice,

    Earlier Version of Windows
  Microsoft Windows Vista
```

Figure A.3 Windows Boot Manager appears when you turn on your PC and offers you a choice of operating systems. If you don't choose within 30 seconds, the computer chooses for you. To change the default OS, choose Start > Control Panel > System and Maintenance > System > Advanced System Settings > Advanced tab > Settings (below Startup and Recovery) > System Startup.

Choosing an Installation Type

If your PC is running Windows XP, choose one of the three installation types in **Table A.1**. If you're running any version of Windows, choose a clean install or dual boot. If your target PC has a blank drive, your only choice is a clean install.

✔ Tip

- The upgrade version of Windows Vista is cheaper than the full version, but if you ever need to install the upgrade version on a clean drive, you must first install the older Windows version and then install Vista on top of it (one reason to take care of your old Windows discs).

Table A.1

Windows Vista Installation Types

INSTALLATION	DESCRIPTION
Clean install	Installs a fresh copy of Vista on your hard drive, replacing any existing operating system and erasing all files on the drive. During a clean install, you reformat or repartition your hard drive, wiping out all its accumulated crud, including outdated drivers, fragmented files, incompatible programs, and stale registry entries. A clean install has a restorative effect on a PC that's grown sluggish over time.
Upgrade	First, check "Upgrading to Windows Vista" in the introduction to see whether your current Windows version qualifies for the upgrade to Vista; if not, you must perform a clean install. Upgrading preserves your existing settings; installed programs; and data files, including your personal desktop elements, Favorites list, and everything in your personal folder. Windows also attempts to upgrade device drivers to Vista-compatible versions. Upgrading saves you from rebuilding or transferring your files and settings but doesn't invigorate your PC the way a clean install does. Before you upgrade, use Upgrade Advisor to flag potential problems. Following the upgrade, you may find that Upgrade Advisor missed some problems. If a program runs poorly under Vista, try reinstalling it, or look for an update on the publisher's website.
Dual boot	If you want to preserve your existing copy of Windows *and* run Vista, you can set up your PC to maintain both of them side by side. Each time you turn on your PC, it asks you which operating system to run (**Figure A.3**). Dual booting is useful if you have a critical piece of hardware or software that runs only on the older OS, or if you're not sure whether you want to use Vista as your everyday OS and want to be able to fall back on the older one.
	Never install both OSes on the same hard-disk partition. Even if Windows let you do it, it would be a disaster—and technical-support people usually don't even answer questions about such setups. Instead, take one of the following paths:
	◆ Buy a second hard drive, and use it for one of the two OSes.
	◆ Partition your existing disk—that is, divide it so that each portion functions as though it were a separate disk, with its own icon and drive letter in the Computer folder. The Windows installer offers a disk tool that can create, extend, delete, and format partitions, but see "Managing Disks" in Chapter 20 for recommendations on better partitioning software.

Installing Windows Vista

To install Windows Vista, follow the steps below for your installation type.

To upgrade to Windows Vista:

1. Insert the Windows installation disc into your computer's DVD or CD drive.

2. On the Install Windows page, click Install Now (**Figure A.4**).

3. On the Get Important Updates for Installation page, choose whether to get the latest Vista updates during installation or wait until later (**Figure A.5**).

4. On the Type Your Product Key for Activation page, type your 25-character product key (**Figure A.6**).

5. On the Please Read the License Terms page, click I Accept the License Terms.

Figure A.4 This window is the starting point for installing Windows Vista.

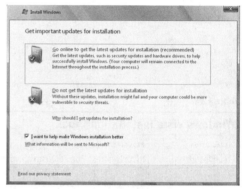

Figure A.5 If you're not online, choose Do Not Get the Latest Updates for Installation. Windows will prompt you to get them later.

Figure A.6 If you want to test-drive Windows Vista before you commit to it, leave the Product Key box blank and uncheck Automatically Activate Windows When I'm Online.

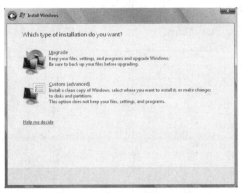

Figure A.7 This page is the branching point for doing an upgrade or clean install.

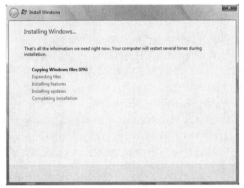

Figure A.8 All installations converge on this page. Installation takes about a half-hour. You'll have to go through one more short wizard before you can use Vista.

✔ Tips

- If you see a compatibility report during installation, you can resolve any issues after installation completes.

- Windows Firewall is turned on by default after all installations. See "Using a Firewall" in Chapter 13.

6. On the Which Type of Installation Do You Want? page, click Upgrade (**Figure A.7**).

7. Follow the onscreen instructions (**Figure A.8**).

To do a clean install or a dual-boot install:

1. Insert the Windows installation disc into your computer's DVD or CD drive and then do one of the following:

   ▲ If your PC already has an OS installed, and if you don't want to partition, go to step 2.

   ▲ If your PC doesn't have an OS installed, or if you want to partition, restart your computer with the Windows disc inserted in the drive. This causes your PC to start (boot) from the disc. If you're prompted to press a key to boot from DVD or CD, press any key. If the Install Windows page appears (refer to Figure A.4), go to step 2. If that page doesn't appear, and you're not asked to boot from a disc, use BIOS to change the startup drive (see the sidebar "Booting from the Windows Disc"). Restart your PC and then start Windows from the installation DVD or CD as described previously.

continues on next page

2. On the Install Windows page, follow any instructions that might appear and then click Install Now (refer to Figure A.4).

3. On the Get Important Updates for Installation page, choose whether to get the latest Vista updates during installation or wait until later (refer to Figure A.5).

4. On the Type Your Product Key for Activation page, type your 25-character product key (refer to Figure A.6).

5. On the Please Read the License Terms page, click I Accept the License Terms.

6. On the Which Type of Installation Do You Want? page, click Custom (Advanced) (refer to Figure A.7).

7. On the Where Do You Want to Install Windows? page (**Figure A.9**), do one of the following:

    ▲ If you don't partition your hard disk, click Next to start the installation.

    ▲ If you have an existing partition and want to dual-boot, install Windows on a partition other than the one containing the existing version of Windows. Select the target partition and click Next to start the installation.

    ▲ If you want to partition, start Windows from the installation DVD or CD. If you didn't begin installation this way, follow the instructions for booting from the disc in step 1 and then follow the onscreen instructions. On the Where Do You Want to Install Windows? page, click Drive Options (Advanced), click the option that you want, and then follow the onscreen instructions. Click Next to start installation.

8. Follow the onscreen instructions (refer to Figure A.8).

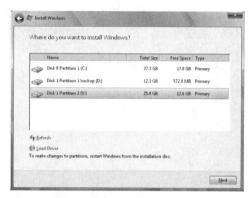

Figure A.9 What you do here depends on whether you want to partition or dual-boot.

Booting from the Windows Disc

If your computer doesn't give you the option to boot from a CD or DVD at startup, use BIOS to select the CD or DVD drive as the startup drive. *BIOS* (basic input/output system) is the set of low-level hardware routines that your computer invokes at startup. The procedure varies by computer, so check the manufacturer's instructions or website.

Here's a typical way to change the startup drive:

1. Turn on your computer, insert the Windows installation disc, and then restart your computer.

2. Look for a startup (boot) menu and choose BIOS Setup, BIOS Settings, or something similar.

3. When the BIOS menu appears, look for an option named Boot Order or something similar.

4. Select your CD or DVD drive as the first startup device.

5. Save your settings and exit BIOS setup.

    Don't mess with any other BIOS settings unless you know what you're doing.

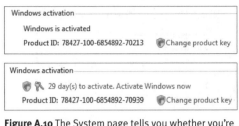

Figure A.10 The System page tells you whether you're activated (top) or not (bottom) and, if not, counts down the days until Windows locks you out.

![Activate Windows now notification balloon]

Figure A.11 Windows nags you to activate.

Activating Windows Vista

Activating Windows prevents you from running the same copy on more than one computer. During installation, Windows examines your PC; computes a unique identifier by using the system time and data about key internal parts (hard drive, video card, motherboard, memory, and so on); and sends this identifier, along with your 25-character product key, over the internet to Microsoft, thereby activating Windows Vista.

To check whether Windows is activated, choose Start > Control Panel > System and Maintenance > System (or press Windows logo key+Break); then look in the Product Activation section (**Figure A.10**). If you skipped activation during installation (refer to Figure A.6), reminders pop up occasionally on the taskbar (**Figure A.11**). Click a reminder or the link in Figure A.10 (bottom) to start the Windows Activation wizard. You have 30 days to activate; if you don't, Windows will stop working.

Later, if you install the same copy of Windows on another PC without uninstalling the first one, Microsoft will discover your duplicity during activation and lock you out of Windows. Unless you activate Vista on the second PC, lockout occurs automatically in 30 days.

✔ Tips

■ Activation is anonymous and transfers no personal information to Microsoft.

■ Bulk-purchased business, government, and school copies of Windows are exempt from activation, and many new PCs come with a preactivated copy.

ACTIVATING WINDOWS VISTA

Transferring Existing Files and Settings

Windows Easy Transfer is a step-by-step program for transferring files and settings from one computer running Windows to another. You can choose what to transfer: user accounts, internet favorites, email contacts, and so on. You also can choose the transfer method (Easy Transfer Cable, network, CD, DVD, USB flash drive, or external hard disk).

You can transfer from a PC running Windows 2000 (files only), XP, or Vista to another computer running Vista. Start Windows Easy Transfer on the computer running Vista and follow the onscreen instructions. (If you upgraded from XP to Vista, your files, settings, and programs were transferred automatically.)

You can copy Easy Transfer to your old PC by using a CD, DVD, network connection, or USB flash drive. If you are using an Easy Transfer Cable (available in computer stores), use the CD that came with the cable to install both Easy Transfer and any drivers on your old computer before plugging in the cable.

To use Windows Easy Transfer:

1. Choose Start > All Programs > Accessories > System Tools > Windows Easy Transfer.

   If a security prompt appears, type an administrator password or confirm the action.

2. Follow the onscreen instructions (**Figure A.12**).

✔ Tip

■ If you're chucking your old computer, check the phone directory or the web for recycling programs in your area (try www.eiae.org). Be sure to shred the files on all your hard drives before you disown your PC (see "Deleting Files and Folders" in Chapter 5).

Figure A.12 You can transfer your settings, files, or both.

INDEX

C

INDEX

INDEX